# THE NEW IRANIAN LEADERSHIP

# THE NEW IRANIAN LEADERSHIP

## *Ahmadinejad, Terrorism, Nuclear Ambition, and the Middle East*

YONAH ALEXANDER AND MILTON HOENIG

PRAEGER SECURITY INTERNATIONAL
Westport, Connecticut • London

**Library of Congress Cataloging-in-Publication Data**

Alexander, Yonah.
The new Iranian leadership : Ahmadinejad, terrorism, nuclear ambition, and the Middle East / Yonah Alexander and Milton Hoenig.
p. cm.
Includes bibliographical references and index.
ISBN-13: 978–0–275–99639–0 (alk. paper)
1. Ahmadinejad, Mahmoud. 2. Presidents—Iran—Biography. 3. Iran—Politics and government—1997– 4. Iran—Foreign relations—1997– 5. Nuclear weapons—Iran. 6. Iran—Foreign relations—Middle East. I. Hoenig, Milton M. II. Title.
DS318.84.A36A44 2008
955.06′1092—dc22 2007039690

British Library Cataloguing in Publication Data is available.



Library of Congress Catalog Card Number: 2007039690
ISBN-13: 978–0–275–99639–0

First published in 2008

Praeger Security International, 88 Post Road West, Westport, CT 06881
An imprint of Greenwood Publishing Group, Inc.
www.praeger.com

Printed in the United States of America

The paper used in this book complies with the Permanent Paper Standard issued by the National Information Standards Organization (Z39.48–1984).

10 9 8 7 6 5 4 3 2 1

# Contents

# Preface

An old Persian proverb teaches us that "events are constantly unlike one another." Indeed, historical patterns cannot be repeated because what has already happened in the past provides no assurances that tomorrow will bring similar or identical occurrences. Additionally, each epoch gives birth to its own leaders, policies, and actions in the struggle for power within and among nations. And yet, it is assumed that wise rulers can benefit from yesterday's lessons, do what is prudent and accountable to confront immediate challenges, and understand that there are adverse consequences for crafting and implementing radical strategies when war and peace are concerned.

Can the validity of this assumption be examined in light of the ancient and contemporary experiences of Iran, Shiite Islam's most significant geopolitical and economic power in both the Middle East and throughout Islamdom?

At the beginning of the twenty-first century, the published and unpublished record of this experience is documented in a vast outpouring of literature on Iran from both official and unofficial sources. Thousands of studies, reports, articles, and general works have been produced by scholars, reporters, and politicians focusing on various aspects of a broad panoply: Persian history originating in antiquity; the Islamic background, characterized by the unending theological conflict between the Shiites (partisans of Ali, Prophet Mohammed's cousin and son-in-law) and the Sunnis (those who follow the tradition) that has lasted over 1,300 years; the Pahlavi dynasty personified by the rise and fall of Shah Mohammed Reza Pahlavi; and the emergence of the new theocratic regime in Tehran under the Ayatollahs since 1979.[1]

What is of grave concern to the world community are Iran's roles in international terrorism and its development of weapons of mass destruction, particularly the regime's expanding nuclear program. These challenges have been intensified with the election of President Mahmoud Ahmadinejad in 2005. Since assuming office, the new Iranian leader has reversed the seemingly more moderate policies of his predecessors and projected himself onto the international scene with headline-grabbing statements and speeches regarding the State of Israel and Judaism, open defiance of UN Security Council resolutions directed at Iran's nuclear capabilities, and antagonism toward the interests of the United States, the European Union, and other states in the Middle East, potentially leading to tragic consequences for all concerned.

Ahmadinejad's apparent vision of his country becoming the dominant power in the region, capable of expanding its terrorist-sponsored activities in Iraq, Lebanon, and the Palestinian territories is only one of the latest examples of Iran's nearly three-decades-long record of the "wild card" in the international system. Perhaps the most disturbing dangers posed by contemporary Iran under Ahmadinejad are those relating to the safety, welfare, and rights of ordinary people in the Middle East; the stability of the state system in the region; the movement toward democracy; and perhaps even the survival of civilization itself.

This book is not a comprehensive history of Persia-Iran from time immemorial. Rather it is an effort to provide a profile of the current leadership's policies and actions against the background of its record since the fall of the Shah and the ensuing confrontation with the United States, the "great Satan," as perceived by the Ayatollahs and most recently depicted by Ahmadinejad and the new Iranian rulers.

The rationale for undertaking such a study seems self-evident in light of the complexity of the relationship between Shiite theology of apocalyptic visions that see universal chaos in preparation for the return of the Hidden Imam and nonreligious political decision-making such as the motivations for Iran's security policies, including terrorism sponsorship and nuclear program development. After all, the Shia-Sunni and Persian-Arab tensions and conflicts only underscore one segment of the nature of the Iranian challenge to the entire international community. Better understanding of the extent of the religious, political, and military roles of President Ahmadinejad and the Supreme Leader Ayatollah Ali Khamenei, as well as other individuals operating within the government structure, is an important element in crafting a coherent and realistic strategy in coping with Tehran's dangers facing the Middle East and other regions.

The book is divided into seven chapters, dealing with aspects of Iran's history, governmental structure, leadership profiles, state-sponsored terrorism, terrorist networks (focusing on Hizballah and Hamas), nuclear ambitions, and military capabilities (ballistic missiles: chemical, and biological). Two appendices are provided. The first includes the record of Iran's leadership policy pronouncements and the international reactions to the nuclear crisis. The second appendix consists of a nuclear chronology from August 2002 to July 2007. A selected bibliography, as a reference for further study and research, as well as an index are incorporated in the volume.

Since the manuscript was submitted to the publisher in late summer 2007, a number of recent developments in September and October have been noteworthy. A brief selection of policies and actions of Iran, several states, and the United Nations follows.

A. Iran

- President Ahmadinejad boasted that Iran is running more than 3,000 centrifuges used to enrich uranium and is installing more every week.[2]
- Iran's Foreign Ministry warned that it will review its cooperation with the International Atomic Energy Agency to consider "new options" if the UN Security Council passed a third sanctions resolution.[3]
- Ayatollah Ali Khamenei replaced Yahya Rahim Safavi, who served as chief commander of the Islamic Revolutionary Guard Corps (IRGC), with General Mohammed Ali Aziz Jafari (who commanded the Revolutionary Guards ground forces for thirteen years).[4]
- Ayatollah Ali Khamenei compared President George W. Bush to Adolf Hitler and predicted that he would eventually be brought to trial as a war criminal.[5]
- An Iranian Web site, affiliated with the Tehran regime, reported that 600 Iranian Shihab-3 missiles were pointed at targets throughout Israel.[6]
- President Ahmadinejad, in a television program, appealed to the American people saying that he wanted peace and friendship with the United States despite mounting tensions between the two countries.[7]
- At a speech at the United Nations General Assembly, President Ahmadinejad stated that he considered the dispute over his country's nuclear program "closed" and vowed to disregard the resolutions of the Security Council, which he said was dominated by "arrogant powers."[8]
- Ali Larijani, Iran's chief negotiator, who has been a key figure in attempts to broker a compromise with the West over the nuclear dispute, resigned, and was replaced by Saeed Jalili, possibly indicating a major shift in Tehran's policy.[9]

B. The United States

- United States District Judge, Royce C. Lamberth, ruled that Iran must pay $2.65 billion to the families of the 241 American servicemen who were killed in October of 1983 when two truck bombs struck the U.S. Marine barracks in Beirut.[10]
- In a *Report to Congress on the Situation in Iraq*, presented by the top U.S. commander in Iraq, General David H. Petraeus, it was observed that "Malign actions . . . especially, by Iran" fuel violence undertaken by "foreign and home-grown terrorists, insurgents, militia extremists, and criminals." General Petraeus specifically reported that "we have also disrupted Shia militia extremists, capturing the head and numerous other leaders of the Iranian-supported Special Groups, along with a senior Lebanese Hizballah operative supporting Iran's activities in Iraq."[11]

- The United States Senate passed a provision urging the Bush administration to designate the IRGC as a "terrorist organization" because of its support of networks from Gaza to Afghanistan. Also, the House of Representatives was considering a bill that strengthens U.S. tools to cut off funds for Iran's nuclear program.[12]
- President George W. Bush raised the challenge of a nuclear Iran as a top foreign policy topic of the United States, asserting at a news conference: "If you're interested in avoiding World War III, it seems like you ought to be interested in preventing them from having the knowledge necessary to make a nuclear weapon."[13]
- The United States announced new sanctions against elements of Iran's government, including the Islamic Revolutionary Guard Corps and the Ministry of Defense, designating them as proliferators of weapons of mass destruction and ballistic missile technology. The sanctions also targeted, among other entities, three major state-owned Iranian banks suspected of involvement in terrorist group financing. The sanctions cut off access to the American financial system and froze any assets held in the United States.[14]

C. The United Kingdom

- Tony Blair, the United Kingdom's former prime minister, accused Iran of backing terrorism and warned that the world is facing a situation akin to "rising fascism in the 1920s."[15]

D. France

- The French Foreign Minister, Bernard Kouchner, asserted that the world should be ready to go to war with Iran over its nuclear weapons program if diplomacy fails.[16] President Nicolas Sarkozy also stated Iran's development of nuclear weapons is "unacceptable" to France.[17]

E. Russia

- Vladimir Putin, Russia's president, during a visit to Tehran stated that Iran's "peaceful nuclear activities must be allowed" and cautioned against using force to resolve the crisis.[18] He also submitted a new nuclear proposal to Khamenei, bypassing Ahmadinejad.

F. The United Nations

- The five permanent members at the United Nations Security Council determined that they would delay their decision on whether to impose tougher sanctions on Iran over its nuclear program.[19]

G. International Atomic Energy Agency (IAEA)

- Mohamed ElBaradei, the head of the IAEA, the United Nation's nuclear watchdog, stated that he has no evidence that Iran is working actively to develop nuclear weapons. He also expressed concern that if the rhetoric escalates then "we will end up into a precipice, we will end up into an abyss . . . the Middle East is in a mess . . . we cannot add fuel to the fire."[20]

It is against the record of nearly three decades of adverse U.S.-Iranian relations that the future resolution of this crisis must be assessed. The challenge to Iran, America, and the entire international community will be to determine whether negotiations and peaceful means are the preferred tools of the policymakers in lieu of utilizing the instruments of war with grave regional and global consequences. What is certain, however, is that the Iranian dilemma will clearly become not only a major foreign policy issue for America in an election year, but inevitably will also constitute a global security concern for the foreseeable future.

In sum, let all the parties involved recall the wise observation of Kalif-Mouawia, the founder of the Omayah Dynasty in 660 AD: "I never use my sword where the stick suffices, nor my stick where the tongue is enough; and if it is only a thread that binds me with my opponents, it will never be broken: if they pull it, I let it; and if they relax it I straighten it."

# Acknowledgments

Any book published reflects a personal journey of its author or authors. This book is no exception. Professor Yonah Alexander's interest in Iran began over fifty years ago, as a graduate student at the University of Chicago and Columbia University, focusing on international affairs and the Middle East. Conducting research at the United Nations in New York City in the early 1960s afforded him an opportunity to meet with Iranian representatives to the world body who enlightened him with the diplomatic history of both ancient Persia, beginning with Cyrus the Great in 550 BCE, and modern Iran.

One of the lessons, based on this dual "old-new" experience that impressed him at the time was the Persian proverb observing that "even with the strength of an elephant and the paws of a lion, peace is better than war." In fact, Fereydoun Hoveyda, the then Permanent Representative of Iran to the United Nations, contributed an article to the first issue of *Terrorism: An International Journal*, which was founded and edited by Professor Alexander and published in 1977. Ambassador Hoveyda's contribution was titled, "The Problem of Terrorism at the United Nations," an issue that some thirty years later is still challenging the international community.

In 1968, Professor Alexander visited Tehran, conducted research in the country, and established academic links with educational institutions and scholars. His other academic activity is related to teaching and lecturing in the region and elsewhere. For example, in 1977 Professor Alexander developed a summer academic program on "Islamic Civilization" in the non-Arab Middle East, including Turkey, Iran, and Israel. His other offerings included the 1995 seminar on "Democracies' Responses to Iranian Terrorism," cosponsored by The George

Washington University (Terrorism Studies Program) and the Center for International and Strategic Studies. Most recently, in 2006, he sponsored a seminar titled, "Middle East Challenges and Opportunities in 2007," focusing on Iran. It was conducted in cooperation with the International Center for Terrorism Studies at the Potomac Institute for Policy Studies and the Inter-University Center for Terrorism Studies. Professor Alexander also worked closely with the United States Congress on Iranian-related issues. For instance, in 1985 he prepared a report with his colleague Dr. Ray S. Cline on "State-Sponsored Terrorism" at the request of the Subcommittee on Security and Terrorism (Committee on the Judiciary of the United States Senate). He also testified before Congress on such topics as "Iran: A Quarter-Century of State-Sponsored Terror" before a February 2005 joint hearing of the Subcommittee on the Middle East and Central Asia and the Subcommittee on International Terrorism and Nonproliferation within the Committee on International Relations, House of Representatives.

Professor Alexander coedited four studies relevant to the issue of Iran, terrorism, and nuclear threats. They include: *The United States on Iran: A Documentary History* (with Alan Nanes), University Publications of America, 1960; *Nuclear Terrorism: Defining the Threat* (with Paul Leventhal), Pergamon-Brassey's, 1986; *Preventing Nuclear Terrorism* (with Paul Leventhal), Lexington Books, 1987; and *Super Terrorism: Biological, Chemical, and Nuclear* (with Milton Hoenig), Transnational, 2002.

Dr. Milton Hoenig, a nuclear physicist, has been working on issues related to weapons of mass destruction, nuclear terrorism, and nuclear nonproliferation. He was technical advisor to the International Task Force on Prevention of Nuclear Terrorism, and he is coauthor of the *Nuclear Weapons Databook, vols. 1–3*, Ballinger, 1984–1987, and *Super Terrorism: Biological, Chemical, and Nuclear*, Transnational, 2002. Dr. Hoenig has written widely in his field and has made presentations in Vienna, Tel Aviv, Montevideo, La Paz, Chapel Hill, and Las Vegas.

The authors wish to acknowledge the contributions of all those who participated in this project over the past six years, with special emphasis given to those who were involved during the 2005–2007 period. Special gratitude goes to Jack Baber (Alumnus, Rhodes College) for his dedicated and extraordinary efforts in conducting research and preparing the manuscript for publication. Without his professionalism and perseverance throughout, this project could not have been completed in such a timely manner. David Kugel (Alumnus, Johns Hopkins University) also provided updated research to the original manuscript. Most recently, the authors were assisted by: Brett Wallace (Alumnus, The George Washington University), Steven Lockfield (Alumnus, London School of Economics and Political Science), Mark Graham (University of New Hampshire), and Michael Atkinson (Cabrini College). Mention should also be made of the research assistance provided by the following individuals: Andrew Fulton (Alumnus, Hamilton College), Colin Costello (Georgetown University), Jack Mountjoy (Whitman College), Alexandra Wald (Vanderbilt University), Ian Mulderry-Hoffer (University of Connecticut), Nick Quon (Loyola Marymount University), Robert Daniels

(Wake Forest University), Gregory Kruczek (Pennsylvania State University), Ann Koppuzha (Georgetown University), Patricia Rueda (American University), Deandra Perruccio (Assumption College), Michelle Phillips (University of Iowa), Lauren Kari (Tufts University), Aaron Epstein (Rice University), Alicia Miller (Alumna, University of Western Kentucky), and Sandra Beutler (Alumna, Dartmouth College). Many thanks also go to numerous colleagues in the Middle East, Europe, Asia, and the United States who contributed their knowledge and wisdom to our understanding of Iran and its policies. In particular, we acknowledge the research effort and guidance of Clare Lopez, Vice President of The Intelligence Summit and former Executive Director of the Iran Policy Committee.

Finally, several academic institutions and a number of individuals have provided encouragement and support for this project over the years. We are most appreciative of the contributions of Michael S. Swetnam, Chairman and CEO of the Potomac Institute for Policy Studies, and Professor Edgar H. Brenner, Co-Director of the Inter-University Center for Legal Studies at the International Law Institute. The Inter-University Center for Terrorism Studies and The George Washington University's Terrorism Studies Program also assisted in the realization of this project.

# 1

# Historical Perspectives

The Iran, or Persia as it was also known, that entered the twentieth century appeared to many to be the "sick man of West Asia." While the Qajar dynasty had succeeded in unifying the country by 1785, it had reached the height of its power by the middle of the previous century.An autocracy founded in both tribal Persian traditions and Shi'ite Islamic law, successive members of the Qajar family line had become progressively corrupt or inept in ruling their territory.

Iran's geographic position also made it an important strategic actor and the subject of external influence and intervention, with the British and the Russians representing two of the most influential European great powers with strategic interests in Iran. The British sought to protect trade routes to India while the Russians desired to expand their territory into northern Iran. Iranian attempts to play off the two sides often ended poorly, and foreign agents were sometimes implicated in the struggles for succession to the throne.

It was then, at the turn of the century, that various members of Iranian society started fomenting what would eventually expand into a full-scale revolution aimed at changing the established political order. Inspired by the writings of Mirza Malkom Khan, intellectuals and others began to develop transformative ideas of Iranian government, which sought to throw off the yoke of foreign domination in Iranian domestic politics. Throughout Iran, they formed secret societies to consider political alternatives without government knowledge. They failed to agree on a specific course of action, but it took only one of these bodies to initiate what became known as the "Constitutional Revolution."[1]

At the time of the 1905 revolution, Muzaffar al-Din Shah held power and was to be succeeded by Mohammed Ali Shah in 1907. Muzaffar al-Din did little to satisfy the nonviolent revolutionaries, but Mohammed Ali made a variety of promises in attempting to placate the revolutionaries. In an effort to provide further evidence of the depth of foreign interference in Iran and the problems it created, he confronted these activists, now known as the *Majles*, head-on. In 1908, the revolution ultimately turned violent when, supported by the Russian Army, Mohammed Ali attacked the Majles and tried to destroy the movement. This strategy failed, and instead galvanized public support for the Majles and their goal of a parliamentary monarchy. In 1911, from exile in Odessa, Mohammed Ali invaded Iran at the head of another Russian-supplied army, only to be defeated again.[2]

Concurrently, British influence in Iran deepened to the point that London provided a home for exiled "constitutional refugees" during the revolution.[3] More significantly, Iran entered Britain's strategic national security sphere with the formation of the Anglo-Persian Oil Company (APOC) in 1909.

Burgeoning internal opposition to the Shah's complacent position vis-à-vis external influence could not prevent Iran from remaining largely under foreign control. Strategic interests of the great powers during World War I, led the British and Russians to fight both the Germans and the Turks in Iran, despite Iran's professed neutrality in the conflict.

British dominance in Iran continued unabated until 1921, when Reza Khan-Mirpari, a career soldier, launched a coup against the last Qajar Shah. and appointed his ally Seyyed Zia'eddin Tabatabai as Prime Minister. In 1925, Reza Shah was elected by the Majles as the head of a new monarchy and adopted the dynastic name of Pahlavi.

The new ruler worked with the Majles to institute several domestic reforms, including the formation of the Iranian National Bank, the construction of the Trans-Iranian Railway, and the establishment of Tehran University. The deserved credit for these achievements, however, was due to Abdolhossein Khan Teymourtash, Reza Shah's Minister of Court. Even after Teymourtash's death in 1933, reforms continued, including the development of a relatively modern medical system and public health code.

World War II gave rise to another period of significant foreign influence in Iranian politics. As a result of Reza Shah's declared neutrality during the conflict, the Allied forces of the United Kingdom and Soviet Union occupied Iran in August 1941. Looking to avoid further humiliation, Reza Shah abdicated, and the Allies, seeking to solidify their strategic position, quickly placed his son, Mohammed Reza Shah, on the throne.[4] What is significant in this connection, however, is the role the United States played in Iran from the first decade of the twentieth century to World War II.

The very entry of the United States into close diplomatic relations with Iran prior to World War II came about because the Iranians judged the United States to be a truly friendly party. Appreciated of Washington's noninterventionist attitude, Iran began looking to the United States to offset British and Russian influence. World War II presented the first opportunity for U.S. involvement in Iran, during which American noncombatant forces were stationed in the country.

After the war ended, political tension and popular dissatisfaction with British control of Iran's oil industry led to the rise of the National Front political party as well as the appointment of Dr. Mohammed Mossadegh as prime minister in 1951. Dr. Mossadegh, appealing to nationalist sentiments within Iran, advocated legislation to dismantle the Anglo-Iranian Oil Company (AIOC), in which Great Britain held significant influence, and nationalize the company under the National Iranian Oil Company (NIOC).[5] Subsequently, economic and political instability resulted from the failed oil industry negotiations, which included an unsuccessful attempt at reconciliation at the United Nations. Following the unsatisfactory resolution of the Anglo-Iranian oil dispute, and the fear of an immediate or potential Soviet takeover, the United States intervened in Iranian internal affairs in mid-August 1953. Several months earlier, in February 1953, the American CIA and British MI-6 collaborated in a covert effort, Operation AJAX, designed to support a coup leading to dismantling of the Mossadegh regime and the return to power of the pro-western Shah. Subsequent to the successful coup, Dr. Mossadegh was convicted of treason, imprisoned, and placed under house arrest, where he remained until his death in 1967. However, despite numerous economic missteps, his stance against foreign political influence made him an enduring national hero, an image solidified by his abrupt, foreign-orchestrated departure from Iranian politics.[6]

The years immediately following World War II were marked by a substantial strengthening and expansion of U.S.-Iranian ties, a development primarily motivated by escalating U.S.-Soviet rivalry. The United States sought to minimize Soviet influence in the Middle East and, more importantly, to safeguard the West's oil supplies. The Shah's return to power on August 22, 1953 secured American influence in the region. Almost immediately following the coup, Iran received $45 million in foreign aid and, in 1954 the United States acquired a 40 percent share of Iranian oil. However, the United States' central foreign policy objective with regard to Iran centered on countering potential Soviet aggression in the region and, as such, support for the pro-western Shah became a linchpin of this containment strategy.

Fearful of political opposition, in 1957, the Shah created the internal security force, SAVAK (Organization for Intelligence and National Security), designed to dissuade political opposition, often by intimidation and force. The CIA and the Israeli Mossad aided the organization to ensure the rule of the pro-western Shah, which subsequently added up to feelings against the countries that helped the SAVAK. Notorious for brutal tactics including arrests, torture, and beatings, SAVAK targeted anyone who spoke out against the regime. These draconian methods and blatant disregard for human rights eventually became an issue under the Carter Administration.

The United States' defeat in the Vietnam War weighed heavily on the ability of U.S. foreign policy to combat communist threats around the world. The war aroused considerable domestic opposition that many, both in America and abroad, wondered whether the United States would be able to keep the policy commitments it had made to assist those countries whose security might be threatened by future communist aggression. The Nixon Administration, recognizing this dilemma, developed a new policy, which encouraged regional allies to adopt more responsibility for collective security. They would receive U.S. arms, but not necessarily direct U.S. military involvement. The Nixon Doctrine thus proclaimed a more cautious role for the United States.

In the early 1960s, the Shah sought to implement a series of economic and developmental reforms that would introduce western economic theories to Iran. The Shah hoped these reforms would help bring economic and industrial modernization while increasing his political stability. The largest initiative during this period was in land reform in which millions of sharecropping farmers became landowners, to the detriment of the elite.[7]

The Ayatollah Rouhollah Musavi Khomeini, a rising theological authority, publicly denounced the Shah's new economic package and urged citizens to protest the reforms. From 1963 to 1964, Khomeini gave speeches and released manifestos publicly denouncing the Shah, accusing him of surrendering Iranian sovereignty in favor of self-interested goals and practicing unconstitutional methods. In the summer of 1963, SAVAK killed thousands of unarmed protesters and worked to shut down networks of the Tudeh party.[8] The Shah, facing serious political unrest, ordered Khomeini into exile on November 4, 1964 in a hope of regaining some political stability. This strategy backfired, instead serving to glorify Khomeini among his followers.

Iran intensified its arms acquisition program as a result of the quantum increase in oil prices adopted by the Organization of Petroleum Exporting Countries (OPEC) in 1973. The regime generated roughly $20 billion in annual revenues a year after the price hike. Moreover, beginning in 1972, the Nixon Administration, seeking to establish a stronger pro-western presence in the region as a counter to Soviet advances, agreed to the Shah whatever non-nuclear arms he desired. By 1976, Iran had an estimated 3,000 tanks, 890 helicopter gunships, over 200 advanced fighter aircraft, the largest fleet of hovercraft of any country, 9,000 antitank missiles, and more military equipment either on hand or on order.[9] The sale of weapons and technology, oil revenues, as well as American investment in Iranian banks created strong economic ties, and relations between the United States. Not only was there close cooperation in the economic field, but Iran was also provided with U.S. general support in its efforts to become the Persian Gulf's regional predominate power.

This special bilateral relationship between the United States and the Shah was short-lived, however, as the economic situation became increasingly fragile. Although military sales strengthened Iran's security, its economy began to suffer. Evidently, the allocation of substantial oil revenue to military procurement damaged Iran's economic development program, and, hence, contributed substantially to the revolution that eventually overthrew the Shah. As the Carter Administration came into office in January 1977 with its increased emphasis on human rights, the bilateral special relationship became more problematic in light of the United States' substantial military assistance to the Shah's regime.

Toward the end of the 1970s, the Shah's effective suppression of secular dissidents encouraged new development of religious opposition to the regime. Indeed, misreading the strength of this movement led to the Iranian Revolution and subsequent exile of the Shah. One particular event is noteworthy. In January 1978, the leading semiofficial newspaper, *Ettela'at*, printed an article that violently attacked the exiled Ruhollah Khomeini residing in Paris. This publication instigated a massive demonstration, in Tehran on September 8, 1978, calling for the return of the Ayatollah. The incident escalated when the army fired upon the demonstrators, and some in the crowd returned fire. The bloody event, known as Black Friday, symbolized the beginning of the monarchy's downfall.[10] In January 1979, the Shah left Iran for an "extended rest." He never returned, and his departure marked the end of a close American-Iranian relationship lasting more than thirty years. Subsequently, Ayatollah Khomeini returned to Iran from his exile in France and assumed power.

On November 4, 1979, the "Students Following the Line of the Imam" (SFLI) attacked and seized the U.S. Embassy in Tehran. Wielding machine guns, they took 63 embassy personnel hostages and obtained classified documents, which were being shredded by the staff as the attack occurred. Khomeini praised the takeover, referring to the United States as "the Great Satan." His support undoubtedly prolonged the crisis, which otherwise would have been short-lived, and expanded his grip on power. Whether Khomeini directed the seizure of the U.S. hostages, or whether the attack was instigated independently by the militant "students," is a question that remains unanswered. In any event, the seizure of the hostages became the axis around which all U.S.-Iranian relations subsequently revolved.

Initially, President Carter publicly ruled out the use of force to secure the hostages' release while making clear that the United States would not submit to the militants' demands for the return of the Shah to Iran. He also blocked Iranian assets in the United States and severed diplomatic relations with Tehran. Moreover, at the United Nations, the United States demanded sanctions against Iran. Additionally, Carter took Iran to the World Court, where American attorneys obtained judgment ordering Iran to release the hostages. None of these other diplomatic measures had any practical outcome.

Frustrated beyond endurance, the United States finally launched a daring hostage-rescue mission, Operation Eagle Claw, in April 1980 that failed after an American helicopter collided with a transport plane in a blinding sandstorm at the rendezvous point inside the Iranian desert, killing eight U.S. servicemen. The mission only served to intensify Iranian convictions of an impending U.S.-led coup and solidified Khomeini's hold on power.

The major challenge to the revolutionary regime was, however, Iraq's September 22, 1980 invasion of Iran. The war, fought over territory disputes, lasted for eight years and resulted in over 1 million deaths. Iran initially attributed Iraqi leader Saddam Hussein's aggression to U.S. encouragement aimed at weakening Tehran and forcing it to release the hostages. Nevertheless, as Khomeini's Islamic revolution gained strength, it soon became apparent that the war was fought more over political strategy and ideological considerations. It is not surprising, therefore, that the United States faced a major foreign policy challenge. Concerned with the likelihood of destabilizing the fragile Middle East power balance, Washington played to both sides throughout the Iran-Iraq war, ensuring that neither side would emerge a regional hegemon.

Domestically, Abolhassan Bani Sadr, a former foreign minister, became the first elected president of Iran with Khomeini's support in January 1980. While the constitution provided that the presidency was the only high office directly elected by the people, it also ensured that de facto power was held by the Ayatollah and the Council of Guardians. This guaranteed that president would never circumvent the *ulama* and religious leadership. Khomeini had no intention of relinquishing power to a non-Islamic form of government as he believed the role of the ulama was to "oversee the work of the Prime Minister or of the President of the Republic, to make sure they . . . don't go against the law; that is, against the Qur'an."[11] When Bani-Sadr attempted to form seemingly "secular" presidency, he was impeached by the Majles and then fled to Paris. Sadr was later succeeded by Sayyed Ali Khamenei, who led the presidency largely in conformity with Khomeini's ideological views.

Meanwhile, the hostage crisis was finally resolved with signing of the Algiers Accords on January 19, 1981. The accords stipulated, in part, that in exchange for the hostages' release, the United States would not intervene in Iran's internal affairs, would unfreeze Iranian assets and lift trade sanctions, and that both governments would cease litigation surrounding the hostage crisis. The hostages were released minutes after President Ronald Reagan was sworn into office on January 20, 1981.

## IRAN-CONTRA AFFAIR

The 1979 overthrow of Anastasio Somoza by the communist Sandinistas in Nicaragua increased American fears of Soviet expansion throughout Central America. Additionally, the U.S. apparent support of Iraq during the Iran-Iraq war as well as the Soviet presence in Afghanistan concerned Washington that Iran may turn to the Soviet camp, thus undermining American influence in the Persian Gulf and ceding further ground to the Soviet sphere. The Reagan Administration therefore attempted to undermine Soviet influence in both regions and sought to make inroads with Iranian "moderates." However, the policies enacted to achieve these goals ultimately undermined America's credibility.

More specifically, in 1986, the Reagan Administration was rocked by two scandals: first, the covert resupply of the Contras, an anticommunist guerrilla group in Nicaragua, and second, the sale of weapons to Iran in exchange for the release of hostages. These transactions were closely linked: funds from the weapons' sales were illegally transferred to fund the Nicaraguan Contras. This foreign policy debacle, known as the Iran-Contra affair, led to the indictment of several top officials, and haunted the remaining term of the Reagan Administration.

Several aspects in connection with this affair are noteworthy. The Soviet Union's presence in Afghanistan intensified U.S. fears that Soviet influence in Iran would threaten U.S. regional interests. The Reagan Administration, therefore sought to improve relations with Iran and influence the release of American hostages, believing that eliminating restrictions on weapon sales would achieve both ends simultaneously.

Thus, the administration formulated a plan it believed would serve both U.S. and Iranian interests. In August 1985, weapons began flowing from the United States to Iran via Israel. Publicly, the United States undertook a trade and weapons embargo against Iran, yet privately it supplied Iran with various weapons. Some million dollars were skimmed off the arms deals and funneled to the Contras in Nicaragua. After numerous shipments and blundered negotiations, the United States was only able to obtain three hostages.

Clearly, the media's revelations of the hostages-for-arms deal, particularly the illegal actions by senior administration members, shocked the American public. The incident had indeed scarred the United States and severely undermined its credibility in its fight against terrorism.

## POST-KHOMEINI IRANIAN LEADERSHIP

During the 1980s, the Ayatollah Khomeini's reign in Iran was consumed largely by the Iran-Iraq war and a series of domestic Islamic consolidations. Although the Ayatollah died on June 3, 1989, his Islamic Republic has succeeded him to the present day. After his death, Ayatollah Sayyed Ali Khamenei, the former two-term president, was named the Supreme Leader of the Islamic Republic, and remains so today. Hashemi Rafsanjani, who campaigned on economic reforms for the new Republic, was elected president soon after Khamenei's ascension. Rafsanjani's goals largely focused on rebuilding a paralyzed Iranian economy devastated by the Iran-Iraq war. Rafsanjani also aimed to decentralize large industry, and to eliminate mismanagement and corruption. However, many of his initiatives were stalled by those Islamic clerics who feared privatization in the nationalized economy.[12] In addition to his efforts at economic reform, the relatively moderate Rafsanjani also attempted to support a women's movement in Iran, a move that gained little sympathy among the conservative Islamic leadership.

President Rafsanjani's lack of domestic success was mirrored by a difficult relationship with the United States. Rafsanjani grew frustrated with the United States' refusal to unfreeze Iranian assets after the release of Western hostages in Lebanon.[13] The United States, however, cited charges of Iranian support for international terrorism as well as its insistence on building a nuclear program.[14]

In reply, Rafsanjani publicly denied that Iran was attempting to acquire or construct nuclear weapons and accused the United States of trying to block peaceful nuclear programs vital to Iranian economic expansion.[15] Ultimately, Rafsanjani's popularity as president greatly diminished during his second term after he was unable to complete many of his far-reaching economic reforms. Indeed, when he attempted to introduce a second five-year economic reform plan, the legislation was blocked completely by Ayatollah Khamenei.

Currently, Rafsanjani still serves in high political office of the Iranian government. Rafsanjani and his followers are known to lean toward the right on most political and religious issues, largely when considering Iran's legal and education system. "Rafsanjanists" also tend to be opposed to strict social code in Iran, especially on topics related to women's education. Many youths in Iran today have tended to identify with moderate leaders and have sought this change through presidential office.[16]

When Rafsanjani's second term ended in 1997, he was unable to run again due to Iran's two-term limit and Seyyed Mohammed Khatami was elected on May 23, 1997 to succeed him. According to election results, there was a 91 percent voter turnout, up from 53 percent in the previous election. Khatami enjoyed widespread popularity during his campaign. In an opening speech, Khatami called for a rapprochement with Western governments, including the United States, as long as they respect Iran's dignity and national interests: "If we do not have relations with an aggressive and bullying country such as America, it is due to the fact that America does not respect those principles."[17] Khatami became one of the first figures in postrevolutionary Iran to consider developing a formal U.S.-Iranian relationship. In fact, he improved relations with the United States by inviting the American national wrestling team to compete in Tehran in 1998. During this event, an American flag was raised in honor of the athletes while the U.S. national anthem played, marking the first time U.S. athletes had been allowed to compete in Iran in almost two decades.[18] However, the reformist efforts were opposed by Khamenei and other conservatives serving on the Guardian Council.

A significant ideological clash developed between the reformists and the conservatives, leading to plotting and undertaking terrorist activities within the country. Members of Hizballah, were linked to fires and bombings of newspapers and magazines printing reformist materials as well as a break-in at a dormitory at the University of Tehran. There radicals beat and killed students who had protested against a bill passing through the Majles that would have drastically reduced press freedom. President Khatami denounced the attacks while Khamenei supported the activities, asserting that "today the enemy is striking Islam from home."[19] The Council of Guardians, along with other conservatives, mobilized the Iranian Revolutionary Guard Corps in fear of an insurrection after a series of protests involving over ten thousand students opposing conservative oppression. However, Khatami was not willing to lead a popular revolt, hoping instead to reform Iran through the current political system rather than risk thousands of Iranian lives in a violent confrontation.

After Khatami failed to capitalize on his wide popularity, Ayatollah Khamenei tightened his hold on the reformist agenda. President Bill Clinton's administration, wishing to develop a better relationship with Khatami, partially lifted its trade embargo with Iran. Moreover,, Secretary of State Madeline Albright issued an admission of U.S. involvement in the 1953 Mossadegh coup. The United States rationalized that these symbolic gestures would motivate a positive dialogue between the two countries.[20]

Iran, however, rejected these moves. On October 30, 2001, Khamenei threatened to dismiss any Iranian official who attempted to circumvent his authority in creating a bilateral relationship with the United States.[21] The remainder of Khatami's second term was directed by the Council of Guardians, who steadfastly refused to relinquish any real power to the presidency. During that period, Iran also expanded its support of international terrorist organizations, including Hizballah.

Additionally, evidence surfaced that Iran had secretly established advanced nuclear programs in two locations: a facility in Arak for plutonium upgrades, and a second in Natanz, designed for advanced uranium enrichment. After President George W. Bush labeled Iran as part of an "Axis of Evil" in his 2002 State of the Union address, President Khatami also abandoned his efforts at improving relations with America. "When a big power uses a militant, humiliating and threatening tone to speak to us, our nation will refuse to negotiate or show any flexibility," Khatami declared.[22] To be sure, the majority of Iranians were disappointed with Khatami's failed attempts to liberalize Iran and shift more power from the Council of Guardians and Ayatollah Khamenei to the office of the president. However, Khatami never planned to operate outside of the established constitution to reach his goals. His work within the limited parameters of his office led to his downfall. Conversely, Khatami's constrained approach was to the conservatives' advantage in their efforts to control Iranian legislation and limit reforms.

The 2005 Iranian election featured seven candidates who were approved by the Council of Guardians to run for the office of the president. After the first set of elections did not give any candidate a majority victory, a second runoff election was held. Akbar Hashemi Rafsanjani, the former Iranian two-term president running under a reformist agenda, and Mahmoud Ahmadinejad, the ultraconservative mayor of Tehran, emerged as the leading candidates for the presidency.[23]

Ahmadinejad won the runoff election with an approximate 62 percent of the votes, despite Rafsanjani's warnings that Ahmadinejad would rule Iran with an Islamic radicalism reminiscent of the Taliban regime. However, the victory was not without controversy. Mehdi Karrubi, one of the reformist candidates, accused the election of being rigged, and a number of signs validated his argument. Despite the controversy, the vote was certified and Ahmadinejad began his term on August 3, 2005. With his election, the prospect of an improvement in U.S.-Iranian relations seemed far less likely while Tehran's drive for developing a nuclear program would undoubtedly accelerate. Underscoring this bleak outlook, in the first press conference after his election, Ahmadinejad stressed the importance nuclear technology played in Iran to generate electricity.

The election of Mahmoud Ahmadinejad strengthened the ability of the Council of Guardians and Ayatollah Khamenei to craft conservative legislation with far fewer political obstacles. On the day of his election, after receiving approval from Khamenei, President Ahmadinejad kissed the hand of the Ayatollah, publicly demonstrating his allegiance to the leader. Indeed, Ahmadinejad was the first president to ever make this gesture, providing an unmistakable signal of the collaborative future between the Islamic conservatives now ruling Iran.

The presidency of Mahmoud Ahmadinejad has taken a dangerous and drastic turn since the efforts of former President Khatami to normalize Iran's relationship with the West and create a more open Iranian society. With the support of Ayatollah Khamenei, Ahmadinejad has been able to pass numerous conservative legislative proposals with ease. Within months of taking office, Ahmadinejad passed a law that banned all Western music from Iranian airwaves, a move that reminded many of Ayatollah Khomeini's bans on music over two decades ago and the associated harshness of Iranian Islamic government control.[24]

To date, Ahmadinejad has continued along this authoritarian path, stifling moderate views and behavior in Iran. For instance, *Shargh*, one of Iran's leading reformist newspapers, was banned from circulation because of its critical remarks toward Ahmadinejad.[25] On September 5, 2006, Ahmadinejad called for the removal of liberal and secular professors from Iranian universities.[26] Ahmadinejad's actions have made many U.S. officials fearful that Iranian society will become even more religiously radical. However, the most alarming aspect of Ahmadinejad's conservative agenda has been his steadfast support of Iran's nuclear enrichment program and his refusal to shutdown nuclear enrichment operations or complying with International Atomic Energy Agency (IAEA) inspections. Furthermore, Iran has funded, trained, and supplied weapons to Hizballah in Lebanon, which is accused of conducting terrorist activities in Iraq subsequent to the 2003 U.S.-led Operation Iraqi Freedom, and has supported Palestinian extremist groups such as Hamas in their war against Israel.

Both President Ahmadinejad and Ayatollah Khamenei have denied Iran's desire to develop nuclear weapons, stating, "We do not need a nuclear bomb . . . we consider a nuclear weapon against Islamic rules."[27] Both leaders have insisted that Iran's nuclear ambitions are solely dedicated to the development of civilian nuclear energy sources. However, the presence and suspected capabilities of Iran's nuclear facilities (and its continued refusal to cooperate with IAEA inspections) has led U.S. officials to believe that the nuclear program is anything but innocent. Indeed, U.S. officials believe Iran hopes to acquire nuclear weaponry as a means to intimidate its Arab Middle Eastern neighbors, resist Western demands, and establish itself as a regional hegemon.

The prospect of an Iran armed with a nuclear weapon becomes all the more terrifying when considered in light of Iran's sponsorship of terrorist organizations and President Ahmadinejad's vitriolic and hostile remarks toward Israel. The president of Iran has continuously made statements referring to the holocaust as a "myth" and has asserted that Israel "must be wiped off the map of the world."

The following chapters discuss in great detail the nature of Iran under President Ahmadinejad, particularly focusing on governmental structures and leadership, the terrorism dimension, and Iran's nuclear ambitions. Indeed, the challenge confronting the international community regarding Iran is twofold: first to determine whether Iran is crossing the "red line" of regional and global security concerns, and second to decide what unilateral or multilateral options are available to confront the dangers posed by the Islamic Republic in the twenty-first century.

2

# Iran's Government Structure

## IRAN'S GOVERNMENT STRUCTURE

From the time of antiquity, many attempts have been made by political philosophers to define and classify the "state" and its "government." One of the oldest treatments of these concepts was provided by Aristotle. He organized "states" on the basis of their intentions and "end goals." Among his classifications of states, he listed "monarchy," "tyranny," "aristocracy," "oligarchy," "democracy," and "anarchy." This approach was criticized subsequently because some governments included the characteristics of more than one form. A more modern perspective of "state" and "government" was introduced over a century ago in *Webster's International Dictionary*.[1] Its definition, however simplistic, asserted that a "state" is a "political body or body politic; the whole body people who are united under one government; a nation." The meaning of the term "government," however, was given a more elaborate treatment:

1. The act of governing, the exercise of authority, the administration of laws, control, direction, and regulation.
2. The mode of governing, the system of polity in a state, and the established form of law.
3. The right of power of governing, and authority.
4. The person or persons authorized to administer the laws, the ruling power, and the administration.
5. The body politic governed by one authority.

While the foregoing descriptions are relevant to a larger or smaller degree to contemporary times, Iran's governmental structure, policies, and activities over the past nearly three decades are rather unique. For example, Iran represents the only theological Shiite state in the community of nations, including the Muslim world. More specifically, Iran is a theocracy, and its legal framework is formulated in accordance with the precepts of religious jurisprudence and Shiite traditions. The 1979 revolution effectively changed the regime and established a governmental structure as developed by Ayatollah Khomeini in his 1970 political treatise, Islamic Government (*Hukumat e-Islami*). The guidelines set forth in this treatise emphasized support for a theocratic government structure and its perseverance within the political sphere, and, following the revolution, a state constitution was written to reflect these concepts.

The following discussion describes in great detail the roles of Iran's leadership as well as the nature of the executive, legislative, and judicial branches. Special attention is paid to those bodies that are connected with Iran's terrorist activities and nuclear ambitions.

## THE SUPREME LEADER

In the absence of a true Imamate, leadership of the state is passed to a single executive, the *vali-e-faqih*, or Supreme Leader. According to Khomeini's interpretation of theocratic rule, the Supreme Leader is intended as the highest religious and political authority in the state, based on his mastery of religious law and practice.[2] Since his authority is divine, and thus infallible, no aspect of legislation or state practice may be implemented contrary to his ruling or religious opinion. According to the constitution, the Supreme Leader is responsible for "general policies of the Islamic Republic of Iran," which include all aspects of domestic and foreign policies. It should be noted that Khomeini's interpretation of executive authority within the theocracy has many detractors within the worldwide Shi'a clergy, who view the political and religious spheres as separate—and not intertwined—entities.[3] It is thus not surprising that the Islamic Republic has consistently undermined, and outrightly suppressed, these dissenting views to the largest extent possible.

The Supreme Leader is under consistent review by the Assembly of Experts, a group composed of the clerical establishment. Since the revolution, there have been only two Supreme Leaders of the Islamic Republic: Ayatollah Khomeini held this office until his death in 1989 and his successor, Ali Khamenei, was appointed to the position by the Assembly of Experts shortly afterwords. Despite the clear hierarchy in Shi'ite religious doctrine, Khomeini chose a successor who was neither the anticipated replacement in terms of religious expertise nor an accepted expert and "source of emulation" (*marje taqlid*) to his followers. Thus, Khomeini's endorsement of Khamenei—a clear supporter of the regime though not a religious expert—was interpreted by many as an attempt to ensure the continuation of his personal policies rather than an attempt at installing a "correct" successor of Shiite jurisprudence. Several scholars have further noted that this perceived lack of religious legitimacy has constrained Khamenei's ability to impose policies, which he considers the proper application of political Islam within the political sphere.[4]

The Supreme Leader has approximately two thousand representatives, spread out across the various sectors of the government. These representatives have the power to intervene in any aspect of the legislative process on behalf of the Supreme Leader if they deem it necessary. The Supreme Leader is also commander-in-chief of the armed forces and controls the Islamic Republic's intelligence and security operations; he alone can declare war or peace. He has the power to appoint and dismiss the leaders of the judiciary, the state radio and television networks, and the supreme commander of the Islamic Revolutionary Guard Corps (IRGC). He also appoints six of the twelve members of the Council of Guardians, the body that oversees the activities of Parliament and determines the qualifications of all candidates who run for public office.[5]

## THE PRESIDENT

The president of the Islamic Republic, though only the second-highest authority in the land, wields considerable power within the country. He is a representative of the people, and is thus elected by a common majority. Each presidential term lasts four years, and no president may be elected to more than two full terms.

According to the constitution, the president must possess the following qualifications: He must be of Iranian origin and nationality; he must possess adequate administrative and managerial skills, piety and trustworthiness, a satisfactory personal history, and a belief in the Islamic Republic's fundamental principles and the official religion of the country.[6] Presidential candidates are subject to the scrutiny of the Council of Guardians of the Constitution, which reserves the right to disqualify candidates they deem unsatisfactory. In the 2005 elections, more than two thousand individuals applied for nominations, yet only eight were granted the right to proceed to the election.[7]

The president is responsible for setting the country's economic policies. He has nominal rule over the Supreme National Security Council and the Ministry of Intelligence and Security, though his authority is still subject to the Supreme Leader's approval. The president signs and supervises the implementation of laws passed by the *Majles* (the Iranian Parliament, see below), signs treaties and other international agreements ratified by the Majles, receives foreign ambassadors, and endorses those Iranian ambassadors posted abroad.[8] His responsibilities also include the administration of the country's budget and development plans ratified by the Majles. Eight vice presidents as well as a cabinet of twenty-two ministers serve under the president. The Council of Ministers must be confirmed by the Majles, though their decisions are subject to the Council of Guardians' veto.

## THE COUNCIL OF MINISTERS

At present, there are twenty-two members of the Council of Ministers. In the past, they were overseen by the prime minister of the Islamic Republic; however, when that post was abolished in 1989, the responsibilities of appointing and dismissing cabinet members moved to the presidency. Thus, all ministers are currently appointed by the president and approved by the Majles. Still, because the ministers' positions are dependant on their cohesion with a political hierarchy responsible for their appointment, that hierarchy (in particular, the Supreme Leader) is able to exert a great deal of influence upon their decisions.

Several ministries, within the scope of their duties, have been involved directly in the support of terrorist organizations: The Ministry of Intelligence and Security (or MOIS, officially founded in 1984) has retained alleged ties to known terrorists. Most notably, several allegations have been made regarding the ministry's role in facilitating the December 1988 bombing of Pan American airlines Flight 103 over Lockerbie, Scotland, and according to western intelligence sources, the ministry paid as much as $2 million to the perpetrators after its completion.[9]

Through the Foreign Ministry, many terrorists enjoy the cover of diplomatic immunity. They are supplied with diplomatic passports and, on occasion, have been granted access to the "diplomatic pouch" of various embassies. The trials of five men (one Iranian and four Lebanese) accused of the September 1992 assassination of Kurdish opposition leader Sadegh Sharafkindi and three colleagues in the Mykonos Café in Berlin, revealed the involvement of the Iranian Foreign Ministry and members of the executive branch, including Ayatollah Khamenei and former President Rafsanjani.[10] The criminal trials following several other incidents, including a thwarted plot to bomb the U.S. Embassy in Kuwait City in August 1983, and the bombing of the Jewish community center in Buenos Aires, Argentina in July 1994, yielded proof that the Foreign Ministry had been directly involved in the implementation of these attacks. Regarding the latter incident, in November 2006 the Argentinean government demanded the extradition of Rafsanjani for trial, citing his direct involvement.[11]

## THE SUPREME NATIONAL SECURITY COUNCIL[12]

The Supreme National Security Council is the body through which the president coordinates foreign and military policies with the Supreme Leader. Although by definition an arm of the judicial branch, this council is effectively administered by the president of the Republic.

The Council is supposed to ensure the national interest and maintain the Islamic values of the Republic within the cabinet.[13] According to Article 176 of the constitution, the Supreme National Security Council is accountable for "preserving the Islamic Revolution, territorial integrity, and national sovereignty." The Council is headed by the president, as stated, and its members are all established public servants. These include the Speaker of the Majles; the head of judiciary; the chief of the combined general staff of the armed forces; the ministers of foreign affairs, interior, intelligence; and the commanders of the Islamic Revolutionary Corps and the regular military. The president, as the leader of the Council, personally upholds—and executes in full—the Supreme Leader's foreign policy choices.

## THE LEGISLATIVE BRANCH

There are three houses in the Iranian legislative branch: the Parliament, the Council of Guardians, and the Expediency Council. While they are all subject to the rulings of the Supreme Leader, they all have considerable power over policymaking, subject to his approval.

### Parliament

The Iranian parliament, or Majles, consists of 290 members who are elected every four years. Before running for parliament, all Majles candidates must be approved by the Council of Guardians. The stated criteria for candidates include, among others, professing an irrefutable belief in the Islamic faith and state.[14] Elected members are regional representatives of the various Iranian provinces and all are elected by popular majority. The Majles is led by a speaker along with two deputy speakers. The speaker is responsible for running the meetings of the Majles; however, in his absence, the two deputy speakers will conduct the meetings. All ministers are appointed by the president, but must be approved by the Majles.

The Majles is responsible for approving international treaties, protocols, agreements, and contracts formulated on behalf of the Republic. All deliberations of the Majles must be open unless the president, a member of the Council of Ministers, or ten members of parliament call for a closed meeting. If a closed meeting is called, a three-fourths majority is needed to pass the legislation. The Guardian Council participates in any voting procedure conducted during these closed meetings.[15]

The Majles' legislative authority is subordinate to the rulings of the Council of Guardians, who can veto any proposed legislation they deem contrary to the spirit of the constitution. Given the overwhelmingly conservative makeup of the Council, whose officials are elected in part by the Supreme Leader, it has proven exceptionally difficult to reform existing legislation and create a more liberalized political construct. Indeed, during the term of the 2000 Majles—arguably the most reformist parliament in the Republic's history—a full 40 percent of the body's legislative decisions were overturned by the Council of Guardians.

The change in the Majles' makeup over the past several elections is striking. The 2000 Majles had an overwhelmingly secular representation (170 of 270 seats), while only 14 percent of the representatives were from the clergy. Conversely, the 2004 elections saw a return of the clerical majority, with the conservative party attaining 156 of the 290 seats. The return of the conservative bloc in parliament can be attributed both to the renewed stringency of the Council of Guardians, who disqualified more than 2400 potential candidates, and to the new rise in nationalistic tendencies, which emphasizes a traditionalist approach to foreign policy and an emphasis on collective, Iranian empowerment.

### Council of Guardians

The Council of Guardians consists of twelve jurists, all of whom are required to have achieved sufficient training in religious jurisprudence. Six of the Council's members are appointed by the Supreme Leader from among the clerical elite, while the remaining six are nominated by the judiciary and voted on by the Majles. The Council of Guardians is responsible for interpreting the constitution, and ensures that legislation passed by the Majles is consistent with Islamic law and the Constitution of the Islamic Republic. Any piece of legislation that does not adhere to these precepts is returned to the Majles for further revision. In addition, the Council is responsible for approving any presidential, parliamentary, and Assembly of Experts nominees before their names can appear on the ballot. The Council has been known to reject large numbers of candidates seeking to run for public office, regardless of the office sought by the candidate. Most recently, in the 2005 presidential elections, the Council barred more than two thousand individuals from running.[16]

### Expediency Council[17]

The Iranian Expediency Discernment Council of the System was established in 1988 by Khomeini after officials complained that the legislative system was constantly being coerced by the Council of Guardians. Thus, the Expediency Council is responsible for mediating legislative disagreements between the Majles and the Guardian Council, and acts as an advisory council to the Supreme Leader at the latter's behest. Originally, the Council comprised thirteen members when it convened. These included six members of the clergy (appointed by the Supreme Leader), six public officials (the president, the prime minister, the Majles Speaker, the supreme court chief justice, the prosecutor general, and a specific representative of the Supreme Leader), and the Majles member whose legislation was overturned. In 1997, Khamenei expanded the Council to thirty-four members, twenty-five of whom were appointed to five-year terms. While, in theory, the Expediency Council only intercedes on behalf of the legislative branch, in practice, it acts as a mediator between all bureaucratic entities, including the executive branch. Furthermore, the Council's composition is such that its rulings almost entirely mirror the legal opinion of the Supreme Leader and the Council of Guardians.[18]

## ASSEMBLY OF EXPERTS

The Assembly of Experts is a clerical council responsible for electing the Supreme Leader of Iran. Though members are elected by popular vote, all candidates are subject to disqualification by the Council of Guardians. Furthermore, because all members are part of the clerical establishment (and thus already affiliated with the ruling class), the supposed system of "checks and balances" expected from the mechanism of a popular vote is effectively nonexistent.

The Assembly of Experts convenes every six months to review the activities of the Supreme Leader in power and decide whether to further extend his term. Since its inception, the Council has never challenged any decisions retroactively or otherwise, and only installed a new Supreme Leader after the death of his predecessor.

## THE JUDICIAL BRANCH[19]

The judiciary is responsible for maintaining the rule of law and enforcing order within the Islamic Republic. The executive branch, through the Ministry of Justice, is responsible for all judicial appointments. Women are not allowed to serve as judges in the Islamic Republic; Shirin Ebadi, the 2003 Nobel Peace Prize laureate, was forced to give up her post as president of the Tehran city court following the revolution.

The courts retain regional jurisdiction over civil and criminal issues, but legal aspects of constitutional affairs are referred to the Council of Guardians. Justices are required to undergo legal and religious training prior to their appointments and are also subject to the approval of the Council of Guardians.

The Supreme Leader—through the Ministry of Justice—appoints the head of the judiciary (comparable to a chief justice), and he, in turn, elects the head of the Supreme Court and the chief public prosecutor.[20] The judiciary head is the highest judicial authority and is appointed to a five-year term. It also ensures that the law is properly enforced and that individual and public rights are protected. The judiciary is the sole body charged with investigating and ruling on criminal and civil matters. Trial by jury does not exist in Iran, though Article 168 of the constitution does permit such trials in specific cases. The judiciary also nominates six members of the Guardian Council.

There are three different courts within the judiciary: the Public Courts oversee civil and criminal cases; the Revolutionary Courts only try cases involving crimes against national security, narcotics smuggling, and other acts that weaken the Islamic Republic; and the Special Clerical Court (SCC), which operates separately from the other courts, is used to try crimes committed by clerics. Additionally, all rulings in the revolutionary and clerical courts are final and cannot bebreak; overturned.

At present, court seats are ostensibly dominated by the conservative camp. This is a major point of contention between the state and the reformist movement, to the point that reformers regard recourse to litigious arbitration as an ineffective and irrelevant means of dispute resolution.

## THE IRANIAN MILITARY

The conventional Iranian military—separate from the Islamic Revolutionary Guard Corps—is composed of three separate branches: the army, navy, and air force. Prior to the Islamic Revolution, the military was an extensively funded institution, which benefited from preferred arms trade agreements with the United States. At present, with an ongoing Western embargo on arms sales to the Islamic Republic, the Iranian military is reliant on domestic weapons production to maintain its military capabilities. Suffering from a deficiency of advanced technological expertise and human capital, the Iranian military's technological capacity has diminished substantially. In addition, political tendencies have led to the diversion of defense expenditures away from the conventional military toward the much larger, and more effective, IRGC.

## ISLAMIC REVOLUTIONARY GUARD CORPS[21]

The Islamic Revolutionary Guard Corps is the largest component of the postrevolutionary Iranian military and has a vast array of duties. Originally established by Khomeini as an instrument to preserve and enforce the directives of the nascent Islamic government, the Iranian constitution grants the IRGC the authority and responsibility to "maintain Iran's religious nature and spirit."[22] Though created primarily for the purpose of maintaining domestic security, the IRGC has branched out considerably, providing assistance and services to other Shi'a communities around the world as the government feels necessary.

The IRGC is a paramilitary force composed of five branches. These include an air force, navy, and ground forces separate from their regular Iranian military counterparts, as well as a special forces unit, the al Quds Force, and a civilian militia, the Basij Corps. The largest branch among the ground forces is the Basij corps, a volunteer force responsible for maintaining domestic order. Additionally, the IRGC's navy possesses far more advanced capabilities than those of the conventional Iranian Navy, as evidenced by their ability to capture fifteen British sailors and Royal Marines patrolling Persian Gulf waters in support of Operation Iraqi Freedom in March 2007.[23]

A uniquely intimate relationship exists between the Iranian political elite and the IRGC. This stems from the fact that most of Iran's political leaders were, at one time, IRGC members. For example, more than eighty members of the Majles have served in the IRGC, and President Ahmadinejad was a Basij volunteer, stationed in the western city of Kerman-shah during the Iran-Iraq war. Additionally, former IRGC commander Ezatullah Zarghami was named chief of Iran's national television and radio company in May 2004.[24]

Due to its close relationship with the Supreme Leader, the IRGC plays a prominent role in Iranian domestic and foreign affairs. The IRGC currently maintains 120,000 troops among an estimated twelve to fifteen divisions deployed in eleven security regions within Iran.[25] These forces are augmented by a separate, civilian offshoot of the IRGC known as the Basij Corps. Organized in 1980, the *Niruyeh Moghavemat Basij,* or Mobilization Resistance Force (aka Basij Corps) was formed as a volunteer paramilitary militia, which numbered some three million by the mid-1980s. These highly motivated, ideologically fanatical armed irregulars were utilized in suicidal "human wave" attacks against Iraqi forces during the Iran-Iraq war. Additionally, they mobilized thousands of armed government supporters in 1999 to suppress widespread nonviolent student demonstrations in which dozens were killed and hundreds jailed.[26]

The IRGC maintains autonomous institutions and facilities, including separate Iranian prisons. Domestically, these prisons are often utilized as centers of dissident repression in which internal opposition is quelled through coercive, and often violent, means. The IRGC also plays a supervisory role in Iran's nuclear program, and, more generally, is believed to be in charge of Iran's chemical, biological, and nuclear weapons programs as well as the country's operational chemical and biological weapons inventories and missile forces.[27] The latter group includes the operational air force unit responsible for Iran's Shahab missile development program.[28] The Shahab 3, first introduced into active service in 2002, has a range of over 1,300 miles, allowing it to strike anywhere within Israel.

Internationally, the IRGC promotes the exportation of the revolution and supports substate organizations loyal to its theocratic Shiite ideology. IRGC intervention in other countries' internal affairs is legitimized by Article 154 of the Iranian constitution, which charges the IRGC with the responsibility of aiding the "oppressed" people of the world. Ayatollah Khamenei once declared, ". . . exporting the revolution is like glitter of the sun whose rays . . . brighten the entire world."[29] IRGC personnel operate globally via front companies and nongovernmental organizations, maintaining contacts with officials from trading companies, banks, cultural centers, as well as representatives of "charitable" organizations including the Foundation of the Oppressed and Dispossessed (*Bonyad-e-Mostafazan*) or the Martyrs Foundation.[30] These influential Iranian institutions help families of those killed in the revolution as well as redistribute goods and money to lower-class families. Their funds help run social and financial services of the Shiite community including religious schools, hospital clinics, and building projects. Religious *hawzats* and mosques are vital in the indoctrination process of new "recruits." Ayatollah Mehdi Karrubi and Hojjatolislam Mohammad Ali-Rahmani currently lead these.[31] Additionally, in August 2006, it was revealed that the Martyrs Foundation reserved up to $2 million for distribution as compensation payments to bereaved families of Hizballah fighters killed in the 2006 Israel-Hizballah war.[32]

Specifically, two IRGC directorates are responsible for international activities: the Committee on Foreign Intelligence Abroad, which is tasked with foreign intelligence collection, and the Committee on Implementation of Actions Abroad, which, along with the elite al-Quds Force, supports and maintains an extensive international network of terrorist organizations, including Palestinian Islamic Jihad, Hamas, and the Palestinian Front for the Liberation of Palestine—General Command.[33] Its most notable achievement, however, has been providing the founding force of Lebanese Hizballah. Even today, the IRGC retains an extensive role in this group's operations. It is alleged that during the July–August 2006 Israel–Hizballah conflict that IRGC members were directly involved in combat operations, fighting alongside Hizballah guerrillas against the Israeli Defense Force. Israeli officials also reported that IRGC advisors in Lebanon assisted Hizballah guerrillas in firing two Iranian-made C802 anti-ship missiles at Israeli Naval vessels, one of which heavily damaged an Israeli Navy ship, the INS *Hanit*, which was enforcing a naval blockade of Lebanese ports.[34] In addition, Iranian-made long-range rockets and artillery were used by Hizballah throughout the conflict. Finally, the IRGC was found to be the source of the armaments supplied to Hamas via the *Karine A*, a weapons transport ship bound for the Palestinian territories that was intercepted by Israel in 2002.

Moreover, a former IRGC officer confirmed that the IRGC runs numerous camps and training centers both within Iran and abroad in locales such as Lebanon's Bekaa Valley. The camps are operated by the IRGC's al-Quds Force, which is responsible for extraterritorial special operations, and they offer instruction in terrorist tactics. The al Quds Force uses "the facilities of Iranian embassies or cultural and economic missions or a number of religious institutions such as the Islamic Communications and Culture Organization to recruit radical Islamists in Muslim countries or among the Muslims living in the West."[35] This same source estimates that the IRGC, with Foreign Ministry assistance, smuggled as many as fifty individuals into Iran for training in March 2006. Other trainees are supplied by their respective terrorist organizations.[36]

## Ministry of Intelligence and Security

Since 1979, the Iranian regime has maintained a formidable intelligence organization, the Ministry of Intelligence and Security (MOIS) or *Vezarat-e Ettela'at va Amniat-e Keshvar* (VEVAK), tasked with both domestic and foreign responsibilities in support of the Islamic regime. A successor to the Shah's intelligence service, SAVAK, and originally known by the acronym *SAVAMA*, the organization was reorganized in 1983–1984 as the Ministry of Intelligence and Security.[37] Domestically, MOIS is tasked with the monitoring, control, and suppression of internal dissidents. Internationally, its responsibilities include intelligence collection in support of terrorist movements as well as harassment and, at times, outright assassination, of regime opponents.[38]

MOIS operates under the direct supervision of the Supreme Leader Ayatollah Ali Khamenei and enjoys access to a secret budget. Operatives coordinate closely with the Iranian Foreign Ministry to conduct intelligence activities abroad, using Iranian embassies worldwide as intelligence-gathering hubs and for the diplomatic cover afforded agents involved in intelligence collection or terrorist activities.[39] MOIS operatives also utilize nonofficial covers, posing as employees of Iran Air (the Iranian state airline) and foreign branches of Iranian state-controlled banks, and as students, merchants, mechanics, businessmen, bank clerks, and, notably, members or former members of opposition groups (such as the *Mujahideen-e-Khalq* (MEK) or "People's Muhajedeen of Iran") while operating abroad.[40]

In the 1980s, the MOIS was directed to conduct a far-reaching political assassination campaign against the new regime's opponents, targeting supporters of the late Shah, exiled leaders of the MEK and prominent members of the Kurdish-Iranian underground who had fought against the ayatollahs' regime.[41] MOIS agents conducted attacks across Asia, Europe, the Middle East, and even inside the United States. Overall, it is estimated that MOIS agents have committed over eighty assassinations of Iranian dissidents worldwide since 1979.

In addition to outright assassinations, MOIS agents have also conducted traditional intelligence gathering, disinformation, and subversive operations against individual regime opponents and opposition governments. To enhance these capabilities, during the 1980s, Iranian MOIS operatives were trained in psychological warfare and disinformation techniques by instructors from Eastern Bloc countries using methods developed by the Soviet KGB.[42] In Europe, the organization established intelligence networks targeting Iranian refugees, political exiles, and others affiliated with regime opposition groups. According to European intelligence and security services, current and former MEK members, and other dissidents, these intelligence networks shadow, harass, threaten, and, ultimately, attempt to lure opposition figures and their families back to Iran for prosecution.[43]

Additionally, these networks attempt to entice or coerce former opposition group members into denouncing and vilifying their former compatriots. In 2002, for instance, MOIS agent and former MEK member Mohammad Hossein Sobhani was dispatched to Europe by MOIS deputy chief Mohammad Reza Iravani to recruit other former MEK members to denounce the group through elaborate disinformation campaigns designed ultimately to alienate MEK supporters, among them European and U.S. lawmakers. Sobhani continues to operate in Europe with other MOIS agents, under Iravani's direction, among them Karim Haqi.[44]

Another example of these subversive activities emerged in May 2005. The MOIS demonstrated the true extent of its reach with a carefully crafted disinformation campaign, which succeeded in duping a prestigious American nongovernmental organization (NGO), the New York City-based Human Rights Watch (HRW), into publishing a report detailing alleged human rights abuses committed by MEK leadership against dissident members.[45] The report was allegedly based upon information provided to HRW by known Iranian MOIS agents who were former MEK members working for the Iranian intelligence service. The MOIS, via this purportedly legitimate HRW report, sought to persuade several U.S. Congress members to reconsider a bill renewing opposition to the theocratic regime as well as financially supporting regime opposition groups including the MEK.[46] Additionally, in May 2005, Iranian officials feared the prospect that U.S. officials might decide to remove the MEK from the Department of State's Foreign Terrorist Organizations (FTO) list, a move which would have repealed various U.S.-imposed sanctions on MEK activities. Indeed, shifting the opinion of American presidential administrations, congressional, and other government leadership figures against this very capable opposition group has been critical to the Islamic regime's strategy for maintaining its grip on power. Influencing American academia, media, and NGOs, as evidenced by the HRW case, is merely the first step toward that objective.

Aside from subversive operations directed against individuals, groups, or government leadership figures opposed to the regime, the MOIS also collects what can be considered "traditional" intelligence on opposition governments and institutions, including the United States. In June 2004, two "security guards" from Iran's United Nations mission in New York City were expelled from the United States after the Federal Bureau of Investigation (FBI) repeatedly warned the Iranians against allowing their UN mission personnel to wander about the city videotaping such sites as the Statue of Liberty, major bridges, and the New York City subway system.[47]

In short, the Ministry of Intelligence and Security has remained an extremely effective, secretive, and vital organ of the Islamic regime's security apparatus.

# 3

# Iran's Leadership Profiles

It is a truism that a leader's role in shaping history is as significant as that of circumstances, coincidences, or the interplay of political, social, economic, and military forces. The experience of the Islamic Republic of Iran from the Ayatollah Khomeini to Mahmoud Ahmadinejad clearly demonstrates that personalities and their national interests and convictions can exert unique influence on issues of war and peace. This chapter focuses on some of the major religious and political figures who have led the country for nearly three decades. In addition to presenting profiles of these leaders, a selection of their statements has been incorporated for the purpose of highlighting specific policy dispositions on various matters, including terrorism, the Middle East conflict, and nuclear ambition.

## GRAND AYATOLLAH RUHOLLAH MUSAVI KHOMEINI

Grand Ayatollah Ruhollah Musavi Khomeini was the first Supreme Leader of the Islamic Republic of Iran and the driving force behind the Islamic Revolution of 1979. He instituted the theocratic structure of the current regime and is directly responsible for many of the existing trends in its current foreign and domestic policy.

Khomeini was born in the village of Khomein, south of Tehran, in 1900. An orphan at an early age, he attended the theological school in Arak, where he specialized in Arabic literature. Following the migration of many Shi'a theologians to the seminaries of Qom, Khomeini gradually advanced within the ranks of the clerical hierarchy there, and was appointed a *mujtahid* (one qualified to interpret religious law) by his tutors in 1927.

By the early 1960s, Khomeini had begun to challenge the secular Iranian regime led by the Shah Mohammed Reza. Under the tutelage of Ayatollah Kashani, one of the fiercest anti-establishment clerics of the period, Khomeini soon emerged as the prime spokesman for the religious community of Iran. Following the Shah's inauguration of the White Revolution in 1963—and the subsequent protests and riots in Iran's urban areas—Khomeini was placed under arrest, only to be freed after additional riots broke out demanding his immediate release. Nonetheless, by the end of the year, the Shah had forced Khomeini into exile. He first moved to Turkey, and later to Najaf, Iraq. However, after Iraqi President Saddam Hussein expelled him in 1978 at the behest of the Shah, Khomeini settled in Neauphle-le-Château, in northern France for the remainder of his exile.

While in exile, Khomeini continued to broadcast his virulent rhetoric, maintaining his position as the foremost advocate for Iranian regime change. After a popular uprising in late 1978, the Shah abdicated, leaving behind a fragile government that inevitably collapsed in early 1979. With no real regime capable of preventing his return, Khomeini arrived in Iran on February 1, 1978 and was subsequently named leader of the Islamic Republic, a position he held until his death a decade later.

Under his rule, the Iranian regime adopted a rebellious, anti-western foreign policy position, often disregarding international laws and norms, in support of its own regional aspirations, a position which has led to its present "pariah" status. Chief among his most notorious actions, he failed to prevent (and some claim tacitly supported) the November 1979 civilian attack on the American embassy in Tehran. Additionally, he continually refused to negotiate a cease-fire during the 1980–1988 Iran-Iraq war, even responding to Iraq's use of chemical weapons with unconventional weapons of his own. He issued several religious edicts pronouncing death sentences upon international figures he believed had usurped Islam, the most notable of which was the fatwa calling for the assassination of author Salman Rushdie for his controversial work, *The Satanic Verses*. Khomeini also wholeheartedly embraced the concept of "exporting the revolution" beyond Iran's borders, in which he consistently appealed to the Shi'a communities in Iraq, Lebanon, Kuwait, and Bahrain to overthrow their Sunni-dominated governments and install theocratic Shi'ite regimes. To realize this vision, Khomeini expanded the IRGC to include various international cells and established the terrorist group Hizballah in order to maintain its interests in the Levant.

Khomeini died in 1989 and was succeeded by Ayatollah Sayed Ali Khamenei. To this day, Khomeini remains the primary source of inspiration for any initiative supporting Iranian political or strategic expansion. His legacy firmly underpins modern Iranian political discourse and he is revered throughout the Shi'ite world as the harbinger of Iranian and Shi'a dominance on the international scene.

## Statements

### Regarding Democracy

- "Don't listen to those who speak of democracy. They all are against Islam. They want to take the nation away from its mission. We will break all the poison pens of those who speak of nationalism, democracy, and such things" (in a meeting with Iranian students and educators, Qom, [3] March 13, 1979).[1]
- "Those who are trying to bring corruption and destruction to our country in the name of democracy will be oppressed. They are worse than Bani-Ghorizeh [4] Jews, and they must be hanged. We will oppress them by God's order and God's call to prayer"—Ayatollah Khomeini (in a talk at the Fayzieah School, Qom, August 30, 1979).[2]

### Concerning the U.S. Embassy in Iran

- "We shall not stop fighting until we defeat [the U.S.] and cut its head in the area and lead weak people to victory. We do not differentiate between the aggressor East and criminal West . . . "[3]
- "If the United States wants to attack us . . . we cannot restrain the students, who are very emotional now, from blowing up the embassy. We will all be killed, and the hostages will also be killed."[4]
- "Our future relations with the United States will depend entirely on the American government," he said. "If the United States government stops interfering in our affairs and respects our nation, we will deal with it accordingly."[5]
- "But we cannot sit idlehanded [sic] when the United States is weaving conspiracies against us. We demand that the United States should extradite the criminal Shah to us, and the British government should extradite criminal Bakhtiar."[6]

### Involving the United States

- "God willing, the warrior Iranian people will maintain their revolutionary and sacred rancor and anger in their hearts and use their oppressor-burning flames against the criminal Soviet Union and the world-devouring United States and their surrogates." "As long as I live, I will not allow the real direction of our policies to change."[7]

### Regarding Islam

- "Those who know nothing of Islam pretend that Islam counsels against war. Those [who say this] are witless. Islam says: Kill all the unbelievers just as they would kill you all! Does this mean that Muslims should sit back until they are devoured by [the unbelievers]? Islam says: Kill them, put them to the sword and scatter [their armies]. . . . Islam says: Whatever good there is exists thanks to the sword and in the shadow of the sword! People cannot be made obedient except with the sword! The sword is the key to Paradise, which can be opened only for the Holy Warriors! There are hundreds of other [Qur'anic] psalms and Hadiths [sayings of the Prophet] urging Muslims to value war and to fight. Does all this mean that Islam is a religion that prevents men from waging war? I spit upon those foolish souls who make such a claim."[8]

### *Other Statements*

- "Dear students, you must watch the behavior and the activities of your teachers and professors so that if, God forbid, they say something wrong, you see them deviating, right away you must report them to the responsible officials. Teachers and professors, you must be alert to watch your own colleagues to see if some of them are trying to teach deviating thoughts during their lessons to the children of our Islamic nation so that they can be stopped. If this does not work, directly communicate with officials. My dear children, you too take care of one another in the best possible way, and if you observe that some enemies in the appearance of friends or schoolmates are trying to attract your friends, introduce them to the responsible officials, and try to do all these things very secretly. Committed mothers and fathers, watch the comings and goings of your children and observe their activities"—Ayatollah Khomeini (in a message on the first day of the school year, Qom, September 23, 1982).[9]

## AYATOLLAH SAYYED ALI KHAMENEI

Ayatollah Sayyed Ali Khamenei is the current Supreme Leader of Iran. Born into a poor family in 1939 in Mashad, he joined the Mashad theological seminary and studied Islamic jurisprudence there until 1958. After a brief visit to Najaf, Iraq, he continued his advanced studies in the city of Qom. Khamenei first became politically active while studying under Ayatollah Khomeini in Qom during the early 1960s. He joined Khomeini's revolutionary movement, becoming a well-known figure within opposition circles. Consequently, he was also well known to the Shah's security forces, having been arrested several times during the late 1960s and 1970s.[10]

After his release, he was briefly deported to the southwest province of Iranshahr and placed under government supervision. In 1978, during the period between the Shah's abdication and Khomeini's eventual return, he was appointed to the Islamic Revolutionary Council (at the behest of Khomeini), which was established to restore order and facilitate the creation of the Islamic Republic. After briefly serving as the secretary of defense in 1980, he was nominated to the presidency later that year, again at Khomeini's behest, and won in a landslide vote. He retained this position for nine years, and served as both the president and the head of the Expediency Discernment Council of the System in 1989. After Khomeini's death, he was appointed the new Supreme Leader of Iran by the Assembly of Experts—this despite his lesser position within the accepted clerical hierarchy.

Under his rule, Iran has expanded its sphere of influence and networks designed to promote Shi'a dominance in the region. After his ascension, which coincided with the election of the new President Akbar Hashemi Rafsanjani, the Iranian intelligence apparatus began a concerted effort to attack Iran's international opposition, and was deemed responsible for numerous assassinations of Kurdish and secular Iranian dissidents.[11] It was also under his rule that Iran's official patronage of the Hamas movement in Palestine began as well as the expansion of Hizballah into a political movement within Lebanon. To this day, Khamenei remains the highest authority in the Iranian decision-making process, and the current policies of the regime may well be considered a reflection of his personal approach to foreign policy.

## Statements

### *Israeli-Palestinian Conflict*

- "Think of the Palestine of the 1940's: a land in the heart of the Arab world, a poor country with a weak government and an unaware nation and some neighbors installed by colonial powers. The wealthiest and most evil Western government with the greatest stockpile of arms and weapons, provoked by the Zionists, took it away from Muslims and entrusted it to a racist, belligerent and terrorist party which received support from all Western countries and from both of the world's two political blocs that were at odds with each other."[12]
- "We in the Islamic Republic of Iran, and surely multitudes of Muslims and broad-minded individuals across the world, share in your grief and suffering. Your martyrs are our martyrs; your affliction and agony is also ours, and your victory is our victory."[13]
- "Israel must be wiped out from the map of the world."[14]
- "Iran's stance has always been clear on this ugly phenomenon [i.e., Israel]. We have repeatedly said that this cancerous tumor of a state should be removed from the region."[15]
- "The world of Islam should show a serious reaction to the Zionist regime's insult to Al-Aqsa Mosque."[16]

### *Conflict between Lebanon and Israel*

- "They (Israel) want Lebanon to be a meat in their mouth, but the powerful Hizballah has prevented their dream from being realized."[17]

- "The crimes and the atrocities in the recent weeks in Palestine and Lebanon have proved again that the existence of Israel in this region is an evil and cancerous being and an infected tumour."[18]
- "The Islamic world states are proud of the courageous resistance by Hizballah against the Zionist (Israel) aggressors."[19]
- "Blamed U.S. for "supporting the killing of innocent children, women and men with such a boldness."[20]

### *Relations with the United States*

- "The bitter and venomous taste of Western liberal democracy, which the United States has hypocritically been trying to portray through its propaganda as a healing remedy, has hurt the body and soul of the Islamic Ummah and burned the hearts of Muslims. Iraq and Afghanistan and Lebanon, Guantanamo and Abu Ghuraib [sic] and other secret dungeons and, above all, the cities in the Gaza Strip and the West Bank have shown to our nations the real meaning of 'liberty' and 'Western human rights,' the most shameless and impudent propagator of which is the American regime. Today, Western liberal democracy is as disgraced and detested in the Islamic world as was the East's socialism and communism yesterday."[21]
- "The world of Islam has been mobilized against America for the past 25 years. The peoples call, "death to America." Who used to say "death to America?" Who, besides the Islamic Republic and the Iranian people, used to say this? Today, everyone says this."[22]
- "The torment of the Iraqis, of the Palestinians, and even of the Americans are the direct outcome of liberal Western democracy, and this must serve as an important lesson to the rest of the world, [which must] open its eyes and understand that those who call themselves advocates of human rights and democracy are in fact the main supporters of crimes against humanity."[23]
- "Your government today is the most hated government in the history of the United States. They announced it to the world in their own opinion polls. . . . "[24]
- "Compare this with our own government. Our government is one of the most popular governments since the [1906] constitutional revolution."[25]

### *Concerning the War on Terror*

- "America does not have the competence to guide a global movement against terrorism, and the Islamic Republic of Iran will not participate in any move which is headed by the United States."[26]
- "The Americans are convinced that they will easily win the war in Iraq. But they will not see that day. As the Imam [Khomeini] said, 'One day the U.S. too will be history.' "[27]
- "In Iraq, you failed. You say you have spent $300bn to bring a government into office that obeys you. But it did not happen. In Palestine, you made

every attempt to prevent Hamas from coming to power and again you failed."[28]

### On Nuclear Weapons

- "We do not negotiate with anybody on achieving and exploiting nuclear technology.... But if they recognize our nuclear rights, we are ready to negotiate about controls, supervisions and international guarantees."[29]
- "We have no problem with the world. We are no threat whatsoever to the world and the world knows it.... " [30]
- "The other suggestion is that Iran is seeking a nuclear bomb. This is an irrelevant and wrong statement, it is a sheer lie. We do not need a nuclear bomb. We do not have any objectives or aspirations for which we will need to use a nuclear bomb. We consider using nuclear weapons against Islamic rules.... "[31]
- "We think imposing the costs of building and maintaining nuclear weapons on our nation is unnecessary. Building and maintaining such weapons is costly. In no way do we deem it correct to impose these costs on the people."[32]
- "Negotiation with the United States has no benefits for us."[33]
- "The Iranian government and the Iranian nation will never ever bow to pressure by the United States or any other states over its nuclear technology ambitions."[34]
- "Those countries which now threaten us with sanctions should know that such threats will have no impact and not intimidate us, but in return encourage Iranian youth to improve their own scientific capabilities."[35]

### Energy

- "Our government has healthy and good relations with European countries. These relations with Europe will be even better in the future, when gas plays a more important role as a source of energy. They need our gas."[36]
- "In order to threaten Iran, you [America] say that you can secure the energy flow in the region. You are wrong. Beware that if you make the slightest mistake over Iran, the energy flow through this region will be seriously endangered. You will never be capable of providing energy security in this region. You are not capable and you should know this."[37]

## MAHMOUD AHMADINEJAD

Mahmoud Ahmadinejad is the current President of the Islamic Republic of Iran. He is a longtime member of the Iranian civil service and served as mayor of the city of Tehran prior to his appointment to the presidency.

Born in 1956 outside Tehran, he became active in Iranian politics from an early age, eventually joining the revolutionary movement that propelled Khomeini to power. After the Islamic Republic's inception, he founded the Islamic Association of Students at the Iran University of Science and Technology. Reports of his direct involvement in the 1979 attack on the U.S. embassy in Tehran and the planned, simultaneous attack on the Soviet embassy have been disproved by many eyewitnesses, including former hostages. Nonetheless, Ahmadinejad's activities during that period remain ambiguous, and his involvement in specific acts of terrorism, while speculated upon, remains unverified.

In 1986, during the Iran-Iraq war, Ahmadinejad volunteered to join the Islamic Revolutionary Guard Corps' (IRGC) special forces.[38] While serving in the IRGC, Ahmadinejad worked in the intelligence and security apparatus before becoming one of the senior officers of the Special Brigade of the Revolutionary Guards. While serving in this position, Ahmadinejad was stationed in Ramazon Garrison, which is reported to have been the headquarters of the Revolutionary Guards' Extraterritorial Operations.[39]

In addition to his military background, Ahmadinejad has a long history of civil service. In 1993, he served as cultural advisor for the Ministry of Culture and Higher Education. Following this, he was appointed governor-general of Ardabil province, where he remained until 1997. In that year, he also received a Ph.D. in engineering and traffic transportation planning from the Iran University of Science and Technology. In April 2003, Ahmadinejad was elected mayor of Tehran by the Tehran City Council. As mayor, he overturned many of the reformist policies enacted by the liberal parliament and president elected during the late 1990s in favor of returning the Republic's capital to a more traditionalist culture with overtly Islamic features. He remained in this post until 2005, whereupon he was groomed by the conservative establishment for the upcoming presidential elections.

Early indicators of the 2005 elections did not favor Ahmadinejad, a hard-line conservative, who trailed the moderate favorite, Ali Akbar Rafsanjani, in all public opinion polls. After taking second place in the initial ballots, however, he proceeded to win the runoff elections by a wide margin. Many analysts believe his victory was due, in part, to his image as a working-class reformer unblemished by the corruption allegations hampering more elitist candidates, including the moderate Rafsanjani.[40]

Since his appointment as president of the Islamic Republic, Ahmadinejad has maintained the same conservative approach that categorized his mayoral administration: His policies emphasize a broadening of the welfare system and a reallocation of wealth to Iran's working class. Concurrently, he supports the strengthening of Iran's Islamic character and restoration of its past military and cultural dominance in the region. Thus, in practice, he has taken conservative positions vis-à-vis Iranian foreign policy, favoring the expansion of Iran's nuclear program, openly denying Israel's right to exist, and supporting Shi'a constituencies throughout the Middle East, particularly in Lebanon and Iraq. He has clashed on numerous occasions with the international community, which accuses him of, among other transgressions, refusing to comply with various international accords and practices, including the Nuclear Non-Proliferation Treaty (NNPT), and of publicly denying the occurrence of the Holocaust. While he has faced significant criticism both at home and abroad, he is still supported by the higher echelons of the Iranian government establishment, including the Supreme Leader and many members of the Revolutionary Guard Council.

## Statements

### *Israeli-Hizballah-Lebanon Crisis*

- "Today, it has been proven that the Zionists are not opposed only to Islam and the Muslims. They are opposed to humanity as a whole. They want to dominate the entire world. They would even sacrifice the Western regimes for their own sake."[41]
- "To attack another country in this way will not solve anything, instead it will make the problems more complicated. Those who think that by oppressing a nation they can create a foothold for themselves are making a big mistake. There is an expression in Persian: He who raises the wind will get a hurricane. And this hurricane is just round the corner in the Middle East, and it will be harsh and destructive for the enemies of humanity."[42]
- "There are also some countries that claim to be democracies and supporters of freedom and human rights but which keep silent when this regime [Israel] bombs Lebanon in front of their eyes and slaughters people in their houses."[43]

### *Israeli-Palestinian Conflict*

- "The skirmishes in the occupied land are part of a war of destiny. The outcome of hundreds of years of war will be defined in Palestinian land. As the Imam said, Israel must be wiped off the map."[44]
- "The real Holocaust is what is happening in Palestine where the Zionists avail themselves of the fairy tale of Holocaust as blackmail and justification for killing children and women and making innocent people homeless."[45]
- "Today there is a strong will . . . to remove the Zionist regime and implement a legal Palestinian regime all over Palestine. The continued survival of this regime (Israel) means nothing but suffering for the region."[46]
- "I am reminding them to stop the crimes of this corrupt government before it is too late, and open the way for a government arising from the votes of the indigenous people of Palestine, all over Palestine."[47]
- "The waves of fury of Muslim nations will not be confined within the boundaries of the region, and the people who close their ears to the cries

of the Palestinians and blindly support this regime will be responsible for the consequences."[48]

- "Ever since the Palestinian nation focused attention on promotion of an Islamic atmosphere and attitude, day-to-day success and progress have been witnessed among Palestinians."[49]
- "They should not let things reach a point where an explosion occurs in the Islamic world. If an explosion occurs, then it will not be limited to geographical boundaries. It will also burn all those who created [Israel] over the past 60 years."[50]

### *Israel*

- "Remove Israel before it is too late and save yourself from the fury of regional nations."[51]
- "The basic problem in the Islamic world is the existence of the Zionist regime, and the Islamic world and the region must mobilize to remove this problem."[52]
- "The biggest threat today for the region is the existence of the fake Zionist regime."[53]
- "... the Zionist regime behaves like Hitler."[54]
- "The survival of this regime is not possible without oppression and aggression."[55]
- "Despite the barbaric and criminal nature of the occupiers of Jerusalem, the regime and its Western supporters do not even have the power to give Iran a nasty look."[56]
- "Zionism is a Western ideology and a colonialist idea... and right now it massacres Muslims with direct guidance and help from the United States and part of Europe... Zionism is basically a new [form of} fascism."[57]
- "Jews [i.e. anti-Zionist Jewish groups such as Neturei Karta] throughout the world have been supporting Palestine for the past 70 years. On the geographic map of the region, there is no country called 'The Zionist Regime'...."[58]
- "The oppressing regime in occupied Palestine is the most important obstacle, and causes the Islamic nation collective concern. Judicious removal of this fear [i.e. Israel] will pave the way to the appearance of Islam's power in successful management of global [matters]. It is unnecessary to point out that there is no logical way to recognize this false regime. The acceptance [of the existence] of [this] oppressing regime means making humanity despair of attaining viable peace and tranquility, and giving a seal of approval to oppression, arrogance, and domination. The only way—which is both the wise way and is compatible with the international rules—is the return of the Palestinian refugees, [and] the holding of a referendum with the involvement of all the original Palestinians, including Muslims, Christians,

and Jews, in order to determine the type of regime in all of Palestine, whose capital is holy Jerusalem."[59]

### Syria

- "[Syria is] the steadfast party confronting Israel and the defender of Islamic vigilance."[60]
- "Common threats to Iran and Syria require joint cooperation from the two countries more than ever."[61]
- "Cooperation between Iran and Syria would be effective in the region and entire Muslim World and there is no limitation in this respect."[62]

### Iraq

- "The American government has all sorts of allegations but never shows any documents or proof. If there is insecurity in Iraq, the first ones to suffer from it are the neighboring countries like Iran."[63]

### United States

- "One day all supporters of Israel, especially the U.S., should be held accountable."[64]
- "God willing, with the force of God behind it, we shall soon experience a world without the United States and Zionism."[65]
- "[The U.S. and their allies are] themselves engaged in nonpeaceful nuclear activities. They expand them day by day. Another indication of that is that in the Middle East region they have equipped some powers and some groups with nuclear weapons, and they themselves test new types of weapons of mass destruction every day."[66]
- "Britain and the United States are accomplices of the Zionist regime in its crimes in Lebanon and Palestine."[67]
- "The US and UK do not deserve to be permanent member of the Security Council. They have abetted Israeli war crimes and should stand trial. . . . They are contemplating to spread the flames of war throughout the Middle East, but, they should fear the fury of the nations."[68]
- "We are after a multipolar rather than a unipolar world."[69]

### Nuclear Ambitions

- "Our religion prohibits us from having nuclear arms. Our religious leader has prohibited it from the point of view of religious law. It's a closed road. We even don't need it; we can guarantee our security in other ways . . . During the past two years, more then 1,200 inspections have taken place in our country. More than 1,030 documents have been given to the IAEA. All the IAEA cameras are fixed on our facilities, and the IAEA supervisors can control every action within our facilities. We have proven amply that we are conforming to regulations."[70]

- "They ask us why we have started [nuclear] research. Our reply is that there is no limitation to research. There are no limits imposed on research in the Nuclear Non-Proliferation Treaty nor in the Additional Protocol. Nor have we made any such commitment."[71]
- "The people of Iran will not give up their right to exploit peaceful nuclear technology. . . . They are not intimated by the arrogant uproar and propaganda today."[72]
- "Those handling the talks are terrified, and before they can even sit down at the negotiating table they retreat 500 kilometers. . . . A popular and fundamentalist government will quickly change that."[73]
- "Iran is ready to transfer nuclear know-how to the Islamic countries due to their need."[74]

### *Iranian Foreign Policy*

- "Those who insulted the prophet should know that you cannot obscure the sun with a handful of dust. The dust will just get back and blind your own eyes."[75]
- "We increasingly see that people around the world are flocking towards a main focal point—that is the Almighty God. My question for you is, 'Do you not want to join them?"[76]
- "I have said in Tehran, and I say it again here – I say to the leaders of some Western countries: Stop supporting these corrupt people. Behold, the rage of the Muslim peoples is accumulating. The rage of the Muslim peoples may soon reach the point of explosion. If that day comes, they must know that the waves of this explosion will not be restricted to the boundaries of our region. They will definitely reach the corrupt forces that support this fake regime."[77]
- "Anybody who recognizes Israel will burn in the fire of the Islamic nation's fury, any (Islamic leader) who recognizes the Zionist regime means he is acknowledging the surrender and defeat of the Islamic world."[78]
- "A nation which is armed with faith and martyrdom will never experience defeat and submission"[79] (September 26, 2006).
- "The enemies of the Islamic Republic (of Iran) are furious because the Iranian nation has dared to grow its self-confidence out of their domination sphere."[80]
- "Some of the Islamic countries are exposed to threats from the superpowers. If the enemies of Islam, and those who wish it ill, do not come up against a suitable reaction on the part of the Islamic countries, there will be no end to their trespassing. A threat to [any] Islamic country must be seen as a threat to all Islamic countries. A joint defensive and security alliance, and its ratification, will prevent these threats."[81]

## SEYYED MOHAMMAD KHATAMI

Seyyed Mohammad Khatami is an Iranian cleric and a former president of Iran. He studied theology at Qom, achieving the high rank of "*mujtahid*." During the 1970s, Khatami chaired the Islamic Center in Hamburg, Germany, where he remained until the 1979 Islamic Revolution.

During the 1980s, Khatami served in a number of positions within the government, first as a member of the Majles General Assembly, and later as Minister of Islamic Culture. He served as a member of President Rafsanjani's cabinet during the latter's presidential term until 1997, when Khatami himself was elected president. His election to the presidency signaled a period of popular sentiment favoring reformist domestic policies. However, his direct subordination to the more conservative Supreme Leader Khamenei greatly inhibited his ability to impose any lasting reforms from his post. Moreover, the elected parliament of 2004, which was dominated by the conservative political faction, overturned many of Khatami's reform proposals—some even retroactively. He stepped down from the presidency after serving for the maximum two terms allowed under the Iranian constitution, and was succeeded by Mahmoud Ahmadinejad in 2005.

### Statements

#### *Regarding Democracy and the Elimination of Reformists*

- "No problem will be solved through the superficial elimination of a group.... [S]uch tendencies would go into hiding and grow up at great cost."[82]

#### *Iraq*

- "All should cooperate with the Iraqi nation to keep Iraqi borders secure and prevent the activities of terrorist groups."[83]

## AKBAR HASHEMI RAFSANJANI

Akbar Hashemi Rafsanjani is the head of the Expediency Discernment Council of the System, and one of the most notable Iranian public figures to emerge from the 1979 revolution. His past positions include the Speaker of the *Majles* Assembly, vice chairman of the Assembly of Experts and president of the Republic from 1989 to 1997.

Rafsanjani comes from a family of pistachio farmers, which is at present one of the world's largest independent suppliers. He studied theology at the Qom seminary alongside the late Khomeini. During the 1970s, he was a well-known detractor of the Shah's regime, and spent almost three years in jail for activities associated with the Mojahedin-e-Khalq (MEK) organization, then an anti-Shah organization, which would later become one of the largest dissident groups opposing the current Iranian theocracy.[84] Together with Ali Khamenei, he was appointed to the Islamic Revolutionary Council and became the first Speaker of parliament for the Islmaic Republic. It is said that he was one of the driving forces able to finally convince Khomeini to agree to the 1988 cease-fire in the Iran-Iraq war. After Khomeini's demise, he replaced Khamenei as president following the latter's appointment as Supreme Leader, and became the first Iranian president to serve his entire term (his immediate predecessors had been removed and assassinated, respectively).

Rafsanjani has been linked to various terrorist activities conducted under Iranian sponsorship. Throughout the 1990s, Rasfanjani's name was linked to the attacks on the Khobar Towers in Saudi Arabia (1996)[85] and the Jewish community center in Buenos Aires, Argentina (1994). Regarding the latter, the Argentinean government recently demanded his extradition along with several other high-ranking Iranian officials.[86] In 2000, a local journalist, Akbar Ganji, accused Rafsanjani of killing eighty writers, an accusation Rasfanjani denied. Ganji, however, was sentenced to jail for "spreading propaganda about the Islamic regime"[87] after the intelligence officer who was supposed to testify against Rasfanjani at trial mysteriously died in jail.

In 2005, Rafsanjani ran in the presidential elections on a platform calling for a more liberal approach to both Iranian economic and foreign policies and, despite previous assertions of his involvement in international terrorist activity, the western press generally hailed him as the most desirable candidate.[88] In spite of being the favorite candidate in the initial balloting, he was decisively defeated by Mahmoud Ahmadinejad in the runoff election. He currently serves as Head of the Expediency Discernment Council of the System, and continues to be the leading voice within the establishment promoting economic reform and a more liberalized economic policy. He also serves as deputy chief of the Assembly of Experts.

## Statements

### *Israel*

- "If one day, the world of Islam comes to possess the weapons currently in Israel's possession—on that day this method of global arrogance would come to an end. This is because the use of a nuclear bomb in Israel will leave nothing on the ground, whereas it will only damage the world of Islam."[89]

### *Nuclear Ambitions*

- "My words to America, and Europe as well is that you are dealing with a strong, zealous, Muslim and faithful nation, you are dealing with a nation that believes in its own rights and relies on its own rights and nothing more, Instead of bullying, we had better negotiate, cooperate and remove any possible ambiguities. This way, neither will you be humiliating a nation nor will we trouble anyone else. God willing, through their negotiations they [the West] will reach a similar conclusion and will neither trouble the world nor any region."[90]

### United States

- "I would like to tell the White House categorically that their way and their threats are futile . . . Iran is not the appropriate place for acts of adventurism . . . We advise you to enter through the gate of peace. You should realize that this revolution is permanent and here to stay and you should recognize the Iranian nation's right."[91]
- "I believe that if the Americans renounce their hostile stance and show goodwill, the road will be prepared for negotiations."[92]

### Iraq

- "We congratulate this patient, impregnable and alert people, who managed to tread such a path while their country was under occupation. We hope that they will continue their resistance to stop the Americans from hoping and desiring to control the parliament and government by relying on their military presence and occupation of Iraq. Because that is why the Americans entered Iraq, to bring the country under their control."[93]

### Iranian Foreign Policy

- "[I call for] prudence . . . so that we can have a presence and help people without being accused of engaging in terrorism, without anyone being able to call us fanatics."

### Future of Iran

- "The West is drumming up confusion and pandemonium in their newspapers by saying that after these elections, the Government of Iran will become more and more Westernized. That is a lie."[94]

### IAEA Recommendations on Iran

- "If they adopt what Europeans have proposed and open our case's path even in the form of report to the UN Security Council, they will in fact commit a big mistake."[95]

## MANOUCHEHR MOTTAKI

Manouchehr Mottaki is the current Minister of Foreign Affairs of the Islamic Republic of Iran, appointed directly by President Ahmadinejad. Previously, Mottaki served as a member of parliament as the representative of the Islamic Consultative Assembly in 1980. He has had a long career as a diplomat for the Islamic Republic, serving as ambassador to both Turkey (1985–1989) and Japan (1994–1999). He was forced to leave his Turkish post in 1989 after the Turkish government became aware of his involvement in several terrorist plots.[96] In 1999, Mottaki began work as an advisor to the foreign minister, a position he held until 2001, when he would be appointed the deputy head of the Islamic Culture and Communication Organization as well as the head of both the Seventh Majlis' National Security and Foreign Policy Committee and the NPT Working Group. He held these positions from March 2004 to August 2005 before being appointed Minister of Foreign Affairs.[97]

### Statements

#### *Nuclear Ambitions*

- "Iran does not intend to halt the process of nuclear negotiations with the EU. It believes that if the Europeans make a positive proposal they could open a new chapter in Iran-EU ties."[98]
- "We stress that after the resumption of activity at Esfahan nuclear installation, we should hold unconditional negotiations. Iran's transparent, reasonable and legal attitude will persuade the European side to join the talks."[99]

#### *Iran's Foreign Policy*

- "In our foreign policy, we must pay attention to kindness and justice. This itself can prepare the stage for attracting Iranian expatriates and foreign investment. . . . Our foreign policy must be dynamic and have a mechanism which befits international relations. We pursue rational and transparent policies and call for structural changes in this domain."[100]

## MOSTAFA POUR-MOHAMMADI

Mostafa Pour-Mohammadi is the current Minister of the Interior of Iran. Pour-Mohammadi was born in 1959 in the holy city of Qom. He studied theology in Qom, Tehran, and Mashhad.[101] Prior to being appointed minister, Mohammadi served as the prosecutor for Khuzestan, Bandar Abbas, Kermanshah, and Mashhad during the Iranian Revolution from 1979 to 1986.[102] He was also a prosecutor for the armed forces in 1986 and the head of foreign information from 1990 to 1999. Other posts he has held include that of deputy information minister from 1997 to 1999 and leader of the Board of Trustees of Center for Islamic Revolution Documents. Mohammadi served as the deputy minister of foreign relations from 1997 to 1999. In 2003, Supreme Leader Khamenei appointed him head of the political and social department of his office.[103]

## MOSTAFA MOHAMMAD NAJJAR

Mostafa Mohammad Najjar is the current Minister of Defense. After completing his education, Najjar joined the IRGC in 1980 and has held various positions within the IRGC throughout the Republic's history. In 1981, he was named the director of the Central Cooperative Department, overseeing medical treatment, social work, housing, and physical education.[104] He headed the Middle East Directorate in 1982, and, by 1985, was the director of IRGC's first hardware manufacturing program, the Hadid Industrial Group. He was also the deputy director of IRGC's military hardware office from 2002 to 2005.[105] Before President Ahmadinejad appointed Najjar as defense minister, he was the deputy head of the School Association for Special Education (SASED) for Planning and Development.[106]

### Statements

#### *Nuclear Ambitions*

- "Access to nuclear energy is an inalienable right of Iran and we shall safeguard it by our presence at international organizations and through diplomacy and confidence building measures. From an Islamic viewpoint, military and non-peaceful use of nuclear technology is *haram* [religiously forbidden]."[107]
- "Iran merely wants nuclear energy for civilian application and the welfare of citizens and does not need nuclear arms."[108]

#### *Iranian Foreign Policy*

- "We follow detente with active diplomacy in a bid to help strengthen peace and stability in the region."[109]

#### *Iraq*

- "Those who commit terrorist acts are real enemies of the ideal of the Iraqi people . . . the security, defense and economic agreements which have already been signed by the two countries show Iran's strong determination to help restore security and peace in Iraq."[110]

### *Iran-Iraq War*

- "Our martyrs taught the world that Iran is alive and dynamic and makes every sacrifice to defend its national and Islamic values . . . they taught the nation the lesson of self-belief and as a result Iran has made progress in the field of modern equipment for defense forces."[111]

### *Islamic World*

- "We look forward to seeing the Islamic world removed from danger and the ummah growing in dignity at this sensitive time in history when the Islamic world is being targeted by numerous conspiracies, and our thanks to God for His blessings and hopes for greater vigilance, unity and cooperation among Islamic governments and nations."[112]

## GHOLAMHOSSEIN MOHSENI-EJEIE

Gholamhossein Mohseni-Ejeie is the current Minister of Intelligence. He was born in Ejiveh and received his Master's degree in International Law from the Haghani School in Qom. He is a cleric and previously served as the judiciary chief's representative to the Ministry of Intelligence and Security from 1991 to 1994. He also served as the prosecutor general for the Special Tribunal for Clergyman under presidents Rasfanjani and Khatami and as the head of the Judicial Complex for Government Employees. Finally, he was the leader of Gholamhossein Mohseni-Ejei, a conservative religious tribunal.[113]

## ALI LARIJANI

Ali Larijani was appointed secretary-general of the Supreme National Security Council (SNSC)—and, more pertinently, Iran's chief nuclear negotiator—by Khamenei in 2004.

Prior to this position, Larijani served as head of the Iranian broadcasting network from 1994 to 2004. Larijani was responsible for introducing "Islamicised" television to Iran, heavily censoring internal Iranian television and radio. In some instances, Larijani completely removed foreign broadcasts that did not follow the policies of the supreme leader. Larijani also censored printed news in Iran, ensuring that antigovernment stories were not published.[114]

Larijani has maintained a successful political career, which essentially began after the 1979 Islamic Revolution,[115] and, indeed, he comes from a prominent family of clerics and public servants (his father achieved the rank of Grand Ayatollah). In 1981, Larijani was the director of External Programs for the Islamic Republic of Iran Broadcasting (IRIB).[116] From 1982 to 1991, Larijani held the positions of deputy minister of social affairs; deputy minister of posts, telegraph, and telephones, and the acting chief of staff of the IRGC.[117] After serving as the minister of cultural and Islamic guidance from 1991 to 1993, Larijani again changed posts, becoming director of the IRIB.[118]

### Statements

#### *Nuclear Ambitions*

- "We should hold discussions [with the outside world] aimed at achieving agreements which would secure our interests and guarantee our security. More important than the principle of dialogue are the goals and outcomes of dialogue. Dialogue itself is a political message."[119]
- "America and its European allies have no intention of coming to terms with Iran and they will put an end to the talks only if Iran relinquished enrichment."[120]
- "Anybody interested in non-conventional or illogical, irrational [moves] would definitely receive an appropriate response."

#### *Iran's Cooperation on the Nuclear Issue*

- "Iran is looking for ways and means to start negotiations."[121]

#### *United States*

- "The U.S. is seeking to control the Islamic Republic of Iran and so it is intensifying its threats, but developing our capabilities can help reduce the threats."[122]

#### *United States' Military Presence in the Middle East*

- "We don't accept the relationship between the U.S. and the countries of the region . . . If you talk to Arab leaders here, you can sense that they aren't happy with the current situation. They feel the Americans are bullies. They don't want the U.S. ambassador ordering them around."[123]

## GHOLAM-ALI HADDAD-ADEL

Gholam-Ali Haddad-Adel is the current Speaker of the Majlis. Elected on May 29, 2004, he is the first noncleric speaker of the Majlis since the 1979 Revolution; however he is a firm proponent of policies based on Islamic law. Haddad-Adel was born in 1945, holds a Bachelor of Science in Physics and a Ph.D. in philosophy. Haddad-Adel's son is currently married to Khamenei's daughter.[124]

### Statements

#### *Nuclear Ambitions*

- "Iran has always been ready to hold negotiations on nuclear issue rationally and based on international regulations."
- "The IAEA has repeatedly announced Iran had no diversion in its peaceful nuclear program but anti-Iran sanctions are raised while several countries in Asia have nuclear bombs. . . . China, India, Pakistan, North Korea and the Zionist regime possess nuclear bombs. Japan has repeatedly announced it enjoys potentials to produce nuclear bombs."
- "The Zionist regime admitted it has nuclear bombs but no one opposed to the issue."[125]

## ABDOLREZA RAHMANI-FAZLI

Abdolreza Rahmani-Fazli is the current secretary and deputy head of the Supreme National Security Council. Prior to joining the Supreme National Security Council, Fazli was the deputy head of the IRIB. He also served as the head of the planning department and as the deputy head of the political affairs department.[126]

## YAHYA RAHIM SAFAVI

Yahya Rahim Safavi is the current chief commander of the IRGC. Ayatollah Ali Khamenei appointed Safavi as the chief commander on September 9, 1997. Before his appointment, Safavi had served as an IRGC commander for sixteen years. He is currently the longest serving military officer in Iran.[127]

Safavi has had a long and distinguished Iranian military career. At a young age, Safavi joined an "underground movement," which the Republic would credit with hastening the Shah's removal from power.[128] Following Khomeini's return, Safavi was hired to travel to Turkey to purchase weapons, which were used to supply the collective that would later comprise the nucleus of the IRGC[129]; Safavi was then appointed to a command post at Isfahan.[130] With the outbreak of the Iran-Iraq war, Safavi was deployed to Paveh (Iranian Kurdistan) and later to Khuzestan in 1982.[131] Returning to Tehran in 1988, Safavi was appointed to the IRGC general staff and, more significantly, commander in chief of the armed forces.[132] Five years later, in 1993, Safavi rose to be Rezai's top deputy and, in 1997, Khomeini appointed him head of the IRGC.[133]

### Statements

#### *Nuclear Ambitions*

- "They [U.S.] know quite well that we are not planning to acquire nuclear weapons. The objective of the work in Iran, which is fully supervised by the International Atomic Energy Agency, is firstly to generate peaceful energy. Our activities are controlled by the agency. They are only seeking some pretext. They are better informed than us on the fact of the matter."[134]

#### *Arab Sentiment toward U.S./Israeli Presence in Region*

- "Today, the hearts of people in the Middle East are filled with hatred of America and Israel."[135]
- "We must keep the hatred of America burning in our hearts until the moment of revenge arrives."[136]

## GHOLAMREZA AGHAZADEH

Gholamreza Aghazadeh currently heads the Atomic Energy Organization of Iran. Previously, Aghazadeh was the Iranian minister of oil. Aghazadah is responsible for reaffirming Iran's commitment to a nuclear power program.[137]

## MOHAMMAD MOHADDESSIN

Mohammad Mohaddessin is the current Foreign Affairs Committee chairman of the National Council of Resistance. He was born in 1955 in Qom. He studied Electrical Engineering and was deeply involved in the anti-Shah movement. During the revolution, he was arrested by the SAVAK (Organization for Intelligence and National Security) in 1976 and was released after the Shah's regime fell in 1979. Following the revolution, Mohaddessin was appointed to be the head of the political section of the Mohadedin and in 1992 he was appointed as the head of the Foreign Affairs Committee. Uniquely, Mohaddessin publicly disagrees with the Islamic fundamentalist beliefs which currently underpin Iranian policy, and has given speeches and written statements to that effect.[138]

## AYATOLLAH SEYED MAHMOUD HASHEMI SHAHROUDI

Ayatollah Seyed Mahmoud Hashemi Shahroudi has been the head of the judiciary since 1999. He was born in 1948 and studied religion and science in Najif. In 1979, Sharoudi began teaching and researching at the Qom Theology Center. Past posts held by Sharoudi include member of the Guardian Council, member of the Leadership Experts Council, member of Management Supreme Council of Hozeh Qom, and deputy chairman of the Instructors Society of Hozeh Elmieh Qom.[139]

## JAMAL KARIMI-RAD

Born in 1956 in the Qazvin province, Jamal Karimi-Rad received his Bachelor of Arts in Judicial Sciences (affiliated with Faculty of Judicial Sciences) as well as two postgraduate degrees: one from the State Management Educational Center in 1999 and another in International Law from Tehran University in 2000.[140] Over the course of his career in the judicial services, Karimi-Rad has held various, and often overlapping, positions. He was the assistant prosecutor in the Public and Revolutionary Court as well as the public prosecutor in Kurdistan.[141] Karimi-Rad has also served as the head of bench 1 of the justice court in Zanjan province, the head of Qazvin province's revolutionary court, article 49 court, and appeals court.[142] In addition to these roles, Karimi-Rad also served in the Justice Department in Zanjan province and as the director general of the State Punishment Department in Qazvin province.[143] Further, Karimi-Rad has held a dual position as a member of the Select Committee at judiciary branches in both Zanjan and Qazvin provinces. He has also held the titles of judgment disciplinary prosecutor and head judiciary spokesman since 2003.[144] Currently, Karimi-Rad is Iran's Minister of Justice.

### Statements

#### *Islamic Dress Code*

- "How could we condone anyone whose reckless behaviour or action promotes decadence and undermines societal values? Crimes that take place in the presence of the officers, such as improper observance of the Islamic dress code, are regarded as crimes and must be dealt with in accordance with the law."[145]

#### *Nuclear Ambitions*

- "The [EU human rights] resolution is part of the ongoing scenario to increase pressure on Iran over the nuclear issue. Unfortunately, today human rights is used as a political lever by the West to put pressure on independent states."[146]

#### *Human Rights*

- "The representatives of the EU must present evidence . . . they cannot use human rights as an excuse to exercise political pressure. Why don't the

European representatives issue such statements for the deprived people of Iraq and Palestine? Of course the Europeans want freedom in subjects such as sex, tribal affairs and religious minorities . . . but freedom in these subjects does not seem very wise and it is also very difficult to achieve."[147]

# 4

# State-Sponsored Terrorism and Iran's Role

## STATE-SPONSORED TERRORISM: CONCEPTS, NATURE, AND OUTLOOK

The conceptual debate surrounding what constitutes terrorism becomes considerably less clear when it is linked to other terms that are traditionally associated with the broader spectrum of modern violent conflict. For instance, the notion of state-sponsored terrorism, which is commonly known as a form of secret or undeclared warfare, is often used when it is internationally inconvenient to designate a violent act as terrorism outright. Conversely, given the nature of modern conflict, the concept of "peace" is merely a euphemism since, in both official and popular phraseology, it is in fact the absence of declared war, *not* the absence of violent conflict, which defines today's notion of peace.

As Carl von Clausewitz said long ago, "War is a mere continuation of policy by other means," and, in other words, "an act of violence intended to compel our opponent to fulfill our will."[1] State-sponsored terrorism is precisely such a pursuit of policy, or, conversely, such a policy is a continuation of war by other means.

Because of fears of military escalation in today's "small wars," it has become common to refer to this kind of violence as "low-intensity conflict" (LIC). This is the most appropriate term for this form of undeclared, regional violent conflict, provided that, contrary to its seemingly benign description, it is understood that such conflict can be extremely intense, destructive, and destabilizing.

Additionally, this Clausewitzian formula on war captures the rationale of state-sponsored terrorism because both forms of conflict have as their ultimate objectives the compulsory submission of the enemy to the will of the aggressor.

A dramatic example of this reality is the 1983 bombing of the U.S. Marine headquarters in Beirut, Lebanon. The U.S. Department of Defense commission investigating the incident concluded:

> The systematic, carefully orchestrated terrorism, which we see in the Middle East represents a new dimension of warfare. These international terrorists, unlike their traditional counterparts, are not seeking to make a random political statement or to commit the occasional act of intimidation on behalf of some ill-defined long-term vision of the future. For them, terrorism is an integrated part of a strategy in which there are well-defined political and military objectives.[2]

Terrorism, therefore, can be another tool with which nations project military and political power. When that tool is successfully employed in areas of important national interest to the United States, it presents significant challenges to the U.S. Government. Chief among them is selecting the most appropriate response strategy, whether this involves overt military force or other, less direct countermeasures such as economic sanctions or political pressure. It is essential to address the question of where state-sponsored terrorism fits into the spectrum of modern conflict, which ranges from isolated individual acts of violence (domestic crime), to traditional diplomatic and economic international pressures, to organized military hostilities between political entities, or overt warfare. In fact, terrorism may fit into any of the intervening categories commonly identified as LIC. It is an instrument that can be brought into action whenever a state wishes to project its power into the territory of another without accepting the responsibility, accountability, and risks of overt belligerency. Thus, a state resorts to terrorism after calculating that clandestinely directed political violence can most efficiently achieve its policy goals.

## Defining Low-Intensity Conflict

Romantic observers of international affairs have asserted that terrorism is "the poor man's form of warfare," the ultimate weapon of a weak entity motivated by a righteous cause to redress grievances against an established authority. The resultant destruction is condoned in view of the group's ultimate goal(s), regardless of whether those goal(s) are realistic or whether the harm done to society far outweighs any potential political or economic gains. Some writers and officials maintain, for instance, that terrorist tactics used against strong adversaries by repressed peoples suffering from discrimination, political restraints, or injustices should, at a minimum, be excused or, at most, be actively supported by the international community. Terrorists, they say, need only determination, dedication, and righteous political motives to merit concrete forms of assistance, including funding, weapons, logistical support, sanctuary and training, from supportive states. This is the view of maverick nations like Iran, Syria, Sudan, Cuba, and North

Korea, who condone terrorist campaigns as part of a preferred, cost-effective, reduced-risk strategy, and often refer to this form of politically expedient violence as "justifiable war."

From a different angle, LIC is justified and utilized by states who view open hostilities as politically, economically, and militarily impractical. Indeed, modern weapons are so expensive and destructive that a number of nations, ideologically inclined to fight and destroy other states they perceive as enemies, systematically restrict themselves to LIC. They attack their enemies, but confine their violence to the lower end of the conflict spectrum, well away from the high intensity of open, organized military hostilities. Their initial aim is often simply to create a climate of social discontent and fear amongst their adversary. In this context, the psychologically destabilizing impact of terrorism can be an integral element in any phase of low-level conflict. Indeed, terrorist actions may prove the tipping point in these small-scale hostilities conducted in favor of conventional, full-scale military operations.

The U.S. Army definition of LIC clearly articulates the challenges it presents. LIC is:

> A broad term describing political-military struggle, short of conventional warfare between national armed forces, to achieve political, social, economic, or psychological objectives. It is often protracted and ranges from diplomatic, economic, and psychosocial pressures through terrorism to insurgent war. The military aspects of LIC are characterized by constraints on the level of violence, weaponry, and tactics. LIC includes such activities as demonstrations of forces, security assistance, peacekeeping, rescue operations, terrorism counteraction, special operations, and limited direct use of regular military forces.[3]

Thus, the broad spectrum of conflict reveals the dilemmas inherent in the semantic overlap and deliberate confusion of these terms. Diplomatic pressures include economic sanctions and military persuasion of the kind implicit in the demonstration of armed force capabilities or presence, such as, "showing the flag" or "rattling the saber." This kind of international behavior is continuous and normal, and, in truth, there is a strong streak of veiled hostility in most relationships between nations. Diplomacy is the way through which international conflicts are managed at the lowest level of the spectrum of conflict. If successful in avoiding a recourse to any kind of violence, diplomacy is credited with keeping the peace, or, in other words, confining international conflict to fundamentally nonviolent dimensions.

At the opposite end of the spectrum lies overt military hostilities, the last recourse of a sovereign political entity seeking to achieve its strategic objectives in opposition to those of another. These hostilities may be large or small in scale and scope, and their destructive potential is often dictated solely by the lethality of the weapons available. War may be declared, although since the end of World War II, hostilities have usually been fought undeclared. While overt hostilities create a climate of organized violence in which terrorism can occur, these individual acts are no longer the strategically important element of the conflict. Instead, the risk of escalation to greater and greater destructive capabilities is paramount among combatants' considerations. Therefore, state-sponsored terrorism is, in many ways, a preferred substitute for overt hostilities, the strategy *par excellence* of unscrupulous states engaged by choice in the midrange of conflict.

A brief further description of each phase of LIC in which violence is customarily employed clarifies the relationship between conflict and state sponsorship of terrorism.

## Insurgency

Insurgency is a condition of armed revolt against a recognized government that does not reach the proportions of organizing a revolutionary government or so being recognized as a military belligerent. Its targets are usually military forces or installations, and it follows international rules of armed conflict. It actively seeks a basis of popular support for its espoused goals and, if successful, eventually conducts guerrilla military operations with the goal of organizing a revolutionary regime.

Resorting to terrorist methods can be extremely tempting to an insurgent group, particularly if a foreign state offers assistance in such tactics. However, these methods cannot be condoned, no matter how theoretically noble the insurgents' objectives may be. Much like those states who actively support terrorist acts, insurgents who employ terrorist methods often become pariahs within the international community.

Insurgency without terrorist acts is merely the first phase of a legitimate attempt at revolution in which military violence is used for specific political and military gains, rather than for the sole purpose of spreading fear. Indeed, the revolutionary attempt may succeed or fail, regardless of whether it adopts or eschews terrorist methods. Additionally, external support for an insurgency will normally depend on whether its goals are politically compatible with the values and strategic concerns of the nation contemplating providing that assistance.

## Guerrilla Military Operations

Guerrilla warfare, literally "a little war," is one of the oldest forms of conflict. With the rise of Leninist and Maoist models of Communism, and particularly in view of Soviet direct or indirect support of guerrilla armies in various noncommunist countries in the post-World War II period, the meaning of the term has been increasingly associated with terrorism. The popularization of the term "urban guerrilla," which indeed means a terrorist acting in the anonymity of the big city, is partially to blame for this association. In fact, classical guerrilla operations may or may not employ terrorist tactics and methods.

> Guerrillas, while "irregular," are organized and operate from large bases (which they may move). . . . Guerrillas may be supported by, or may support, a regular military force, aim to develop into a regular force themselves, and strive for occupation and power.
>
> Terrorists are on the road, or in safe houses, or they hide abroad. . . . Terrorists aim to terrorize, i.e., largely at psychological effects. If they kill, instead of unknown citizens, prominent persons, military, economic, and political leaders, they want to maximize the psychological effects, and possibly to achieve limited political effects.[4]

These distinctions suggest that guerrilla military operations are part of a campaign of combat against state authorities and armies, a campaign that seeks full-scale revolution but is hobbled by insufficiently numbered, unorganized fighting forces incapable of effectively moving into a final political showdown or decisive violent confrontation with the state. Guerrilla military operations may progress to this revolutionary attempt at seizure of power, or, conversely, they may drop back to the sporadic, harassing operations best defined as insurgency. On the whole, guerrilla operations are considered a legitimate form of conflict if they confront oppressive dictatorships while avoiding the temptation to employ terroristic methods, and, most especially, refusing assistance from nations utilizing terrorist methods.

## Political Revolution

A revolution is a basic transformation of the politicial, economic, or social principles and institutions in a state, resulting from the overthrow of an established governmental order. It may be helped by outside forces, including foreign states. For example, eighteenth-century France secretly provided money and military assistance to the American colonies engaged in revolution against Great Britain. However, such secret intervention is not considered terrorism unless terrorist methods are employed.

A revolution typically involves a popular uprising and the use of violence against the governing elite. When revolutionary leaders are able to occupy principal posts within the government of a state, they may then participate in policymaking in an attempt to achieve some of their goals.

However, in light of the more militant revolutionary traditions of Lenin, Mao, and Castro, this is only a temporary step on the path to total political control, for "[t]he ultimate objective is the total destruction of the society, the government, and the administration of the area in which the conflict is occurring."[5]

## NATURE OF STATE SPONSORSHIP

With this background on the spectrum of conflict, it is now important to clearly define the exact nature of state-sponsorship of terrorism as a method by which a state engaged in LIC achieves its strategic goals.

State sponsorship of terrorism is defined as a government's direct or indirect encouragement of official or nonofficial groups to exercise psychological or physical violence against political opponents, adversarial governments, or other entities for the purpose of coercion and widespread intimidation designed to bring about a desired political or strategic objective. State sponsorship of terrorism is unique in that the groups carrying out the violence are furthering the policy of an established government located outside the territory in which the conflict occurs. Additionally, what distinguishes the use of terrorism from more conventional forms of coercive force at a sovereign state's disposal is the option of plausible deniability, or a complete absence of public accountability. The secretive operational methods employed by state-sponsored terrorists (who range from individual foreign nationals to entire client states) afford sponsoring nations such as Iran the ability to avoid admissions of warlike behavior and evade accountability in the court of international opinion.

The degrees to which a state's involvement with a terrorist group can be reasonably considered "official" vary greatly, ranging from the direct or indirect provision of both moral and material support to direct psychological conditioning, political indoctrination, and propaganda support. Indeed, for the state sponsor, the actual initiation of a terrorist campaign signals the fruition of a long and complex development process. For the terrorist receiving support, external assistance from an organized government in control of sovereign territory and state institutions is an enormous advantage as they strive to create a favorable political climate in which to strike effectively.

Generally, however, if a government is to be held responsible internationally for the actions of a terrorist organization, its assistance to that group has to be measured in concrete terms, e.g., its direction of activities, its supply of funding and armaments, and its use of national assets and territory for training and intelligence activities. Such intimate involvement, however, is usually accompanied by an ideological, religious, or political affinity between a sponsoring government and a group, as well as mutually beneficial propaganda support. However, rather than mere rhetoric, a state's role as "accomplice" or "accessory to the crime" constitutes the most convincing and concrete evidence of terrorism sponsorship.

In international affairs, it is not commonly understood that the domestic criminal law concept of conspiring to commit a crime is itself illegal. This elementary concept, applicable to state sponsorship of terrorism, must be established in international opinion because it justifies self-defense measures and retribution. A terrorist group acting in conjunction with, or on behalf of, a foreign government can be used to affect a target country's political stability, commercial ties, and diplomatic relations in ways that direct military confrontation cannot, or will not, achieve, and this effect can be seen regardless of whether or not a state of war exists between the sponsor and target government. Indeed, state sponsorship of terrorism is most detrimental to democratic institutions in cases short of outright warfare.

A prime example of this dynamic is Iran's activation of terrorist cells among Shi'ite Muslim populations throughout the Middle East. Before the Islamic Jihad made international headlines with the suicide truck bombings of U.S. installations in Lebanon, Iran had used its terrorist network as a complement to its war against Iraq. Iraqi Shi'ites, recruited and trained by Iranians, carried out urban guerrilla actions in Baghdad and against other key vulnerable points of Iraq's economy. Terrorist operations were directed against Middle Eastern governments backing Iraq as well as against diplomatic and commercial assets of Iraq's European arms suppliers, namely France. Thus, a ripple effect of violence was felt far beyond the immediate conflict zone.

## FORMS OF STATE SPONSORSHIP

The Cold War struggle between democratic, Western nations and the Communist bloc, dominated by the Soviet Union, provided fertile ground for state sponsorship of terrorism. State sponsorship most often took the form of ideological encouragement and material support provided by Communist governments to various Marxist terrorist groups active around the world. However, since the end of the Cold War, the politically motivated ideological links underpinning national support for terrorist organizations have been replaced by politico-religiously-motivated relationships between radical Islamic regimes and violence-prone Muslim fundamentalist movements.

Once a group identifies ideologically and psychologically with a certain government, it is fairly simple for that government to direct, or at least influence, the actions of that group. Often, official statements of hostility toward a certain target category, such as American imperialism, are sufficient to inspire attacks against assets or symbols of the mutually perceived enemy, regardless of any direct external guidance or control.

After a cooperative relationship is established, intelligence, diplomatic, or even high-level political contacts are maintained between the sponsor government and the terrorist group. A sponsor government can, at this point, facilitate any or all levels of material aid necessary for a group's survivability, expansion, and operational capability. Such government aid can range from lending sanctuary to individual members of a terrorist organization to the establishment of a full range of propaganda and logistical support facilities for the movement.

Islamic and Palestinian terrorist factions can, for example, rely on such support in Iran and Syria. Additionally, most leftist terrorist organizations operating in Latin America, and even some in Europe, can make use of similar facilities in Cuba.

When such an intimate level of dependency is reached between a sponsoring government and a terrorist organization, the latter can become an agent or instrument of state policy. The sponsor government can begin to directly fund, or even contract out, certain terrorist operations in support of its broader strategic objectives.

## STATE SPONSORSHIP OF TERRORISM BY MULTIPLE GOVERNMENTS

To be sure, there are situations in which two or more governments have been involved in a terrorist operation. This situation derives from the nature of the international terrorist network, which involves links between many governments.

The activities carried out in the name of Islamic Jihad and other Middle Eastern groups, which have usually involved more than one government, clearly illustrate this multifaceted support network. The truck bombing of U.S. installations in Lebanon and the mining of the Red Sea were both claimed by Islamic Jihad, Iran–Syria and Iran–Libya, respectively.

Syrian intelligence officers also guided the operation against the U.S. Marine headquarters in Beirut, facilitating contacts between the Shi'ite extremists and Syrian guerrilla operatives who provided the explosive and technical expertise for wiring the truck bombs.

Such double and triple involvement of governments in Islamic Jihad operations stem from their cooperation in forming this particular terrorist network. Before Islamic Jihad operations expanded to their present scope, Syria advised and assisted in the recruitment of terrorist operatives in support of Iranian efforts to mount Shi'ite guerrilla offensives against Iraq as well as other, more conservative Persian Gulf states. Following Israel's invasion of Lebanon in 1982, Libya also became involved in sponsoring Islamic Jihad, reportedly by providing Palestinian operatives to train Shi'ite guerrilla cadre in Iran. Syria apparently also acted as middleman in these Iranian-Libyan exchanges.

The Iranians have also been interested, and indeed active, in forming such connections. During their occupation of Lebanon in 1982, the Israelis uncovered documents recording the activities of Iranian Embassy officials who were developing contacts with Palestinian guerrilla organizations. The record also indicates that an Iranian official involved in this operation was also working as a double agent for the Soviet Union.[6] This latter connection is significant in view of the creation of yet another terrorist entity involving radical Shi'ite members of Lebanon's Communist party. The Revolutionary Organization of Socialist Muslims[7] reportedly played a role in the guerrilla resistance to Israeli forces in South Lebanon during the 1982 to 2000 occupation.

## FUTURE OUTLOOK

State-sponsored terrorism has taken on new tactics and new dimensions. Operations have become more effective, wider in scope, and more sophisticated, resulting in higher destructive potential. The 1983 truck bombing of U.S. installations in Lebanon succeeded in reducing Western leverage, and in that country, shifted control of events away from the moderates toward more radical forces.

Also, the lessons that terrorists and their state sponsors are drawing from Lebanon are that high-explosive attacks against strategic installations with maximum casualty levels are successful.

Finally, state-sponsored terrorism facilitates the availability of sophisticated armaments as well as opportunities to train in their use. Additionally, this phenomenon makes the use of weapons of mass destruction (WMD) more likely and, indeed, there is little question that if nuclear, chemical, or biological weapons were to become available to governments such as Iran's, they would be deployed via terrorist operations. However, whether Iran or some other terrorist-sponsoring government manages to acquire WMD through other channels is another question entirely.

Notwithstanding this nightmarish threat of "super terrorism," it can be assumed that the United States' adversaries will continue to utilize terrorism—"warfare on the cheap"—as a significant strategic tool of their foreign policy. A realistic American response to this challenge must, therefore, become a national security priority.

The following section provides selected examples of Iranian direct and indirect involvement or alleged involvement in terrorist activities in the Middle East and beyond. Additional treatment of Iran's terrorism role, focusing on both Hizballah and Hamas, is presented in Chapter 5.

## SELECTED IRANIAN DIRECT AND INDIRECT TERRORIST ACTIVITIES

### Iran's Responses to the Publication of Salman Rushdie's *The Satanic Verses*

- *February 1989*: The 15 Khordad[8] Foundation places a $1 million bounty on Salman Rushdie's head. In November 1992, the price is doubled to $2 million.
- *February 12–13, 1989*: Riots protesting the publication of Salman Rushdie's *The Satanic Verses* in Kashmir and Islamabad, Pakistan led to the death of six people. On February 26, 1989, the British Council Library in Karachi, Pakistan is bombed and one security guard is killed.[9]
- *February 28, 1989*: Offices of the *Riverdale Press* weekly newspaper in New York are firebombed, causing severe damage to the premises. The attack was apparently in response to an earlier editorial defending Rushdie's right to freedom of speech.[10]
- *July 3, 1991*: Ettore Capriolo, the Italian translator of Salman Rushdie's novel *The Satanic Verses*, is stabbed in his Milan, Italy apartment and is seriously injured. Italian police told the Associated Press (AP) that he was

stabbed by an Iranian who had previously asked Capriolo for Rushdie's address.[11]

- *July 12, 1991*: Hitoshi Igarashi, the Japanese translator of *The Satanic Verses*, is stabbed to death at Tsakuba University in Tokyo, Japan.[12]
- *October 12, 1993*: William Nygaard, publisher and translator of *The Satanic Verses*, is seriously injured by gunmen in Oslo, Norway.[13] Official investigations show that "all speculation is in the direction of a link with Iran."[14]

## Global Iranian-Sponsored Terrorist Operations

### *Middle East*

*Cyprus*

- August 26, 1989: Bahman Javadi, a member of the underground Iran Communist Party and its Komala Kurdish guerrilla forces, was shot and killed by two gunmen in Larnaca, along with another man who was wounded. Swedish authorities warned Cypriot police shortly before the killing that Javadi was under threat and should be protected.[15] Western investigators also believed the Iranian government ordered the attack.[16]

*Lebanon*

- *September 4, 1981*: The French ambassador to Lebanon, Louis Delamare, was assassinated as he drove home in West Beirut. It was assumed that the assassination was a response by extremists to the French government's decision to grant political asylum to Iran's deposed president, Abolhassan Bani Sadr.[17]
- *April 18, 1983*: A car bomb exploded in front of the U.S. Embassy in Beirut,[18] Lebanon, killing sixty, including seventeen Americans.[19] The Iranian-sponsored Islamic Jihad claimed[20] responsibility with cooperation from the Iranian Revolutionary Guard.[21] CIA's Near East Division chief, Robert Ames, was one of the casualties.
- *March 8, 1986*: Four French TV workers were kidnapped in Lebanon. The pro-Iranian Revolutionary Justice Organization claimed responsibility for the kidnapping. Three of the hostages were released after France repaid a 1975 loan from Iran.[22]
- *November 8, 1989*: Mohammed Ali Marzouqi, the personnel officer for the Saudi Embassy in Syria, was killed by three gunmen in Beirut. Islamic Jihad, an Iranian-backed terrorist group, said in a statement that it had carried out the assassination to avenge the executions by Saudi Arabia of several convicted terrorists a month earlier.[23]

*Saudi Arabia*

- *November 13, 1995*: Six people—five of whom were U.S. citizens—were killed and sixty injured when a car bomb exploded in Riyadh.[24] Four Muslim militants, who acknowledged ties to external Islamic groups, were convicted by the Saudi government and later executed.[25]
- *June 25, 1996*: A car bomb exploded outside the al-Khobar apartment complex which was housing U.S. military personnel for the U.S. air base in Dhahran, killing 19 and injuring 389.[26]

*Turkey*

- *May 16, 1985*: Colonel Behrouz Shahverdi, an army officer who was close to former Iranian Prime Minister Shahpour Bakhtiar, was murdered in Istanbul.[27]
- *December 23, 1985*: Aziz Moradi, a former colonel in the Shah's army and an associate of former Prime Minister Shahpour Bakhtiar, was shot point blank at an airport in an Istanbul suburb.[28]
- *October 24, 1986*: Ferzan Ahmed Hamid Monfared, former bodyguard of the Shah and a colonel in the Shah's army, was shot by two men while waiting at a bus stop in front of a primary school in Istanbul.[29]
- *October 11, 1988*: Turkish customs officers stopped an official diplomatic car registered to the Iranian consulate in Istanbul near the border with Iran and found the Turkish representative of the Mojahedin-e Khalq, Abdol Hassan Mojtahedzadeh, bound and gagged in the trunk.[30] Five members of the Iranian diplomatic mission fled the country rather than face charges of kidnapping; the Turkish police believed that this incident was linked to the four assassinations of Iranian expatriates in previous years.[31]
- *March 14, 1990*: Hossein Mir-Abedini, a senior member of the Mojahedin-e Khalq, was shot on his way to the Istanbul airport along with another man. Information appearing in the Turkish press identified one of the assassins as an agent of the Iranian Ministry of Intelligence and Security in coordination with the Iranian consulate.[32]
- *September 4, 1990*: Turan Dursun, editor for a banned publication critical of Islam, was shot to death outside his home in Istanbul.[33] In 1996, Irfan Cagirici was arrested for the killings of Dursun, Cetin Emec (in March 1990), another prominent columnist for the Turkish media, and for the kidnapping and murder of Akbar Ghorbani [aka Mansour Amini], the Mojahedin-e Khalq representative in Ankara (in June 1992). During the trial, it was reported that Irfan had links with the Iranian government and was trained in Iranian camps.[34]
- *December 26, 1992*: Major Abbas Gholizadeh, former bodyguard of the Shah, was abducted.[35] In late January 1994, the leader of Islamic Action,

a Turkish fundamentalist group, Mehmet Ali Bilici, admitted to having received more than $37,500 for the kidnapping and to having turned him over to Iranian intelligence agents, who were believed to have interrogated, tortured, and killed him.[36]

- *January 24, 1993*: Ugur Mumcu, a Turkish journalist and outspoken opponent of Iranian-style Islamic fundamentalism, was killed by a car bomb in Ankara. Turkish authorities said the killers had links with Iran.[37] In 2002, four men were sentenced to death for the bombing, as part of a group of twenty defendants on trial for the murders of four people as part of a campaign to install Islamic rule in predominantly Muslim Turkey with Iran's support.[38]
- *August 28, 1993*: Mohammad Ghaderi, former member of the Kurdish Democratic Party of Iran (KDPI) living in Turkey, was kidnapped.[39] Ten days later his body was found mutilated.[40] His death was later cited in a United Nations Commission on Human Rights (UNCHR) report saying Iran must stop its intelligence agents from targeting political opponents living outside the country.[41]
- *August 28, 1993*: Behran Azadfer, an Iranian leader and dissident of the government, was shot in his home in Ankara by two men. Turkish police also arrested members of the Muslim extremist group Islamic Action, whose members were believed to have received training in Iran, for killing one of the dissidents.[42]
- *January 4, 1994*: Taha Kermanj, a leading member of the KDPI, was killed in Corum. A United Nations report suggested "the possible involvement of Iranian government agents."[43]
- *February 20, 1996*: Zahra Rajabi, a former member of the Leadership Council of the Peoples Mojahedin Organization of Iran, a popular opposition movement in Tehran, and Abdolali Moradi, a sympathizer of the same organization, were fatally shot in Rajabi's Istanbul apartment. An Istanbul court sentenced an alleged Iranian agent to thirty-three years and four months in jail for the killing.[44]

### *Iraq*

- *August 4, 1994*: Ghafur Hamzeh'i, leader of the KDPI, a member of the party's Central Committee in Baghdad, was killed outside his home by terrorists from the Islamic Republic of Iran. The KDPI is the largest Kurdish movement in Iran. Hamzeh'i joined the democrat party [KDPI] in 1977, was a member of its Central Committee in 1983, and was responsible for foreign relations of the party and held that post until his assassination.[45]
- *July 9, 1995*: Gunmen shot dead Sayyed Hussein Sudeiry, Ibrahim Suleimi, and Bari Ali Kartabar, three officials of Iran's main armed opposition group, the People's Mojahedin, in Baghdad, Iraq. Mojahedin spokesman Farid Slimani accused the Iranian embassy of "directing" the attack.[46]

- *March 7, 1996*: Hamed Reza Rahmani, a Mojahedin member and Iranian opposition figure, was shot in the head and killed in Baghdad. The killing was initially blamed on agents from Tehran.[47]
- *March 18, 1996*: Osman Rahimi, Taher Azizi, Hassan Ebrahimzadeh, and Faramarz Keshavarz, all four members of the KDPI, were fatally shot outside the city of Erbil. The KDPI accused the Iranian government of carrying out the attack.[48]
- *August 19, 1997*: Saeed Moradi, Ali Zokaleh, and Isma'il Namaki, all members of the KDPI, were killed during the armed attack against the bus in which they were traveling. The KDPI is the largest opposition movement in Iran.[49]
- *June 9, 1999*: Fariba Mozarmi, a senior militant for the People's Mojahedin group, was killed when a car bomb detonated near a bus carrying several Mojahedin members out of Baghdad. A spokesman for the Mojahedin-e Khalq held the "clerical regime of Iran's Ministry of Intelligence and Security" responsible for the attack.[50]

*Iran*

- *February 19, 1979* :[51] Rev. Aristou Sayyah, an Iranian Anglican priest, was killed in the town of Shiraz, Iran.[52]
- *October 26, 1979*: Bishop Hassan Dehqani-Tafti, bishop of the Anglican Church in Iran, survived an assassination attempt in his house; however, his wife was injured in the hand. Following the attempt, he fled to London.[53]
- *May 6, 1980*: Bahram Deghani Tafti, 24, and son of Anglican Bishop Deghani Tafti, was ambushed and shot dead. He was a member of the religious minority in Iran, which sought to preserve and teach its religious heritage. Iran represses and strictly regulates non-Muslim groups with such practices by restricting where and when religious services are held as well as making its members carry religious affiliation identification cards.[54]
- *June–October 1980*: Iranian authorities took over Anglican hospitals and missionary houses in Shiraz and Isfahan. Anglicans are a minority religious group in Iran, which has constantly faced discrimination and repression at the hands of the Iranian regime.[55]
- *November 8, 1993*: "The Hizballah Committees" threw grenades at French Embassy and Air France offices in Tehran because of French support for Mojahedin-e Khalq.[56]

*Kuwait*

- *April 5, 1988*: A Kuwaiti Airlines plane en route from Thailand to Kuwait was hijacked and flown to Mashhad, Iran. The Iranian House Speaker, Ali Akbar Hashemi Rafsanjani, offered asylum to the hijackers in return for the hostages' release. After two Kuwaiti hostages were killed, hijackers released the prisoners in Algeria and flew to Lebanon.[57] Imad Mughniyah, who was behind the hijacking, is today head of the Iranian-backed Hizballah's overseas operations.[58]

*Egypt*

- *July 3, 2005*: Ihab el-Sharif, Egyptian Ambassador to Iraq, was abducted. His captors, members of Al-Qaeda,[59] reported that he was killed four days later, though his body was never found. An article in *Al Ahram* claimed that members of the Iranian Intelligence Services were behind the kidnapping, apparently in response to Egypt's support for the U.S. invasion of Iraq.[60]

*United Arab Emirates*

- *June 4, 1989*: Ataellah Bayahmadi, the chief covert intelligence operative of the Paris-based Flag of Freedom organization, was shot and killed during a meeting with Iranian military officers in Dubai. Western investigators believed he was lured into a trap by Iranian officials.[61] The suspected killer was supposed to have met with Iran's consul general in Dubai, Hamid Asraf Islami, around the time of the killing.[62]

## Asia

*Pakistan*

- *July 9, 1987*: Iranian refugees, suspected of being opponents of Ayatollah Khomeini, were attacked with rockets and grenades in Karachi and Quetta. Two were killed and twenty-two injured.[63]
- *December 3, 1988*: Iranian refugees were shot at by a masked gunman as they were outside of the United Nations office in Karachi. One person was killed and five others wounded. The gunman fled in a car after the incident.[64]
- *September 14 1989*: Hossein Keshavarz, a Mujaheddin sympathizer, was fatally shot in Karachi, Pakistan.[65]
- *June 6, 1993*: Mohammad Hassan Arbab, member of National Council of Resistance of Iran, was assassinated in Karachi by two masked gunmen. A Pakistani newspaper accused the Iranian consulate in Karachi for planning the assassination.[66]

## Europe

*Germany*

- *July 31, 1984*: An Air France jet hijacked by the "Islamic Organization for Liberation of Palestine," landed in Tehran and was blown up by hijackers; no casualties.[67]

- *January 16, 1987*: Ali Akbar Mohammadi, the former pilot for the Speaker of Iran's parliament, Hashemi Rafsanjani, was shot and killed by two gunmen in Hamburg. He defected the year before from Iran and flew a plane to Baghdad, Iraq, and applied for political asylum in West Germany.[68]
- *August 8, 1992*: Fereydoun Farokhzad, an Iranian singer and opposition figure, who worked from exile against the Islamic theocracy, was stabbed to death at his flat in Bonn, Germany.[69]
- *September 17, 1992*: Four leading dissidents and members of the KDPI against the Iranian regime were assassinated in the Mykonos Café in Berlin, including the Secretary-General of the KDPI, Dr. Sadeq Sharafkandi.[70] Two Iranian diplomats were later implicated in the assassination on December 29 of that year.[71]

*Italy*

- *March 16, 1993*: Mohammad Hussein Nagdi, Mujaheddin official, was shot to death in Rome by motorcycle gunman. No arrests.[72]

*Belgium*

- *March 13, 1996*: Customs officials in Antwerp found weapons sent from the Iranian ship "Kalahdoos." When the ship was detained in Hamburg, two of the crew were found to be the members of Iranian intelligence.[73]

*France*

- *December 7, 1979*: Shahriar Shafiq, nephew of the Shah, was murdered outside his sister's Paris apartment by a single gunman.[74] An Iranian suspect would be returned to French authorities after fleeing to Britain. Muslim militants in Iran had vowed to kill the Shah and other members of his family who fled the country in January 1979.[75]
- *April 25, 1980*: A bomb exploded in the Toulouse offices of an American agriculture company. Credit for the bombing was taken by a group called "Self-Defense Against All Authority" in response to America's intervention in Iranian affairs.[76]
- *July 18, 1980*: Failed assassination attempt on former Prime Minister Shahpour Bakhtiar in his apartment Paris. Bakhtiar was not harmed but the attack resulted in the deaths of a French policeman and a neighbor. It was also in this apartment that the National Movement of the Iranian Resistance (NAMIR), the first prodemocracy opposition movement to Iran's theocracy, was founded in August 1980.[77]
- *February 7, 1984*: Ali Golam Avazi, head of Iranian Ground Forces under the Shah, was assassinated in Paris along with his brother. Two groups, the Islamic Jihad and the Revolutionary Organization for Liberation and Reform, claimed responsibility for the killings.[78]

- *February 8, 1984*: The United Arab Emirates' ambassador to France, Khalifa Ahmed Abdel Aziz Mubarak, 38, was shot in the back of the head while leaving his Paris home.[79] The group, the Arab Revolutionary Brigades, a Palestinian group which is said to be funded by Iran, claimed the murder for the expelling of Palestinians from the UAE.[80]
- *October 24, 1990*: Cyrus Elahi, director of the Flag of Freedom Organization of Iran and a supporter of the late Shah, was fatally shot in the hallway of his apartment. In its judgment in 2000, a U.S. District Court ordered Iran to pay the damages of $311 million to Elahi's brother, Daryosh Elahi, a professor at Harvard University.[81]
- *April 18, 1991*: Abdorrahman Boroumand, an Iranian lawyer and prodemocracy activist, was stabbed to death in the lobby of his Paris apartment. Along with Dr. Shahpour Bakhtiar, Boroumand played an active role in the creation and development of NAMIR (National Movement of the Iranian Resistance).
- *August 8, 1991*: Shahpour Bakhtiar, former prime minister under the Shah, and his aide, Sorush Katibeh, were stabbed to death in Bakhtiar's home outside of Paris. In December 1994, three Iranians were convicted for the murder, including the Paris bureau chief of the Islamic Republic Broadcasting Network and a member of the Iranian diplomatic mission to Switzerland.[82]
- *May 28, 1996*: Reza Mazlouman, who served as deputy education minister under the Shah and had political refugee status in France, was shot to death at his apartment near Paris.[83] An Iranian with links to the government was convicted of conspiracy in 2002, and an arrest warrant for the then Iranian minister of information and security, Hojatoleslam Ali Fallahian was issued, but never complied with.[84]

*Austria*

- *July 20, 1987*: Hamid Reza Chitgar, an outspoken human rights activist against Tehran's government and head of the Iranian National Resistance opposed to the Islamic government of the Ayatollah Ruhollah Khomeini, was found murdered in a central Vienna flat. He was shot in the back of the head and had been dead for about two months.[85] Political motives linked to Iran were suspected.[86]
- *July 13, 1989*: Abdol Rahman Qassemlou, the secretary-general of the Kurdistan Democratic Party of Iran, was killed in Vienna along with two other dissidents, where he was scheduled to meet a delegation sent by the then Iranian president Akbar Hashemi Rafsanjani.[87] The Austrian foreign minister, Alois Mock, said shortly after the murders that he thought Iran was probably responsible. The killers may have been linked to a radical Iranian faction seeking to discredit President Rafsanjani.[88]

*Switzerland*

- *April 24, 1990*: Kazem Rajavi, representative of the opposition National Council of Resistance of Iran and formally Iran's first ambassador to the U.N., was fatally shot in his car while he was driving home in Coppet. Swiss police charged Ali Fallahian, who previously headed Iran's Ministry of Intelligence and Security, with masterminding the assassination.[89] Arrest warrants were issued for thirteen Iranians travelling on diplomatic passports.[90]

*United Kingdom*

- *August 19, 1986*: Bijan Fazeli, a 22-year-old actor and writer, who had used propaganda films to criticize the Iranian government, was killed by a car bomb that exploded outside his father, Reza Fazeli's video shop in London.[91]
- *July 18, 1987*: Amir Hossain Amir-Parviz, former agriculture and development minister under the Shah and head of the London office of the former prime minister, Shahpour Bakhtiar's Paris-based Iranian National Movement, was severely injured in a car bomb attack. A group called the Guardians of the Islamic Revolution claimed the attack as part of the fight against the "monarchists."[92]
- *October 2, 1987*: Ali Tavakoli-Nabavi, a known critic of the Iranian regime, and his son were found dead in their London apartment.[93] The "Guardians of the Islamic Revolution" claimed responsibility for the killing.[94]

### United States

- *July 22, 1980*: Ali Akbar Tabatabai, an Iranian cleric and critic of Ayatollah Khomeini was shot in his Bethesda, Maryland home. The assassin, Daoud Salahaddin, was apparently acting at the behest of the Iranian government.[95]
- *October 22, 1982*: Daniel Jordan, a leader in the Bahai faith from California was assassinated by Iranian terrorists; his body was later found in a Stamford, Connecticut, parking lot.[96] Followers of the Bahai religion had been severely persecuted in Iran under the orders of the Ayatollah Ruhollah Khomeini.[97]

# 5

# Iran's Terrorist Network: Hizballah and HAMAS

Iran's terrorist record for nearly three decades is rather transparent. It includes, as has been documented previously, a broad array of lawless activities in the Middle East and beyond. It is sufficient to mention Iran's violations of fundamental human rights of its own citizens; establishing, encouraging, directing and supporting both indigenous and foreign terrorist groups; cooperating directly and indirectly with various factions of al Qaeda and other *jihadist* movements in Iraq and elsewhere; and undermining efforts to stabilize the region in general, and to sabotage the Israeli-Palestinian peace process, in particular.

There is ample evidence exposing this clandestine web of Iranian networks comprised of various Islamist-based groups, both Shiite and Sunni. This chapter presents a detailed profile of two notorious and dangerous terrorist movements: Hizballah and Hamas. Although these two groups maintain different theological and political dispositions, Iran has traditionally provided both with financial, organizational, and operational assistance, including arms, training, intelligence and safe haven. This chapter covers selected perspectives on Hizballah and Hamas, including background, ideology, organizational structures, leadership, funding, strategies and activities. Special emphasis is placed on the Middle East conflict and its implications for regional and global security concerns.

## HIZBALLAH (HIZ B'ALLAH OR "PARTY OF GOD")

### History

Hizballah was founded in June 1982, amidst the Lebanese civil war and in response to the Israeli invasion of Lebanon that same year. It began, first and foremost, as an umbrella organization, comprising several radical Shi'ite Muslim groups. Many Shi'ites saw the Israeli Defense Forces' (IDF) invasion, and the subsequent establishment of their proxy Southern Lebanon Army (SLA), as worthy causes for holy war (*jihad*) against their invaders. Accordingly, Iran sent fighters from its Islamic Revolutionary Guard Corps (IRGC) to assist in the establishment of an organization, which would represent Shi'ite interests both within the context of the civil war and the Israeli incursion. Iran, moreover, hoped to expand its influence among the international Shi'ite population and gain status and recognition as the unofficial spokesman of the Shi'a community.

Aside from the initial 1,500 members of the IRGC who comprised the bulk of the militia force in its early stages, Hizballah's membership was drawn primarily from two groups: First, from a collection of fundamentalist splinter groups and breakaway factions of the larger (and overtly secular) AMAL organization, who objected to AMAL's ad hoc alliance with Christian forces affiliated with Israel. The second group was a merger between Hussayn Musawi's "Islamic AMAL" organization (another AMAL splinter group who welcomed the IRGC's arrival in Lebanon) and the Lebanese branch of the Da'wa party.

Hizballah quickly became the vanguard of terrorist groups operating within Lebanon, responsible for nearly 90 percent of the attacks on international peacekeepers and foreign armies in Lebanon throughout the 1980s. During the civil war, Hizballah established its strongest support base among impoverished Shiite youth. With the Lebanese government proving incapable of protecting legitimate ownership rights, the economically disadvantaged Shi'ite population benefited from an elaborate reallocation of land and buildings in Hizballah-controlled areas. This effort, when combined with its Islamist Shi'ite doctrine (detailed below), created an ample supply of potential recruits to be used against Hizballah's enemies and gave the group a "singular capability to strike wherever it wished, [a capability which] other less fanatical militias" lacked.[1] Indeed, with Iranian-allied-Syria's dominance of the Lebanese political and social landscape during the later stages of the civil war, Hizballah was able to strengthen its position over other, more moderate Shi'ite organizations, including AMAL.[2] Even after the 1990 Ta'if Accords called for a full disarmament of all nonstate militia groups, Syria's continued dominance of the Lebanese political landscape ensured Hizballah's continued growth and expansion, particularly in the Shi'ite dominated south.[3] After the end of the Lebanese civil war in 1990, Hizballah continued its armed struggle on the premise that Israel, along with the mostly Christian SLA, still occupied southern portions of Lebanon.

During the 1990s, the group expanded its arsenals and recruiting networks and established social service organizations for residents of southern Lebanon, while remaining committed to its goal of derailing any potential Arab-Israeli peace accord. To this end, Hizballah participated in a variety of attacks on Israeli forces and civilians, at times with remarkable impact on Lebanese and Israeli public opinion. After the signing of the Oslo peace accords between the Israelis and the Palestinians in 1993, Hizballah grew even more determined to retain its influence within the Arab-Israeli conflict. As such, the number of Hizballah attacks on Israeli targets grew from 63 in 1992 to a high of 344 in 1995.[4] Indeed, throughout the mid-1990s, the Hizballah-Israeli conflict was characterized by a series of attacks and counterattacks, occasionally accompanied by brief and unofficial truces or cease-fires. There were two major watershed events during the period between Israel's first incursion into Lebanon and its withdrawal in May 2000: The first was the July 1993 Israeli-led Operation Accountability, an IDF operation targeting Hizballah militants in southern Lebanon, which ended in a verbal agreement between the two sides on the rules of engagement within the conflict. Secondly, Operation Grapes of Wrath in April 1996 involved an intensive Israeli air and artillery bombardment of Hizballah positions and infrastructure in southern Lebanon. Following this second strike, a codified set of agreements, based on those achieved after Operation Accountability, was put in place and, to a certain extent, both sides complied with the agreed-upon stipulations. In addition, the 1990s also saw Hizballah's "graduation" to the arena of international terrorism, most notably attacking Israeli and Jewish targets in Latin America.

Israeli public opinion, over time, turned against the increasingly costly stay in Lebanese territory. This culminated in 1999 with the election of Ehud Barak to the Israeli premiership, largely based on his campaign promise to withdraw all Israeli forces from Lebanon "by June of 2000." True to Barak's pledge, Israeli forces completed their withdrawal—in full and in accordance with United Nation's supervision—on May 23, 2000. Still, Hizballah adamantly maintained that Israel remained an occupying force, citing a small area along the Syrian-Lebanese-Israeli tri-border—known as the Sha'aba Farms—as proof of Israel's continued occupation. In addition, Israel's withdrawal from the southern region, coupled with the disbanding of the SLA, created a significant power vacuum in the region. This facilitated Hizballah's efforts to redeploy along the Israeli-Lebanese border and continue its conflict on the basis of Israel's alleged occupation. In October 2000, Hizballah initiated a cross-border incursion and took hostage three Israeli soldiers, who were conducting a routine border patrol.

Hizballah continues its armed struggle against the Jewish state on the premise of liberating the Sha'aba Farms from Israel. It has conducted several cross-border attacks throughout the decade, including sniper and rocket attacks on Israeli military bases and civilian targets along the border. In July 2006, Hizballah conducted a daring daylight cross-border raid into Israeli territory targeting IDF soldiers patrolling the northern border with Lebanon. Hizballah soldiers killed three and kidnapped two IDF soldiers, sparking a swift response from the Israeli military and a month-long war between Hizballah guerrillas and IDF forces.

Massive Israeli air, land, and sea attacks on Hizballah targets and civilian infrastructure in Lebanon resulted in over a thousand deaths, injuries to thousands more, and the flight of some 900,000 Lebanese from their villages and towns. Hizballah, on the other hand, utilized an active force of some 3,000 combatants, along with reserves of several thousand others, to combat the IDF. It also fired several thousand of its short- and long-range rockets and missiles at both Jewish and Arab civilian targets in northern Israel, displacing some 333,000 people to safer areas outside missile range. Hizballah perceived the war with Israel a major triumph. In a speech aired on Hizballah's Al Manar TV on August 14, 2006, Hizballah secretary-general Hassan Nasrallah declared, "We are facing a strategic and historic victory. This is not an exaggeration. This is a victory for Lebanon—all of Lebanon—for the resistance, and for the entire nation."[5]

Despite this claim, the "Second Lebanese War" resulted in no decisive victor from a military perspective. The new strategic arrangements established by the United Nations following the war's cease-fire changed Hizballah's favorable military position due to the deployment of an expanded United Nations Interim Force in Lebanon (UNIFIL) and Lebanese force in south Lebanon. Nevertheless, a year later, Nasrallah still warned that should Israel launch another war in Lebanon, it would force a "surprise that will change the fate of the region."[6] Considering Iran's continued supply of a wide variety of arms to Hizballah, the likelihood of the deployment of weapons of mass destruction in a new confrontation is of particular security concern to Israel.

It is significant to note, however, that simultaneously with its terrorist and military activities against Israel and other western targets, Hizballah has worked hard to integrate itself into the post-civil war political landscape of Lebanon, and has been active in the political process since 1992. This move was an important shift as the group had previously rejected political participation on the grounds that it was counterproductive to the goal of establishing an Islamic republic in Iran's image. Nevertheless, the call to integrate politically came at the behest of both the Syrian and Iranian governments. Hizballah won eight of 128 seats in Lebanon's 1992 parliamentary election, seven seats in the 1996 elections, and twelve seats in the 2000 elections following Israel's withdrawal. In addition, the group has bolstered both its membership and popular support for its anti-Israeli agenda by expanding its network of public services, including schools, mosques, clinics, hospitals, and community centers throughout its traditional Lebanese strongholds.

## Ideology

Hizballah is a political, social, economic, and military organization whose focus and general identity in Lebanon resembles the militancy and ideology of the Iranian revolution. The organization is primarily inspired by the radical Shi'ite Islamist philosophy of the late Iranian revolutionary leader Ayatollah Khomeini, and sees "the Iranian regime as the vanguard and new nucleus of the leading Islamic State in the world."[7] Hizballah is dedicated to the removal of all non-Islamic influences from the Middle East as well as the global exportation of their Iranian-inspired Islamic revolution, the final result of which is a worldwide Islamic republic headed by Shi'ite clerics and governed by Shi'ite Islamic law (*Ja'fri Sharia*).

Hizballah subscribes to traditional Shi'ite religious doctrine and the religious hierarchy that governs it spiritually. The success of the Islamic revolution proved a watershed in recent Shi'a history, wherein religious activism supplanted the previous norm of "disassociation" (that is, keeping quiet about the Shi'a belief system in the face of a dominant Sunni majority). Since its inception, Hizballah has embodied this new approach as well, acting as both an interest group for the underrepresented, though demographically dominant, Shi'a populace in Lebanon and an extension of Shi'ite regional influence into the Levant. This helps explain Hizballah's eventual foray into national politics and its political ideology as concurrent with its religious agenda.

This transformation highlights two unique aspects of the Shi'a doctrine and their importance in the present context: An absolute clerical hierarchy that is absent in Sunni Islam and the role of martyrdom in Shi'a tradition. The Shi'a hierarchy has two strands, the first of which being the Imamate, the spiritual leadership descending through the lineage of the movement's founder, Ali ibn-abi-Talib, and ended in 874 A.D. when the twelfth descendant went into a state of "occultation".[8] In the absence of the Imamate, a traditional clergy is tasked with leading the community, with the most prominent leaders attaining the unofficial rank of *marja taqlid* ("source of emulation"). This carries many implications for the general populace, who view their religious authorities as exemplary to the point of blind obedience. Currently, the absence of a dominant religious authority in Lebanon has led the Shi'a populace to emulate lesser religious authorities within Lebanon—who gain legitimacy through their political activism—or toward the clerical leadership in Iran, home to the majority of the world's Shi'ite population. Either way, both Lebanese and Iranian sources lend support to Hizballah's militant tactics and sanction its militia in all its endeavors. In particular, religious leaders who have become worthy of worship and emulation include the late Ayatollah Ruhollah Khomeini and, within Lebanon, Sheikh Al-Musawi, Sheikh Hassan Nasrallah, and Sheikh Muhammad Hussein Fadallah.

The second trend in contemporary Shi'ism is the reemergence of martyrdom as a worthy practice. The origins of this cult of martyrdom derive from the legend of Ali's son Hussayn dying on the battlefield in defense of the Shi'a tradition. The leaders of the Islamic revolution in Iran (most notably Ayatollah Khomeni) centralized this issue and numerous times applied its lessons to the dynamic between the monarchy and the populace. Later still, during the Iran-Iraq war, Khomeini responded to the threat of chemical weapons attacks by urging Iranian soldiers to run into the clouds of gas rather than surrender. Hizballah has since espoused the importance of martyrdom as a tenet of Shi'ite political discourse. This has served to legitimize the extremist tactics it utilizes, particularly suicide bombings and close-range attacks (where the chance of incurring casualties is much greater).

## Objectives

The original agenda of Hizballah since the early 1980s centered on the eviction of Israeli military forces from Lebanon and, in the long-term, the conversion of

Lebanon into an Islamic state. Indeed, Iran's stated desire of destroying Israel and expanding its Islamic revolution throughout the Middle East is principally implemented via state-sponsored terrorism conducted through groups such as Hizballah. The group's stated objectives, according to its 1996 Electoral Program, include:

1. The removal of all western influences from Lebanon and the region, to include the liberation and sovereignty of all claimed lands, the protection of Lebanese civilians, public relations campaigns with the Lebanese people, and more "state involvement" in this liberation struggle.
2. Creation of an Islamic republic in Lebanon modeled after the Islamic Republic of Iran and established on the concept of *vali e-faqih*, or political rule of the Islamic jurist. Specifically, this process would include the abolition of political sectarianism, a balanced electoral system, and the patronage-based government bureaucracy currently ruling Lebanon.
3. Liberation of Al-Quds (Jerusalem) via proxy Palestinian rejectionist groups such as Hamas and Palestinian Islamic Jihad (PIJ).
4. The creation of a pan-Islamic International Community.

## Organizational Structure

Hizballah is governed by the *Majlis al-Shura* (decision making council; an oligarchy of religious authorities) with an executive *Shura* administering the organization's daily activities. The politburo administers the regional command structure as well as several sub-organs. The organization is subdivided into intelligence, security, and military wings.

### *Majlis al-Shura*

Convened on May 28, 1986, the Majlis al-Shura is the supreme decision-making authority and consists of seven committees: ideological, financial, military, political, judicial, informational, and social affairs. Each of these committees is replicated in regional areas. In 1989, the Executive Shura and a Politburo were added. The Supreme Shura Council, consisting of seventeen members, meets frequently to set policies, and makes decisions based on majority vote. However, in the case of a deadlock, they are referred to the vali al-faqih, Ayatollah Ali Akbar Khamenei in Iran, as the definitive jurisconsult.[9]

### *The Executive Shura*

The Executive Shura, under the control of Secretary-General Hassan Nasrallah, oversees daily Hizballah activities, conducts meetings, and makes all financial, military, judicial, social, and political decisions.

### The Politburo

The Politburo is a supervisory body appointed by the Shura Council that guides three areas of Hizballah activity: the Enforcement, Recruitment, and Propaganda department, the Holy Reconstruction department, and the Security Branch. The Politburo convenes once every three months and passes its decisions to the regional districts accordingly.[10]

### Regional Command

Hizballah command structure reflects its foundation, as the organization is a combination of the fighters from the Beka'a Valley in eastern Lebanon, Beirut, and from southern Lebanon, all subject to the Shura and ultimately, Iran. Sheikh Muhammad Hussein Fadlallah acts as the overall spiritual guide of Hizballah.

In the past, the Beka'a Valley wing has been headed by Sheikh Subhi al-Tufayli and by Hussein al-Musawi (before his assassination via an Israeli air strike). In Beirut and the surrounding suburbs, the organizational leaders are Sheikh Ibrahim al-Amin, the official spokesman, and Sheikh Hassan Nasrallah, who took over the position of secretary-general after Mussawi's death.

Sheikh Raghib Harb headed the southern branch until his death in 1984. After his death the command was split between the Nabatiyya and Sidon-Zahrani districts, which are now headed by Sheikh Afif al-Nabulsi and Sheikh Muhammad Fannish, respectively.

### The Military Wing[11]

Hizballah's military wing is also known as the Islamic Resistance Movement. The military wing is subdivided into three regions: the southern district of Beirut; Jabel Amil (the south Lebanon region); and the Beka'a Valley. Hassan Nasrallah and Sheikh al-Amin head the southern Beirut command. Sheikh Nabil Qaouk, who also controls the Lebanese National Army units in southern Lebanon, commands the southern Lebanon military wing. Sheikh Husayn al-Khalil, who also commands the Special Security Apparatus in the region, currently heads the Beka'a Valley region.

Each command maintains both regular and motorized infantry units of 252 men each. Specifically, the southern Beirut command has two infantry battalions, one of which is mechanized; the Beka'a Valley command has seven infantry battalions, three of which are mechanized; and the southern Lebanon command has seven infantry battalions, five of which are mechanized.

### Special Security Apparatus

The Special Security Apparatus (SSA) has several responsibilities, most notably, to carry out all overseas military strikes ordered by the Majlis al-Shura. The current head of the SSA is security and intelligence director Imad Moughniyeh; his deputy director is Abd al-Hadi Hamadi. Within the Majlis al-Shura, and in each regional area, there is a separate body responsible for intelligence and security matters. These are subdivided into the central security apparatus, the preventative security apparatus, the intelligence apparatus, and the overseas security apparatus.[12]

1. The National preventative security apparatus is currently operated by Muhammad Hammud and is responsible for ensuring the personal security of prominent Hizballah clergymen.
2. Internal security and intelligence is currently operated by Salah Nun and is responsible for upholding the political and religious reliability of its membership.
3. Hizballah National Central security apparatus is currently operated by Sheikh Hussein Khalil and is responsible for the infiltration and liquidation of any military or political opponents in Lebanon.
4. Overseas security apparatus[13] encompasses several cells that are somewhat independent from the center. However, they still maintain some connections with the center, and are commanded by the following:
   a. North America: Imad Moughniyeh.
   b. South/Central America: Hussein Khalil.
   c. Asia: Muhammad Haydar.
   d. Europe: Kharib Nasser and Abd al-Hamadi.
   e. Near East: Abd al-Hadi Hamadi.
   f. Middle East: Ibrahim Aqil.

## Special Operations Command

Generally speaking, control over Hizballah's special operations is maintained by the SSA, which is supported by Iranian and Syrian intelligence. However, many of the Special Operations divisions work independently in order to minimize the likelihood of leaks or intelligence infiltration.

Hizballah Special Operations forces that are sent overseas are trained in the culture, language, and customs of the host country and can remain dormant there for long periods of time. For instance, operatives infiltrating Israel dress like Israelis, speak fluent Hebrew, and may reside in Israel for long periods of time. Al-Qaeda, the Armed Islamic Group (GIA), and other terrorist organizations have adopted similar tactics elsewhere.

There are two forms of Special Operations units within the military wing of Hizballah: the Special Forces Infiltration unit, which is a paramilitary unit designed to infiltrate, destroy, or assassinate targets, and the Jihad Special Forces, more commonly known as "suicide terrorists."

The known Jihad Special Forces units consist of the following:

1. The Islambouli Brigade: Named for the assassin of former Egyptian leader Anwar Sadat, the brigade receives specialized training in assassinations and suicide attacks for the purpose of attacking world leaders.

2. The Jerusalem Brigade: Fifty-six men per company; divided between the Fathi Shkaki company and the Yahya Ayyash company.
3. The Martyr Abbas Mussawi Brigade: Two suicide companies of approximately fifty-six men per company.[14]

## Leadership

### *Sheikh Muhammad Husayn Fadlallah*

Sheikh Muhammad Husayn Fadlallah heads the Leadership Council and is the spiritual leader of the movement. Although he was born and educated in Iraq, Fadlallah serves as the highest religious authority of the Shi'ite community in Lebanon, where he wields great religious and moral influence.

### *Said Hassan Nasrallah*

In February of 1992 Said Hassan Nasrallah was unanimously elected commander of operations after Hizballah Secretary-General Abbas Mussawi was killed in an IDF helicopter raid on February 16 of that year. Nasrallah was reelected to this post in 1993, and has served in this capacity ever since. Like his predecessor, he was a founding member of the "Islamic Resistance" (the group which carried out terrorist operations in southern Lebanon). Born in 1960, he was a key figure in the AMAL movement before joining Hizballah in 1982.

### *Sheikh Subhi Tufayli*

Born in 1948 in the Beka'a Valley, Sheikh Subhi Tufayli, was educated in Najaf, Iraq and Qom, Iran. He was a former member of the Supreme Shura and leader of the Beka'a Valley region along with Musawi. He was also acting secretary-general from 1989–1991. A staunch traditionalist, he contested Nasrallah's choice as secretary-general Nasrallah's faction fought against Hizballah's involvement in Lebanese parliamentary elections. In 1998 he was expelled from Hizballah mainly for his opposition to Hizballah's entry into "mainstream" politics. He appears to have split from Hizballah to form the "Revolution of the Hungry" in the Beka'a Valley.

### *Sheikh Na'im Qasim*

Sheikh Na'im Qasim is the deputy secretary-general, directly under Hassan Nasrallah. After finishing his clerical training at the age of thirty, Qasim joined the AMAL movement at the outset of the Lebanese civil war in 1975. After rising through AMAL's ranks, he left the group following the disappearance of the party's founder Imam Musa al-Sadr in 1978. When former AMAL members formed Hizballah in the early 1980s, Qasim joined their ranks, becoming an active member in 1989. Under Hizballah's first secretary-general, Sheikh Subhi al-Tufayli, Qasim became deputy president of the Executive Council. Later, when Abbas al-Musawi became secretary-general, Qasim was chosen as his deputy. Following al-Musawi's assassination by the Israelis, and Nasrallah's appointment as secretary-general, there was significant controversy over the fact that Qasim was passed over and left as the deputy secretary-general. It is believed Nasrallah's stronger connections to the Iranian regime, and Grand Ayatollah Ali Akbar Khamenei in particular, hastened his rise to secretary-general in spite of Qasim's seniority within the organization.[15]

### *Sheikh Sayyid Ibrahim Al-Amin Al-Sayyid*

Sayyid originates from the Beirut region and is the official spokesman for Hizballah.[16] He was elected to the Lebanese parliament in 1992, and remains a member of the Supreme Shura and Politburo.

## Other Key Operational Leaders

### *Imad Moughniyeh*

Moughniyeh is currently the security and intelligence director of the Special Security Apparatus, the Hizballah arm responsible for its international terrorist activities. He originally joined the AMAL movement during the Lebanese civil war, but later affiliated himself with Hizballah after the PLO's expulsion from Beirut. Moughniyeh initial contact with the Iranian regime came in the Iranian Embassy in Beirut via Anis Nacchache, a Lebanese militant, who attempted to assassinate former Iranian Prime Minister Shahpour Bakhtiar in Paris.[17] He served for a brief period as a member of Yasser Arafat's Force 17 bodyguard while Arafat was still based in Lebanon.[18] After receiving military training in Iran, Moughniyeh participated in guerrilla raids against Iraqi forces during the Iran-Iraq war. He was later appointed Hizballah's intelligence chief and also acted as a personal bodyguard to Sheikh Hassan Fadlallah, Hizballah's spiritual leader.[19] Moughniyeh exceptional field command and leadership abilities eventually propelled him to SSA chief. In this role, he established terror cells in Europe, the United States, Southeast Asia, West Africa, and South America's tri-border region. Moughniyeh is also suspected of planning the 1983 bombing of the U.S. Marine barracks in Beirut, which killed 241 U.S. servicemen as well as the June 1985 hijacking of TWA Flight 847, in which one U.S. citizen was murdered; an act for which he was indicted by the United States and placed on the FBI's most-wanted list of terrorist suspects.[20] Under his direction, in 2002, the Palestinian Authority sought to acquire from Iran the *Karine A*, a vessel used in the attempted smuggling of a massive weapons cache to Palestinian militants. The shipment was intercepted by the Israeli Navy. Additionally, Moughniyeh is strongly suspected of having planned and participated in the July 2006 kidnapping of two Israeli soldiers along

Israel's northern border with Lebanon that precipitated a month-long war between Israel and Hizballah.[21]

## Hizballah Funding

Hizballah is believed to hold between $10 million and $600 million in annual revenue, with the most reliable reports estimating Hizballah's budget at around $230 million. The majority of the group's holdings come from Iranian and Syrian direct deposits of cash that arrive by military air transport in diplomatic pouches. Additionally, several Saudi businessmen are believed to have donated between $15 million and $36 million per year to Hizballah in the past.

Hizballah's money is maintained in several banks, including two of Lebanon's main banks: the Byblos Bank, which is headquartered in Beirut and has branches in Syria, and the Banque Saradar S.A.L, having headquarters in Beirut as well as several overseas branches.[22] Both banks are linked to several other Middle Eastern banks where money is deposited from worldwide terrorist organizations and donors.

In addition to these multiple worldwide bank accounts, Hizballah receives much of its funds through the Hawala banking network, an Islamic practice involving unofficial loans and transactions. Because no questions are asked and no written records are kept, Hawala transactions are ideal for forwarding funds to terrorist cells in foreign countries to finance their activities. It is no surprise that this system comprises the bulk of the financial network through which Hizballah's most militant branches are financed, specifically its Special Operations Command units abroad.

## Hizballah Activity in Latin America

The so-called "Tri-Border Area" (TBA), a region plagued by a variety of criminal and terrorist enterprises, comprises the cities of Puerto Igauzu (Argentina), Foz do Iguazu (Brazil), and Ciudad del Este (Paraguay). The region possesses a significant Muslim population, particularly those of Lebanese origin, and thus constitutes an ideal environment for radical Islamist proselytizing, fund-raising, and recruitment. The homogenous and secluded expatriate enclaves of this region allow terrorists to effectively conceal their illegal activities from local law enforcement.[23] The existence of widespread political and governmental corruption also facilitates relatively unimpeded criminal and terrorist activity and movement into and out of the area.

Hizballah, in particular, is known to have operated in the region since 1992. Investigations into the 1992 attack on the Israeli embassy and the 1994 attack on the Asociación Mutual Israelita Argentina (AMIA), Jewish Community Center in Buenos Aires, Argentina, traced both bombings back to Hizballah cells operating in the TBA.[24] Hizballah cells have engaged in money laundering, document forgery, supply of weapons, and narcotics trafficking as well as attacks in the area on local business or community leaders opposed to their activities. A cell led by Assad Mohamed Barakat, a Lebanese expatriate who was identified as Hizballah's military operations chief in the TBA, was responsible for raising revenues in support of Hizballah operations in the Middle East. In addition, Imad Moughniyeh, Hizballah's foreign operations chief, visited the region several times in preparation for the two Argentinean bombings.

Illegal narcotics production and distribution, principally heroin and cocaine, also heavily finance Hizballah terrorist activity. Western intelligence sources estimate that Hizballah's drug route begins in South America, with specific drug ties with Colombia, Peru, and Brazil. The group imports the morphine base used in the production of heroin from Far East countries as well as from Pakistan, Iran, Turkey, and Syria.[25] The drugs are manufactured in laboratories in the Beka'a Valley and exported by air or sea or via Syria. Some analysts believe that Syria serves as a transit station for both incoming and outgoing drugs, and provides protection for the drug traffic. Israeli sources estimate the profits from the drug trade at billions of dollars a year. Some estimate that Syria alone earns close to $1 billion a year from this trade, and it is clear that its drug trafficking has substantially increased the country's budget and enriched many of its presidential loyalists.[26]

## Hizballah's Iranian Relationship

Hizballah's operational command maintains close relations with Iran's embassies in Beirut and Damascus, as well as the *Pasdaran* (IRGC). The Pasdaran is involved in supplying Hizballah's Special Security Apparatus (SSA) with training, military equipment, and financial backing.

Iran is still Hizballah's primary source of support and reportedly provides an estimated $50–600 million annually. Iran also pays the militiamen $150–200 per month. Additionally, the Iranian government supplies the group with weapons and ammunition. It is estimated that in January 2002, IRGC maintained 2,200 permanent members in Baalbek. However, according to an April 2005 *Washington Post* report, the number of Guard advisors fell to less than fifty following Israel's withdrawal in 2000.[27] Much of Iran's support for Hizballah is facilitated by Iran's Damascus embassy, rather than its embassy in Beirut, due to past AMAL-Hizballah clashes in Beirut and the risk of jeopardizing Iran's diplomatic mission in Lebanon. The Iranian military attaché in Damascus coordinates activities between the Pasdaran contingent in the Beka'a Valley and its headquarters in the Syrian border village of Zebdani. It also organizes training exercises between Iranian and Hizballah military personnel. As a result of its success in bringing about Israel's withdrawal from Lebanon, Iran views Hizballah as a model for leadership within the current Israeli-Palestinian struggle.

## Selected Key Hizballah-Iranian Connections

### *Muyhammad Haydar*

Haydar was formerly Hizballah's main Pasdaran liaison.

### *Ali Akhbar Mohtashemi*

Mohtashemi is the former Iranian ambassador to Syria and former interior minister. He was instrumental in the founding of Hizballah in 1982, and has maintained close relationships with Sheikh Hassan Nasrallah and Sheikh Subhi Tufayli.[28] He is believed to have acted as the central Iranian conduit between Hizballah and the Iranian regime in Hizballah's October 23, 1983, suicide bomb attack on the U.S. Marine barracks in Beirut, Lebanon, which killed 241 servicemen.[29] He allegedly instructed the IRGC's Lebanese representative in Beirut to move forward with the planned attack and later met with Nasrallah and Tufayli. In addition, he is the secretary-general of the International Islamic Support for the Palestinian Resistance Conference hosted in Tehran.[30]

### *Ayatollah Ali Montazeri*

Montazeri was the official successor to Khomenei in Iran and head of the office of the Islamic Liberation Movements, but was dismissed in March 1989. Despite his dismissal, he was able to use the Ministry of Islamic Guidance to help support Hizballah's social institutions in Lebanon. Montazeri was placed under house arrest for six years after criticizing Iran's Supreme Leader Ali Khamenei's rule.[31] In written answers to journalists' questions ahead of the February 2000 elections, he came out strongly against clerical interference in government, the key issue in the struggle between the reformers and conservatives in Iran. However, he upheld the principle of clerical supervision to ensure that legislation and government policy remain in line with Islamic principles.[32]

### *Mohammed Ali Siobhan*

Siobhan is the current Iranian ambassador to Lebanon. Three Iranian intelligence officers represent him from the Sevak, most notably Hussein al-Khalil.[33]

### *Qassem Soleimani*

Soleimani is the commanding general of the Al-Quds (Jerusalem) Force of the IRGC active in Lebanon[34] and is charged with overseeing the IRGC's extraterritorial operations. According to *Time* magazine, he serves as a special advisor to Supreme Leader Ayatollah Ali Khamenei on the issues of both Iraq and Afghanistan. Under Suleimani, and his predecessor Ahmad Vahidi, the Al-Quds Force has been linked to nearly every instance of Iranian-backed terrorism over the last decade, including the 1994 bombing of the Jewish Community Center in Buenos Aires, Argentina, that killed 85 and injured 230.[35]

### Organizational Structure

Hizballah has an estimated 600–800 active members as well as 4,000–5,000 militia in paramilitary reserve units in Southern Lebanon.

### Areas of Operation

Hizballah operates principally from locations within Lebanon, including the Beka'a Valley, southern Beirut, and southern areas of Lebanon. In addition, Hizballah operates terrorist cells in Europe, Africa, South America, North America, and Asia.

### Headquarters

- Baalbek in the Beka'a Valley, Lebanon—Training headquarters for Hizballah.
- South Beirut, Lebanon—Operational and administrative headquarters and the operational command center.
- Nabatiyya, Lebanon—Southern Lebanon regional headquarters.
- Tehran, Iran—Liaison with government regarding policies, support, and terrorist activities.

### Capabilities and Tactics

#### *Military Capability*[36]

According to various reports, Hizballah possesses the following military technologies and capabilities:

- Several M113 armored personnel carriers
- Ultra-light aircraft
- SA-7, SA-18, Stinger antiaircraft missiles
- ZU-23X2 and 57 mm air defense artillery
- C-802 antiship missiles[37]
- RPG-7v and Saghegh antitank missiles
- AT-3 Sagger, AT-4 Fagot and TOW antitank guided missiles (ATGM's)
- 144 Chinese type 63–107 mm artillery guns
- 81 mm, 120 mm mortars
- 72–6 × 6 mounted 122 mm BM-21 multiple rocket launchers

- 7500–107 mm and 121 mm Katyusha style man-portable bombardment rockets
- 240 mm Fajr-3; 333 mm Fajr-5 artillery rockets
- AK-47/74 assault rifles
- RPK-74 squad automatic weapon (SAW), RPD-47 SAW, AKM submachine gun
- Vz-24 rifle
- M-16A2 and Galil assault rifles
- Uzi Submachine guns
- 40 mm grenade launchers

### *Tactics*

As an organization with both social, nationalist and Islamist agendas, Hizballah utilizes a wide range of institutions and tactics to promote its ideological goals.

On the military front, Hizballah was the first terrorist organization in the world to make regular use of suicide bombing as a tactic. Within Lebanon, it has implemented a wide range of strategies within its guerilla-esque framework against the Israelis and its Lebanese rivals; using car bombs, Katyusha rocket launchers, artillery, roadside bombs, antiaircraft and antitank missiles to attack its opponents. In addition, Hizballah fighters have engaged in several high-profile close-range attacks, including assaults on military installations and sniper attacks on a number of military and civilian targets. The military wing oversees the majority of the Hizballah's military technology and has amassed a considerable arsenal, including heavy artillery to support their operations. Since 1994, Hizballah operatives have increasingly utilized antiaircraft missiles to engage IDF aircraft over Lebanon in an effort to deny the Israelis air superiority during battles between Hizballah ground forces, IDF, and SLA units. These missiles may include the U.S. Stinger and the Russian SA-18 portable antiaircraft missiles.

On the international scene, the special infiltration forces and special operations units are of a more clandestine nature than their counterparts in Lebanon. Special operations forces undergo training in the culture, customs, dress, and language of the country they are to infiltrate. They also learn to operate the weapons systems of the host country. Special infiltration forces, when attempting to cross into Israel, usually dress in camouflage fatigues, IDF uniforms, or the regional military uniforms, and cover their faces with ski masks and hoods so as to remain unidentifiable before reaching the border. They also utilize weapons and radios of the country they are infiltrating. The Jihad special forces units wear green or black clothing and are wired with Semtex, C-4, or C-9.[38] The Hizballah special security apparatus includes a psychological warfare department (also known as the Hebrew observation department) headed by Ahmad Ammar. Its mission is to broadcast Hizballah propaganda and to gather information from Israeli sources. The unit scans the Internet, radio waves, microwaves, military networks, satellite transmissions, and UHF and VHF frequencies.

Hizballah's political wing operates in the form of a grassroots movement, maintaining a cohesive and dependent popular base to ensure its continued relevance and legitimacy within the political sphere. Hizballah operates a wide array of social institutions throughout areas with a large Shi'ite population. These include: hospitals, schools, social halls, and public works. Following the 2006 Israel-Lebanon War, Hizballah-operated relief crews were among the largest and most enthusiastic groups to aid in the reconstruction of southern Lebanese villages damaged in the fighting.

Hizballah also has its own radio (Radio Nur) and television network (Al-Manar, "The Beacon"), which disseminate the group's message. In addition to the straightforward Islamic programming that dominates the daily schedule, Al-Manar also includes a substantial amount of anti-Israel and antisemitic propaganda. Due to its seamless incorporation into general programming, this propaganda is often well received by the station's viewers. Past Al-Manar programs have included a miniseries on the Jewish people, specifically recalling the Passover blood libel, a fictitious account wherein Jews use the blood of Christian children as a main ingredient in the special Passover bread. In a March 2002 speech before thousands of spectators and Al-Manar viewers commemorating the eighth night of the Shiite holiday of Ashura, Nasrallah unequivocally outlined his views, stating:

> . . . the main source of evil in this world, the main source of terrorism in this world, the central threat to international peace and to the economic development of the world, the main threat to the environment of this world, the main source of . . . killing and turmoil, and civil wars and regional wars in this world is the United States of America. . . . The American political discourse is to terrorize the countries of the world. . . . America is a beast in all meanings of the word. A beast that is hungry for power and hungry for blood.[39]

Nasrallah regularly uses Al-Manar as a pulpit to denounce the State of Israel, thereby reinforcing a key tenet of Hizballah's *raison d'être*. In a video entitled "Death to Israel," Nasrallah states:

> We have a faith in which there is no doubt, and a commitment in which there is no hesitation. And our commitment is to the resistance, to its rifles, its bullets, and the blood of its mujaheddin. Death to Israel! No one has the right to give up a single grain of sand from the land of Palestine, and no one has the right to erase even a single letter from the name of Palestine. Israel is utterly null and void, and it's a raping, deviant, occupying, terrorist, cancerous entity that has no legitimacy or legality at all, and never will.[40]

The station additionally supports other groups calling for Israel's elimination by allotting substantial airtime to leaders of Palestinian extremist groups, such as Hamas and Islamic Jihad. Following the events of September 11, 2001, the role of Al-Manar shifted appreciably. Instead of focusing exclusively on the situation in Lebanon and the Palestinian-Israeli conflict, Al-Manar widened its focus to include the newly declared U.S. "War on Terror" as well as the U.S. presence in the Middle East. Following the U.S.-led invasion of Iraq, Al-Manar's new theme became "death to America" and it subsequently began to call for suicide attacks against the "Great Satan" as well as Iraqi resistance against coalition forces in Iraq.

Through the use of modern satellite technology, Al-Manar has developed a truly global audience and has significantly impacted public opinion throughout the Middle East. The station is among the top five most-watched television stations in the region and is also believed to have an additional ten million viewers throughout the world. Along with this worldwide reach, Al-Manar still maintains a loyal audience within Lebanon, and is considered to be the third most popular station in the country, according to Lebanese television officials. Al-Manar's Lebanese channel usually tends to be more sectarian and Shiite dominated than its internationally focused satellite channel.

Currently, Al-Manar has an annual budget of roughly $15 million. Although it receives significant funding from Iran, Palestinian, and Shiite donors and through advertisements from Arab and western corporations, Al-Manar is closely linked with Hizballah. According to Nayef Krayem, the station's former general manager, "Al-Manar gets its political support for the continuation of the channel from Hizballah. It gets money from the shareholders who are leaders in Hizballah [and] they breathe life into one anther. Each provides the other with inspiration. Hizballah uses Al-Manar to express its views. Al-Manar in turn receives political support for its continuation."[41] Thus, it is clear that Hizballah heavily controls Al-Manar's content and agenda. Since its foundation, Al-Manar has grown to become an indispensable instrument in Hizballah's propaganda machine, used to promote its worldview and advance its militant plans, not only in Lebanon, but throughout the broader Middle East and Muslim world.

## The Hizballah–Israel Summer 2006 War

The summer 2006 war between the Israeli Defense Forces (IDF) and Hizballah revealed the Lebanese militant organization's effective efforts at improving both its defensive and offensive military capabilities since the IDF's withdrawal from southern Lebanon in May 2000. With Syrian and Iranian (particularly IRGC) assistance, Hizballah utilized the intervening six years of relative calm to build up an advanced arsenal as well as organize itself much like a modern army, complete with specialized intelligence, antitank, explosives, engineering, and communications units. In addition, it established an elaborate network of defensive positions throughout southern Lebanon, its traditional stronghold, specifically designed to exploit both this indigenous environment and IDF tactical weaknesses.

With a force estimated by Israeli intelligence to number between 2,000 and 4,000 fighters, roughly the size of a Syrian army division, Hizballah's arsenal proved quite capable against one of Israel's most formidable and vaunted military technological developments, the Merkava Mark IV main battle tank. Hizballah's antitank missiles, primarily of Russian and Iranian origin, are wire or laser guided with ranges of up to two kilometers.[42] In addition, militants utilized antitank missiles to target buildings in which IDF infantry units sought shelter, emerging briefly from tunnels dug into the hilly terrain to fire shoulder-launched missiles before disappearing again, thus achieving tactical surprise that effectively countered Israel's overwhelming superiority in firepower. Combined with such advanced weaponry, these tunnel networks, which included storage rooms, barracks, and modern communications equipment, made the IDF campaign, fought among a largely pro-Hizballah populace, extremely difficult.[43]

According to Israeli intelligence, the IRGC is also suspected of having provided on-site training and assistance in several areas of the conflict. Most notably, Iranian soldiers are suspected of being behind an attack on an Israeli naval vessel, firing radar-guided, ground-to-ship C802 missiles and causing serious damage to an Israeli destroyer. Iranian Air Force officers repeatedly visited Lebanon to train Hizballah in the use of Iranian-made, medium-range Fajr-3 and Fajr-5 missiles; however, U.S. intelligence officials believe there was no evidence that the small contingent of Iranian operatives in Beirut directed Hizballah's actions.[44] Hizballah militants used this expanded arsenal to great effect, striking IDF tanks with large roadside bombs planted in anticipation of the IDF's combined arms infantry–armor assault, wounding IDF infantry with sniper fire accurate to 600 yards, and, according to one IDF tank company commander, damaging or destroying around 20 percent of his unit's Merkava tanks with antitank missiles.[45]

Overall, Hizballah's expanded arsenal, advanced training and familiarity with its environment made it an extremely formidable force in this conflict. Timur Goksel, a former senior political advisor to UNIFIL, tasked with monitoring the Lebanese-Israeli border, described Hizballah much as the Israelis do: careful, patient, attuned to gathering intelligence, and respectful of Israeli firepower and mobility.[46] Furthermore, he states, "Hezbollah [sic] . . . studied asymmetrical warfare . . . and [had] the advantage of fighting in their own landscape, among their people, where they prepared for just what the Israelis [did]—enter . . . behind armor on the ground . . . [thus] drawing them in to well-prepared battlefields," and considerably equalizing the battle space in its favor.[47] In short, after fighting the Israelis for eighteen years, Hizballah "is not afraid of the Israeli Army anymore," Goksel concludes.[48] Indeed, the latest conflict proved to be anything but a clear victory for either side, with Israeli government officials and its public expressing frustration at the IDF's ineffective military campaign, while Hizballah claims victory by virtue of its continued existence and operational capability.

## Selected Chronology

**April 18, 1983—Beirut, Lebanon:** A large vehicle packed with explosives detonates in the U.S. embassy compound, killing sixty-three people, including the driver and seventeen

Americans. American investigators soon discovered that both Iran and Syria were involved in planning the blast. In May 1983, U.S. intelligence intercepted a preattack cable from the Iranian foreign ministry to the Iranian embassy in Syria, approving payment for a terrorist attack in Beirut. Intelligence suggested that Syrian and Iranian-backed Hizballah guerrillas, operating in Lebanon under the nom de guerre "Islamic Jihad," carried out the attack.[49]

**October 23, 1983—Beirut, Lebanon:** A large truck loaded with 2,500 pounds of TNT crashes through the main gate of the U.S. Marine headquarters and explodes, killing 241 U.S. servicemen and the driver. Two minutes later, another truck packed with explosives slams into a French paratrooper base two miles away, killing 58 soldiers and the driver. U.S. officials cast their suspicions upon Iran, Syria, and Iranian-backed Hizballah guerrillas in the Syrian-controlled Beka'a Valley of Lebanon.[50]

**December 12, 1983—Kuwait City, Kuwait:** An explosives-laden truck crashes into the compound of the U.S. embassy annex. The blast kills four and injures at least sixty-two. Within a week of the bombing, Kuwait announced the arrest of ten Shiite Muslims with ties to Iran. The ten (seven Iraqis and three Lebanese) were members of the Al Dawah (the Call) Party, a radical Islamic group supported by Iran and tied to Hizballah.[51]

**March 16, 1984—Beirut, Lebanon:** Three armed men kidnap the Central Intelligence Agency's Beirut Station Chief, Lt. Col. William F. Buckley, as he leaves his apartment in West Beirut. Buckley is murdered on October 3, 1985 after being tortured while in captivity. Islamic Jihad, an often used alias for Hizballah, claimed responsibility, stating that his murder was in retaliation for an Israeli attack on a Palestine Liberation Organisation (PLO) camp in Tunisia.[52]

**September 20, 1984—Beirut, Lebanon:** A van laden with explosives swerves around several barricades and U.S. soldiers, entering the compound at the relocated U.S. embassy in East Beirut. The resulting explosion, thirty feet from the embassy annex, kills thirteen, including the driver. In early October 1984, U.S. officials stated that evidence pointed to Hizballah involvement, with the Iranian government providing the explosives via Syria.[53]

**April 12, 1985—Madrid, Spain:** A bomb explodes in a restaurant popular with American servicemen in Madrid, Spain, killing 18, all Spaniards, and injuring 82, including 15 Americans. Within days, Islamic Jihad, a Hizballah alias, claimed responsibility in Beirut.[54]

**June 1, 1985—Beirut, Lebanon, and Algiers, Algeria:** Trans World Airlines Flight 847, bound for Rome, is hijacked over the Mediterranean Sea and ultimately ordered to land in Beirut. The hijackers demand fuel and the release of some 766 captives, mostly Shiites militants held by Israeli forces in southern Lebanon. One American Navy diver is killed. The hostages are eventually freed after being bussed to Damascus in a deal releasing the 766 Lebanese detainees in Israel. Mohammed Hamadei (aka Hammadei, Hammadi), a member of Lebanese Hizballah, led the hijackers. In addition, three members of Hizballah, Imad Moughniyeh, Hasan Izz-al-Din, and Ali Atwa, are put on the FBI's list of 22 most-wanted terrorists for their roles in the hijacking.[55]

**February 17, 1988—Lebanon:** U.S. Marine Corps Lieutenant Colonel W. Higgins is kidnapped and murdered by Hizballah while serving with the United Nations Truce Supervisory Organization (UNTSO) in southern Lebanon.

**March 17, 1992—Buenos Aires, Argentina:** Terrorists attack the Israeli embassy, killing twenty-nine people and leaving more than one hundred wounded. Islamic Jihad (aka Hizballah) was found responsible. Several suspected participants were traced back to a Hizballah cell operating from the tri-border region of South America.[56]

**July 25–August 1, 1993—South Lebanon:** Israel launches "Operation Accountability" in retaliation for a number of cross-border rocket attacks by Hizballah. The operation included extensive aerial and artillery assaults by Israel, and concluded only after a verbal agreement was reached between the two sides.

**July 18, 1994—Buenos Aires, Argentina:** A car bomb destroys the Argentine Israeli Mutual Association (AMIA) Community Center. Eighty-six people are killed and over two hundred are wounded. Both Israeli and American intelligence agencies have attributed the bombing to terrorists connected with the Hizballah, possibly acting under direct orders from Tehran.[57]

**October 29, 1994—Nabatiyya, Lebanon:** Hizballah fighters launch a close range attack on an IDF outpost on the Dabsha Mount in South Lebanon, killing an Israeli soldier. Hizballah's videotaping of the event shows a flag being planted on the outpost prior to the guerillas' retreat. Widespread broadcasts of the footage enflamed Israeli public opinion and raised questions as to the continued Israeli presence in Lebanon.

**June 25, 1996—Dhahran, Saudi Arabia:** Two men detonate a fuel truck loaded with explosives outside the fence of a U.S. military housing complex in Dhahran, Saudi Arabia, killing nineteen American servicemen and wounding over five hundred people at the Khobar Towers apartment complex.

In March 1997, Hani Abdel Rahim Sayegh, a Saudi dissident suspected in a bombing in Ottawa, Canada, identified an Iranian connection to the Khobar Towers attack:

- Sayegh linked a senior Iranian intelligence officer, Brig. Ahmad Sherifi, and a local cell of Saudi Hizballah to a "conspiracy" to attack U.S. targets in 1995, according to various news reports.
- Sayegh himself served as a driver of the car used to signal the driver of the truck carrying the bomb at Khobar Towers, officials said.
- Sayegh was later deported to Saudi Arabia after he reneged on a deal to cooperate with the U.S. investigation of the incident and prosecutors found insufficient evidence to prosecute him.[58]

**April 11–April 27, 1996—Southern Lebanon:** Israel launches "Operation Grapes of Wrath" in response to a cross-border rocket attack by Hizballah. The sixteen-day operation combined aerial and artillery bombardments of Hizballah targets and incurred hundreds of civilian casualties. The operation ended after a memorandum of understanding was signed between the two parties, based roughly on uncodified agreements that ended Israel's Operation Accountability in 1993.

**August 10, 1996—Southern Lebanon:** Hizballah guerrillas detonate a roadside bomb killing and wounding several Israeli soldiers on patrol.[59]

**January 29, 1997—Southern Lebanon:** Three Israeli soldiers are killed, and a fourth wounded, after Hizballah militants detonate a roadside bomb in IDF-controlled southern Lebanon. Militants stated the attack was to mark the Islamic holy month of Ramadan.[60]

**September 7, 1997—Ansariyyah, Lebanon:** A botched Israeli raid leads to a firefight in which twelve Israeli naval commandos are killed. A year later, a deal was reached wherein the two sides concluded an exchange for their respective soldiers' remains.

**January 8, 1998—Jezzin, Lebanon:** Hizballah is suspected of placing several roadside bombs along the Roum-Jezzine road, one of which specifically targeted South Lebanon Army official Emile Nazr, whose niece and nephew were killed in a separate roadside bombing the same day.[61]

**March 31, 1998—Hasbayya, Lebanon:** A roadside bomb explodes near the village of Kaoukbaba, killing five civilians and wounding one. Investigations revealed this bombing occurred simultaneously with a Hizballah mortar attack on a Norwegian United Nations peacekeeping force post.[62]

**October 11, 1998—al-Rayhan, Lebanon:** Hizballah militants fire mortar shells and rockets into a southern Lebanese village, wounding two people.[63]

**December 23, 1998—Kiryat Shmona, Israel (northern Israel):** Hizballah fires between twenty and thirty Katyusha rockets at the northern Israeli town of Kiryat Shmona, wounding at least thirteen and causing extensive damage. Hizballah claimed the attack was in retaliation for the killing of a Lebanese woman and her six children in an Israeli air raid the previous day.[64]

**February 28, 1999—** Brigadier General Erez Gerstein of IDF, commander of the Lebanon liaison unit, and three other soldiers are killed by an explosive device detonated on their convoy by Hizballah.

**January 30, 2000—** Aqel Hashem, deputy commander of the Israeli-allied South Lebanon Army is killed by a roadside bomb. Hizballah claimed responsibility for the attack.

**May 25, 2000—** Israel completes its withdrawal from all sovereign Lebanese territory in accordance with U.N. Security Council Resolution 425 (later confirmed by the U.N. Secretary General on June 16, 2000).

**October 7, 2000—Sheb'aa Farms:** Three Israeli soldiers are ambushed by Hizballah fighters along the Israeli border after a roadside bomb detonates alongside their patrol vehicle. The three kidnapped soldiers are transferred into Lebanon and held hostage awaiting an eventual exchange with the Israeli government. In 2004, the bodies of the three soldiers were exchanged for 432 Palestinian and Lebanese prisoners held in Israeli prisons.

**August 7, 2001—South Lebanon:** Two houses belonging to senior members of the former Israeli-allied South Lebanon Army are destroyed by bombs.[65]

**August 10, 2003—Shlomi, Israel (northern Israel):** Haviv Dadon, an Israeli teenager, is killed and five others were wounded when Hizballah fighters shelled the northern border town of Shlomi from southern Lebanon in the most serious attack since the IDF withdrawal from Lebanon in May 2000. Hizballah claimed the attack was in retaliation for the killing of one of its security officials, Ali Hussein Saleh, in a car bombing.[66]

**April 7, 2005—Northern Israel:** Hizballah operatives kidnap two Israeli-Arabs, holding them for four days in order to interrogate them in the hope of gaining intelligence on Israel. Israeli officials believed no security information was compromised.[67]

**July 12, 2006—Northern Israel/Southern Lebanon:** Hizballah attacks two IDF Humvee patrol vehicles operating along the northern Lebanese-Israeli border with the aim of kidnapping IDF soldiers in order to force a prisoner exchange. The well-executed attack kills three IDF soldiers, wounding three others and two IDF reservist noncommissioned officers, Ehud Goldwasser and Eldad Regev, taken captive. After realizing IDF soldiers had been kidnapped, additional IDF units pursued the Hizballah attackers into Lebanon and were themselves attacked, where five were killed.

**July 12–August 14, 2006: Israel-Hizballah War ("Second Lebanon War"):** Calling the kidnapping of two IDF soldiers by Hizballah operatives on July 12, 2006 "an act of war," Israeli Prime Minister Ehud Olmert launches an offensive targeting Hizballah throughout Lebanon. The IDF offensive targeted a broad range of Lebanese and Hizballah installations, from Katyusha rocket positions to Beirut's Rafik Hariri International Airport to Lebanese roadways leading to Syria, which, according to Israel, were used by Hizballah to rearm and resupply its forces during the conflict. The initial IDF response included air strikes and an intensive artillery bombardment of Hizballah positions in southern Lebanon. Israel later staged a full-scale ground invasion targeting hardened Hizballah fighting positions in southern Lebanon as well as a naval blockade of Lebanese ports designed to interrupt Hizballah's resupply routes. Hizballah responded by fiercely defending the southern Lebanese towns it controlled and firing hundreds of Katyusha rockets into northern Israel throughout the duration of the conflict. After over a month of fighting and a series of unmet Israeli ultimatums outlining ceasefire conditions, chief among them the return of the kidnapped IDF soldiers, hostilities were ended by U.N. Security Council Resolution 1701. The resolution called for the disarmament of Hizballah, the withdrawal of Hizballah and Israeli forces, and the deployment of Lebanese Army troops with an expanded UNIFIL contingent into southern Lebanon. By December 3, 2006, all IDF forces had withdrawn from southern Lebanon. However, subsequent to the conflict, both UNIFIL and the Lebanese government refused to effectively disarm Hizballah.

**November 21, 2006—Beirut, Lebanon:** Lebanese Industry Minister Pierre Amine Gemanel, a prominent Christian politician and well-known opponent of Syria, is shot down by gunmen in a Beirut suburb. Syrian involvement, through Hizballah, was highly suspected. Gemanel is the fifth anti-Syrian to be killed in Lebanon in the past two years.[68]

**June 13, 2007—Beirut, Lebanon:** Walid Eido, a Lebanese anti-Syrian member of parliament, is killed near Beirut in a car bombing that claimed eleven victims. One of Eido's sons as well as his two bodyguards, also died in the bombing. Though Syria and Hezbollah were suspected, both denied any involvement in the incident.[69]

**January 11, 2007—Zarat, Israel:** The IDF finds abandoned weaponry, including rockets, launchers, Lao missiles, submachine guns, carriers, etc., while searching the area of Zarit, where two Israeli soldiers were abducted on July 12, 2006. The examination of the equipment indicated that it was abandoned by Hizballah soon after the abduction.[70]

**January 26, 2007— Israel:** The IDF discovers two connected bunkers that were used by Hizballah as a base for its operations. The bunkers were safely detonated by the IDF.[71]

**February 5, 2007—Jerusalem, Israel:** The IDF finds explosive devices near the border with Lebanon. Explosive ordnance disposal teams succeed in safely detonating the four devices that, in the military's opinion, targeted Israeli military patrols. Israel strongly suspected Hezbollah of planting these explosives,[72] and declared that if more devices were to be found, they would destroy the Hizballah military position erected close to the border in the Aytarun and Maroun al-Ras area.[73]

## HAMAS[74]

Hamas (an acronym for the Arabic phrase *Harakat al-Muqawama al-Islamiyya*, meaning "The Islamic Resistance Movement") is a Sunni-Islamist organization dedicated to armed Palestinian resistance against Israel. Extensively funded by Iran, Hamas is committed both to the destruction of the state of Israel and absolute opposition to the establishment of any non-Islamic entity on lands once controlled by the great Islamic empires of historical Palestine. In its resistance to Israeli sovereignty, Hamas has employed a variety of terrorist tactics against the Israeli civilian population, the most notorious of which is its use of suicide bombers.

### History

Hamas is an offshoot of the Palestinian Muslim Brotherhood organization, which was first established in 1977 after Israeli Prime Minister Menachem Begin licensed the group's operations within Israel. In doing so, Begin hoped to counterbalance the influence of Yassir Arafat's Fatah movement and the PLO within the West Bank and Gaza. Ironically, the group would evolve into a far more serious threat to Israeli security in later years. Hamas matured as a terrorist organization after the outbreak of the first *Intifada* in 1987. Previously, the Muslim Brotherhood had established various social and religious institutions as alternatives to the existing secular institutions, and Hamas grew to become the dominant faction in a number of public forums, most notably the student council body of the Islamic University in Gaza.

Hamas's position within Palestinian society grew continuously throughout the first *Intifada*. Its founders, led by the spiritual leaders Ahmed Yassin and Abdel Aziz Rantisi, sought to capitalize on Israel's previous indifference to its activities and undermine Fatah as the sole representative of the Palestinian people. Its various militant activities, coupled with its growing social services network, substantially increased its popularity, primarily within the Gaza Strip. Hamas's activity against Israel expanded in scope, from shootings at roadside patrols to the kidnapping and execution of two Israeli Border Patrol officers. By 1988, Hamas began carrying out attacks within Israel proper, including knife attacks on Israeli civilians in West Jerusalem. Hamas's successes led to numerous violent confrontations with their Fatah rivals, which were completely separate from their joint anti-Israeli conflict from 1987 to 1993. Also notable among Hamas's activities at the time were the persecution and execution of both Palestinians and Israeli Arabs accused of collaborating with Israeli security forces.

In 1988, the official Hamas charter was published. It stated unequivocally then—as it does today—that the destruction of Israel and its replacement with a Sunni-Islamic state is the group's primary objective, and that violent "struggle" is the only acceptable means of achieving this end. The Hamas charter views all Islamic lands as religious endowments (a*wqaf*); this territory is not subject to non-Muslim governance and is not to be abused for secular purposes. Israel saw a precipitous rise in the number of Hamas attacks from this period onward, indicative of both its past success and the popular momentum surrounding its activities. In response, Israel began to expand its counterterrorist efforts against the group. It finally arrested Sheikh Ahmed Yassin, the spiritual leader of the movement, convicting him of conspiring to kill Israeli citizens and sentencing him to five life sentences in 1989.

In 1991, Hamas established an official military wing, dubbed the *Izz al-Din al-Qassam* brigades, named for a legendary Palestinian military commander of the 1930s. Headed by Yahya Ayyash (also known as "The Engineer" for his bomb-making skills), this group would ultimately be responsible for the vast majority of attacks against civilians in the following years. The first Hamas suicide attack, carried out in April 1993 at the Mehola junction near the city of Jericho, wounded eight people. From this point on, concurrent with the PLO's more conciliatory stance during the negotiation of the Oslo peace accords, Hamas rose to become the principle terrorist organization in the West Bank and the Gaza Strip, ultimately solidifying its legitimacy as a resistance movement and expanding its mandate as the spokesman for the Palestinian people.

Several other factors contributed to Hamas's rise to power. Under Yasser Arafat's leadership, the PLO suffered several significant setbacks in its ability to establish a Palestinian state, the most serious of which resulted from Arafat's alignment with Saddam Hussein during the Gulf war in 1990. Later, when Arafat adopted a policy of negotiations over a two-state solution, Hamas became the prime advocate for unwavering resistance against the Israeli presence in Palestine. The slow pace of the peace process throughout the 1990s and the lack of tangible benefits ceded to the Palestinian population enabled Hamas to achieve high popular standing among the Palestinian populace, this despite the improved chances for peace with Israel. Yet intra-Palestinian conflict continued, including the death of Hamas's top bomb-maker, Muhyi a-din Sharif in March 1998, an assassination that was ultimately traced to Fatah loyalists.[75]

Throughout the Oslo peace accord negotiations from 1993 to 1999, Hamas continued to assert its opposition through indiscriminate violence. It carried out numerous devastating attacks against Israeli military and civilian targets, within both the occupied territories and Israel proper. Israel's responses to these attacks were facilitated by its control of large portions of the West Bank and the Gaza Strip, though its diplomatic concessions to the Palestinian leadership under Arafat would, at times, undermine its strategic counterterrorism objectives. Israeli counterterrorist actions did achieve some positive results, such as the assassinations of Yahya Ayyash in 1995 and Adel Awadallah in 1997. However, a similar September 1997 "targeted killing" attempt on Khaled Mashaal, head of Hamas's Jordanian branch, produced catastrophic results. The botched operation ended with the arrest of two Israeli Mossad agents in Amman, Jordan. They were eventually returned to Israel in exchange for the release of Ahmed Yassin. Mashaal, meanwhile, was expelled from Jordan in 1999 and moved to Damascus, Syria, where he resides to this day.

Hamas capitalized on the breakdown of the peace process and the outbreak of a second Intifada in September 2000 by expanding both its network and the scope of its attacks. Consequently, it began to receive increased funding from its patrons in Syria and Iran. Israeli retaliation against Hamas under Prime Minister Ehud Barak was restrained, even as Yasser Arafat began to release Hamas detainees held in Palestinian jails in order to allow them to regroup and continue their terrorist activity. In the following months, Barak opted for a return to diplomatic negotiations with Arafat after it was decided that he was incapable of reigning in Hamas and its operations. This policy failed and ultimately led to Barak's defeat in the 2001 Israeli parliamentary elections.

Under the new Prime Minister Ariel Sharon, Israeli counterterrorism efforts grew more aggressive. Following Israel's January 2002 seizure of the munitions ship *Karine A* en route from Iran to the Gaza Strip (and the subsequent public diplomatic backlash against the Palestinian authority), Israeli policy began to shift from reliance on its defensive intelligence network to offensive operations. Sharon increased the size of IDF ground forces within the West Bank and Gaza and projected a strong airpower presence around the Palestinian territories. This allowed Israel to regain control of almost all the autonomous areas handed over to the Palestinians during the previous decade's peace negotiations. Sharon also favored a strategy of maintaining encirclement around populated areas designed to isolate and incapacitate Palestinian terrorist groups, as well as a policy of "targeted killings" against senior Hamas members and military commanders. Although condemned by the international community as "illegal" policies, these actions severely degraded Hamas's operational capabilities and led it to divert funds from terrorist operations to security details tasked with protecting the group's senior leadership. In March 2002, after a terrorist attack at a Netanya hotel on the eve of the Jewish Passover holiday, Sharon launched Operation Defensive Shield in an attempt to incapacitate Hamas's infrastructure. This was the largest military action of the second Intifada, and inflicted hundreds of casualties on both sides.

Given Sharon's new offensive approach, Hamas changed its tactics on the diplomatic front by offering a cease-fire in the form of a *hudna* (truce, as opposed to peace treaty) agreement. From 2002 onward this hudna was offered several times to the Israelis—and even implemented twice on a tentative basis—but both times it was voided before it expired due to violations by both sides. Yasser Arafat's death in November 2004 left a profound power vacuum and led to an internal power struggle within Fatah, which continues to the present day. The loss of the iconic Palestinian leader precipitated a general popular shift away from Fatah (and its failed domestic policies) toward Hamas. Furthermore, Arafat's death from natural causes, when contrasted with the Hamas leadership's assassinations as "martyrs of the resistance," only broadened Hamas's popular mandate.

Israel's "Disengagement Plan" from the Gaza Strip in the summer of 2005 bolstered Hamas's image and solidified its dominant position atop the Palestinian resistance to Israel. Despite vociferous denials by the Israeli government, the Palestinian public perceived Israel's withdrawal as direct result of the tenacity of the "armed resistance" of which Hamas was unequivocally the prime instigator. Therefore, it is not surprising, in hindsight, that Hamas was able to achieve a majority victory in the Palestinian parliamentary elections of January 2006. Nonetheless, the international community was shocked by the result and was presented with a serious dilemma: the Islamic party was elected legitimately through a democratic process, yet it refused to recognize Israel as a sovereign nation and renounce terrorism. Thus, immediately following the election, the Quartet (the collective title of the European Union, Russia, the United States and the United Nations) effectively cut off financial aid to the Palestinian government and issued a joint statement, saying that "there is a fundamental contradiction between armed group and militia activities and the building of a democratic state."[76]

In the months after the elections, the economic situation of the Palestinian government under Hamas has become dire. With no funds available to pay the salaries of its 100,000 public servants (including almost 80,000 members of the various security services), strikes and violent demonstrations have become a common occurrence throughout Gaza and the West Bank. In view of the Quartet's embargo, the Palestinian public has responded with even more virulent anti-western sentiment and deep-seeded distrust of Western peace mediators. Moreover, the government's continued refusal to contain terrorist attacks originating in the Palestinian territories has sparked renewed clashes between the Israelis and the Palestinians. The most noted of these was the June 25, 2006 kidnapping of IDF Cpl. Gilad Shalit from within Israel by the Popular Resistance Committees, an amalgam of Hamas and Fatah militants.

While it has been said that the mandate afforded Hamas through the election was a response to increasing bureaucratic corruption in Fatah, and it was originally hoped that the group's incorporation into the democratic process could serve to moderate its rhetoric and polices, it is apparent that the burdens of governance have not yet changed the organization's position on the use of indiscriminate violence as a means of resistance. The messages communicated by key Hamas policymakers have been inconsistent, ranging from a refusal to ever recognize Israel's sovereignty to offers of a "ten-year truce" after a withdrawal to the pre-1967 Six-Day War borders. It also appears unlikely that the Iran–Hamas connection will remain intact if the latter disbands its terrorist operations. Indeed, Hamas has gone to great lengths to maintain this link, suffering the burden of an international embargo and virtual economic collapse. These close relations are predicated on mutual animosity toward Israel, and if Hamas were to moderate its position, Iran would merely divert its funding to other terrorist outlets (such as the Palestinian Islamic Jihad). Thus, Hamas elects to maintain its Iranian alliance, refusing to recognize any non-Palestinian government west of the Jordan River and continuing to champion violent resistance against Israel.

Of particular concern more recently has been the violent takeover of the Gaza Strip by Hamas in June 2007, during which Hamas militants brutally defeated the Fatah movement's security forces, transforming the area into a more dangerous security challenge than ever before. According to Israeli intelligence reports, over the course of two months in the summer of 2007, Hamas smuggled some twenty tons of explosives into the Gaza Strip.[77] Its current military capabilities include antiaircraft missiles, antitank rockets, and most likely guided missiles. Moreover, Hamas's armed wing, the *Izz Al-Din Al-Qassam* brigades, has recently become most active in some areas of the West Bank, despite the efforts of Palestinian Authority President Mahmoud Abbas to maintain stability in the territory and advance the ongoing peace process with Israel.

## Ideology

Hamas is an extremist Islamist organization. As such, it dedicates itself to the principles of political Islam: imposing the Sunni *shari'a* (Islamic law) within its realm and liberating all Islamic lands from the control of those they view as un-Islamic. Israel is the major challenge to the Hamas ideology as it represents the most blatant example of an illegitimate entity on Islamic soil. Hamas's theoretical ideology is outlined in its 1988 charter.[78] Selected excerpts are included below:

The motto of Hamas is "God is its target, the Prophet is its model, the Qur'an its constitution: Jihad is its path and death for the sake of God is the loftiest of its wishes."[79] Hamas states that its objective is "to bring about justice and defeat injustice, in word and deed."

*Preface*: "Israel will exist and will continue to exist until Islam will obliterate it, just as it obliterated others before it." (A quote from Hassan al Banna, founder of the Egyptian Muslim Brotherhood)

*Article 6*: "The Islamic Resistance Movement is a distinguished Palestinian movement, whose allegiance is to Allah, and whose way of life is Islam. It strives to raise the banner of Allah over every inch of Palestine, for under the wing of Islam followers of all religions can coexist in security and safety where their lives, possessions and rights are concerned. . . . "

*Article 11*: "The Islamic Resistance Movement believes that the land of Palestine is an Islamic Waqf consecrated for future Muslim generations until Judgment Day. It, or any part of it, should not be squandered: it, or any part of it, should not be given up."

*Article 13*: "There is no solution for the Palestinian question except through Jihad. Initiatives, proposals and international conferences are all a waste of time and vain endeavors. The Palestinian people know better than to consent to having their future, rights and fate toyed with."

*Article 28*: "The Zionist invasion is a vicious invasion. . . . It relies greatly in its infiltration and espionage operations on the secret organizations it gave rise to, such as the Freemasons, the Rotary and Lions clubs, and other sabotage groups. All these organizations, whether secret or open, work in the interest of Zionism and according to its instructions. . . . "

*Article 31*: "The Islamic Resistance Movement is a humanistic movement. It takes care of human rights and is guided by Islamic tolerance when dealing with the followers of other religions. It does not antagonize anyone of them except if it is antagonized by it or stands in its way to hamper its moves and waste its efforts. Under the wing of Islam, it is possible for the followers of the three religions—Islam, Christianity and Judaism—to coexist in peace and quiet with each other."

*Article 32*: "After Palestine, the Zionists aspire to expand from the Nile to the Euphrates. When they will have digested the region they overtook, they will aspire to further expansion, and so on. Their plan is embodied in *The Protocols of the Elders of Zion*, and their present conduct is the best proof of what we are saying."

## Organizational Structure and Funding

The organizational structure of Hamas can be broken down into its "internal leadership," or those members within the West Bank and the Gaza Strip, and its "external leadership," or those members residing outside the Palestinian territories, mainly in Syria. The Syrian government enables the Hamas leadership and its terrorist commanders to conduct various activities from within its territory, including the formulation of the Hamas operational strategy, distribution of its global propaganda, the training of terrorist operatives in Syrian-based camps, global funding of terrorist activity, and provision of economic aid toward arms and ammunition purchases.

Although he was not necessarily involved in all of the group's activities, Sheikh Ahmad Yassin represented the hierarchical apex of the organization until he was killed by an Israeli air strike on March 22, 2004. Since then, the overall leadership of the organization has transferred to the external leader, Khaled Mashaal, currently based in Damascus, Syria. His second-in-command, also in Damascus, is Moussa Muhammad Abu Marzouq. Theoretically, both the internal and external wings of the group have equal input on all issues of interest and impact to Hamas. However, recent events have shown that it is the external leadership that maintains overt authority over the group's decision-making cycle. Since the external leadership is both less threatened by potential Israeli responses to their activities, as well as more responsive to Syrian and Iranian pressure, it normally takes a more rigid and radical approach to the group's potential areas of activity. The internal leadership, which faces the reality of the Palestinian situation and the direct ramifications of any violent activity, is, at times, more pragmatic in its approach.

Within the Gaza Strip and the West Bank, the organizational framework comprises a parallel hierarchy determined by the functions of both public and covert activity. Down to the cell level, subdivisions are determined by region, district, and respective villages. The primary goal of the public arm of Hamas is to expand the ranks of the movement through social action. Hamas's public arm can be broken down into several groups: The first network is that of the Hamas's *Da'awa* or "infrastructure," which engages in recruitment, distribution of funds, and the domestic dissemination of Hamas's ideological message. The second network promotes "popular uprising" and agitation against Israel (specifically in relation to Israel's occupation of the West Bank and Gaza), usually appearing in the form of protests and rallies. Third is the Hamas's *Aman* or "security" network that acts both as a peacekeeper and territorial "police force" tasked with establishing and maintaining Hamas areas of control with regard to other power-seeking organizations within the Palestinian territories (mostly Fatah). In addition, the Aman network is known to gather information on collaborators with the Israeli security services and target them specifically.

It is noteworthy that in its early years, Hamas's funding came primarily from the oil-rich Gulf monarchies, which provided concurrent funding to many Islamist groups engaged in militant activities (including the Palestinian Islamic Jihad). In a 2002 interview, Khaled Mashaal recalled how the connections many Hamas members made during their stay in Kuwait facilitated attempts at fundraising in the Arab world. By the early 1990s, however, Hamas expanded its network to include many other outlets for funding and military aid. Some of these funding sources included Sudan (under the Islamist leadership of Hassan al-Turabi), Syria, Kuwait, the United Arab Emirates, and Yemen, where the organization maintained a number of its training camps, as well as Iran, which became an official patron in a much publicized 1992 agreement. Originally, it was declared that Iranian support for the group would only reach approximately $30 million.[80] Due to the outbreak of the second Intifada in 2000, that number has greatly increased. Hamas's annual budget is presently estimated at between $50 million and $90 million[81]—by all accounts, Iran is Hamas's largest state sponsor and one of its staunchest supporters within the diplomatic arena. In any case, its enlarged network led to Hamas representatives maintaining offices in most of these host countries, as well as in Jordan, before King Abdullah outlawed the group in October 1999.

Hamas's network of financial sources, operating within the framework of *Da'awa* activity, is pervasive, extending throughout the region and globally, with estimated annual revenues in the tens of millions of dollars. Several of the key financiers of Hamas include:

a. A considerable proportion of the aforementioned funds originate from various sources in the Gulf States (the Gulf Cooperation Council States). Most of the funding is from Saudi Arabian sources, totaling around $12 million per year.
b. Iranian contribution is estimated at $3–30 million a year. In 1993, for example, Iran provided Hamas with $15 million in order to undermine the Olso Agreement between the PLO and Israel.
c. Charitable associations in the territories have been raised for Hamas through mosques (a convenient domain for fundraising and recruitment of members) and through charitable associations and foundations.
d. Charity associations overseas, throughout Europe and the United States, have been active for many years.
e. Fundraising abroad and in the territories, acting sometimes as a cover for other charity objectives and later funneling money illegally to Hamas activists.

The "charity" organizations (*Jamayath Hiriya)* and "committees" (*Lejan Zekath*) that openly fund Hamas activities within the Palestinian territories operate in concert with covert illegal fundraising operations throughout the world. These networks or charity associates also serve to mask financial movements of the Hamas leadership abroad, while actually transferring funds to Hamas operatives worldwide and providing opportunities to recruit new members. While a significant portion of the funds accrued through "charitable donations" does in fact fund legitimate institutions in the Palestinian territories, it is nearly impossible to determine which portions fund terrorist activities and which do not. Common methods of transferring funds to Hamas include the use of moneychangers, checks drawn on foreign accounts, fraudulent foreign business accounts, and direct cash transfers.

Donations to Hamas are, for obvious reasons, "off-the-books" transactions. Hamas acquires additional funds through charitable donations under the auspices of traditional Islamic tithing (*zakat*) and through a number of nongovernmental organizations that funnel portions of their humanitarian aid provisions directly to the organization. Since financial accountability rarely exists within these non-profit organizations, most of the monies reach Hamas with little difficulty. Hamas also receives funds through several outlets outside the Middle East.[82] The most well-known of these was the U S.-based Holy Land Foundation for Relief and Development, which was shut down and outlawed by the U.S. government following the September 11, 2001 terrorist attacks. Lesser known organizations include the (also defunct) Al Aqsa Education Fund, the Quranic Literacy Institute, and the Al-Haramein Foundation. Similar organizations exist in Europe as well, including the Commite de Bienfaisance et de Secours aux Palestinians in France and Interpal (the Palestinian Relief and Development Fund) in the United Kingdom.

In addition to its ideological and fundraising activities, Hamas has developed an elaborate military component that is composed of various armed militias loyal to its leadership. Of these, the *Izz Al-Din Al-Qassam* brigade is the most well known. It was founded in 1992 by Yahya Ayyash, a prominent Hamas militant, and was composed of two earlier militant wings of Hamas: the "Palestinian Holy Fighters" (*Al-Majahadoun Al-Falestinioun*), which combats external enemies of Hamas, and the internal security section (*Jehaz Aman*), which is responsible for domestic security.

The *Al-Majahadoun Al-Falestinioun* was originally founded in 1982 by Sheikh Ahmed Yassin to arm Hamas supporters against rival Palestinian factions. This internecine conflict was predicated on an old position of the original Muslim Brotherhood, which stipulated that a purge of dissenting elements "from within," i.e., within the Islamic *umma*, must precede any armed struggle against external forces. However, once the first Intifada broke out in 1987, Al-Majahadoun Al-Falestinioun expanded its attacks to include external, Israeli targets, carrying out bombings, ambush attacks on Israeli patrols, and kidnappings and executions of Israeli citizens.[83]

The *Jehaz Aman* unit was also established by Yassin along with two close associates, in 1986. The original purpose of this unit was to collect information on Palestinians believed to be acting as "collaborators" for Israel. Yassin, acting on the recommendation of Jehaz Aman leadership, issued a *fatwa* (religious edict) condemning all "collaborators" and "heretics" to death, and assassination squads were later assembled to execute any Palestinian collaborators. Later, this group would be incorporated into the Al-Majahadoun Al-Falestinioun organization. Today, most of Hamas's armed factions fall under the umbrella of the *Izz al-Din al-Qassam* brigade, which has been responsible for almost every terrorist attack carried out by Hamas since the end of the first Intifada.

## Leadership Profiles

### *Khaled Mashaal*

Khaled Mashaal is head of the political bureau of Hamas, the de facto head of the "external leadership," and currently resides in Damascus.[84] As a student at Kuwait University in 1971, he became active in Islamic and Palestinian politics and joined the Muslim Brotherhood branch there. Under his leadership, the group acted as a serious contender for dominance of the Palestinian agenda against Yasser Arafat's PLO. When Hamas was founded, he formed the Kuwaiti branch of the organization while teaching physics at Kuwait University. Following the 1991 Gulf War, Mashaal moved to Jordan, where he continued to act as head of the political bureau of the organization. In 1999, after surviving an Israeli attempt on his life two years earlier, he was expelled from Jordan by royal decree, along with several other key members of the external leadership. Since that time, he has enjoyed Damascus' patronage and support, allowing him to lead the organization with virtual impunity. Following the January 2006 election victory, Mashaal claimed that Hamas would neither disarm nor formally recognize Israel, though he has tentatively supported a political alliance with Fatah in order to ensure popular unity. In the aftermath of Hamas's takeover of the Gaza Strip in June 2007, relations with Palestinian Authority President Mahmoud Abbas have again deteriorated to the point of open confrontation between Abbas' Fatah movement and Hamas.

### *Ismail Haniyeh*

Ismail Haniyeh is a former Prime Minister of the Palestinian National Authority and a current senior member of the Hamas organization.[85] His headquarters are in Gaza. Haniyeh was born in the Sha'ti refugee camp in Gaza, and graduated from Gaza City's Islamic University with a degree in Arabic literature. One of approximately four hundred people expelled by Israel to Lebanon in 1992, Haniyeh returned to Gaza the next year and became the dean of the Islamic University, where he also led the Hamas student movement. His close ties with Sheikh Ahmed Yassin led to his promotion to chief of Yassin's office in 1998. While Haniyeh has never explicitly contradicted the stated agendas of the movement as per its charter, he is considered to be among the more moderate of the prominent members of the organization. In the past, he has advocated some level of dialogue with Israel, even indicating a need to amend Hamas's position if only to improve the Palestinians' international standing. However, since Hamas assumed control of Gaza in June 2007, Haniyeh has faced renewed political and legal challenges from Fatah leadership as well as a deteriorating security and economic situation in the area.

### *Sheikh Ahmad Yassin*

Ahmad Yassin was the spiritual leader of Hamas, and was widely involved in the organization's terrorist activities, until his death in 2004. Yassin previously headed the Gaza branch of the Muslim Brotherhood. He was arrested in 1984 and released the next year as part of a prisoner exchange. He was imprisoned again in 1989 for the abduction and murder of two Israeli soldiers, and was released in 1997. Throughout his incarceration, Yassin maintained a high degree of influence over Hamas's ideology and activities. He was killed in an Israeli air strike, along with several other members of the Hamas leadership, in March 2004. In a statement after his death, an IDF spokesman referred to Yassin as "personally responsible for numerous . . . terror attacks. . . . "[86]

### Abdel Aziz Rantisi

Abdel Aziz Rantisi, one of the founding members of Hamas, was born in 1947 and began studying pediatrics at the University of Alexandria.[87] There, he was introduced to Islamic political theory, and, upon his return to Gaza, founded the Gaza Islamic Center in 1973. Along with the other founding members, he first became involved in Islamic politics through the Palestinian Muslim Brotherhood. During the first Intifada, he was jailed multiple times and expelled to Lebanon in 1992 for publicly inciting terrorist attacks. He remained a key decision maker in the organization until he was killed by an Israeli air strike in 2004.

### Mahmoud Al-Zahar

Mahmoud al-Zahar was the foreign minister of the Palestinian government until 2007, and one of the founding members of the Hamas organization. He graduated from the University of Cairo with a degree in Medicine in 1971, and, upon arriving in Gaza, joined a branch of the Palestinian Muslim Brotherhood. His activities there brought him in touch with the rest of the Hamas leadership, particularly Abdel-Aziz Rantisi.[88]

In the early years of the organization, Zahar was considered one of the more moderate voices in the group, until Israel expelled him and scores of other Hamas members to Lebanon in 1992. Upon his return, however, he became far less amenable toward the Jewish state and began to exhibit far more extremist views regarding the nature of Palestinian resistance. Since then, he has been one of the most high profile members of Hamas, appearing frequently on the media outlets to express Hamas's position as events unfolded.

Despite his seniority in Gaza, Zahar was ninth on Hamas's list of candidates in the 2006 Palestinian elections, most likely due to his reputation as a "hardliner." On the day of the elections, Zahar stated on Al-Manar TV that "we will not recognize the Israeli enemy's [right] to a single inch." However, in later interviews with Haaretz and CNN, Zahar stated that a Palestinian state could be established based on the borders which existed prior to the 1967 Arab-Israeli war, albeit only as an interim measure.

### Mohamad Deif

Mohamad Deif is a senior commander of the *Izz al-Din al-Qassam* brigades in the Gaza Strip. He is believed to be the mastermind behind numerous terror attacks, including suicide operations in Tel Aviv and Jerusalem. Deif is in charge of the Izz al-Din al-Qassam, the leadership of which he acquired after the death of Salah Shehaddeh in July 2002 (though Hamas has never formally acknowledged any replacement to Shehaddeh). He is one of Israel's most wanted men, and has survived six IDF assassination attempts. The last of these, on July 13, 2006, purportedly rendered him paralyzed on his right side.

It has been reported that Deif, unhappy with the January 2006 truce announced by Hamas, decided to split from the group to join Al-Qaeda cells being established in the Gaza Strip. However, this was denied by the Izz al-Din al-Qassam brigades, and has since been discredited by Israeli security sources' reports, as well as a videotape Deif released several months later.

### *Yahya Ayyash*

Yahya Ayyash (aka "the Engineer") was one of the most prominent members of the *Izz al-Din al-Qassam* brigades, and one of its most effective bomb makers. He studied at Beir Zeit University and received a Bachelor's degree in electrical engineering in 1988. It was under his command that Hamas's first suicide attack was launched. In later years, bombings that he had orchestrated would cause the deaths of more than seventy Israelis. He was assassinated in January 1996 through an elaborate plan in which Israeli intelligence installed an explosive device in his cell phone. His death, along with those of his protégés in subsequent IDF killings, significantly reduced the quality of Hamas's incendiary devices during the second Intifada.

### *Adel Awadallah*

Adel Awadallah was a senior member of the *Izz al-Din al-Qassam* brigades, pivotal in the regional commands of Judea, Samaria, and Jerusalem. He excelled at procuring and transporting armaments throughout the West Bank, as well as money laundering. He was also instrumental in securing international funding for Hamas. It was revealed after he was killed by Israeli soldiers in September 1998 that Awadallah had been planning to attack Israel by contaminating the public water supply with chemical weapons. A Hamas handbook, *The Mujahedin Poisons Handbook* (1996), had been placed on the organization's website. The twenty-three-page manual included instructions for making homemade poisons, toxins, gases, and other materials.[89]

### *Moussa Muhammad Abu Marzouq*

Moussa Muhammad Abu Marzouq is the deputy head of Hamas's political bureau, and serves at present as the second-in-command to Khaled Mashaal in Damascus, Syria. Born in Gaza in 1951, Abu Marzouq graduated from Cairo's Ein Shams University in 1977 with a degree in engineering. He lived in both the United States and Jordan for many years and in 1991 received a Ph.D. in industrial engineering in the United States. While in the United States, he founded the Holy Land Foundation for Relief and Development, a major fundraising outlet for Hamas. In July 1995, Marzouq was arrested at John F. Kennedy International Airport when his name appeared on the Immigration and Naturalization Service's terrorist "watch list." Subsequent Israeli extradition requests sought to tie him to 10 separate attacks carried out by the military wing of Hamas between 1990 and 1994. Marzouq was expelled from the United States, and subsequently was expelled from Jordan as well, before settling in Damascus. In 2004, a U.S. court indicted him *in absentia* for coordinating and financing Hamas activities; Syria has yet to extradite or expel him.[90]

### *Muhyi a-din Sharif*

A Hamas bomb maker, Sharif died in Ramallah on March 29, 1998 while preparing for a suicide attack against Israel. He was the apprentice to Yahya Ayyash, the "Engineer." After his autopsy it was discovered that a bullet, not the accidental explosion of the bomb that he was working on, had killed him. Hamas immediately blamed Israel for his death, an accusation that Israel denied.[91] Subsequent police investigations into Sharif's death found that five members of Hamas were responsible.[92] Imad Awadallah, one member accused, was believed to have had disagreements with Sharif over the allocation of Hamas's funds.[93]

### *Mustafa Qanu'*

Mustafa Qanu' is Hamas's official representative to Syria. In October 1995, along with Imad al-Alami, he was the key ambassador to Iran during an instrumental meeting with the Iranian officials that further solidified the connection between Hamas and the Islamic Republic.[94]

### *Imad al-Alami*

Imad Khaled Fayeq al-Alami is the official envoy to Jordan and currently resides in Amman. He is a civil engineer, was a member of the executive committee of the Engineers Union in Gaza, and reportedly maintained a very close relationship with Ahmed Yassin. After being deported from Gaza in 1990, he took up residence in Amman before moving to Tehran, and then Damascus. He was the head of Hamas's interior committee.[95] Al-Alami has had oversight responsibility for the military wing of Hamas within the Palestinian territories. As a Hamas military leader, al-Alami directs the movement of personnel and funds to the West Bank and Gaza. Consequently, the U.S. Treasury Department has classified him as a "specially designated global terrorist" (SDGT), freezing his U.S. assets and prohibiting transactions with U.S. nationals.[96]

### *Ibrahim Ghawsha*

Ibrahim Ghawsha, a Jordanian citizen, is considered to be the official spokesman of Hamas and a member of Hamas's senior leadership. He was detained in Jordan in early September 1997 for issuing statements promoting anti-Israeli violence.[97]

### *Mohammad Amin Nazzal*

Mohammad Amin Nazzal began work for Hamas in 1989 and received his first significant post as a member of the politburo in 1992.[98] As the group's working representative in Jordan, Nazzal publicly stated in 1993 his support for a Palestinian state in the West Bank and Gaza as the first steps in the liberation of Palestine. During the 1999 attempt by Jordanian security forces to reign in Hamas, Nazzal was forced to relocate first to Syria and later to Lebanon, where he continues to engage in inter-Palestinian dialogue.

### Selected Chronology[99]

**February 16, 1989—Hodaya, Israel:** Avi Sasportas, an IDF solider, was kidnapped and murdered at the main junction of the city.

**May 3, 1989—Ashkelon, Israel:** Ilan Sa'adon, an IDF solider, was kidnapped and murdered while hitchhiking to his home.

**July 28, 1990—Tel Aviv, Israel:** A Canadian tourist, Marnie Kimelman, was killed by a bomb detonated on a popular tourist beach.

**December 14, 1990—Jaffa, Israel:** Three workers at a local aluminum factory were murdered.

**October 11, 1991—Tel Hashomer, Israel:** Two IDF soldiers, Master Sergeant Aaron Agmon Klijami and Sergeant Shmuel Michaeli, were run over and killed by a terrorist who deliberately drove his vehicle into a queue of soldiers at a hitchhiking station at the Tel Hashomer army base. Eleven other soldiers were injured.

**May 17, 1992—Bet Lehe'ya, Gaza:** David Cohen, from Moshav Te'asshur, was shot and killed by the Izz al-Din al-Qassam brigades in the Gaza Strip.

**May 24, 1992—Bat Yam, Israel:** A fifteen-year-old girl from Bat Yam, Helena Rapp, was stabbed to death by a Hamas activist. The murderer was apprehended on the spot.

**May 27, 1992—Gush Katif, Gaza:** Shimon Barr, the rabbi of Darom Village, was stabbed to death. The murderer, a member of the Izz al-Din al-Qassam brigades, was quickly apprehended.

**June 22, 1992—Rimal, Gaza:** A policeman and an Israeli civilian were injured by shots that were fired from a speeding car at a police building in the Rimal district by fugitives belonging to the Izz al-Din al-Qassam brigades.

**June 25, 1992—Saja'i'a, Gaza:** Two Israeli civilians were stabbed to death in a packinghouse near the Saja'i'a neighborhood. The murders were perpetrated by the Izz al-Din al-Qassam brigades. The same day a resident of Ma'ale Levona was injured while traveling with his family to Jerusalem by an axe-wielding assailant from the village of Sanjiel. The assailant was shot, wounded, and apprehended.

**September 18, 1992—Tel Aviv, Israel:** Alon Caravani, IDF soldier, was kidnapped by members of the Izz al-Din al-Qassam brigades. They gave the hitchhiking soldier a lift in their car. He was stabbed and thrown out of the vehicle.

**September 22, 1992—Jerusalem, Israel:** A border policeman, Avinoam Peretz, was shot and killed at Shoefat junction in French Hill. The murderer claimed that he was recruited by the Izz al-Din al-Qassam brigades.

**October 21, 1992—Hebron, Israel:** Shots were fired from a speeding car at an IDF vehicle at the southern entrance to Hebron. An IDF soldier and a female officer were injured. The Izz al-Din al-Qassam brigades took credit for the attack.

**October 25, 1992—Hebron Israel:** Shots were again fired from a speeding car at an IDF observation post near the Cave of Patriarchs in Hebron. One IDF reserve soldier was killed and another solider wounded. The Izz al-Din al-Qassam brigades took credit for the attack.

**November 1992—Or Yehuda, Israel:** Izz al-Din al-Qassam brigade activists planned a car-bomb attack in a heavily populated area in the center of the country. The car was detected in Or Yehuda and, after a pursuit, it was stopped and the bomb was defused. Two of the terrorists in the car were apprehended and admitted affiliation with the Izz al-Din al-Qassam brigades.

**December 7, 1992—Saja'i'a, Gaza:** Shots were fired from a speeding car at an IDF vehicle on patrol on the Gaza bypass road, near Saja'i'a junction. The three IDF reserve soldiers in the vehicle were killed. The Izz al-Din al-Qassam brigades took credit for the attack.

**December 12, 1992—Hebron, Israel:** Shots were fired at an army jeep in Hebron. An IDF reserve soldier was killed and two others were injured, one of them critically. The Izz al-Din al-Qassam brigades took credit for the attack.

**December 13, 1992—Lod, Israel:** A border policeman, Nissim Toledano, was kidnapped on his way home. A group of fugitives from the Izz al-Din al-Qassam brigades took credit for the incident. They demanded the release of Hamas leader Sheikh Ahmad Yassin from prison. Nissim Toledano's body was later found near Jerusalem.

**September 24, 1993—Basra, Israel:** Yigal Vaknin was stabbed to death in an orchard near his trailer home, close to the village of Basra. A squad of Hamas' Izz al-Din al-Qassam brigades claimed responsibility for the attack.

**October 24, 1993—Gaza:** Two IDF soldiers were killed by a squad from the Izz al-Din al-Qassam brigades. The two soldiers entered a vehicle with Israeli license plates outside a Jewish settlement in the Gaza Strip. The vehicle's occupants were apparently terrorists disguised as Israelis. Following a brief struggle, the soldiers were shot at close range and killed. Hamas publicly claimed responsibility for the attack.

**November 7, 1993—Hebron, Israel:** Efraim Ayubi of Kfar Darom was shot to death by terrorists near Hebron. Hamas publicly claimed responsibility for the murder.

**December 1, 1993—Ramallah, West Bank:** Shalva Ozana, 23, and Yitzhak Weinstock, 19, were shot to death by terrorists from a moving vehicle, while parked on the side of the road to Ramallah because of engine trouble. Weinstock died of his wounds the following morning. The Izz al-Din al-Qassam brigades claimed responsibility for the attack, stating that it was carried out in retaliation for the killing by Israeli forces of Imad Akel, a wanted Hamas leader in Gaza.

**December 6, 1993—Hebron, Israel:** Mordechai Lapid and his son, Shalom Lapid, age 19, were shot to death by Palestinian terrorists. Hamas publicly claimed responsibility for the attack.

**December 23, 1993—Ramallah, West Bank:** Eliahu Levin and Meir Mendelovitch were killed by shots fired at their car from a passing vehicle in the Ramallah area. Hamas claimed responsibility.

**December 24, 1993—T-Junction, Gaza:** Lieutenant Colonel Meir Mintz, commander of the IDF special forces in the Gaza area, was shot and killed by terrorists in an ambush on his jeep in the Gaza Strip. The Izz al-Din al-Qassam brigades publicly claimed responsibility for the attack.

**January 14, 1994—Erez, Israel:** Grigory Ivanov was stabbed to death by a terrorist in the industrial zone at the Erez junction, near the Gaza Strip. Hamas claimed responsibility for the attack.

**February 13, 1994—Beitunya, West Bank:** Noam Cohen, member of the General Security Service, was shot and killed in an ambush on his car. Two of his colleagues who were also in the vehicle suffered moderate injuries. Hamas claimed responsibility for the attack.

**February 19, 1994—Ariel, Israel:** Zipora Sasson, resident of Ariel and five months pregnant, was killed in an ambush in which shots were fired at her car. The terrorists were members of Hamas.

**April 6, 1994—Afula, Israel:** Seven civilians were killed in a car-bomb attack on a bus in the center of the city. Hamas claimed responsibility for the attack. Ahuva Cohen Onalla, wounded in the attack, died on April 25.

**April 7, 1994—Ashdod, Israel:** Yishai Gadassi, 32, was shot and killed at a hitchhiking post at the Ashdod junction by a member of Hamas. The terrorist was killed by bystanders at the scene.

**April 13, 1994—Hadera, Israel:** Another suicide bombing on a bus in Hadera killed four civilians and one solider. Hamas claimed responsibility for the attack.

**May 29, 1994—Gaza:** Staff Sgt. Moshe Bukra, 30, and Cpl. Erez Ben-Baruch, 24, were shot dead by Hamas terrorists at a roadblock, one kilometer south of the Erez checkpoint in the Gaza Strip.

**July 19, 1994—Rafiah, Gaza:** Lt. Guy Ovadia, 23, of Kibbutz Yotvata, was fatally wounded in an ambush near the Rafiah settlement. Hamas took responsibility for the attack, saying it was a response to an earlier "massacre" at the Erez checkpoint.

**August 14, 1994—Kissufim, Gaza:** Ron Soval, 18, was shot to death in an ambush near Kissufim junction. Hamas claimed responsibility.

**October 9, 1994—Jerusalem, Israel:** Ma'ayan Levy, 19, a solider, and Samir Mugrabi, 35, were killed in a terrorist attack in the Nahalat Shiva section of downtown Jerusalem. Hamas claimed responsibility for the attack.

**October 14, 1994—Gaza:** Cpl. Nahson Wachsman, 20, who had been kidnapped by Hamas, was murdered by his captors. In addition, Captain Nir Poraz, 23, was killed during the course of an unsuccessful IDF rescue attempt.

**October 19, 1994—Tel Aviv, Israel:** Twenty-one Israelis and one Dutch national were killed in a suicide bombing attack on the No. 5 bus on Dizengoff Street.

**November 19, 1994—Netzarim, Gaza:** Sgt. Maj. Gil Dadon, 26, was killed at the army post at Netzarim junction by shots fired from a passing car. Hamas claimed responsibility for the attack.

**January 22, 1995—Netanya, Israel:** Two consecutive bombs exploded at the Beit Lid junction near Netanya, killing eighteen soldiers and one civilian. The Islamic Jihad claimed responsibility for the attack. This was a joint operation with Hamas.

**July 24, 1995—Ramat Gan, Israel:** Six Israeli civilians were killed in a suicide bomb attack on a commuter bus.

**August 1995—Jerusalem, Israel:** Rivka Cohen, 26, Hanah Naeh, 56, Joan Davenney, 46, and Police Chief Superintendent Noam Eisenman, 35, were killed in a suicide bombing of a Jerusalem bus.

**January 16, 1996—Hebron, Israel:** Two IDF soldiers were killed when terrorists fired on their car on the Hebron–Jerusalem road.

**January 30, 1996—Jenin, West Bank:** An Israeli solider was stabbed to death at the liaison office in an army camp south of Jenin.

**February 25, 1996—Ashklon, Israel:** Sgt. Hofit Ayyah, 20, was killed in an explosion set off by a suicide bomber at a hitchhiking post outside Ashklon. Hamas claimed responsibility for the attack.

**February 25, 1996—Jerusalem, Israel:** Seventeen civilians and nine soldiers were killed in a suicide bombing on bus No. 18 near the Central Bus Station. Hamas claimed responsibility for the attack.

**March 3, 1996—Jerusalem, Israel:** Sixteen civilians and three soldiers were killed in a suicide bombing on bus No. 18 on Jaffa Road.

**March 4, 1996—Tel Aviv, Israel:** Twelve civilians and one soldier were killed when a suicide bomber detonated a 20-kilogram nail bomb outside Dizengoff Center.

**March 21, 1996—Tel Aviv, Israel:** Michal Avrahami, 32, Yaek Gilad, 32, and Anat Winter-Rosen, 32, were killed when a suicide bomber detonated a bomb on the terrace of a crowded cafe. Forty-eight others were wounded.

**June 26, 1996—Jericho, Israel:** Two soldiers and one civilian were killed as they were ambushed along the Jordan River north of Jericho by terrorists who infiltrated from Jordan.

**April 10, 1997—Kfar Tzurif, West Bank:** The body of IDF Staff Sgt. Sharon Edri, missing for seven months, was found buried near the village of Kfar Tzurif. Edri had been kidnapped and murdered by a Hamas terrorist cell in September 1996 while hitchhiking to his home in Moshav Zanoah.

**July 30, 1997—Jerusalem, Israel:** Sixteen people were killed and one hundred seventy-eight wounded in two consecutive suicide bombings in the Mahane Yehuda market. The Izz al-Din al-Qassam brigades claimed responsibility for the attack.

**September 4, 1997—Jerusalem, Israel:** Seven people (including three suicide bombers) were killed and one hundred eighty-one wounded in three suicide bombings on the Ben-Yehuda pedestrian mall. The Izz al-Din al-Qassam brigades claimed responsibility for the attack.

**July 19, 1998—Jerusalem, Israel:** A devastating car bombing on the city's main avenue was narrowly averted when a van loaded with explosives failed to detonate. A policeman managed to extinguish the fire with a hand-held fire extinguisher. The driver, a Palestinian, was rushed to the hospital in critical condition.

**August 5, 1998—Yitzhar, West Bank:** Two men, Harel Bin-Nun, 18, and Schlomo Leibman, 24, were shot and killed while patrolling the Jewish settlement's borders.

**August 20, 1998—Tel Rumeiyde, Israel:** Rabbi Schlomo Raanan was stabbed to death in his home by a Hamas terrorist. The attacker entered the house through a window and escaped after throwing a Molotov cocktail that set fire to the house.

**August 27, 1998—Tel Aviv, Israel:** A small bomb placed in a garbage dumpster near Allenby Street exploded during the morning rush hour, injuring fourteen people. One woman was seriously injured, and two moderately. The eleven other victims suffered only light injuries.

**September 24, 1998— Jerusalem, Israel:** An IDF soldier was injured when a bomb exploded in a bus station near Hebrew University.

**September 30, 1998—Hebron, Israel:** Fourteen IDF soldiers and eleven Palestinians were wounded when a terrorist hurled two grenades at a border police jeep. The patrol shot the attacker in the leg and pursued him into the Palestinian-controlled part of Hebron, but he managed to escape.

**October 1, 1998—Hebron, Israel:** Thirteen soldiers and five Palestinians were injured in a grenade attack. A Palestinian from the H-1 area threw two grenades at an IDF unit, injuring several soldiers and bystanders, but managed to escape back into the Palestinian-controlled section of Hebron.

**October 13, 1998—Jerusalem, Israel:** One Israeli civilian was killed and another critically wounded following a shooting at a swimming spring in the Jerusalem Hills. The attackers were ambushed by two men who opened fire on them at close range before escaping in one of the victim's cars.

**October 19, 1999—Jerusalem, Israel:** At least fifty-nine people were wounded in a rush-hour grenade attack at the Central Bus Station. The Palestinian attacker was subdued by the crowd, who soon put him into the custody of a civil guard officer.

**October 29, 1998—Gush Katif, Gaza:** A Hamas-affiliated suicide bomber driving a vehicle laden with explosives attempted to collide with school bus carrying children from Kfar Darom. An army jeep escorting the bus intercepted the attacker as he detonated the explosive device. One solider was killed and several others were injured.

**August 10, 1999—Nahshon, Israel:** Six Israelis were wounded when a man deliberately steered his vehicle into a crowd. Initially, the man hit two female Israeli soldiers. Shortly after speeding off, he returned and injured four more. A police officer soon shot and killed the assailant.

**October 31, 1999—Tarkumiyah, Israel:** Five Israeli civilians were injured when a bus en route from Kiryat Arba to Jerusalem was ambushed by several gunmen. Though the perpetrators escaped into the surrounding area, Hamas is believed to have been behind the attack.

**November 7, 1999—Netanya, Israel:** Three pipe bombs exploded during rush-hour at a busy intersection in the center of the city, injuring twenty-seven. A fourth bomb, apparently intended to detonate when rescue workers arrived on the scene, was discovered and defused by a police bomb squad. Hamas claimed responsibility for the attack.

**September 28, 2000—Netzarim, Gaza:** One IDF soldier was killed and another wounded when a roadside bomb detonated just outside the Jewish settlement. The soldiers were escorting a civilian convoy at the time of the attack. Hamas operatives are believed to be responsible for the bombing.

**November 2, 2000—Jerusalem, Israel:** A car packed with explosives blew up near the city's main outdoor market, killing two and injuring ten. The attack, believed to be the work of Hamas, killed Ayelet Levy, the daughter of former cabinet minister Yitzhak Levy.

**November 13, 2000—Ofra, West Bank:** Three people were killed and eight were injured when terrorists opened fire with automatic weapons in two consecutive attacks. One assault was on the car of an Israeli civilian, while the other was directed at a bus carrying IDF personnel. The assailants are believed to have been Hamas operatives.

**November 20, 2000—Gush Katif, Gaza:** Two civilians were killed and twelve were injured when a car bomb went off as a school bus from Kfar Darom passed. The bus was deliberately targeted, as the device was not detonated until after a military escort ahead of the bus had already passed. Hams is believed to be responsible for the attack.

**November 22, 2000—Hadera, Israel:** Two people were killed and fifty-five were injured after a bomb was detonated next to a crowded bus during the evening rush hour. Hamas is believed to have been behind the attack.

**December 22, 2000—Jordan Valley, West Bank:** A Palestinian suicide bomber wounded three patrons of a roadside café near Mehola Junction. Remains of an explosives belt discovered at the scene suggested that it was similar to those used by Hamas bombers in the past.

**January 1, 2001—Netanya, Israel:** Twenty people were injured by a car bomb at a busy intersection in the city center. Hamas is believed to be responsible for the attack.

**February 8, 2001—Jerusalem, Israel:** Four people were injured by a car bomb in the ultra-orthodox Mea She'arim neighborhood. While the Popular Palestinian Resistance Forces claimed responsibility, Israeli intelligence indicates that the group is likely a cover for Hamas (or, alternatively, Islamic Jihad).

**March 1, 2001—Mei Ami, Israel:** One person was killed and nine were injured when a minivan exploded near the Mei Ami junction. Hamas was linked to the attack.

**March 3, 2001—Netanya, Israel:** A suicide bomber killed himself and three others while mingling with a crowd waiting to cross an intersection. The attack, which also wounded over sixty people, took place in the main commercial center of the city.

**March 27, 2001—Jerusalem, Israel:** One person was killed and twenty-eight were injured when a suicide bomber targeted a bus in French Hill. Hamas claimed responsibility for the attack.

**March 28, 2001—Kalkilya, West Bank:** Two teenagers were killed and four were injured when an Izz al-Din al-Qassam brigades suicide bomber blew himself up near a busy bus stop frequented by students.

**April 22, 2001—Kfar Saba, Israel:** A suicide bomber killed a doctor and wounded sixty others at a bus stop in an attack that was one of three attacks in just three days. Hamas claimed responsibility for the bombing.

**May 18, 2001—Netanya, Israel:** Five were killed and over seventy were injured as the result of a suicide bomb attack outside a shopping mall. Hamas claimed the bombing was retribution for the killing of five Palestinian police officers earlier in the week.

**May 25, 2001—Netzarim, Gaza:** A truck carrying explosives attempted to ram an Israeli military outpost near the Netzarim Junction. Soldiers fired on the vehicle as it approached, setting off the explosives before they reached their target. The attacker, Hussein Nasser, was a member of Hamas. The group claimed that the attack was timed to coincide with the first anniversary of Israel's pullout from southern Lebanon.

**June 1, 2001—Tel Aviv, Israel:** Twenty-one people were killed and more than 120 others were wounded when a Palestinian suicide bomber detonated an explosives belt outside the Dolphinarium, a popular beachfront nightclub. Both the Palestinian Islamic Jihad (PIJ) and Hamas claimed responsibility for the blast.

**June 22, 2001—Dugit, Gaza Strip:** Two IDF soldiers were killed and one was wounded after a Palestinian suicide bomber lured them to his booby-trapped jeep bearing Israeli license plates. Israeli forces responded to the attack by using tanks and heavy machine gun fire against Palestinian militants, wounding three. Hamas claimed responsibility for the attack.

**July 16, 2001—Bethlehem, Israel:** Israeli helicopter gunships opened fire on a suspected Hamas safe house with air-to-surface missiles. Israeli security forces claim that Oman Sa'ada and Taha Aruj, both senior Hamas operatives, were killed in the strike.

**July 31, 2001—Nablus, West Bank:** Six Hamas members, including senior Hamas leader Jamal Mansour, were killed as a result of an Israeli Air Force strike.

**August 9, 2001—Jerusalem, Israel:** Fifteen Israelis were killed and 130 were injured by a suicide bomb attack in a Sbarro restaurant. Hamas and Islamic Jihad both claimed responsibility. The Israeli government responded to the attack by seizing the Palestinian Authority's unofficial foreign ministry in East Jerusalem, as well as ordering an air strike on a Palestinian police station in Ramallah.

**September 9, 2001—Nahariya, Israel:** Hamas recruit Muhammad Saker Habisi carried out a suicide attack on the platform of the Nahariya train station, killing three Israelis and wounding ninety-four others. The same day, thirteen others were also injured in a suicide bombing just south of the city in which the attacker prematurely detonated his device after spotting a police vehicle. Gunships of IDF responded with four missile attacks against Fatah offices in Ramallah and El Bireh.

**September 11, 2001—Jenin, West Bank:** IDF forces surrounded the entire town of Jenin, which has been a major staging area for suicide attacks within Israel. Nine Palestinians were killed.

**October 2001—West Bank:** The Israeli General Security Service (Shabak, or formerly Shin Bet) arrested more than twenty Hamas operatives over the course of a month, dealing a blow to organization's infrastructure. Israel claimed that the men were taking orders directly from Hamas headquarters in Syria.

**October 2, 2001—Elei Sinai, Gaza:** Hamas gunmen killed two Israelis and wounded thirteen others after infiltrating the Jewish settlement. Hamas took responsibility for the attack.

**November 4, 2001—Jerusalem, Israel:** Palestinian terrorists opened fire on a municipal bus in the northern part of the city, killing two and injuring forty. Both Hamas and the PIJ claimed responsibility for the attack.

**November 24, 2001—Nablus, West Bank:** Mahmoud Abu Hanoud, head of Hamas's military operations in the West Bank, was killed by Israeli helicopter fire.

**November 27, 2001—Gush Katif, Gaza:** A Hamas gunman opened fire on a convoy near the Gush Katif Junction, killing one Israeli and wounding three others.

**December 1, 2001—Jerusalem, Israel:** Two suicide bombings within the city's pedestrian mall resulted in the deaths of 10 people and the wounding of 180 others. A car bomb, which detonated as rescue workers arrived, caused no casualties. Hamas and the PIJ both took responsibility for the bombings.

**December 2, 2001—Haifa, Israel:** A suicide bomber affiliated with Hamas killed fourteen and injured more than sixty at a bus stop in the Halissa neighborhood.

**December 12, 2001—Emmanuel, West Bank:** Ten people were killed and thirty others were wounded when terrorists employed a roadside bomb, anti-tank grenades, and small arms fire against a bus and several passenger cars. Fatah and Hamas both claimed responsibility.

**December 22, 2001—Israel:** Hamas announced that it would temporarily halt mortar attacks and suicide bombings within the Jewish state.

**January 9, 2002—Southern Israel:** Four Israeli soldiers and two Palestinians died in a firefight in the area where the borders of Israel, Gaza, and Egypt converge. Palestinian gunmen initiated the battle and Hamas claimed responsibility.

**February 11, 2002—Beersheba, Israel:** Two IDF soldiers were killed and four were wounded when Hamas operatives opened fire on IDF Southern Command headquarters in the Old City.

**February 11, 2002—Negev, Israel:** For the first time, Palestinian terrorists fired Kassam -2 rockets into Israel, targeting different points in the Negev. Hamas is believed to have been responsible.

**March 9, 2002—Jerusalem, Israel:** Eleven people were killed and fifty-two were wounded when a suicide bomber attacked the popular Moment Café in the city center. The military wings of both Hamas and Fatah claimed responsibility for the attack.

**March 27, 2002—Netanya, Israel:** A suicide bomber killed at least twenty-five and injured one hundred seventy-two at the Park Hotel. The attack coincided with the start of the Jewish holiday of Passover. Hamas claimed responsibility for the bombing.

**March 31, 2002—Haifa, Israel:** Twenty-five people were killed and forty were wounded when a suicide bomber detonated an explosive device inside a crowded restaurant. Hamas stated that it carried out the attack to avenge Israel's recent incursion into the West Bank town of Ramallah.

**April 10, 2002—Haifa, Israel:** An explosion aboard a commuter bus killed eight and injured fourteen. Hamas and the PIJ claimed responsibility.

**April 11, 2002—Dura, West Bank:** Akram al-Atrash, leader of the Izz al-Din al-Qassam brigades, was killed in a firefight with Israeli forces.

**June 18, 2002—Beit Safafa, Israel:** Nineteen people were killed and seventy-four were wounded when Muhamed al-Ral detonated a bomb shortly after boarding a bus at Patt Junction in Beit Safafa, an Israeli-Arab neighborhood near Gilo. Al-Ral had infiltrated the Jerusalem city limits from Nablus early that morning.[100]

**July 16, 2002—Emmanuel, West Bank:** Seven were killed and twenty-five were injured after a roadside bomb was detonated next to an armored bus entering the West Bank settlement of Emmanuel. The three attackers were dressed in Israeli army uniforms and opened fire on fleeing civilians following the blast. While several groups claimed responsibility, the attack was believed to be perpetrated by the same Hamas cell responsible for previous attacks on residents of Emmanuel in December 2001.[101]

**July 16, 2002—Jerusalem, Israel:** Four Israelis and five Americans were killed when a bomb exploded in the cafeteria of the Frank Sinatra International Student Center at Hebrew University. The bomb was planted by a Hamas member who was an independent contractor working at the school as a painter. At least fifteen other cell members from East Jerusalem and Ramallah were arrested in the ensuing weeks.[102]

**August 4, 2002—Safed, Israel:** On a day in which several separate terrorist attacks shocked the state of Israel, a suicide bomber killed himself and eight others when he detonated a bomb aboard a bus leaving the Meron Junction Station. The Hamas leadership immediately claimed responsibility for the bombing, which was apparently in response to a recent Israeli air strike that had killed the organization's top military commander as well as fourteen others.[103]

**November 21, 2002—Jerusalem, Israel:** A bomb was detonated aboard a bus filled with schoolchildren, killing eleven people and wounding fifty others in the Kiryat Menachem neighborhood. The suicide attack was perpetrated by Nael Abu Hailil, a member of the Izz al-Din al-Qassam brigades. Hailil detonated the device during rush hour to maximize its destructive potential.[104]

**March 5, 2003—Haifa, Israel:** Fifteen Israelis were killed and at least forty were wounded as a result of a powerful blast aboard a bus carrying high school and college students. The explosion occurred in the busy downtown Carmel Center and damaged many surrounding buildings. Several Hamas spokesmen praised the attack. Israeli forces responded by initiating operations in the Jabaliya refugee camp, ostensibly aimed at eliminating senior Hamas activists and destroying weapons caches.[105]

**May 17–19, 2003—Hebron, Israel:** An attack in Hebron was the first of the deadly wave of suicide bombings that began in mid-May. Two civilians were killed when a blast rocked Gross Square; the bomber was a student at Hebron's Polytechnic University. The following day, May 18th, seven were killed and twenty wounded in a bus bombing near French Hill in Jerusalem. Only half an hour later, another would-be bomber was killed after being intercepted by police at a security checkpoint in north Jerusalem. These two terrorists were also students at the Polytechnic University. On May 19th, three members of the IDF were wounded in the southern Gaza Strip after a Palestinian man detonated explosives while riding a bike past a military vehicle in Kfar Darom. Hamas claimed responsibility for all of the attacks.[106]

**June 11, 2003—Jerusalem, Israel:** Seventeen people were killed and 150 wounded when a member of Hamas dressed as an ultraorthodox Jew detonated a bomb aboard a bus outside of the Klal building on Jaffa Road. Samir Ahmed Atresh and Omar Salah Muhammad Sharif were later arrested by Israeli authorities for allegedly helping to outfit the bombers responsible for the June 11th and May 18th attacks, and escorting them to their targets.[107]

**September 9, 2003—Rishon Lezion, Israel:** Nine members of the Israeli Defense Forces were killed and at least fifteen others were wounded following a suicide bombing just outside the Tzrifin army base. The bomber, a member of Hamas, detonated the device across the street from the base, a popular spot from which many soldiers and patients of the nearby Assaf Harofe Hospital hitchhike. The attack was the first bombing since a series of Israeli assassination attempts directed against top Hamas leaders the previous weekend.[108]

**August 31, 2004—Beersheba, Israel:** Two suicide bombings were carried out almost simultaneously aboard commuter buses. Hamas claimed responsibility for the bombings, which left at least fifteen dead and eighty injured. The militant Islamic group soon distributed leaflets in Hebron, which claimed that the bus bombings were a response to Israel's assassination of top Hamas leaders, namely Sheikh Ahmed Yassin and Abdel Aziz Rantisi.[109]

**January 13, 2005—Karni Crossing, Israel/Gaza Border:** Three terrorists detonated a bomb on the Palestinian side of Karni Crossing between the northern Gaza Strip and Israel, blowing a hole in the security checkpoint shortly before its closure. The bombers arrived by truck and detonated their device after attaching it to a gate through which goods are transferred across the border. Following the blast, the men, clad in bulletproof vests and armed with automatic rifles and hand grenades, stormed through the gate and opened fire on truck drivers and Port Authority employees, killing six and wounding five Israelis before being killed by IDF forces. The attack was a joint operation of Hamas and the Fatah al-Aqsa Martyrs Brigade, and forced the closure of several border crossings between Gaza and Israel.[110]

**August 28, 2005—Beersheba, Israel:** A Palestinian man detonated an explosive device outside a public bus station. The suicide bomber seriously injured two security guards and eight others. The attack marked the first such bombing since Israel's historic withdrawals from all twenty-one of its Gaza settlements and four West Bank settlements.[111]

**January 2006:** Following a landslide electoral victory on January 25, 2006 in which Hamas gained clear control of the Palestinian Authority, it instituted a policy of restraint with regard to terror attacks, specifically in its utilization of rocket attacks and suicide bombings within Israel. This was partly the result of Hamas attempts to heighten its operational capabilities within the Gaza Strip, as well as focus on violent inter-Palestinian clashes with Fatah security forces. While the organization worked to solidify its legitimacy in leading the Palestinian Authority, it continued to encourage terror attacks by other radical groups such as Islamic Jihad and the Fatah al-Aqsa Martyrs Brigade.[112]

**June 26, 2006—Karem Shalom Crossing, Israel/Gaza Border:** A collaboration of several terror groups joined Hamas forces in a well-coordinated assault on an Israeli Defense Force position adjacent to this crossing between Gaza and the western Negev. The attackers dug a tunnel under the crossing to outflank the IDF position, and later killed two and wounded three Israeli soldiers. Additionally, IDF Corporal Gilad Shalit was captured and taken into captivity in Gaza.[113]

**April 24, 2007—Israel:** Hamas's Izz al-Din al-Qassam brigades fired rockets and mortar shells into Israel for the first time since a November 2006 conditional cease-fire agreement was effected. Though no injuries were reported, the attacks clearly demonstrated the tenuous nature of the pact.[114]

**June 15, 2007—Gaza Strip:** Hamas claimed complete control of Gaza following several decisive battles against its Fatah rivals. The organization's leaders claimed that a new era had arrived in which the Palestinian territory would be governed by Islamic law. Palestinian President Mahmoud Abbas of Fatah quickly dissolved the young unity government just months after its inception. He declared the Gaza Strip to be in a state of emergency.[115]

# 6

# Iran's Nuclear Ambitions

## IRAN'S NUCLEAR AMBITIONS

### By Every Secret Means

Over much of the past two decades, after failed attempts to buy nuclear fuel cycle technology from the Russia (a gas centrifuge plant) and China (a uranium conversion facility), Iran has sought by every secret means to assemble the elements of an indigenous, independent nuclear fuel cycle, amid heightened concerns that it is seeking to acquire nuclear weapons. Iran's nuclear program is aimed at mastering uranium mining and milling, conversion and enrichment, and fuel fabrication, all at the "front end" of the nuclear fuel cycle. It is constructing or operating a commercial light-water power reactor, a heavy-water production plant, a heavy-water research reactor, and related research and development capabilities. At the "back end" of the fuel cycle, it has performed laboratory-scale experiments related to the reprocessing of irradiated fuel and is carrying out research and development (R&D) in the treatment, storage, and disposal of radioactive waste.[1]

Iran's nuclear program has continued to raise vexing questions for which the International Atomic Energy Agency (IAEA), headquartered Vienna, Austria, and U.S. intelligence would like answers. Since the discovery and acknowledgement of the program overseen by the Atomic Energy Organization of Iran (AEOI) in 2002 and 2003, the IAEA stated and restated its inability to verify the correctness and completeness of the Iran's declarations on the history and scope of its enrichment and fuel reprocessing activities, and the peaceful nature of its program.[2]

Adapted from a map created by Bookcomp, Inc.

Furthermore, there are continuing questions about a secret parallel military nuclear program under the Iran Revolutionary Guard Corps (IRGC) to develop nuclear weapons and their missile delivery systems that remain unresolved. The possible existence of a string of hidden facilities to nurture this program is the subject of much unsubstantiated rumor and revelation.

Yet despite gaps and uncertainties, a considerable amount of information is now known about Iran's official nuclear program, even though it was hidden from the IAEA for eighteen years. Iran did not declare its nuclear fuel cycle activities and experiments to the IAEA until late 2003, in violation of its obligations under the country's Comprehensive Safeguards Agreement with the IAEA under the Nuclear Non-Proliferation Treaty (NPT) of 1970. Iran acknowledged developing two uranium enrichment programs: centrifuge enrichment, over the previous eighteen years with an eye to industrial-scale production of enriched uranium, and laser enrichment, on an experimental scale over the previous twelve years. It admitted producing small amounts of low-enriched uranium (LEU) using both the centrifuge and laser technologies and conceded that it had failed to report to the IAEA a large number of conversion, fabrication, and irradiation activities involving nuclear materials, including the separation of a small amount of plutonium.[3]

As a signer of the NPT, Iran was obligated to renounce any nuclear weapons ambitions and put its nuclear activities under IAEA safeguards. It was remiss in this, at least since 1985, and maybe since the 1970s, going back to the reign of the Shah, when Iran is reported to have sought laser enrichment technology and may have set up a secret nuclear weapons group.[4] Even after the first revelations in August 2002 by the National Council of Resistance of Iran (NCRI), the political wing of the Iraq-based Iranian dissident group, Mujahedin-e-Khalq (MEK),[5] Iran's policy of concealment continued almost totally until October 2003, when it made an extensive declaration in response to a September resolution of the IAEA Board of Governors that set a deadline for disclosure.[6]

In dealing with the IAEA, Iran has not offered the degree of transparency needed to fully understand the scope and rationale for its nuclear activities. Not the least of the unanswered questions is why Iran decided to start its secret uranium centrifuge enrichment program in 1985 in the midst of a draining war with Iraq, when it had no obvious need to do so.[7]

Despite the eighteen-year lapse in declaring its nuclear program, Iran continues to say that the program is peaceful—for civil purposes only, and not for weapons. Yet, its activities raise suspicions because the nuclear technologies it is pursing or has experimented with in the past decades are dual use, related both to civil nuclear power and nuclear weapons. The fact that its declared nuclear program is now under safeguards gives the Iran a justification for claiming the right to pursue all aspects of the civil nuclear fuel cycle but leaves other countries nervous about its underlying intentions.

Instead of building confidence, Iran has wavered in the application of the Additional Protocol to its NPT safeguards agreement that would allow for more intrusive, unannounced inspections, agreeing, first, in 2003, that it would voluntarily abide by the Protocol, and, later, suspending its agreement in retaliation for calls to limit the extent of its nuclear activities. Adherence to the Protocol, which is voluntary because Iran has signed but not ratified it, was last suspended in February 2006 as Iran again prepared to restart uranium enrichment.[8]

Whatever Iran's true motivations, its lack of complete openness presents a picture of a country with questionable intentions and with something to hide. The IAEA's Board of Governors has the power to declare Iran in noncompliance with its safeguards agreement, an act that would in principle automatically refer the matter to the U.N. Security Council for further action. The Board could also take lesser steps to try to coerce additional information and the shutdown of its declared nuclear activities out of a reluctant Iran. Expanded authority for the IAEA to deal with Iran's noncompliance would come only from the U.N. Security Council, and only the Security Council can impose sanctions on Iran under Chapter 7 of the U.N. Charter.[9] The Security Council finally voted sanctions against Iran on December 23, 2006, at the culmination of a period negotiations and compromises ultimately involving all of five permanent members of the Security Council and Germany.

The IAEA has continued to be a major channel for information about Iran's past nuclear activities through its constant and often frustrating dealings with the country since 2002. The situation is reflected in a succession of IAEA reports in which attempts to seek out answers are described in language reflecting Iran's style of deliberate vagueness, using cryptic references such as "intermediary," "foreign intermediary," "supply network," and "procurement network" for contacts and suppliers and leaving the reader guessing about to whom they might be referring. In particular, the A.Q. Khan network is never mentioned explicitly by name as a supplier to Iran, despite the revelations in 2004 about Libya's nuclear program that point to Pakistan's scientist A.Q. Khan and his network as Libya's chief source of centrifuge technology.[10]

At the focus of the IAEA's inspections in Iran are banks of spinning centrifuge machines that enrich a feed of uranium gas. The known centrifuges in Iran are mainly the "P-1" type—of Pakistan origin and obtained via the A.Q. Khan network. Each P-1 centrifuge machine is about two meters tall, ten centimeters in diameter, and spins at 50,000 revolutions per minute. A group of about 164 machines are connected by pipes into a "cascade," and the cascades are further connected, so as to enrich a feed of natural uranium up to any desired level in the fissile isotope uranium-235 (U-235) by separating the U-235 from the predominant, heavier isotope, uranium-238 (U-238). The working centrifuges could be easily hidden by the many thousands and without detection in halls located in secluded or underground buildings.[11] Iran has been working with one centrifuge, or with 10, 20, and up to perhaps 2,000 at a time, but if its plan for a commercial-size plant with up to 54,000 centrifuges eventually bears fruit, machines churning out enriched uranium, either low enriched for reactor fuel or highly enriched for nuclear weapons, would be arrayed in the tens of thousands, like an "army" of terracotta soldiers.

The centrifuges of the P-1 type that Iran has been fabricating and using are similar to the design that the Pakistani scientist, A.Q. Khan, stole from the Urenco enrichment plant in the Netherlands when he was working there in the 1970s and then used in Pakistan's early centrifuge plant. Iran says that it obtained components to build five hundred P-1 centrifuges in 1994—1996 through intermediaries from an unknown source and says that it imported none thereafter. Pakistan replaced the P-1 with the more advanced P-2 centrifuge as the basis of it's enrichment program. Iran has admitted to receiving blueprints for the P-2 around 1995, but it insists that between then and 2002, it did no research and development work with them, whatsoever. This is a claim, one of many, which the IAEA finds difficult to accept and has continued to investigate.[12]

Another question that remains only partly resolved is the origin of some of the uranium particle contamination detected by the IAEA from "swipes" on centrifuge-related equipment in Iran. At various sites in Iran, particles of uranium of various enrichments were found on centrifuge equipment, and their presence could not be explained by any of Iran's declared nuclear activities. Iran adheres to the claim that before April 2006 it had never enriched uranium to greater than 1.2 percent U-235 and explains the highly enriched uranium (HEU)[13] found as already being on the centrifuge components when they were imported. Iran thought it was importing new machines but apparently was getting used P-1 models that Pakistan had replaced, in its own plant, with the advanced P-2 models.

A further puzzle is what went on at the Physics Research Center (PHRC), operated by the Iran Ministry of Defense at a site in Lavizan-Shian in the northeastern neighborhood of Tehran. Suspicions point to activities in a parallel military program. What is known is that once the existence of Lavizan-Shian was revealed in March 2003 as a military nuclear site by the MEK/NCRI group, it was razed, only a few months before IAEA inspectors could make a visit. Dual-use equipment related to uranium conversion and enrichment appears to have been moved to a nearby technical university laboratory. The IAEA has been seeking to interview people involved in the PHRC, and environmental samples have revealed the presence of uranium contamination on the equipment. Still another mystery is why Iran was experimenting with the production of alpha-particle emitting isotope polonium-210, if not set on eventually using it to trigger nuclear warheads, as in early nuclear weapon designs.[14]

One other question, on which the IAEA first reported in November 2005, is the origin of the documents containing offers to Iran of equipment for the casting and machining of uranium metal into hemispherical shapes, equipment that would be used to fabricate a uranium core, or "pit," of an implosion-design nuclear weapon. There are several unexplained documents, one a handwritten one-pager from the supply network and a related 15-page document, as well as the so-called Green Salt Project document. Added to this, there is a laptop computer, allegedly stolen from Iran and loaded with weapons-related data and calculations, that was acquired by U.S. intelligence and shown to IAEA officials.[15]

## THE A. Q. KHAN NETWORK

Iran's nuclear program is suspected to have roots in a proliferation network headed by Abdul Qadeer Khan. Khan, a metallurgist, worked from May 1972 to December 1975 at the Dutch Physical Dynamic Research Laboratory (FDO), an affiliate of Urenco, a Dutch–British–German uranium enrichment consortium.[1] Suspecting increased scrutiny, he suddenly left the company on December 15, 1975, and headed for Pakistan with copies of centrifuge blueprints, designs stolen from Urenco, and contact information for close to 100 companies from which he could obtain centrifuge components and materials.[2] Khan then used this information to kick-start Pakistan's own nuclear program with the production of the P-1 and P-2 centrifuges adapted from German models. Khan obtained materials and centrifuge components for Pakistan's nuclear program in the black market and later used his established channels within the black market to proliferate nuclear technologies and materials, including centrifuge components, design specifications, technical drawings, complete assemblies of both P-1 and P-2 centrifuges, and even blueprints for a nuclear warhead, probably an early Chinese design.[3] Although a market had already existed, Khan integrated the marketplace and made it easier for countries to develop nuclear weapons capabilities by combining the sale of technologies with design, engineering, and consulting services.[4]

The Khan network spread across three continents with nuclear suppliers and manufacturers stationed in over thirty countries.[5] Khan's first client was Iran, with whom he met around 1987.[6] In the 1990s, the Khan network expanded cooperation to include both Libya and North Korea. In addition to the aforementioned countries, offers were also made to Iraq (disclosed in a memo found at the farm of Saddam Hussein's son-in-law Hussein Kamal),[7] Egypt, Syria, and possibly Saudi Arabia.[8] These countries have denied receiving supplies from Khan, and there is currently no evidence that they participated in the network.

There is, however, evidence that implicates several other countries with involvement in the network. Between 1997 and 2003, Khan traveled extensively, making visits to eighteen countries, which led to questions about how vast his network really was.[9] Investigations have revealed that nuclear technologies, blueprints, and centrifuge parts were transferred to both Libya and Iran through middlemen in Malaysia, Turkey, Germany, Switzerland, and the

United Kingdom with transported materials having also passed through the United Arab Emirates, South Korea, Japan, Switzerland, the United Kingdom, Germany, and the Netherlands.[10]

Malaysia was particularly important and Dubai was a central transfer point. As detailed in a February 2004 Malaysian police report, a Khan associate, the Sri Lankan businessman B.S.A. Tahir, arranged for Scomi Precision Engineering, set up in Kuala Lumpur in 2001 and controlled by the Malysian prime minister's son, to manufacture centrifuge parts for the network.[11,12] Another company involved in the network was Tahir's SMB Computers, set up in Dubai as a front for Scomi.

After the United States confronted Pakistan President Pervez Musharraf with evidence about the Khan's centrifuge trade, Musharraf reined him in, and he was relieved of his official duties in 2001. But Khan continued to remain active, filling orders for North Korea and Iran and pursuing a business deal with Libya to supply a turnkey nuclear operation, culminating in December 2002, when Libya began to receive large shipments of centrifuge components. This all came to an end when in October 2003 the United States intercepted the German ship, BBC China, enroute from Dubai to Libya carrying thousands of centrifuge parts manufactured in Malaysia by Scomi Precision Engineering and other parts manufactured in Turkey with papers showing that the

transshipment through Dubai had been arranged by Tahir. Libya saw the light, completely giving up its nuclear program, and it spoke openly to IAEA inspectors about its connections to Pakistan, essentially naming Pakistan and the Khan Laboratories as the supplier. In January 2004, Libya handed over plans for a Chinese-design implosion bomb that apparently had been supplied by the Khan laboratories. In return for a pardon from Musharraf, Khan appeared on television on February 4, 2004 and took blame for all the actions of the network that had brought opprobrium on Pakistan. A national hero, he remains under house arrest. B.S.A. Tahir was arrested and detained in Maylasia in 2004 as a security risk.[13] Malaysian police cleared Scomi of wrongdoing; the company thought the parts were to be used for oil and gas production in Dubai, not shipped to Libya.

Many others, mainly involved in dealings with Libya, have been under investigation, indictment, or on trial. On July 26, 2006, a judge in Mannheim, Germany dismissed the case against Gerhard Lerch, a German engineer who was on trial for the illegal sale of centrifuge equipment. Lerch also was named on a list of suppliers given by Iran to the IAEA at the end of 2003. A prosecution witness at the Lerch trial, British businessman Peter Griffin, himself under periodic investigation as a supplier to Pakistan, has been identified as a participant in the Libyan deal through his company, Gulf Technical Industries. Urs Tinner, a Swiss consultant whose father, engineer Friedrich Tinner, had done business with Khan since the 1980s, was brought by Scomi in 2002 to set up a new plant and procure the highly specialized machines for fashioning centrifuge components. Urs Tinner has been in custody of Swiss authorities since November 2005 awaiting trial and his father Friedrich is also in Swiss custody. Businessman Henk Slebos was convicted in the Netherlands of smuggling nuclear components to Pakistan. In South Africa, businessman Gerhard Wisser, owner of Krisch Engineering, and his employee, Swiss engineer Daniel Geiges, were indicted for illegally shipping vacuum equipment to and from Dubai for the Libyan project.[14–17] Japanese police arrested five officials of the Mitutoyo Company on August 25, 2006 on suspicion of illegally exporting precision measuring devices to Scomi in Malaysia, which shipped one to Libya and possibly used others to make centrifuge parts for the Khan network, as well as making illegal exports of precision devices directly to Iran.[18]

1 Michael Laufer, "A. Q. Khan Nuclear Chronology." *Carnegie Endowment for International Peace,* http://www.carnegieendowment.org/npp/publications/index.cfm?fa=view&id=17420 (July 11, 2006).

2 Ibid.

3 Guarev Kampani, "Proliferation Unbound: Nuclear Tales from Pakistan." *CNS Research Story*, February 23, 2004. <http://cns.miis.edu/pubs/week/040223.htm>

4 Ibid.

5 Dafna Linzer, "Iran Was Offered Nuclear Parts," *Washington Post*, February 27, 2005.

6 Michael Laufer, "A. Q. Khan Nuclear Chronology."

7 David Albright and Corey Hinderstein, "Documents Indicate A.Q. Khan Offered Nuclear Weapon Designs to Iraq in 1990: Did He Approach Other Countries," February 2004 <http://www.isisonline.org/publications /southasia/khan_memo html>

8 Albright and Hinderstein, "Unraveling the A. Q. Khan and Future Proliferation Networks," 113.

9 Ibid.

10 Shi-Chin Lin, "The AQ Khan Revelations and Subsequent Changes to Pakistani Export Controls," *Center for Nonproliferation Studies*, October 2004 <http://nti.org/e_research/e3_54a.html>

11 David E. Sanger, "The Khan Network," Paper presented at the Conference on South Asia and the Nuclear Future, Stanford University, 4–5 June 2004 <http://iisdb.stanford.edu/evnts/3889/Khan_network-paper.pdf>

12 Richard P. Cronin, K. Alan Kronstadt and Sharon Squassoni, "Pakistan's Nuclear Proliferation Activities and the Recommendations of the 9/11 Commission: U.S. Policy Constraints and Options," Congressional Research Service, RL32745, 25 January 2005, 11.

13 William Langewiesche, "The Wrath of Khan," *The Atlantic Monthly*, November 2005.

14 Frederick Lamy. "Export controls violations and illicit trafficking by Swiss companies and individuals in the case of A. Q. Khan network," Geneva Centre for Security Policy, August 19, 2004, www.pircenter.org/data/resources/lamy.pdf

15 "Press Release by Inspector General of Police in Relation to Investigation on the Alleged Production of Components for Libya's Uranium Enrichment Program," *Polis Diraja Malaysia*, February 20, 2004, www.rmp.gov.my/rmp03/040220scomi_eng.htm

16 Steve Coll, "The Atomic Emporium: Iran and the A.Q. Khan Network," *The New Yorker*, August 7 & 14, 2006, pp. 50–63

17 Ellen Nakashima and Alan Sipress, "Insider Tells of Nuclear Deals, Cash," *Washington Post*, Feb 21, 2004.

18 Martin Fackler, "Japan Accuses 5 of Exporting Equipment With Nuclear Uses," *New York Times*, August 26, 2006.

## The Nuclear Program Exposed

Throughout the late 1980s and the 1990s, intelligence reports on Iran's nuclear ambitions focused on its fuel-cycle connected dealings with Russia and China.[16] There were exceptions. In June 1991, for example, reports by Mark Hibbs in the international trade journal, *Nucleonics Week,* described visits to Iran by the head of Pakistan's uranium enrichment program, A.Q. Khan, beginning in 1988 and known to the U.S. government, to meet with officials of the AEOI for the possible purpose of supplying centrifuge enrichment and nuclear weapons technology to Iran. By 2000, the United States had indications that Iran was buying nuclear equipment from Khan and then collected intelligence on construction of heavy-water and centrifuge enrichment plants but held off going public to collect more information.[17]

Still it came as a shock on August 14, 2002, when the Washington DC office of NCRI revealed publicly that Iran was secretly pursuing a number of nuclear projects, including building a underground uranium centrifuge enrichment plant in the desert near Natanz and a heavy-water production plant on a river near Arak. (The Iraq-based, Shia-Marxist, MEK/NCRI group has been on the U.S. State Department's list of terrorist organizations since 1997.[18]) The heavy-water plant was in the Khondab region, approximately 150 miles southwest of Tehran, and the centrifuge plant was in the region near Kashan, about 200 miles south of Tehran and 100 miles north of Esfahan. Because of the high sensitivity of the projects, according to NCRI spokesman, Alireza Jafarzadeh, the activities were covered by two front companies operating out of Tehran, Kala (Kalaye) Electric for the Natanz project and Mesbah Electric for the Arak heavy-water plant.[19]

Construction of the Fuel Enrichment Plant (FEP) at Natanz [began] had begun in [2000] 2001, and the Arak heavy-water plant in 1996. At Natanz, the plans for the FEP called for two large subterranean halls, each 25,000 square meters, in a land area covering 100,000 square meters. Each hall was eight meters (about 24 feet) below ground and was protected by eight-meter thick concrete walls. The Arak heavy water plant had characteristic 48-meter tall towers of a heavy-water production facility.[20] Within a few months, information released by the MEK/NCRI was corroborated from commercial satellite images uncovered by a Washington-based private organization, the Institute for Science and International Security.

The IAEA soon entered the picture and sought to schedule a visit for October 2002 by Director General Mohamed ElBaradei to inspect the sites. The visit was put off until late February 2003, when Iran tried to make amends for its previous secrecy by submitting the declaration to the IAEA for the Natanz plant required by its safeguards agreement. Iran stated that the maximum enrichment would be only 5 percent U-235, sufficient for power reactor fuel, and made assurances that the centrifuge enrichment would be only for peaceful purposes. In addition, Iran confirmed the construction of the heavy-water plant at Arak. Gholam-Reza Aghazadeh, the Iranian vice president and the head of the AEOI, said that over one hundred P-1-type centrifuges were already installed in the small Pilot Fuel

Enrichment Plant (the PFEP) at Natanz and were scheduled to start operating in June 2003. These were the first of the planned one thousand centrifuges in the PFEP, all of which were to be installed by the end of the year. Aghazadeh also informed the IAEA that the underground FEP, which was being built, would hold up to fifty thousand centrifuges when completed.[21]

During the February 2003 visit by the IAEA, Iran also confirmed that the Kalaye Electric Company workshop, on the outskirts of Tehran, was used for making centrifuge components, but it insisted that no testing was done there or at Natanz with actual gasified uranium hexafluoride ($UF_6$) feed.[22] Shortly before, on February 20, 2003 the MEK/NCRI disclosed additional information that Kalaye Electric Company workshops had been registered as a watch factory to cover the centrifuge activities.[23] It was reported that the United States had gotten a tip about uranium enrichment activities at Kalaye Electric Company as early as 2000 but did not push for inspections because the CIA feared exposing its sources. Also, apparently the IAEA had heard about the watch factory cover, but it could not inspect the site without proof that nuclear material was present.[24]

Earlier in the month, Iranian President Khatami had made public other facilities that would complete Iran's nuclear fuel cycle—uranium mining at Saghand, in Yadz, yellowcake preparation in a plant under construction in Ardakan, near Yadz, and the Uranium Conversion Facility (UCF) under construction in Esfahan.[25]

Still, Iran appeared uncertain in its willingness to cooperate. Between February 2003 and October 2003, it took a number of steps intended to conceal the origin, source, and extent of its centrifuge enrichment program. These included denying access to the Kalaye Electric Company workshop to IAEA inspectors in February 2003, refusing to permit the IAEA to take environmental samples there in March 2003, dismantling equipment used at the workshop and moving it to Pars Trash (another subsidiary company of the AEOI located in Tehran), renovating part of the Kalaye Electric Company workshop to prevent detection of nuclear material use, and submitting incorrect and incomplete declarations.[26] The IAEA inspectors reportedly found the centrifuge factory secreted behind a false wall at the electric company.[27] Iran finally relented in August 2003, allowing the sampling at the Kalaye Electric Company in which particles of HEU and LEU turned up on stored centrifuge components.[28]

A big move began on October 16, 2003, when Hassan Rohani, secretary of the Supreme National Security Council of Iran and then Iran's chief nuclear negotiator, announced that Iran would make a full disclosure of its past and present nuclear activities. Rohani's action followed a resolution by the IAEA Board of Governors in September 2003 calling on Iran to provide, by the end of October 2003, a full declaration of all materials and components imported for the enrichment program, giving source and date of receipt, especially for certain equipment and components that IAEA inspectors found had been contaminated with HEU particles.[29]

On October 21, 2003, Iran vice president Aghazadeh submitted a letter to the IAEA providing a "full picture" of Iran's nuclear activities and their "exclusively peaceful character." In the letter, Iran acknowledged that between 1998 and 2002 it had tested centrifuges at the Kalaye Electric Company using $UF_6$ imported in 1991; between 1991 and 2000 it had a laser enrichment program, in the course of which it used 30 kg of uranium metal not previously declared; and between 1988 and 1992 it had irradiated 7 kg of uranium oxide ($UO_2$) targets and extracted small quantities of plutonium.[30]

Before the revelations by the MEK/NCRI of Iran's progress in building a nuclear infrastructure, U.S. attention had been focused mainly on Russia as the supplier of sensitive nuclear technology to Iran. The doocuments provided in October 2003 by Iran to the IAEA reportedly gave an extensive amount of information on a secret procurement network that was the source of blueprints, technical guidance, and centrifuge equipment, without naming Pakistan directly as the supplier. It soon emerged in IAEA investigations that the source of assistance for Iran's centrifuge program was the A.Q. Khan network, operating out of Pakistan through a front company in Malaysia and a storage and distribution center in Dubai, along with a worldwide network of suppliers. Much about the Khan network came to light with the seizure of the German-flagged ship BBC-China on October 4, 2003, carrying a cargo of centrifuge components from Dubai to Libya. Soon this was followed, in December 2003, by Libyan leader Gadhafi's complete abandonment of his secret nuclear program.[31]

Were Iran's intentions peaceful, or otherwise? One response to this question comes from a 2005 interview in Paris with Iranian physicist Alireza Assar, who left Iran in 1992 and in the early 1990s had consulted with the Iran's Ministry of Defense (MOD). He described two parallel programs, the civil program run by the AEOI and organized around the Bushehr nuclear power reactor and the military program, which he claimed was operated by the IRGC and the MOD, to develop the vast uranium enrichment program revealed in 2002. The military program's purpose, he said, was "to produce enough HEU to enable the regime to produce nuclear weapons." The Revolutionary Guard sought to let him know that they had unlimited funds for a research program to produce neutron triggers for nuclear weapons. Assar claimed that Iran had been working for years on the challenge of designing a nuclear warhead small enough to fit in a missile.[32]

An interesting sidebar is provided by a reported offer made in mid-2003 by Iran, and approved by the highest levels of the Iranian government, to open talks with the United States on normalizing relations between the two countries. The offer was transmitted in a fax sent to the U.S. State Department in May 2003 through the Swiss ambassador in Tehran, who represented U.S. interests in Iran. In a cover letter to the one-page Iranian "roadmap," the Swiss ambassador noted that it had been reviewed and approved by Ayatollah Khamenei, President Khatami, and Foreign Minister Kharrazi. Iran proposed a broad dialogue on matters including cooperation on nuclear safeguards, ending support for Hizballah and Hamas, helping to stabilize Iraq, and recognizing Israel. In return Iran sought an end to U.S. sanctions, full access to peaceful nuclear technology, and action to disband the MEK Iranian dissident group, based in Iraq, and repatriate its members to Iran. The offer was not taken up by the U.S. government. The document containing the offer surfaced only in mid-2006, although the approach by Iran had been reported earlier.[33]

On May 11, 2003, it was reported that American forces in Iraq had started disarming the MEK in a gesture following secret talks between Iranian and U.S. diplomats in Geneva, but the talks soon were adjourned after suicide bombings in Saudi Arabia on May 12, 2003 in which, the United States said, al Qa'ida officials harbored in Iraq were implicated. Iran said that the U.S. disarming of the MEK was a sham, but the U.S. State Department insisted that the 3,500-member MEK had been disarmed.[34] Iran suggested privately that it would turn over the al Qa'ida members in exchange for the members of the MEK captured by the United States, but Under Secretary of State Richard Armitage, testifying on October 28, 2003 on renewing the adjourned talks with Iran, ruled out such a deal because of uncertainty how the MEK would be treated.[35]

## A Strategy of Delay

Insights into Iran's reasoning and strategies leading up to its October 21, 2003 declaration are contained in a speech by Hassan Rohani, then the chief nuclear negotiator and secretary of the Supreme National Security Council, dating probably to late 2004, during the Khatami presidency.[36] The speech was published in September 2005 in the *Rahbord* quarterly journal of the Center for Strategic Studies, a research arm of Iran's Expediency Council, shortly after Mahmoud Ahmadinejad assumed the presidency following the June 2005 election. It was possibly leaked in reaction to the hard-line approach taken by President Ahmadinejad and to justify the Khatami regime's decision to sign the Additional Protocol and fully suspend centrifuge manufacture and enrichment activities in November 2004.[37]

In the speech, Rohani explained that because Iran had been denied access to nuclear technology from other countries like China and the Soviet Union in the mid-1980s, it began efforts of its own to develop indigenous technology, going to the black market and to supply networks. He said a decision was made in 1999–2000 to upgrade Iran's nuclear capabilities and that the AEOI then received increased funding and authority. These plans, however, were upset in August 2002 by the revelations of the MEK/NCRI dissident group about clandestine nuclear activities at Natanz and Arak. Also, after the U.S. invasion of Iraq in March 2003, Iran was concerned that the United States, buoyed by the first successes of battle, would raise the Iran issue at the meeting of the IAEA Board of Governors in mid-2003, either as a prelude to sending it to the UN Security Council for sanctions or simply to apply political and economic pressure.

Thus when IAEA Director General ElBaradei reported on the Iran case to the IAEA Board of Governors in June 2003, Rohani states, the decision was made to transfer nuclear issues up to the higher level of the Supreme National Security Council for the resolution of differences between the AEOI and the foreign ministry. One issue being debated was whether Iran should accept the Additional Protocol to its safeguards agreement, as ElBaradei had called for in the June 2003 Board of Governors meeting. This matter took on an air of great importance as the September 2003 Board meeting approached.

Iran's concerns were justified. Rhani states that the strongly worded resolution approved at the September 2003 meeting in Vienna "took us to the doorstep of the UN Security Council." Back in Tehran, for the Supreme National Security Council, finding a solution that would avoid a referral to the UN Security Council was paramount. The matter was taken up at the very top level by "the heads of the ruling system," who considered the pros and cons: an incomplete report might send the case to the UN, but a complete report might also do the same because Iran would be charged with a violation of its safeguards obligations. Rohani argued that the IAEA already was aware of many of Iran's undeclared nuclear activities through routine reports from countries that had nuclear projects with Iran, such as China, or had exported nuclear-related equipment to Iran, such as Russia. For example, Rohani notes, a secret test conducted a number of years earlier by a Tehran professor was written up in a student's dissertation that became available to the IAEA, while another secret project was described in a scientific paper published in an international journal.

At that time, one idea that gained support among Iran's ruling elite was to work with the EU-3, which had proposed that Iran drop its indigenous nuclear fuel cycle. The three European foreign ministers were invited to visit Tehran with the hope of putting a wedge between them and the United States. Rohani states that he reached an agreement with the foreign ministers to resist pressures to take Iran to the UN Security Council, on the condition that Iran would make a complete declaration to the IAEA. Accordingly, says Rohani, Iran presented the IAEA with "a complete picture" in its letter of October 21, 2003 and consequently at the November 2003 IAEA Board of Governors meeting the Europeans upheld their commitment, and the resolution on Iran was not sent to the Security Council.

In his speech, Rohani notes that the process of confidence building with the Europeans was soon undermined by the P-2 centrifuge issue. In December 2003, after the ship *BBC China*, transporting a cargo of centrifuge components to Libya from the Khan network, was intercepted in October 2003, Libya gave up its nuclear program completely and told the IAEA everything it knew about the activities of the network, including the fact that Iran had purchased plans for the advanced P-2 centrifuge from an intermediary, the Khan network. Rohani claims that Iran had provided the IAEA with the same dossier on the intermediary as given by Libya to the Agency, even though it was unaware that the two were using the same middleman. The P-2 centrifuge plans were left out, he says, because the IAEA already had found out about them from Libya. "It became evident to us that they knew about the transaction . . . , but they saw that as a violation, anyway," Rohani states, innocently.

The preliminary agreement reached in Brussels with the EU-3 in June 2004 resulted in only a brief suspension of some activities. Rohani points out that the

Europeans gradually understood and cooperated with Iran's method of operation, which was not to accept suspension in any areas where it had technical problems that were still being ironed out. Thus, in the period during which a suspension of enrichment-related activities was being negotiated with the Europeans, Iran was able to complete the UCF at Esfahan that would provide $UF_6$ feed for the centrifuges at Natanz.

Iran made a distinction, Rohani states, between lying, which he says Iran had not done, and not telling the truth in a timely manner. Rohani bragged of the great progress made by the UCF project in the preceding year (2004) from having nothing but a small amount of $UF_6$ feed imported from China to having all that was needed. Another achievement, Rohani says, was to have gone from some 150 centrifuges when Iran first was negotiating with the Europeans to about 500 operational machines at the time of his speech, a year later. Rohani complains that the United States was telling the Europeans that they have been deceived in the year of negotiations and that the Iranians had taken advantage of them. He states, with assurance, that with all the equipment then in place, Iran could make 3.5 percent enriched uranium in just a few months, if it decided to do so, absent any agreements for suspension.

As the period covered by the Rohani speech ends, pressure is building up, following a resolution at the September 2004 meeting of the IAEA Board. Anticipating the impact of the IAEA's quarterly report to the upcoming November 2004 meeting of the IAEA Board, Iran announced a complete suspension of all enrichment and reprocessing activities on November 14, 2004. This lasted until February 2006, when Ahmadinejad nullified the suspension and, as Rohani had anticipated, Iran was able to reach 3.5 percent enrichment by the following April.

## IRAN'S CENTRIFUGE URANIUM ENRICHMENT PROGRAM

The beginnings of Iran's effort to develop gas centrifuge technology for enriching uranium are traced to a technical literature search begun in 1985. Subsequently in 1987, Iran acquired drawings for the European P-1-type centrifuge, the model used earlier in Pakistan, through the clandestine A.Q. Khan network, together with samples of centrifuge components.[38] Evidence of this transaction is in a one-page handwritten document, the so-called "1987 offer" for a centrifuge enrichment "starter kit" that Iran eventually shared with the IAEA in January 2005.[39] In 1993, Iran again established contact with the supply network, and between 1994 and 1996, it received components for five hundred P-1 centrifuges and apparently a duplicate set of drawings for the P-1 centrifuge design. At the same time, Iran said, the network also supplied design drawings for an advanced European design P-2 centrifuge then used in Pakistan. The information on acquiring the P-2 drawings was not forthcoming until January 2004, after an inquiry by the IAEA.[40] It was omitted from the October 21, 2003 letter, which was supposed to have provided the "full scope of Iranian nuclear activities."

## P-1 Centrifuges

Iran claimed in February 2003, soon after its centrifuge program was exposed, that its first foray into P-1 centrifuge design and research and development work was only in 1997. It started then, they said, first with a literature search, followed by extensive computer modeling and simulation, including the testing of centrifuge rotors in the Plasma Physics buildings of the Tehran Nuclear Research Center (TNRC), using information only from open sources and without using nuclear material as feed. This was met with disbelief among IAEA experts, who concluded that it was not possible for Iran, starting in 1997, to have developed enrichment technology to the level seen at Natanz based solely on open source information, computer simulations, and mechanical testing and without testing the whole process with $UF_6$ feed.[41]

Iran soon amended and corrected its earlier statement in a pattern that would become common. It informed the IAEA in August 2003 that the decision to launch a centrifuge enrichment program had actually been taken in 1985 and that in fact Iran had received drawings of the P-1 centrifuge through a foreign intermediary around 1987. The centrifuge R&D program, Iran stated, was situated at the TNRC between 1988 and 1995 and was moved to the Kalaye Electric Company workshop in 1995. Centrifuge R&D activities then were carried out at the Kalaye workshop between 1995 and 2003, when they were moved to Natanz.[42] Furthermore, in its letter of October 21, 2003, Iran finally acknowledged that a limited number of tests using small amounts of nuclear material ($UF_6$) were conducted at the Kalaye workshop in 1999 and 2002.

Iranian authorities later explained that 1.9 kg of $UF_6$ involved in the Kalaye tests had been taken from material imported from China in 1991, a transaction that itself was not declared to the IAEA until February 2003. Earlier, when the IAEA first did a material accounting, Iran had attributed the absence of this quantity of $UF_6$ from its declared inventory to evaporation loss from leaking valves on the bottles containing the $UF_6$ gas stored in a room under the roof of the Tehran Research Reactor (TRR) building. In fact, the room was contaminated with $UF_6$, but from an unexplained source.[43]

An interview conducted by IAEA inspectors in October 2004 with a former AEOI official who was involved in centrifuge R&D at the Kalaye Electric Company from 1987 until 2001 provided confirmation. The official gave details on the procurement of the P-1 centrifuge design and sample components around 1987, the supply of the duplicate set of P-1 designs and components for five hundred P-1 centrifuges that were delivered through the Khan network to Iran in two shipments in March 1994 and July 1996, and the supply of centrifuge bellows in 1997 to replace poor quality ones previously sent. The AEOI official also confirmed that meetings with the intermediary network continued after 1996 and included discussions on technical issues. In all, Iran said, thirteen official meetings took place with the clandestine supply network between 1994 and 1999.[44]

Iran's actions between February 2003 and October 2003 were intended to conceal the origin, source, and extent of its enrichment program. This included denying inspectors access to the Kalaye Electric Company workshop in February 2003, refusing to permit the IAEA to take environmental samples there in March 2003, and dismantling equipment used at the workshop and moving it to Pars Trash, an AEOI subsidiary company in Tehran.

In addition, Iran renovated part of the Kalaye Electric Company workshop in order to prevent detection of the use of nuclear material, and it submitted incorrect and incomplete declarations to the IAEA.[45] During the August 2003 visit, IAEA inspectors were finally allowed to to take environmental samples at the Kalaye Electric Company workshop, and they noticed considerable renovation to one of the buildings on the site since their earlier visit in March. The renovation was an attempt, the IAEA believed, to conceal activities carried out there and prevent it from seeing and taking samples from equipment in place.[46]

At the Kalaye Electric Company workshop, $UF_6$ gas was fed for the first time into a single centrifuge in 1999 and into as many as nineteen centrifuges in 2002.[47] The construction of the two centrifuge facilities at Natanz, the PFEP and the underground FEP, began in 2001. According to Iran's plans, the holdings of the smaller PFEP would include some 1,000 P-1 centrifuge machines (approximately six cascades of 164 centrifuges each) and the commercial-scale FEP facility was to contain over 50,000 P-1 machines when completed. While Iran placed an upper limit of 5 percent U-235 on the intended level of enrichment at these facilities, as a statement of its peaceful intentions, there is no technical barrier to reconfiguring the centrifuge cascades to enrich uranium to HEU for weapons, should the facility be taken out of IAEA safeguards and inspectors barred. However, in that event, reconnecting the cascades for the production of HEU would probably take several weeks, and enriching enough uranium for a weapon would take a year using a few thousand operating P-1 machines.[48]

## The Paris Agreement and a Period of Suspension

Iran introduced $UF_6$ gas into a centrifuge at the PFEP two years later, on June 25, 2003. By October 2003, the installation of a 164-machine cascade was nearing completion, when, in November 2003, Iran shut down the facility.[49] This occurred in response to a statement issued in Tehran with the foreign ministers of the EU-3 nations on October 21, 2003 in which Iran acted voluntarily to suspend all enrichment-related and reprocessing activities, including the production of feed material.[50] The Tehran statement was a direct response to the September 12, 2003 resolution of the IAEA Board of Governors. Seeing the progress being made, the IAEA Board decided at its November 2003 meeting to put off reporting Iran's noncompliance to the Security Council as the EU-3 and Iran continued negotiations on an agreement to provide confidence that Iran's nuclear activities were entirely peaceful.[51,52]

The measures agreed to in October 2003 were slow to take effect. Only by December 29, 2003 did Iran institute a halt to the testing and operation of all centrifuges at Natanz and the installation of new ones, as well as assuming new contracts for manufacturing centrifuge machines and components.[53] On February 4, 2004, Iran said that in early March 2004 it would finally stop the assembly and testing of new centrifuges and the domestic manufacture of centrifuge components under exiting contracts.[54]

By the end of April 2004, the understanding reached in October 2003 was apparently beginning to breakdown. On April 29, 2004 Iran informed the IAEA that it intended to conduct hot tests on the $UF_6$ production line at the new UCF in Esfahan. In a subsequent exchange with the IAEA, Iran declared that "the decision taken for voluntary and temporary suspension . . . does not include suspension of production of $UF_6$."[55] The IAEA Board's resolution of June 18, 2004 condemned Iran's continued production of centrifuge equipment as well as its decision to generate $UF_6$, and also noted its discovery that Iran had withheld ten assembled centrifuge rotors for research purposes.[56]

Finally, on June 23, 2004, Iran notified the IAEA of its intention to resume, "under IAEA supervision, manufacturing of centrifuge components and assembly and testing of centrifuges."

Iran was granted permission to remove the seals that IAEA inspectors had applied to monitor the brief suspension, and during a July 2004 inspection visit, Iran returned forty seals that had been removed from equipment and centrifuge components at Natanz, Pars Trash, and Farayand Technique. Iran then proceeded to assemble and test centrifuge rotors, which the IAEA said was difficult to supervise, absent the seals.[57]

On September 18, 2004, the IAEA Board passed another resolution, demanding that Iran adhere to its earlier agreement and suspend centrifuge enrichment and production of feed material at the UCF immediately.[58] Then, as the November 29, 2004 meeting of the Board approached, negotiations with the EU-3 materialized in a new framework, the Paris Agreement, which was signed by Iran and the EU-3 on November 15, 2004. The agreement firmly stated Iran's decision to "continue and extend" its suspension of all enrichment and reprocessing activities. It spelled out a voluntary suspension covering all aspects of enrichment, including centrifuge import, manufacture and assembly, and testing, as well as uranium conversion, and all reprocessing activities, including plutonium separation. It also looked to the continuation of negotiations on a "long-term agreement" that would have guarantees on peaceful nuclear technology, economic cooperation, and security issues.[59]

In less than a year, the commitments under Paris Agreement began to unravel. Iran notified the IAEA on August 1, 2005 that it had decided to resume conversion activities at the UCF. Iran started to feed uranium ore concentrate (UOC, yellowcake) into the first part of the process line and send its stock of uranium tetrafluoride ($UF_4$, green salt) into the UF4-to-$UF_6$ process line.[60] It also began the quality control testing of centrifuge components.[61] The IAEA Board reacted by passing a resolution on September 24, 2005 finding that Iran was in noncompliance with its safeguards agreement and declaring a lack of confidence that Iran's nuclear program was exclusively for peaceful purposes. But the Board held back on reporting this lapse to the UN Security Council. Subsequently, the IAEA raised some disturbing questions about Iran's links with the A.Q. Khan network, which had helped build clandestine military nuclear programs in Libya and North Korea.[62]

Finally, on January 3, 2006, Iran informed the IAEA of its intentions to resume enrichment at Natanz. Iran did a substantial renovation of the gas handling system at the Natanz PFEP and some rotor testing at Farayand Technique and Natanz. Then in February 2006, it started enrichment tests at the PFEP, feeding $UF_6$ gas into a single P-1 machine, and later into 10- and 20-machine cascades. In March 2006, Iran completed a 164-machine cascade and began tests with $UF_6$. A campaign involving the completed 164-machine cascade was conducted in April 2006.

The culmination of all this activity was a dramatic speech on April 11, 2006 by President Ahmadinejad, announcing that Iran had achieved a uranium enrichment level of 3.5 percent U-235 at Natanz, or more precisely, 3.6 percent U-235 as declared to the IAEA on April 13, 2006.[63,64] On April 16, 2006, the IAEA observed that two additional 164-machine cascades were under construction, out of the total of six planned. At that time, Iran again began feeding $UF_6$ into a single machine and into the 10-machine cascade. In June 6–8, 2006, it fed $UF_6$ into the 164-machine cascade and on August 24, 2006 resumed feeding $UF_6$ into the 164-machine cascade. Also in June 2006, Iran announced achieving 5 percent enrichment in the 164-centrifuge cascade.[65] A high level of operation was not being sustained; the breadth of activities indicated both successes and continued technical problems.[66] In October 2006, Iran installed and began testing a second 164-machine cascade at the PFEP.[67]

At the end of year, on December 9, 2006, President Ahmadenijad announced that the installation of the first three thousand machines had begun at the underground Natanz FEP plant, with plans to have them operating by March 2007.[68] In reality, progress on centrifuges at Natanz was slow, and this was among Ahmadinejad's many pronouncements that were left unfulfilled.

However, after weeks of limited access inside Iran, inspectors from the IAEA reported that Tehran had succeeded in manufacturing parts for about three thousand centrifuges. The Natanz site in the desert south of Tehran was described as a maze of buildings, barbed wire, and antiaircraft guns.[69] In January 2007, Russia completed the delivery of twenty-nine Tor M-1 air defense systems to Iran for the enrichment plant, designed for protection against aircraft and cruise missiles at altitudes of up to six miles.[70] In early February 2007, Iran installed the first two 164-machine centrifuge cascades in the cavernous subterranean FEP facility.[71]

## Advanced P-2 Centrifuges

Iran has consistently held to the position that its only development work on an advanced P-2 centrifuge was carried out between 2002 and 2003, largely at the workshop of a private company in Tehran under contract with the AEOI and limited to the manufacture and mechanical testing of a small number of modified P-2 rotors. Iran insists that no other work on the P-2 was done prior to 2002 or has been done since 2003. It has rejected any suggestion that it might have a parallel military enrichment program using the P-2, stating that "no other institution, company or organization in Iran has been involved in P-2 R&D" and that "no P-2 R&D has been undertaken by or at the request of the Ministry of Defense." However, in declarations to the IAEA in 2003 on implementing the Additional Protocol to its safeguards agreement, Iran said that it did foresee P-2 related R&D activities in the future.[72] The P-2 centrifuge under optimum operating conditions is estimated to have about twice the separative capacity of the P-1 design.[73]

When, in January 2004, Iran first acknowledged that in about 1995 it had received P-2 centrifuge drawings from a foreign intermediary (the Khan network), it further revealed that in 1999 or 2000 the AEOI had signed the contract with the owner of a private company located in Tehran to develop the P-2 based on a modified design. The drawings were identified by the IAEA experts as being similar to a European advanced design that used maraging steel rotors with bellows. Since Iran was not capable of manufacturing the appropriate maraging steel cylinders with bellows called for in the drawings, the company owner explained that a decision was made to develop a shorter, subcritical carbon composite rotor. The owner said that seven rotors were manufactured, and that mechanical tests were conducted on them without using nuclear material before the work was terminated by the AEOI after June 2003 and the equipment moved to Pars Trash in Tehran, where P-1 centrifuge equipment also was stored and concealed for a period in 2003.[74]

After insisting that it had not received any P-2-related components from abroad, Iran admitted in May 2004 that the private contractor had imported magnets from Asian suppliers, and, as well, had inquired from a European supplier about procuring 4,000 magnets, with the possibility of even larger purchases in the future. These inquiries, as the IAEA noted, were all hardly in keeping with the declared small scale of the program, but Iran has claimed that only a limited number of magnets were actually received. When asked in February 2006 about a possible transaction in 2003 for 900 magnets from a foreign supplier, Iran denied ordering or receiving them.[75] Also, Iran officials clarified that the composite rotors were not manufactured in the workshop of the company, but at a site belonging to Iran's Defense Industries Organization (DIO). International Atomic Energy Agency experts remained skeptical that Iran would hold on to the P-2 design drawings acquired in 1995 until 2001 before starting any work, and they questioned the feasibility of then being able to manufacture the components in less than a year.[76]

When questioned about why the P-2 centrifuge R&D activities had not been mentioned in its October 21, 2003 declaration, Iran gave a grab bag of explanations, including "time pressure," and the argument that only if the Additional Protocol, which was signed in December 2003, had been in force would the information have been required under the safeguards agreement.[77] After reviewing the P-2 drawings, the IAEA experts concluded that they were of the same origin as those provided to Libya.[78] Since Libya had admitted buying a nuclear warhead design from the Khan network as well as parts and diagrams for building more sophisticated P-2 centrifuges, wasn't it likely, thought IAEA inspectors, that Iran had received the same package?[79]

Iranian authorities reiterated that no P-2 centrifuges were obtained from abroad and that all the components were produced domestically with the exceptions of "some raw materials and minor items supplied to the contractor by the P-1 R&D team and a few items that had been purchased from abroad in connection with the P-2 contract, such as bearings, oils and magnets."[80]

In October 2004, the IAEA interviewed the former AEOI official who was said to have originally received the P-2 centrifuge design documents. During these discussions, the official described the negotiations that had led to the supply of the P-2 drawings, recalling that they took place around 1995 or 1996, and he was questioned about the apparent gap of seven years before the R&D test work on the P-2 design had begun. The IAEA repeatedly questioned Iran on information to suggest that P-2 components had possibly been acquired during the period 1995–2002. Iran consistently maintained that no P-2 components were delivered by intermediaries, either with the centrifuge drawings or after, and it repeated that no work on P-2 centrifuges was carried out between 1995 and 2002. Nor, Iran said, did it discuss either P-2 design or the possible supply of P-2 components with the Khan intermediaries during that time.[81]

Interest in the P-2 heightened in the Spring of 2006, when President Ahmadinejad announced, on April 12, 2006, that Iran was conducting research on advanced P-2 centrifuges that would "quadruple the capacity of the P-1."[82] The IAEA asked for clarification of media reports in mid-April 2006 of statements by high-level Iranian officials concerning R&D and testing of P-2 centrifuges[83] and on conducting research on new types of centrifuges.[84] At a press briefing in Paris on August 24, 2006 the MEK/NCRI claimed that Iran was building P-2 centrifuges at a secret Tehran site run by the Iran Centrifuge Technology Company (Sherkate Technology Centrifuge Iran or "TSA") headquartered in Tehran's Yousef Abad district. They claimed that at least fifteen P-2 machines had been built and were being tested with hundreds more expected by 2007, and they identified the assembly site as three hangars on the Tehran–Damavand highway, three kilometers from the Tehran–Pars junction.[85]

## OFFERS BY THE KHAN NETWORK

The period between November 2004 and March 2005 saw developments in four areas related to the IAEA's verification of Iran's P-1 centrifuge enrichment program. These concerned revelations about a 1987 offer for centrifuge-related design, technology, and components; the genesis of a mid-1990s offer of P-1 centrifuge documentation and components for five hundred centrifuges; shipping documents and other documentation related to the delivery of items in connection with the mid-1990s offer; and technical discussions held between Iran and the Khan intermediaries concerning centrifuge enrichment.[86]

## The 1987 Offer

Not until early 2005 did the IAEA see any written evidence to back up Iran's account in 2003 of the beginnings of its centrifuge program. During a meeting in Tehran on January 12, 2005, Iranian officials showed the IAEA a handwritten one-page document, devoid of any dates, names, signatures, and addresses, but said to reflect a 1987 offer by the Khan network for the delivery of a disassembled centrifuge machine, along with drawings, descriptions, and specifications for the production of centrifuges as well as drawings, specifications, and calculations for a "complete" centrifuge plant, and materials for two thousand centrifuges. The document also made reference to auxiliary vacuum and electric-drive equipment, a complete set of workshop equipment for mechanical, electrical, and electronic support, and capabilities for uranium reconversion into metal and metal casting. The last item aroused concern because it may have referred to casting uranium metal into components for nuclear weapons. Iran stated that the network had offered the reconversion unit with casting equipment on its own initiative and that the AEOI had not received it.[87]

The MEK/NCRI took exception to the contention that offers in the one-page document were unsolicited. According to this group, A.Q. Khan visited Iran in 1987 and met with three top commanders of the IRGC, led by Brig. Gen. Mohammad Eslami, who were working on nuclear research.[88]

Despite repeated requests, Iran maintained that no other written evidence existed, attributing this to the secret nature of the program and the management style of the AEOI. More than sixty documents supplied by the intermediaries and relating mainly to the 1987 offer were finally made available to the IAEA in late 2005. These included a drawing of a layout of 6 centrifuge cascades of 168 machines each and a 2,000-centrifuge plant in the same hall.

## The 15-Page Document

Among the more than sixty centrifuge-related documents supplied to Iran by the Khan network was the "15-page document" that appeared to be background and supporting material for the 1987 offer. The 15-page document, among other things, contained a description of the procedures for the reduction of $UF_6$ to uranium metal in small quantities, and it gave procedures for casting enriched and depleted uranium metal into hemispheres, something of direct relevance to the fabrication of nuclear weapons components. It did not, however, include dimensions or other specifications for machined pieces for such components.[89]

Iran has contended that it was given the 15-page document on the initiative of the network and not at the request of the AEOI. However, Iran could not establish when it was received and consistently declined to provide the IAEA with a copy, although it did permit the IAEA to place the document under IAEA seal in January 2006.[90]

During the period between 1995 and 2000, Iran had conducted a series of experiments to reduce $UF_4$ to uranium metal and also made a few attempts at uranium casting and machining, but these did not appear to follow the procedures outlined in the 15-page document. Iran's motivation for conducting uranium reduction experiments was initially to make uranium metal for its laser program and, later, to develop an alternative process for the UCF under construction at Esfahan.[91] However, the 15-page document in Iran was a matter of concern because of its apparent relation to the reference in the original one-page 1987 offer to uranium reconversion and casting, which Iran said was not pursued. The IAEA had seen the same document and other similar ones in Libya after that country revealed its centrifuge enrichment program.[92]

## The Mid-1990s Offer

Between 1987 and mid-1993, Iran contends that it had no contacts with representatives of the Khan network.[93] The "mid-1990s offer" refers to the subsequent approach made by the network in 1994 to supply the components and documentation for five hundred P-1 centrifuges. The offer also included the possible acquisition of P-2 centrifuge technology, but Iran has maintained that no actual P-2 components were delivered—only that drawings for P-2 centrifuge components without specifications were provided in 1994–1995. No further work was said to have been done on P-2 centrifuges until 2002, nor were any discussions on P-2 centrifuges held with network intermediaries during this period, Iran said. But there were questions about whether the Tehran contractor who worked on a modified P-2 design during 2002–2003 had inquired about purchasing magnets for the P-2 during the intervening 1987–1993 period. Moreover, there continued to be conflicting statements by Iran and key network intermediaries on events leading to the offer.[94]

By Iran's account, the network's 1994 offer was made orally to an employee of a company that was set up to purchase computers for the State Organization for Management and Planning (OMP). The matter made its way to the head of the OMP, who then passed it upward until it reached the president of AEOI and resulted in renewed contacts between the AEOI and network intermediaries in 1993. Iran contended there were no written documents on the offer except for shipping documents confirming the delivery of P-1 components in 1994–1995.[95] The IAEA finally received a number of such documents from Iran in January 2005 on the acquisition of centrifuge-related equipment showing four shipments of equipment in 1994 and 1995, along with related customs documents in August 1995, but nothing detailing the actual contents of the shipments. The documents did reveal that deliveries of P-1 components started eight to nine months before Iran's declared date of first meeting between AEOI representatives and network intermediaries—in January rather than October 1994. Further information provided by Iran in April 2005 showed that one of the AEOI representatives had made trips related on the matter in August 1993 and December 1993.[96]

Following the mid-1990s offer, up to ten meetings were held with the Khan network intermediaries during the period 1996 to 1999, Iran said, to discuss the poor quality of the P-1 components that had been supplied and to obtain answers to technical questions about operating the P-1 centrifuges. Iran claimed that at no time in these meetings did it discuss the supply of P-2 centrifuges or components.[97] Despite corroboration with Iran's chronology of events in interviews with Iranian officials and with individuals in the Dubai, where P-1 centrifuges were stored before delivery to Iran, the IAEA continued to question the completeness and consistency of Iran's information provided on the delivery of centrifuge components.[98]

## IRAN'S LASER ENRICHMENT PROGRAM

Using laser light to enrich uranium by selectively removing U-235 atoms from a vapor of natural uranium metal, or removing molecules containing U-235 from a gas of $UF_6$, has been a lure for scientists seeking a "simple" but sophisticated approach to enrichment. Laser enrichment is even less demanding of space than a centrifuge plant and is more economical and efficient, with high "separation factor," unlike centrifuges, which require passage through many machines to obtain a substantial separation of U-235 from U-238. Mostly, laser uranium enrichment has been confined to research and production of less than gram quantities of enriched uranium, with the exception of a failed try at commercialization in the United States.[99]

One essential drawback of laser enrichment is nuclear proliferation – the possibility that a small, hidden laser enrichment plant operating over several years could produce enough HEU for a nuclear weapon or two. This would be done in secret by a nonnuclear weapon state like Iran in a violation of its obligations under the NPT and its safeguards agreement.[100] Suspicions of this sort were raised in 2004 about South Korea by the highly embarrassing revelation that its laser scientists had carried out experiments during 1993–2003 resulting in two-tenths of a gram of enriched uranium.The revelation jolted South Korea's research establishment.[101]

## Small Quantities, Big Secrets

In May 2003 the MEK/NCRI dissident group identified Lashkar Ab'ad and Ramandeh in the Hashtgerd region of Iran as locations of backup facilities to the centrifuge enrichment plants under construction at Natanz.[102] Ramandeh was an AEOI facility that was part of the Karaj Agricultural and Medical Center, which was not previously known to be involved in nuclear fuel cycle activities.[103] Shortly afterward, Iran acknowledged to the IAEA that Lashkar Ab'ad, in fact, was part of its substantial laser program, but claimed it had not done any uranium enrichment using lasers and that, currently, it had no program in laser isotope separation. Subsequenty, on visiting the Lashkar Ab'ad site in August 2003, the IAEA was told by Iranian officials that it had been an AEOI laboratory for laser fusion research and laser spectroscopy and that no nuclear material had been used there in the experiments. Moreover, Iran denied that planned foreign cooperation in laser fusion and laser spectroscopy had ever occurred.[104] To quote from the IAEA's November 2004 report to the Board of Governors,

> Iran's responses between February 2003 and October 2003 to the Agency's inquiry into the possible existence in Iran of a laser enrichment program were characterized by concealment, including the dismantling of the laser enrichment laboratories at the TNRC and the pilot laser enrichment plant at Lashkar Ab'ad and the transfer of the equipment and material involved to Karaj, and by failures to declare nuclear material, facilities and activities.[105]

In the October 21, 2003 letter to the IAEA, Iran acknowledged the extent of its laser enrichment program and that it involved the two established laser enrichment techniques, *atomic vapor laser isotope separation* (AVLIS) and *molecular laser isotope separation* (MLIS). AVLIS, operating at high temperatures, selectively separates U-235 atoms out of uranium metal vapor, while MLIS, operating a near room temperature, does the same for U-235 in molecules of $UF_6$ gas. In the AVLIS process, a high-temperature stream of uranium metal vapor is irradiated by orange light from tunable dye lasers ( which are "pumped" by green light for copper vapor lasers) in order to selectively excite and ionize atoms of U-235, which are then electrostatically deflected out of the vapor stream. In the MLIS process, a stream of $UF_6$ gas just above room temperature is irradiated successively by an infrared laser and an ultraviolet laser in order to selectively split a U-235$F_6$ molecule into a fluorine atom and a U-235$F_5$ molecule, which solidifies and precipitates out of the gas.

Iran's interest in laser enrichment goes back to the era of the Shah before the 1979 revolution. Between 1975 and 1998 Iran concluded separate AVLIS- and MLIS-related contracts with suppliers in four foreign countries:

1. A 1975 contract to set up a laboratory to study the spectroscopy of uranium metal; this was abandoned in the 1980s.

2. A contract in the late 1970s to study the MLIS process. Four carbon [Monoxide] monoxide (CO) lasers and vacuum chambers were delivered, but the project was terminated by the revolution.
3. A 1991 contract with China to establish a Laser Spectroscopy Laboratory (LSL) to study uranium metal and a Comprehensive Separation Laboratory (CSL) at the TNRC to enrich milligram quantities of uranium using the AVLIS process. The contract included the supply in 1993 of fifty kilograms of natural uranium metal. Iran had failed in its safeguard obligations to report the receipt and use of the uranium metal in 1993 and to provide design information for LSL, CSL, and Lashkar Ab'ad. The LSL and CSL were shut down in 2000.[106]
4. A 1998 contract was signed for delivery of laser enrichment equipment and information to Lashkar Ab'ad, but only some equipment was delivered due to export restrictions.

In addition, in March 2001, Russia cancelled sale of laser enrichment equipment to Iran under U.S. pressure.[107]

The CSL facility operated fairly well until 1994, when the foreign scientists completed their work. The contract provided for "getting one milligram uranium enriched with 3 percent concentration of U-235 in no longer than eight hours." The IAEA ascertained that the highest average enrichment achieved was 8 percent with a peak enrichment of 13 percent. Of the 50 kg of natural uranium metal supplied as part of the third contract, 8 kg was used in experiments at the LSL and CSL, Iran said. Five hundred grams of uranium metal were evaporated in the laser experiments and milligram quantities of enriched product were collected, with the wastes discarded mainly at the disposal site in the city of Qom. Laboratory notebooks reviewed by the IAEA indicated that experiments during 1994–2000 were not successful due to problems with the copper vapor lasers, electron beams, and dye lasers.[108]

Iran finally established its pilot laser enrichment plant at Lashkar Ab'ad in 2002. The contract for the supply of AVLIS equipment had been hampered by the supplier's difficulties in obtaining export licenses for copper vapor lasers, dye lasers, collector parts, power sources, and the electron beam gun, so that only some documentation and equipment, including a large process vessel with supporting diffusion pumps, were delivered. As a recourse, Iran installed lasers from the CSL in the pilot scale vessel and was able to carry out runs using a total of five hundred grams of uranium metal feed in December 2002 and January 2003.

IAEA experts concluded that the capacity of the AVLIS installation at Lashkar Ab'ad was about one gram per hour, but that it could not operate continuously. Analyses by the IAEA were consistent with the 0.8 percent U-235 enrichment levels declared by Iran. The equipment was dismantled in May 2003, and the large vacuum vessel was sent into storage at Karaj Radioactive Waste Storage Facility (RWSF), along with some metal that was subsequently transferred to Jabr Ibn Hayan multipurpose laboratories (JHL) at the TNRC. In December 2003, the IAEA visited the mass spectrometer laboratories at Karaj and examined two spectrometers which had not been included in the October 21, 2003 declaration but were used to measure enrichment in the AVLIS program.[109]

In contrast to what actually materialized at Lashkar Ab'ad, the 1998 contract had called for equipment to guarantee 5 kg of product within the first year with enrichments of 3.5–7 percent U-235. The IAEA concluded that, had this system been installed, it would have been capable of producing HEU in gram quantities. Also, the IAEA said, the vacuum vessel-incorporated features peculiar to HEU separation work. Iranian AVLIS researchers claimed ignorance, denying any awareness of the possibility for HEU when the contract was negotiated.[110]

Iran had totally dismantled the laser enrichment projects and removed all related equipment, it said, and there were no plans to resume uranium enrichment using laser isotope separation. Nevertheless, it was continuing laser R&D activities, for example, on copper vapor lasers, an integral component of the AVLIS laser system.[111]

## URANIUM PARTICLE CONTAMINATION

### Clue or Coincidence

Unexpectedly, the IAEA discovered enriched uranium particle contamination on some imported and domestically fabricated centrifuge components in samples taken in Iran at the end of October 2003. This marked the beginning of a lengthy investigation into the source of the contamination. From the start, there was an air of mystery, a result of the fact that earlier in October 2003, Iran had told inquiring IAEA inspectors that all the centrifuges previously used at the Kalaye Electric Company workshop had been scrapped, when, in fact, they had been put in storage elsewhere in Tehran, as Iran admitted only a few weeks later.[112]

### Contamination Found on Centrifuge Parts

The IAEA conducted extensive environmental sampling at locations where Iran declared that centrifuge components were manufactured, processed, and stored, including at Natanz, the Kalaye Electric Company workshop, TNRC, Farayand Technique, and Pars Trash and centrifuge component manufacturing workshops in Iran. Iranian officials explained the presence of contaminating HEU particles by claiming they were on the centrifuge components when they were imported. The officials insisted that during the period in question Iran had not done centrifuge enrichment of uranium beyond 1.2 percent U-235. Nevertheless, whatever the source of the contamination, nuclear material was present that had not been declared by Iran to the IAEA, and this called into question the completeness of Iran's declarations about its centrifuge enrichment activities.[113]

The analysis of the environmental samples by the IAEA revealed contamination with particles of both HEU and LEU. Enrichments ranging up to 70 percent U-235 were found. The cumulative results from sampling, as reported in November 2004, were as follows:

- Predominantly LEU contamination on domestic centrifuge components; LEU and HEU contamination on imported components.
- Contamination found at the PFEP was different from that at the Kalaye Electric Company workshop and its Farayand Technique subsidiary.
- Up to about 70 percent U-235-enriched uranium particles (but practically no depleted uranium) was found in samples from imported components sent to storage at Natanz and Pars Trash from the manufacturing workshops as well as in samples taken from the Kalaye Electric Company workshop and the balancing machines used there.
- An elevated content of the uranium isotope U-236 in the LEU and HEU particles in many samples, suggesting the use of recycled uranium recovered from reprocessing of irradiated reactor fuel as a centrifuge feed. U-236, which has a half life of is 15 million years, is not found natural uranium.
- 36 percent U-235 contamination (in the range of 32–38 percent U-235) found on balancing machines relocated from mainly one room at the Kalaye Electric Company workshop to Farayand Technique. Significantly more particles of 36 percent U-235 at the Kalaye workshop than other enrichment levels.
- Numerous ~54 percent U-235 particles (in the range of 50–60 percent) found on imported components and on tested rotors assembled using the imported components. Some ~54 percent U-235 contamination found at the Kalaye workshop.
- Some 54 percent U-235 particles in chemical traps at the PFEP, which had not yet begun operation when the sample was taken.[114]

The IAEA exchanged data with Pakistan, the presumed source of Iran's P-1 centrifuges. Pakistan said it could not plausibly be the source of all the contamination uncovered in Iran since, for example, the U-236 fraction found in the uranium samples taken in Iran was significantly higher than produced in Pakistan's reactors.[115] Jane's reported in August 2004 that with Pakistan's assistance, IAEA inspectors had confirmed that a sample of HEU enriched to 54 percent U-235 had come from equipment originating in that country. Inspectors also confirmed that a sample of 36 percent enriched uranium was from contamination on Russian equipment that had been supplied to China and then passed on to Pakistan from where it found its way into the Khan network.[116] The 36 percent uranium enrichment level is a known signature of Russia's uranium enrichment operations.[117]

The IAEA eventually reached a conclusion supporting Iran's statement regarding the foreign origin of most of the HEU contamination at the declared centrifuge sites, but it left unresolved the source of the LEU particles as well as some of the HEU particles.[118] It sought to corroborate Iran's claims by taking samples in January 2005, and again in March, at locations in Dubai where Iran said its imported centrifuge components had been stored by the procurement network in the mid-1990s prior to shipment. But these samples did not indicate any traces of nuclear material. Possible explanations given were that the storage sites had been renovated or that the components were not removed from their original wrappings during storage.[119]

Iran's claim of foreign origin of the HEU contamination received support from the positive results of an IAEA analysis of swipe samples taken in May and December 2005 from centrifuge components provided by Libya, which also had been supplied by the Khan network.[120] Still, additional information obtained from Pakistan did not fully explain the presence of some of the HEU and LEU particles. The IAEA concluded in early 2007, the matter could not be further resolved without a full understanding and chronology of Iran's centrifuge enrichment program, which would require Iran to implement the Additional Protocol and any required transparency measures.[121]

## Contamination at Other Places

Enriched uranium contamination showed up in samples taken at other locations besides the declared centrifuge sites, often without any coherent explanation. One puzzler is connected with attempts since 2004 to clarify what the IAEA viewed as efforts by the PHRC at the Ministry of Defense's Lavizan-Shian site to acquire dual-use materials and equipment that could also be used in uranium enrichment and conversion activities. The equipment had been transferred to a nearby technical university when the PHRC was razed, and Iranian officials claimed that it actually had been procured for use by the university and not by the military laboratory. After much delay, the IAEA was allowed to take environmental samples at the university in February 2006 from some of this equipment, and the analysis showed the presence of a small number of natural uranium as well as HEU particles.[122] Resampling in December 2006 showed natural and LEU particles. The presence of the particles of various [enricments] enrichments remained unexplained by Iran.[123]

Still another riddle involved depleted uranium targets that were irradiated at the TRR in the course of plutonium experiments and stored in containers at the Karaj Waste Storage Facility. In late August 2006, the IAEA reported that samples taken a year earlier from one of the containers showed the presence of particles of HEU, indicating some unknown previous use of the containers.[124] In a letter of October 16, 2006 to Iran, the IAEA revealed that further analysis of the samples confirmed the presence of HEU particles and also showed the presence of traces of plutonium.[125] Iran explained the HEU contamination as originating from leaking TRR fuel assemblies fabricated from HEU.[126]

## SECRET NUCLEAR MATERIALS AND EXPERIMENTS

### Iran's Undeclared Uranium Imports

Twelve years after, in late February 2003, Iran finally acknowledged importing 1.8 metric tons of natural uranium in 1991 in various forms from China, something the IAEA had already learned just shortly before from the supplier state. Iran also revealed that the material had been stored in the previously undeclared site, the Jabr Ibn Hayan Multipurpose Laboratories (JHL) at the TNRC. By not reporting this material at the time it was received, Iran had violated its obligations under its NPT safeguards agreement, and it extended that violation by failing to declare the subsequent processing and use of the material, as well as the facilities where it was stored and processed. The fact that the imported nuclear material consisting of

- 1,005 kg natural uranium hexafluoride ($UF_6$),
- 402 kg natural uranium tetrafluoride ($UF_4$, green salt), and
- 401.5 kg natural uranium oxide ($UO_2$)

was not suitable for use directly as the fissile component of a nuclear weapon did not detract, in the IAEA's view, from the seriousness of Iran's failures to report its import and subsequent use in a "timely manner."[127]

An additional 50 kg of natural uranium metal was imported from China in 1993, as Iran informed the IAEA in the October 21, 2003 letter. Of this, 8 kg was for AVLIS laser experiments from 1993 to 2000 in the LSL and CSL at the TNRC, and 22 kg was used during October 2002 – February 2003 in AVLIS experiments at the Lashkar Ab'ad pilot enrichment plant. Iran had failed to report the importation of the natural uranium metal in 1993 to the IAEA and its transfer to laser enrichment experiments.[128]

A decade earlier, both before and after the Iranian revolution, other quantities of uranium had been imported by Iran. The material consisted of 20 kg of depleted $U_3O_8$ and 50 kg of depleted $UO_2$ imported in 1977 (which was exempted from safeguards by the IAEA in 1978), and 531 metric tons of yellowcake imported in 1982 and reported to the IAEA in 1990.[129]

### Conversion Experiments and Target Irradiation

Conversion refers to the sequence of chemical processes that takes uranium ore concentrate (UOC or yellowcake) into gasified uranium (uranium hexafluoride or $UF_6$) [to be fed] for feed into an enrichment plant. It also describes the reverse set of processes going from enriched $UF_6$ to uranium oxide ($UO_2$) or metal for fuel or weapons. The JHL was central in Iran's uranium conversion experiments. Iran disclosed in March 2003 that it had converted almost all of the $UF_4$ imported from China in 1991 to metal in a series of 113 experiments at the JHL in 2000.[130] Iran's rationale for the conversion experiments was that it had made a decision in the 1990s to include a uranium metal production line in the UCF that was to be constructed at the Esfahan Nuclear Technology Center (ENTC), based on the possibility that Iran might want to choose a metal-fueled reactor for its future nuclear power program. Yet another justification given was to produce heavy metal for radiation shielding material.[131]

The primary role of uranium metal in Iran's fuel cycle activities remained for a time clouded in uncertainty. Not until the disclosure of Iran's laser enrichment program in Vice President Aghazadeh's letter of October 21, 2003 to the IAEA did it become clear that the uranium metal was destined as feed for the Iran's AVLIS enrichment process experiments. Iran further reported using an additional 30 kg of undeclared natural uranium metal, imported in 1993, in its AVLIS experiments: 8 kg in 1999–2000 at the TNRC and 22 kg in October 2002–February 2003 at Lashkar Ab'ad.[132]

Most of the imported $UO_2$ remained unused. Iran initially denied using any nuclear material to test even the most difficult conversion processes that would be incorporated at the Esfahan UCF. In February 2003, Iran did acknowledge using some natural uranium at the JHL in tests of parts of the conversion process, such as dissolution of uranium in nitric acid and production of uranyl nitrate, the purification of uranium in pulse columns, and the production of ammonium uranyl carbonate (AUC), a key intermediate stage in conversion processes. Forty-eight kilograms of $UO_2$ were used in those experiments, and the waste was disposed of at Esfahan and Qom.

In April 2003, Iran also admitted to irradiating an additional 1–2 kg of $UO_2$ in undeclared isotope production experiments at the TRR, followed up by separation of the radioisotope Iodine-131 in a lead-shielded hot cell at the Molybdenum, Iodine, and Xenon radioisotope production facility (MIX facility) in Tehran. The nuclear waste from that activity was sent for disposal to Esfahan, Anarak, and Qom.[133]

Later in 2003, Iran acknowledged that it had irradiated seven kilograms of depleted $UO_2$ in targets that were prepared at the ENTC and subsequently reprocessed in shielded glove boxes at the TNRC to recover plutonium.[134]

But Iran denied any need to test other processes, such as the conversion of $UO_2$ to $UF_4$ and $UF_4$ to $UF_6$, important steps on the chemical engineering learning curve. Iran told the IAEA that the process designs and test reports obtained from China were sufficient to allow the AEOI to complete the design and manufacture of equipment for the UCF and that all experimental equipment related to the $UF_4$ and $UF_6$ experiments was dismantled and moved to waste storage at the Nuclear Research Center for Agriculture and Medicine (NRCAM) at Karaj.[135]

The story was changed in August 2003, when Iran admitted to carrying out some "bench scale" (kilogram quantity) conversion experiments. Also, Iran disclosed laboratory-scale $UO_2$ to $UF_4$ conversion experiments in the 1990s at the radiochemistry laboratories at the TNRC using depleted imported $UO_2$ whose absence was disguised as "process loss" in the declaration made to the IAEA in 1998. This material, which was imported in 1977, had been exempted from safeguards on receipt but was returned to safeguards in Iran's 1998 declaration. Iran saw the need to acknowledge the experiments only after the IAEA's July 2003 waste analysis showed the presence of depleted $UF_4$.[136]

Iran further acknowledged in early October 2003 that virtually all the materials important in the stages of the conversion of yellowcake to centrifuge plant feed— ammonium uranyl carbonate (AUC), uranium trioxide ($UO_3$), uranium tetrafluoride ($UF_4$), and uranium hexafluoride ($UF_6$)—had been produced in laboratory and bench-scale experiments between 1981 and 1993 at the TNRC and the ENTC. These experiments had not been reported to the IAEA at the time. Some, such as those involving pulse columns, continued until early 2002. The experiments in fuel cycle chemistry involved the bench-scale preparation of $UO_2$ at the Esfahan ENTC and of AUC, $UO_3$, $UF_4$, and $UF_6$ at the TNRC.[137] The $UF_4$ to $UF_6$ experiments ended in 1993. From 1995 to 2002, Iran developed techniques to convert $UF_4$ to uranium metal, and it did research and development on processes for the UCF between 1997 and 2002.[138]

Initially, Iranian authorities had stated that none of the natural $UF_6$ imported in 1991 had been processed, nor had any been used in centrifuge enrichment tests. Yet, when IAEA inspectors examined the cylinders of $UF_6$ at the JBL in March 2003, they found that one was 1.9 kg lighter than declared, a discrepancy that Iran explained away as due to a leaking valve or evaporation.[139] In fact, the 1.9 kg of $UF_6$ was used for testing centrifuges at the Kalaye Electric Company workshop between 1999 and 2002, as Iran conceded in the October 21, 2003 letter of Aghazadeh to the IAEA.[140]

## Plutonium Production and Separation

In October 2003, Iran revealed to IAEA that between 1988 and 1992 it had irradiated 6.9 kg of depleted $UO_2$ in targets at the five megawatt (MW) TRR. Three kilograms of the irradiated $UO_2$ was processed in a hot cell using three shielded glove boxes at the nuclear safety building of the TNRC in order to separate small quantities of plutonium, which was stored at JHL. The remaining 3.9 kg of irradiated targets was stored in containers at the TNRC. The wastes from the activities were sent to Anarak and Qom.

While the targets were prepared at the ENTC from material that itself had been exempted from safeguards in 1978, under its safeguards agreement, Iran should have reported to the IAEA both the irradiation of the material and the plutonium separation. In 1998, rather than admitting to the true use of the uranium in targets, Iran had declared its absence to the IAEA as process loss. In typical fashion, Iran explained that the target irradiation at the TRR was solely for the production of the fission product isotopes of molybdenum, iodine, and xenon to be stored in the MIX facility. Iran started construction of the MIX facility in 1995, but never commissioned it because the neutron flux of the TRR was not sufficient to permit production of radioisotopes with natural uranium targets.[141]

The separated plutonium was stored in solution as plutonium nitrate in two small bottles, which were provided by Iran to the IAEA for verification purposes in early November 2003. The contents of one of the bottles had completely leaked out into the overpack, making the determination of the original volume of the solution impossible. Iran estimated that approximately 200 micrograms (0.2 of a milligram) of plutonium was present originally in the solution. However, the IAEA calculated that a "substantially" larger amount of plutonium would have been produced under the radiation conditions in the reactor.[142] The IAEA gave an estimate in the milligram range,[143] perhaps 2 milligrams, ten times greater. Iran, after some revisions, conceded the point while arguing that its plutonium separation efficiency was very low.[144]

The IAEA's measurements indicated that the age of the plutonium in solution was less than the 12–16 years claimed by Iran. From its analysis of both the solutions and contamination of the used glove box stored at Esfahan, the IAEA also suggested that there appeared to be other sources of plutonium than just the irradiated targets. This was based on the presence of other plutonium isotopes—Pu-240 and Pu-241—that are produced in uranium target irradiation along with Pu-239. Some of the plutonium contamination in the glove box had a Pu-240 fraction different from that found in the plutonium solution bottles. The presence of only milligram quantities of plutonium in the solution appeared inconsistent with the large amount of americium-241 (Am-241), the decay product Pu-241, found in the glove box. And some only slightly irradiated natural uranium was detected, which Iran explained as coming from the iodine-131 production experiments.[145]

Iran explained the plutonium with the higher Pu-240 abundance and the high Am-241 content as the result of experiments between 1982 and 1984 at the TNRC radiochemistry laboratories on smoke detectors using Am-241 that had been imported before the 1979 revolution.[146] Samples taken from the plutonium solution in September 2004 again confirmed that the age of the plutonium in the bottles appeared to be less than the declared 12–16 years old, meaning that it could have been separated after 1993.

In April 2005, Iran told the IAEA that the plutonium nitrate in the two bottles had been purified and converted into a number of plutonium disks for alpha spectroscopy in the years 1995 and 1998. Iran's reports were rife with inconsistencies. An IAEA analysis of eight of the disks revealed a Pu-240 content that was significantly lower than in the solution in the bottles. The number of unprocessed irradiated $UO_2$ targets stored in four containers at the Karaj Waste Storage Facility, as verified during August 1–9, 2005, was found to be greater than what Iran had declared, and a preliminary assessment indicated that they had been irradiated for a longer period than originally stated by Iran.[147] In April 2006, Iran repeated its earlier explanations of the inconsistencies identified in the plutonium analysis, and the IAEA reported that it was unable to exclude the possibility that the plutonium it had analyzed "was derived from source(s) other than the ones declared by Iran."[148]

Iran portrayed its irradiation experiments as being directed mainly to the production of radioisotopes for medical and industrial uses, while the IAEA was interested in detecting any fuel reprocessing efforts to separate plutonium. This would require hot cells (small reprocessing laboratories) to recover the material from irradiated targets, and the dimensions of the hot cells and their radiation shielding would be an indication of their intended use, whether for small targets or discharged fuel assemblies. The IAEA was interested in the details of Iran's past efforts to procure hot cell windows and manipulators for "long lived" isotopes, which had been abandoned because of procurement difficulties. In August 2004, Iran presented drawings received in 1977 from a foreign supplier for hot cells to be constructed at Esfahan. Iran said it had used these drawings in preparing specifications for manipulators to be used to recover cobalt and iridium radioisotopes in hot cells for the planned IR-40 heavy-water moderated research reactor at Arak.[149]

The IAEA took environmental samples on August 8, 2005 from one of the storage containers at Karaj, and the analysis, completed a year later, indicated the presence of HEU particles. On August 15, 2006, the IAEA requested Iran to provide information about the source of the contamination and the past use of the containers.[150] Iran's reply explained that the containers had been used only for temporary storage of the targets and had been used to store other items.[151] Further analysis of the samples taken at Karaj also showed the presence of plutonium, which had remained undetected in the earlier analysis.[152]

## Polonium-210 Experiments

The IAEA inspectors were in for a small surprise. In September 2003, examining records in connection with Iran's undeclared irradiation of uranium oxide targets in the TRR during the 1989—1993 period, they found references to the irradiation of bismuth metal during the same period. Bismuth is not a nuclear material subject to IAEA safeguards, but its use is of great concern because irradiation of bismuth in a reactor produces polonium-210 (Po-210), an intensely radioactive alpha emitter (its half life is 138.4 days compared to 24,100 years for plutonium-239). Alloyed with beryllium, it was used as the neutron "initiator" in the Nagasaki nuclear bomb and other early nuclear weapon designs to provide a source of neutrons at the opportune moment to start the chain reaction.

In November 2003, Iran informed the IAEA that the bismuth irradiation had been part of a feasibility study for using the Po-210 as a heat source in a radioisotope thermoelectric generator (RTG), i.e., a "nuclear battery,"[153] that would be used in a relatively short-lived spy satellite or as a power source in remote areas. Early on, around 1959, RTGs for the U.S. SNAP-3 satellite program used

Po-210 but soon switched to longer lived plutonium-238 as the heat source.[154] Russia also developed RTGs using Po-210 and two are still in orbit on 1965 Cosmos navigation satellites.[155] Generally, Po-210 is no longer used as a power source.

The rapid death of ex-KGB agent Alexander Litvinenko in London on November 23, 2006 after ingestion of a microgram quantity of Po-210 brought attention to the highly radioactive isotope's potential as a tool in espionage and terrorism. Other than being produced in a reactor, Po-210 occurs naturally in trace quantities in uranium ore, in radium-226, and in tobacco. In submicrogram quantities, it is plated to brushes or other devices that are used to eliminate static in textile mills and on photography.[156] Russia is the main commercial producer for that purpose.

The IAEA learned from interviews in January 2004 with two of the Iranian scientists involved in the bismuth project that two bismuth targets had been irradiated at the TRR and that an attempt to extract Po-210 from one was unsuccessful, while the other was discarded. The scientists reiterated that the polonium was for the development of RTGs, but subsequently, Iranian officials said that the experiments were also part of a study on neutron sources.[157] Attempts by Iran to buy beryllium metal were not successful.[158]

## THE URANIUM CONVERSION FACILITY

Iran dutifully fulfilled its safeguards obligations for the UCF that was under construction fifteen kilometers southeast of Esfahan. It regularly sent design information to the IAEA, starting with the preliminary information in July 2000. Yet, before Iran's declaration of the centrifuge facilities at Natanz in February 2003, the design information on the UCF left out Iran's intention to use the $UF_6$ produced at the conversion facility as feed for an indigenous enrichment plant. Before February 2003, Iran's stated plans called for sending the $UF_6$ produced at the UCF outside Iran for U-235 enrichment and then returning the LEU, and the depleted uranium (DU) from the enrichment plant waste stream, to the UCF for conversion back to low-enriched $UO_2$ for power reactor fuel and to low-enriched or depleted uranium metal.[159]

According to Iran, the design of the UCF was based on designs provided by China in the early 1990s. The AEOI had signed a contract with the China National Nuclear Corporation (CNNC) for construction of a complex, the Esfahan Nuclear Research and Production Center (ENFRPC), including the UCF. Originally, the UCF was to have been constructed by the Chinese company under a turnkey contract, but that was cancelled in 1997, evidently before the supply of any equipment. Then in 1999, Iranian companies began construction on their own, using the supplier's blueprints and equipment test reports. All parts and equipment, Iran claimed, were manufactured indigenously.[160] The first operation at the UCF occurred from March to May 2004, with the conversion of 1.24 metric tons of UOC to natural $UF_6$. The stages involved were the conversion of UOC into $UO_2$ and $UF_4$, and $UF_4$ into $UF_6$.[161]

The production capacity of the UCF plant, as specified in the July 2000 design information, was two hundred metric tons of $UF_6$ per year. The selection of UCF process lines gives some idea of the intended direction of the nuclear program. The lines, using updated design information provided in July 2003, included:

- Uranium ore concentrate to natural $UF_6$
- Natural $UF_6$ to natural $UO_2$
- Low-enriched (5% U-235) $UF_6$ to $UO_2$—30 metric tons per year of $UO_2$
- Natural $UF_4$ to natural uranium metal
- Depleted $UF_6$ to $UF_4$—170 metric tons per year of depleted $UF_4$
- Low-enriched (19.7% U-235) $UF_4$ to 19.7 percent U-235 uranium metal—30 kg per year[162]

IAEA inspectors first became aware of the dedicated line for conversion of natural $UF_4$ to natural metal in 2000. Reference to it subsequently appeared in Iran's April 2003 design update, replacing a line in the 2000 design for converting depleted $UF_4$ to metal, introduced as a way of reducing storage space for depleted $UF_6$, Iran said. The explanations offered for natural metal line were to provide shielding material and to anticipate the possibility of a metal-fueled reactor in Iran's future nuclear power plans. The real reason, however, was to provide the natural uranium metal feed for the AVLIS laser enrichment process, something unknown until the declarations in the October 21, 2003 letter to the IAEA.

The process line for natural $UF_6$ to natural $UO_2$ was added in the 2003 design information to provide fuel for the planned IR-40 heavy-water moderated research reactor. The purpose of the 19.7 percent U-235 line was to accommodate fabrication of LEU fuel for the TRR to replace the initial supply that was fabricated in Argentina from 19.7 percent LEU supplied by Russia. The natural and low-enriched $UO_2$ were to be sent to the fuel manufacturing plant (FMP) planned at Esfahan for fabrication into research and power reactor fuel. Only after the February 2003 declaration of the PFEP and FEP at Natanz did Iran acknowledge its intention to enrich $UF_6$ domestically as feed to the UCF.[163]

As of January 2007, Iran said that it had stored 250 metric tons of uranium in $UF_6$ produced at the UCF in underground tunnels there.[164] On April 8, 2007, at a National Day of Nuclear Technology ceremony in Natanz, AEOI head Reza Aghazadeh said that 270 metric tons of $UF_6$ had been produced over the past year.[165]

## HEAVY-WATER PRODUCTION AND THE ARAK REACTOR

### The Heavy Water Plant

The revelations by the MEK/NCRI in August 2002 referred to Iran's construction of a heavy-water production plant (HWPP) near Arak, in the Khondab region, to produce heavy water (deuterium oxide, $D_2O$) by extracting it from ordinary water, in which deuterium occurs naturally in less than 200 parts per million (ppm). The plant was situated on the river Qara-Chai in order to supply the large amount of needed water. The MEK/NCRI asserted that the plant was a secret AEOI project, outside the supervision of Iran's Organization for Planning and Budget.[166] Iranian Vice President Aghazadeh was questioned by IAEA Director General Elbaradei in September 2002 about the MEK/NCRI report on the HWPP at Arak, as well as the centrifuge enrichment plants at Natanz, and Elbaradei was allowed to visit both the Arak and Natanz sites from February 21 to February 22, 2003, when Iraq confirmed the existence of the facilities there.[167]

Heavy water is not a material that falls under NPT safeguards. However, its primary use is as a moderator in nuclear research and plutonium production reactors and in commercial power reactors that use natural uranium fuel. If it is employed in operations that fall under IAEA safeguards, such as a in a reactor, then its use must be reported to the IAEA. The advantage of deuterium (a heavy isotope of hydrogen) as a reactor moderator is its effectiveness in slowing down neutrons without absorbing them and, thus, allowing the use of natural uranium fuel in the reactor, without any enrichment. Such fuel, however, when irradiated in a reactor for a period of time, is a fertile source of plutonium for nuclear weapons. Canada is the world's largest producer, using the so-called Girdler-Sulphide process to produce high-purity heavy water for its CANDU commercial power reactors.

### The IR-40 Reactor

Iran's acknowledgement of plans for a heavy-water moderated reactor was soon to follow its confirmation of the heavy-water production plant. On May 5, 2003, Iran informed the IAEA of its intention to construct a heavy-water moderated and cooled research reactor at Arak, beginning in June 2004. It would be the 40 MW Iran Nuclear Research Reactor (IR-40), eight times the rated power of the TRR in Tehran. The basic design of the IR-40 was completed in 2002, and a decision was made then to construct it in Arak rather than in Esfahan.[168]

To fabricate the reactor's natural $UO_2$ fuel, Iran planned to begin construction of the FMP in Esfahan in 2003, with operation expected in 2007. The IAEA monitored the ongoing civil engineering construction of the reactor using satellite imagery.[169] In August 2006, it was reported that the reactor would go into operation in 2009, although another report said it would be postponed until 2011.[170] In full operation, the 40 MW IR-40 reactor would be able to produce 10–12 kilograms of plutonium per year, sufficient for two nuclear weapons.

In a letter of August 19, 2003 to the IAEA, Iran provided information on the heavy water requirements of the reactor (80–90 metric tons initially and less than 1 metric ton per year) and on the design capacity of the heavy—water production plant (8 metric tons per year with the option for expansion to twice that capacity). It also stated that production of heavy water was to start in 2004. The Arak heavy—water plant was to be a pilot facility to test the Girdler-Sulfide process.[171] On April 26, 2006, President Ahmadinejad inaugurated the Arak heavy—water plant at doubled capacity of 16 metric tons per year over its startup capacity in 2004.[172]

Iranian officials said that, in planning the IR-40 to meet Iran's needs for medical and industrial isotope production and R&D, they had tried unsuccessfully to acquire a research reactor from abroad. Iran reportedly received blueprints for a heavy-water research reactor from Russia.[173] The only alternative was the indigenously designed IR-40. The 5 MW TRR that it would replace was reaching its safety limits after thirty-five years of operation in a growing suburb of Tehran. The natural $UO_2$ would be produced at the FMP and the Zirconium Production Plant (ZPP) in Esfahan.

The decision to start design of a heavy-water moderated reactor was made in the early 1980s, when Iranian officials were uncertain whether their uranium enrichment plans would succeed. In its October 21, 2003 letter, Iran said that foreign experts had been consulted on some aspects of the design. The decision to construct was made in the mid-1990s, and laboratory scale experiments in heavy-water production were conducted in Esfahan at the ENTC. The production of both "long lived" and "short lived isotopes" was under consideration.[174]

At its meeting on November 23, 2006, the IAEA Board omitted the IR-40 from the list of facilities voted to receive "atoms for peace" technical assistance, apparently over concerns that it would be used as a source of plutonium.[175] Resolutions of the IAEA Board have repeatedly called on Iran to abandon the project. In particular, Iran ignored UN Security Council Resolution 1737, passed on December 23, 2007, which gave it a sixty-day period to halt heavy-water-related activities as well as enrichment and reprocessing. But, as the IAEA reported in February 2007, satellite imagery showed that all the construction and operation activities were continuing.[176]

The capacity of the FMP fuel plant, announced by Iran in August 2004, was to be 40 metric tons of $UO_2$ per year to accommodate the IR-40 (about 10 metric tons of natural $UO_2$ per year) and the Bushehr Nuclear Power Plant (about 25 metric tons of $UO_2$ enriched up to 5 percent U-235 per year).[177]

As for the FMP, on July 25, 2007, the IAEA carried out a physical inventory verification (PIV) at the FMP and found the installation of process equipment there to be in an advanced stage but that the facility was not yet operational.[178]

### *Estimates*

| IR-40 Plutonium Production | |
|---|---|
| Plutonium to be produced | 10–12 kg (22–26.4 lb) per year |
| Nuclear weapons | Enough for two nuclear weapons per year |

## IR-40 Hot Cells—How Many, What For

A review of design drawings by visiting IAEA inspectors in July 2003 and updated design information provided in early August 2003 raised concern because there was no reference to hot cells that would be needed to process irradiated targets, if radioisotope production was indeed one of the purposes of the IR-40. Iran's October 21, 2003 letter to the IAEA stated that design information and dimensions for the hot cells were uncertain and unavailable because of uncertainty about the dimensions of the heavy manipulators and shielded windows that could be procured from abroad. Iran indicated, however, that 9 hot cells were planned: 4 for the production of medical isotopes, 2 for cobalt-60 and iridium-192 sources, 3 for waste processing, with another 10 as backup.[179]

The IAEA appeared to be suspicious of Iran's intentions. Were the hot cells intended for reprocessing the spent fuel, perhaps to recover plutonium, or were they for recovering radioisotopes from special targets after irradiation in the reactor? The IAEA had received information from another state, in connection with Iran's efforts to procure manipulators and leaded glass windows, that showed specifications for hot cells with walls 1.4 meters thick, more appropriate for handling spent fuel than for the stated purpose of radioisotope production.[180]

During an October 2004 visit, the IAEA asked Iran to explain how it could give precise specifications for the manipulators and windows it was trying to procure without having any preliminary hot cell designs. Iran answered that the specifications used were based on the foreign designs provided from the 1970s as well as on hot cells at the MIX facility at the TNRC, and it showed the IAEA drawings of hot cells capable of handling 100 to 10,000 curies of radioactivity[181]

In November 2003, Iran noted plans to construct an additional building at the Arak site to hold hot cells to recover "long lived" radioisotopes, while hot cells in the original building would recover the "short lived" ones, but by May 2004 the additional building was cancelled because of difficulties in obtaining the manipulators and windows from abroad.[182]

## COMMERCIAL NUCLEAR POWER: THE BUSHEHR PLANT

Iran's long standing project to build the 1000 megawatt electrical (MWe) Bushehr Nuclear Power Plant (BNPP-1) near Bushehr, a city on the Persian Gulf about 750 kilometers southwest of Tehran, was started by German company Siemens in 1970 and then abandoned in the early stages of construction following the 1979 revolution. In January 1995, Iran signed an agreement with Russia to complete the project. The one-billion-dollar plant, which is being constructed by the Russian state company, Atomstroiexport, is a third-generation Russian design VVER-1000 reactor. The reactor core is to be loaded with 79.5 metric tons of about 4 percent enriched uranium dioxide ($UO_2$) fuel having a three-year life cycle.[183]

A 2002 report claims that Russian aid to Iran flows through two channels, an open one giving assistance to the construction of Bushehr, and a second, secret channel, through which Russian companies supply technology and parts to assist in the production of nuclear weapons.[184]

Russia sought an agreement to supply the fuel for the Bushehr reactor and take it back when discharged to ensure that Iran could not separate plutonium from the spent fuel and divert it to weapons purposes. On February 27, 2005, Iranian Vice President Gholam-Reza Aghazadeh, head of the AEOI, and Alexander Rumyantsev, chief of the Russian Federal Atomic Energy Agency (RosAtom), signed an agreement on Russia taking back spent fuel.[185] A next step was taken on September 26, 2006, when Russia reached an agreement with Iran to supply about eighty tons of LEU fuel for the Bushehr reactor to Iran by March 2007. The agreement was signed by Sergei Shmatko, head of Russia's Atomstroiexport, and Mahmoud Hanatian, vice president of the AEOI. Even though the enrichment and fabrication of the fuel would be done in Russia, there was some concern in the West that the uranium could be diverted for further enrichment into weapons grade.[186]

Despite constant U.S. pressure on Russia to abandon all nuclear assistance to Iran, Russia kept to the construction schedule. The reactor was scheduled for startup in September 2007 and electricity generation by November 2007.[187] However, a dispute reputedly over Iran wanting to make its monthly $25 million payment in euros rather than dollars delayed shipment of the first LEU fuel loading of about 100 metric tons until mid-2008.[188] Subsequently, Russia was reported to have said that fuel would not be delivered until Iran suspended its indigenous enrichment activities.[189] This hesitancy to complete the reactor and supply the first fuel loading came at a time when Russia was exploring with the IAEA the establishment of an international uranium enrichment center in Siberia.[190]

## URANIUM EXPLORATION, MINING, AND MILLING

Iran's known conventional uranium reserves are very limited and the concentration of uranium in its ore deposits is low. Conventional uranium deposits, worldwide, are found in igneous rock and sandstone. Low-grade uranium is also recovered as a byproduct of phosphate mining for fertilizer.

The AEOI began prospecting for uranium in 1974 and discovered deposits in the central part of the country in Yazd province which holds Iran's largest phosphate deposits, in the Azerbaijan provinces in the northwest, and in the south near the city of Bandar Abbas.[191] It was reported in the 1990s that Iran was receiving assistance in uranium mining and milling from China and Russia.[192] Iran has frequently publicized the discovery of new deposits; for example, in May 2006, Iran announced the discovery of three new uranium deposits in central Iran in the Khoshoumi region and in Chah Juleh and Narigan.[193]

Iran has focused on developing uranium mines in two places, at Saghand in Yazd, with a capacity of fifty metric tons of uranium per year, and Gchine near Bandar Abbas, with a capacity of twenty-one metric tons per year. In the Additional Protocol declarations of May 2004, Iran first provided the IAEA with information on the location, operational status, and production capacity of the Saghand and Gchine uranium mines and mills.[194]

Saghand has two mines, an open pit mine holding 10 percent of the uranium reserves and an underground mine, holding 90 percent of the reserves, with two 357-meter deep shafts sunk into low-grade hard-rock ore bodies. With the infrastructure and shaft sinking essentially completed and tunneling toward the ore bodies begun, ore production was expected to start by the end of 2006. The total estimated reserves at Saghand is 1.58 million tons of uranium ore with an average uranium concentration of 553 parts per million (ppm). The mine's projected annual output of 120,000 metric tons of uranium ore is to be processed into uranium ore concentrate (yellowcake) at the Yellowcake Production Plant (YPP) in Ardakan, nearby the mine in Yazd province. The start up of the Ardakan mill site is was set to coincide with the start of mining at Saghand.[195]

The Gchine uranium mine has a colocated mill, the Bandar Abbas Uranium Production Plant (BUP). The low, variable-grade uranium ore found at Gchine in near-surface deposits is being open-pit mined and processed at the mill. Iran informed the IAEA that mining operations had started there as of July 2004 and that the mill had been hot tested.[196]

Iran also carried out small-scale experiments at the TNRC on recovering uranium as a byproduct from phosphoric acid. In addition, several hundred kilograms of yellowcake were extracted in facilities employing percolation leaching at the Gchine site that were subsequently dismantled.[197]

## Suspicions About the Gchine Mine

The IAEA raised concerns undeclared mining and milling activities at Gchine, hinting at the possibility of a parallel military program there, and it asked to see copies of the original contract between the AEOI and the engineering company that constructed the BUP mill. The IAEA had two questions. Why had the AEOI suspended work at the Gchine project between 1994 and 2000 while pursuing the less promising mine at Saghand?[198] And, once the Gchine project was resumed, how could the newly founded company, which had only limited experience in uranium ore processing, manage to design, procure, build, and test the ore grinding process line for the mill in the short time between 2000 and mid-2001?[199]

In April 2005, Iran provided a copy of the contract with the engineering company, dated June 13, 2000, and some final "as built" drawings. Suspiciously, on some additional drawings shown to the IAEA in August 2005 from the first attempts to construct the process line, the names of the people involved in preparing the drawings and the company were blacked out, as were project numbers and dates, to protect commercial secrets, Iran said. Moreover, Iran produced an abundance of purchase orders placed around 2002 for the later stages of the development of the process line, but it could not provide any purchase orders for the earlier procurement of the equipment for the line. Its explanation was that the new, inexperienced company initially purchased most of the grinding equipment off the shelf.[200]

## Iran's Limited Uranium Resources

The 2003 "Red Book" lists Iran's uranium resources as 1,427 metric tons of known resources and 13,850 metric tons of undiscovered resources (in the estimated and the speculative categories) for a total of 15,277 metric tons of uranium.[201] Iran's known uranium resources would meet the fuel reload needs of the 1,000 MWe BNNP-1, scheduled to go into operation in late 2007, for about six years. Including the "undiscovered" resources, Iranian uranium could supply Bushehr for about sixty years.

The Bushehr core loading of 76.5 metric tons of uranium oxide fuel enriched to about 4 percent U-235 contains 70 metric tons of uranium. Operating on a three-year life cycle, the reactor must be reloaded with about 23 metric tons of uranium in fresh fuel every year. About 53,000 P-1 centrifuges are needed to enrich a single 23-metric ton annual reload, which is about the number Iran says it is eventually planning to install at Natanz. If Iran builds additional nuclear power reactors, more advanced centrifuges with higher separative capacity would be needed at Natanz if the enrichment of their fuel were to be done solely at Natanz. While installing some 50,000 centrifuge machines is unlikely in the near term, the total of known and undiscovered uranium resources would be enough to supply about 74 annual reloads, enough for the forty-year lifetime of the Bushehr reactor and a second one of the same design. Alternatively, the total resources would provide a thirteen-year supply for Bushehr reloads and the initial cores and reloads of six more similar reactors, with one coming on line every two years.[202]

However, long-range plans of Iran for civil nuclear power have called for seven 1,000 MW nuclear power plants by 2020 and twenty plants by 2030.[203] Iran could produce only part of the low-enriched nuclear fuel domestically, based on its mining and centrifuge enrichment capacity.[204] Otherwise, following this schedule and using indigenous uranium alone for the needed fuel reloads would exhaust the total known and undiscovered resources by about 2020.[205]

Inside Iran, the ambitious goals for nuclear power have met with some skepticism due to both its resource limitations and concern that the country is located in a highly active earthquake zone inhospitable to nuclear reactors. It is claimed that one of President Ahmadinejad's first acts was to suppress a report by the Tehran University seismographic center warning of the inability of existing nuclear reactor technology to withstand earthquake tremors.[206]

### *About the Estimates*

| | |
|---|---|
| Uranium Resources— | |
| Iran's known uranium resources | 1,427 metric tons |
| Undiscovered resources | 13,850 metric tons |
| Total | 15,277 metric tons |
| Bushehr fuel[1]— | |
| Annual Bushehr-1 fuel loading | 23 metric tons, 4% enriched uranium |
| P-1 centrifuges required | about 53,000 (for 0.3% tails) |
| Uranium feed needed: | 207 metric tons/yr natural U (in UF6) |
| Nuclear weapons— | |
| One nuclear weapon per year | 15 kg/weapon, 93% enriched uranium |
| P-1 centrifuges required (2 kgSWU/yr): | 1,500 centrifuges (at 0.3% tails assay), full-time operation |
| Uranium feed needed | 3.4 metric tons/yr natural U (in $UF_6$) |
| When might Iran have nukes? | Early in next decade,[2] sooner?[3] or later?[4] |

[1] Iran has contracted with Russia to supply fresh fuel for the BNNP-1 and take back the spent fuel.

[2] V. Adm. Lowell E. Jacoby, director, DIA in statement to Senate Select Committee on Intelligence, February 16, 2005, p. 10.

[3] "The American intelligence community may be seriously underestimating Iran's progress toward a nuclear bomb"—Graham Allison, former Asst. Secretary of Defense, *YaleGlobal*, June 13, 2006; Mossad chief Meir Dagan cited by Yoav Stern, "Mossad chief: Iran will Have a Nuclear Bomb by 2009–2010," *Haaretz* December 18, 2006.

[4] A new National Intelligence Review projects that Iran is about a decade away for a sufficient quantity of HEU. Dafna Linzer, "Iran is Judged 10 Years from Nuclear Bomb," *Washington Post*, August 2, 2005.

## SUSPECT MILITARY SITES AND ACTIVITIES

There are numerous instances of reports of nuclear activities at sites connected with military organizations outside the control of the AEOI and under the jurisdiction of the Defense Industries Organization or the IRGC .

For example, the *Daily Telegraph* of London reported on June 12, 2006 that IAEA experts were pressing Iran for information on a secret military project to enrich uranium to weapons grade. The secret project, code named Zirzamin 27, was said to be located in research laboratories at a secret military base outside

Tehran and operated under the supervision of the IRGC and under the direction of Mohsen Fakhrizadeh, who was identified as head of the Modern Defensive Readiness and Technology Center.[207] The laboratories were said to be located in a hidden 2,200 square meter facility under a lake near the Lashgarak dam, some 20 kilometers northeast of Tehran.[208] Fakhrizadeh was one of the Iranian officials named in the sanctions imposed by the UN Security Council's resolution 1747 on March 24, 2007, where he is identified as a senior scientist in the Ministry of Defense and Armed Forces Logistics (MODAFL) and also as the former head of the PHRC at Lavizan-Shian, the one whom Iran would not allow to be interviewed by the IAEA.[209]

Iran had confided to the IAEA in its October 21, 2003 declaration that seven of the total of thirteen workshops that were involved in the domestic manufacture of centrifuge components for the enrichment program were owned by Iranian military industrial organizations and located on DIO sites.[210] More recently, UN Security Council resolutions 1737 and 1747 of December 2006 and March 2007 cited the involvement of DIO subordinates in making centrifuge components, naming the 7th of Tir entity specifically.[211]

## Physics Research Center PHRC

In March 2003, the MEK/NCRI organization disclosed secret nuclear activities under the MOD at the Lavizan-Shian site in the northeastern part of Tehran. Subsequently, sensitive equipment was removed from the site, and after November 2003 the site was razed in an attempt to eliminate any trace of the secret activities. The leveling of the site was revealed in satellite images released in March 2004. At its June 2004 meeting, the IAEA Board of Governors took up the question of alleged nuclear related activities at Lavizan-Shian and the possibility of a concealment effort indicated by the demolition of buildings. On June 28, 2004, the IAEA was allowed to visit the site and take environmental samples. Iran also provided access to two whole body counters that had been acquired, with trailers, from a foreign source and currently were located at a clinic in Tehran and at Malek Ashtar University of Technology in Esfahan. Only the whole body counter at the Tehran clinic was originally at the demolished Lavizan-Shian site, Iran said, and only its trailer was allowed to be sampled.[212]

Interest focused on the PHRC at the Lavizan-Shian site and evidence of dual-use equipment and possible parallel military and civilian nuclear programs there, particularly in uranium conversion and laser enrichment.[213] According to Iran, the PHRC was established in 1989 to provide scientific advice and services to the MOD and preparedness for responding to casualties from nuclear attacks and accidents. Iran provided a list of the eleven activities that were conducted at the PHRC, but it refused to give the IAEA a list of the equipment used there. It claimed that no nuclear material that might be required to be reported under the NPT safeguards agreement had been used at the PHRC and that no nuclear fuel cycle activities were carried out there. Iran explained that the site had been razed by the municipality of Tehran in a period of two or three months, starting in December 2003, after a decision ordering its return to the municipality for use as a park.[214] Iran noted that three government organizations had been located a Lavizan-Shian between 1989 and 2004. The PHRC, it said, had been terminated in 1998. Then the facility became the Biological Study Center, devoted to biological R&D and "radioprotection" activities, and in 2002, the site was changed again into the Applied Physics Institute, although some biological activities continued there.[215]

The IAEA's analysis of the vegetation and soil samples collected at Lavizan-Shian showed no evidence of nuclear material, but this was not unexpected, since the extensive razing the site would have made the detection of nuclear material in soil samples very difficult. Moreover, the removal of buildings made it impossible to verify what activities had taken place.[216]

With only limited success, the IAEA undertook to acquire additional information and clarification and to interview individuals, including two former heads of the PHRC, who were involved in efforts there to acquire dual-use materials and equipment that could be used for uranium enrichment and conversion activities.[217] In addition, it sought to take samples from the second whole-body counter trailer in Esfahan.[218] On January 26, 2006, Iran provided the IAEA with documents showing the unsuccessful attempts to acquire a number of dual use items—electric drive and power supply equipment and laser equipment, including a dye laser. Other equipment on the list included balancing machines, mass spectrometers, magnets, and fluorine handling equipment, all apparently relevant to uranium enrichment. The documents showed involvement of the PHRC in the procurement effort. Nevertheless, Iran said, the equipment was actually intended for a laboratory at a technical university where a former head of the PHRC was a professor, but it declined to let the IAEA interview him.[219]

In January 2006, the IAEA presented Iran with a list of high-vacuum equipment that had been purchased by the PHRC. The IAEA was allowed to take environmental samples from some of this equipment, which was located at the technical university. It continued, but with little success, to seek out further information on the PHRC's procurement activities and the relation between the PHRC and the technical university.[220]

In a turnaround on February 26, 2006, the IAEA was allowed to meet with one of the former heads of the PHRC. He said that the dual-use equipment and the vacuum equipment had been used for R&D in various departments at the technical university and that his connections through the PHRC had been used to procure the equipment for the university, but he denied any knowledge of the research being done with it. The vacuum equipment, he suggested was being used by the physics department for such benign purposes as vacuum coating and nanotechnology applications.[221] As noted, Iran continued to refuse the IAEA permission to interview the other former head of the PHRC, Mohsen Fakhrizadeh, who was sanctioned for various military-related activities under UN Security Council resolution 1747 voted on March 24,

Finally the IAEA hit onto something. Analysis of the environmental samples taken at the technical university in January 2006 showed the presence of a small number of particles of natural and HEU.[222] Iran continued to deny access to other equipment at the university.[223] Then on November 28, 2006, Iran announced that it would allow the IAEA to take environmental sampling on additional equipment at the university traced to the demolished PHRC.[224]

## The Green Salt Project

The so-called Green Salt Project refers to alleged studies by Iran that came to the attention of the IAEA on the conversion of $UO_2$ to $UF_4$ and on tests of high explosives and the design of a missile reentry vehicle. The source of the IAEA's information was reported to be U.S. intelligence."Green salt" is the name used by metallurgists for uranium hexafluoride ($UF_4$), the intermediate step in conversion of $UO_2$ to $UF_6$, as well as the reconversion of enriched $UF_6$ back to enriched uranium metal. The studies appeared to be related and had a possible secret military to the conversion of uranium to metal and the fabrication of nuclear warhead components.

A January 31, 2006 brief prepared for the IAEA Board provided evidence directly suggesting that this was a separate military project. Iran was shown a copy of a process flow diagram related to bench-scale conversion as well as some communications related to the Green Salt Project at a meeting with the IAEA on January 27, 2006. Iran stated that all of its national nuclear projects were conducted by the AEOI and said the Green Salt documents were fabricated. At a February 26, 2006 meeting, Iran told the IAEA that all its national efforts were centered in the UCF project, and that it would make no sense to develop indigenous conversion when the technology for the UCF had already been obtained from abroad. The IAEA noted that the same company associated with the Green Salt project had been involved in procurement for the UCF and the design and construction of the Gchine ore processing plant.[225]

## The Stolen Laptop Computer

In parallel with the Green Salt Project, U.S. intelligence is reported to have gained possession of a stolen laptop computer, that shed light on Iran's nuclear aspirations. It was passed on in mid-2004 with German help by a contact in Iran and contained more than a thousand pages of documents in Persian that were interpreted to indicate Iranian work from 2001 to 2003 on the design of a Shahab missile nose cone to deliver a compact nuclear warhead, as well as other nuclear weapons activities. The documents detailed computer simulations, calculations, blueprints, experiments and diagnostic information, and include studies of various warhead configurations.[226]

First reference to the documents had been made to reporters by U.S. Secretary of State Colin Powell in a press briefing in November 2004, but at that time U.S. officials downplayed them because they came from a lone source that was described as unvetted and unsolicited.[227]

The documents refer only to "Shahab," but Sandia National Laboratory scientists were reported to have used computer simulations to determine that the laptop drawings were plans by Iranian engineers for expanding the nose cone of the Shahab-3 to carry a nuclear warhead and that they would have been unsuccessful, if implemented.[228] The Shahab-3 is a modified version of North Korea's Nodong missile, which itself is based on the old Soviet-made Scud.

On July 18, 2005, a U.S. team headed by Undersecretary of State Robert Joseph briefed IAEA Director General ElBaradei and other IAEA officials in Vienna on the contents of the laptop in order to convince them that Iran was trying to develop a compact warhead for delivery by the medium-range Shahab-3 missile, with the range to reach Israel and other countries in the Middle East. A test firing by Iran of a Shahab upgrade in 2004 was said to indicate that Iranian engineers had developed an advanced "triconic" nose cone that would improve range and stability but require a more compact warhead, causing some to conclude that the missile had been designed for a nuclear warhead.[229]

A State Department briefing, entitled "A History of Concealment and Conception," was then given to various countries on the IAEA Board of Governors, ahead of the Board meeting in September 2005.[230] On September 24, 2005 the Board passed a resolution condemning Iran for concealment and conception over a long period. But countries other than Britain, France, and Germany were cool to accepting the U.S. intelligence report as an indication of Iran's pursuit of a nuclear weapon.[231] The laptop is said to have also contained studies of essential nuclear warhead features, such as the spherical array of detonators around the layer of chemical high explosive whose ignition creates a shock wave to compress the enclosed fissile nuclear core. Another study was on the stable positioning a spherical "black box," resembling a heavy ball of nuclear material in a nuclear warhead, during a reentry vehicle's descent toward its target.[232] However, any relation to a nuclear weapon is was only by inference, since there was no use of the word "nuclear" and no specific reference to the fissile materials, uranium, or plutonium.[233]

The U.S. briefings contended that the research was commissioned by the IRGC and was carried out in 2001–2003 by a group that works on the Shahab missile. The program's code name is was Project 111.[234] The laptop documents make reference to a blast occurring at 600 meters (roughly 2,000 feet) above the target, an appropriate altitude for maximum damage from a nuclear explosion but of no relevance to detonation of a conventional, chemical or biological weapon.[235] In addition, the documents included sophisticated drawings of a 400-meter subterranean tunnel outfitted with remotely monitored instruments to measure pressure and temperature that appears to have been designed to test a nuclear weapon.[236]

Reports were that the laptop also contained a set of technical drawings for a small-scale uranium conversion facility by a small Tehran design firm, Kimeya Madon, set up in 2001 and operating until the early Spring of 2003. The facility, if constructed, would augment to the capability of the UCF in Esfahan to produce $UF_4$ (green salt), an intermediate step in the production of $UF_6$ gas for centrifuge enrichment, and, according to some U.S. officials, would be part of a secret, parallel military program to produce nuclear weapons. Organizations mentioned in the documents are connected to the IRGC officer, Mohsen Fakrizadeh, indicating that the work may have been done for the IRGC. Fakrizadeh was identified as director of the Project 111 by U.S. intelligence.[237]

### Parchin

On several occasions in briefings and reports the MEK/NCRI made reference to the MOD's military complex at Parchin, located in Varamin about 30 kilometers southeast of Tehran, as being a center of secret nuclear-related activities. In November 2004, Parchin was identified as the location of laser enrichment activities.[238] In September 2005, the assertion was made that Iran had built a tunnel at Parchin to hide its nuclear weapons program. This was augmented in November 2005 to include a series of interrelated tunnels and other underground locations dealing with both nuclear weapons and missile development and dedicated to the production of the nuclear-capable Shahab-3 and Ghadar missiles.[239]

Prodded by open source reports on the presence of dual use military and civil equipment and materials in Iran, the IAEA in October 2004 repeated a request to inspect the Parchin site for undeclared nuclear materials and activities. The IAEA had been permitted to visit another defense site, Kolahdouz, where it did not find any nuclear-related activities, but it was not allowed to visit the Parchin site until January 2005, and only under certain restrictive conditions. The IAEA inspection was limited to any one area out of the four it had previously specified, and it had to agree to limit its visit there to only five buildings in that chosen area. The environmental samples taken in those buildings did not indicate the presence of nuclear material, nor was any nuclear material or dual-use equipment seen there.[240]

On November 1, 2005, the IAEA was able to visit yet another area on the Parchin site. Again, environmental samples did not indicate the presence of any nuclear material, and no unusual activities were observed in the buildings visited there.[241]

## THE CHANGING SCENE

### The Security Council Votes Sanctions

Two years before the Security Council voted sanctions on Iran, the European Union countries of France, Germany, and the United Kingdom (the EU-3) had taken on the task of negotiating a suspension with Iran, and on November 15, 2004, they signed the Paris Agreement with Iran that included the suspension of all enrichment and reprocessing activities.[242] This lasted longer than any other suspension up to that time, but it finally collapsed in early January 2006, when as the Ahmadinejad regime took power, when Iran informed the IAEA that it would shortly be resuming uranium enrichment at Natanz.[243]

Soon after, on February 4, 2006, the IAEA Board passed a resolution to report Iran's nuclear activities to the Security Council and demand a resumption of the suspension of enrichment and reprocessing activities, a halt in the construction of the IR-40 research reactor at Arak, and clarification on certain activities that could have a "military nuclear dimension."[244] Iran not only had restarted feeding its centrifuges at Natanz in February 2006, but on April 13, 2006 Iran reported to the IAEA that an enrichment level of 3.6 percent had been reached, three times Iran's previously claimed enrichment level.[245]

In early June 2006, the EU foreign policy chief Javier Solana presented Tehran with a package of incentives from the EU-3 plus China, Russia and the United States to persuade Iran to halt its enrichment and reprocessing activities in exchange in return for support of its civil nuclear power program, membership in the World Trade Organization, and opening direct talks with the United States,[246] but Iran let the deadline of June 29, 2006 pass without accepting the package.[247]

The six countries then agreed to seek a UN Security Council resolution ordering Iran to freeze its nuclear activities or face the possibility of sanctions,[248] and on July 31, 2006 the Security Council passed resolution 1696 demanding that Iran suspend all enrichment and reprocessing activities by August 31, 2006, with the possibility of economic sanctions if it did not comply.[249] According to one legal opinion, the Security Council resolution overrode, pursuant to Article 40 of Chapter 7 of the UN Charter, any right Iran would have had under Article IV of the NPT to develop nuclear technology.[250] Nevertheless, Iran rejected a suspension in a twenty-one-page response handed out to diplomats on August 22, 2006.[251] In the aftermath, the IAEA Board of Governors declined to provide Iran with "atoms for peace" technical assistance for the IR-40 reactor.[252]

This was a prelude to the UN action on December 23, 2006, when the Security Council voted 15-0 to adopt resolution 1737 imposing mandatory sanctions on organizations and individuals involved in Iran's nuclear and missile programs, in a compromise at the behest of Russia that excluded military action and placed no restrictions on the Bushehr light-water nuclear power plant.[253, 254] Iran's failure to comply was followed by Security Council resolution 1747 on March 24, 2007 with expanded sanctions. Iran appeared to be totally unphased by concern in the West over its nuclear activities, particularly its development of uranium enrichment. For example, it has rejected a proposal for Iranian technicians to participate on Russian soil in enrichment activities for the low-enriched fuel of the Bushehr power reactor.[255]

Resolution 1737's sanctions froze the foreign financial assets of 12 Iranians and 10 organizations involved in Iran's nuclear and ballistic missile programs, with the exception of equipment and fuel for light-water nuclear power plants, namely the Russian-built Bushehr reactor, which was excluded. Originally, a mandatory travel ban was considered, but that was replaced by a notification to be made whenever sanctioned individuals and agency representatives crossed state boundaries. As a last minute concession to Russia and China, the final draft was amended to delete sanctions on Iran's Aerospace Industries Organization (AIO), although its subsidiaries are cited among the sanctioned entities. Ahmad Vahid Dastjerdi, head of the AIO, was blocked from any financial transactions, as were Maj. Gen. Yahya Rahim Safavi, commander of the IRGC, and Gen. Hosein Salimi, who was in charge of the air force branch of the IRGC. Others named include the AEOI vice president for R&D, officials of the Arak reactor and the Natanz PFEP, and the rector of the Malek Ashtar University of Defense Technology in Esfahan.[256,257]

## The Deadline Passes

The list of anctioned organizations included the AEOI, the Mesbah Energy Company, which was cited as the provider for IR-40 Reactor, Kalaye Electric, the Pars Trash Company, Farayand Technique, DIO, which was noted as being controlled by MODAFL, and the 7th of Tir, a subordinate organization of DIO.

Iran again ignored the UN Security Council mandate and instead ramped up its uranium enrichment activities during the sixty-day period following the December 23, 2006 resolution. The deadline expired on February 21, 2007, and President Ahmadinejad, speaking in northern Iran, vowed to continue work on nuclear technology "to reach our right in the shortest possible time," as reported by the student news agency ISNA.[258] When asked in mid-February, 2007 whether it intended to suspend activities identified in resolution 1737 and ratify the safeguards Additional Protocol, Iran's reply was dismissive of the role of the Security Council, stating a "full readiness and willingness to negotiate on the modality for the resolution of the outstanding issues with the IAEA, subject to the assurances for dealing with the issues in the framework of the Agency, without the interference of the United Nations Security Council."[259]

IAEA Director General ElBaradei submitted the required sanctions report to the Security Council on February 22, 2007.[260] Also at the end of February 2007, the IAEA reported on the nuclear-related activities in Iran.[261] At the Natanz PFEP, since November 2006, Iran intermittently fed $UF_6$ into single centrifuge machines and into 10-, 24-, and two 164-machine cascades for enrichment to less than 5 percent U-235. The IAEA verified samples from one 164-machine cascade to be less than 4.2 percent U-235, and in January 2007, Iran provided records on product and tail assays that had been denied to the IAEA inspectors earlier. At the Natanz FEP, in January 2007, Iran informed the IAEA of plans to start feeding UF6 into cascades by end of February 2007, and to progressively install all 18-, 164-machine cascades into the 3,000-machine hall and bring them into operation by May 2007. On January 31, 2007, Iran transferred 8.7 metric tons of natural $UF_6$ to the FEP from the UCF. On February 17, 2007, it informed IAEA inspectors that two 164-machine cascades had been installed in the FEP, and two additional 164-machine cascades were being installed there.

Iran's schedule calling for installation and operation of 3,000 centrifuges at the FEP by May 2007 was two months later than the previously stated goal of March 2007. The 8.7 metric tons of natural $UF_6$ delivered to the FEP would be enough uranium feed for a year's full-time operation of 2,000 P-1 centrifuges, producing enough 90 percent enriched uranium for a nuclear weapon. The imminent installation of four 164-machine cascades at the FEP in addition to the two already at the PFEP would bring the total number of centrifuges installed at Natanz to about 1,000 machines.

The issue of remote monitoring of centrifuge operations at the FEP remained to be resolved. Iran denied the IAEA's request to install remote monitoring cameras, which would transmit data by satellite or cable to IAEA headquarters in Vienna, and asked for legal justification. The IAEA agreed to the alternative of frequent onsite inspection, so long as the number of machines in the FEP did not exceed five hundred, after which all required safeguards measures including remote inspection would need to be implemented.[262]

## More Sanctions

Under strong pressure from the United States, Britain and France, the UN Security Council voted unanimously on March 24, 2007 to adopt resolution 1747, imposing new and toughened sanctions on Iran for failure to suspend its uranium enrichment activities and the construction of the Arak heavy-water moderated reactor. This added to the sanctions voted earlier on December 23, 2006, which ordered countries to stop supplying materials and technology that could contribute to Iran's nuclear and missile programs. By invoking Chapter 7 of the UN charter, both resolutions, were mandatory, but they excluded military action. As before, the required suspensions in the new resolution were a precondition for Iran entering into negotiations with the five permanent members of the Security Council and the EU on its nuclear program, and the resolution also called on Iran to resolve outstanding questions about possible nuclear activities (at the PHRC) and materials (HEU particle contamination) posed by the IAEA.[263]

The new resolution, 1747, resulted from intense negotiations by the five permanent members plus Germany with South Africa, Indonesia, and Qatar, although it was weaker than the one sought by the United States. At the insistence of South Africa, it stressed the importance of a Middle East free of weapons of mass destruction (WMD). Again, the IAEA was to report back in sixty days. If Iran suspended its enrichment program, the sanctions would be suspended; otherwise further sanctions would be considered.

The expanded sanctions in resolution 1747:

- Prohibited the sale or transfer of Iranian weapons to any nation or organization,
- Called on nations to show "vigilance and restraint" in exporting arms (combat aircraft, attack helicopters, tanks, armored combat vehicles, warships, missiles and missile delivery systems, and large caliber artillery) to Iran,
- Extended resolution 1737 by freezing assets of an additional 15 individuals and 13 organizations that were involved with the nuclear and missile programs or were key persons or organizations of the Iran IRGC,
- Froze the assets abroad of Iran's 4th largest bank, Bank Sepah, which already had been sanctioned by the U.S. Treasury Department, in order to isolate it from international financing of Iran's programs,
- Called on countries to voluntarily impose restrictions on travel by individuals subject to sanctions, and
- Called on nations and organizations voluntarily not to enter into new commitment for export credit, grants, or loans to Iran except for humanitarian or development purposes.[264]

The following entities and individuals were sanctioned by the resolution:[265]

- *Entities Involved in Nuclear or Ballistic Missile Activities:* Ammunition and Metallurgy Industries Group (AMIG) Owned by the Defense Industries Organization (DIO); Esfahan Nuclear Fuel Research and Production Center (ENFRPC) and Esfahan Nuclear Technology Center (ENTC), Parts of the Atomic Energy Organization of Iran (AEOI) Nuclear Fuel Research and Production Company; Kavoshyar Company, Subsidiary of AEOI; Parchin Chemical Industries, Branch of DIO; Karaj Nuclear Research Center, Part of AEOI; Novin Energy Company, Operating Within AEOI; Cruise Missile Industry Group; Bank Sepah and Bank Sepah International, Providing Support to Aerospace Industries Group (AIO) and Subordinates, Including Shahib Hemmat Industrial Group (SHIG) and Shadid Bagheri Industrial Group (SBIG); Sanam Industrial Group, Subordinate to AIO; Ya Mahdi Industries Group, Subordinate to AIO.
- *IRGC Entities*: Quds Aeronautics Indutries; Pars Aviation Services Company; Sho'a' Aviation.
- *Persons Involved in Nuclear or Ballistic Missile Activities:* Mohsen Fakhrizadeh-Mahabadi, Senior Scientist, Ministry of Defense and Armed Forces Logistics (MODAFL), Former Head of Physics Research Center (PHRC)—refuses to be Interviewed by IAEA; Fereidoun Abbasi-Davani, Senior Scientist MODAFL—has links to Institute of Applied Physics, works With Mohsen Fakhrizadeh-Mahabadi; Seyed Jaber Safdari, Manager of the Natanz Enrichment Facilities; Amir Rahimi, Head

of ENFRPC; Mohsen Hojati, Head of Fajr Industrial Group; Mehrdada Akhlaghi Ketabachi, Head of SBIG; Naser Maleki, Head of SHIG—also a MODAFL Official overseeing the Shahab-3 Ballistic Missile Program; Ahmad Derakhshandeh, Chairman and Managing Director, Bank Sepah.

- *Key Persons, IGRC*: Brig. Gen. Morteza Rezaie, Deputy Commander IGRC; V. Adm. Ali Akbar Ahmadian, Chief, IGRC Joint Staff; Brig. Gen. Mohammad Reza Zahedi, Commander, IGRC Ground Forces; R. Adm. Morteza Safari, Commander, Basij Resistance Force; Brig. Gen. Qasem Soleimani, Commander, Quds Force; Gen. Zolqadr, IGRC, Deputy Interior Minister for Security Affairs.

President Ahmadinejad responded on April 9, 2007 by announcing, during the National Day of Nuclear Technology ceremony at the Natanz plant, that now Iran "is among the countries of the world that produce nuclear fuel on an industrial scale." The meaning of this statement was unclear. It came on the first anniversary of Iran's announcement of achieving enrichment at Natanz. While Iran's chief nuclear negotiator, Ali Larijani, implied that uranium gas had been injected into three thousand centrifuges assembled underground in the FEP, Russia and France voiced skepticism about any dramatic expansion of Iran's enrichment program, and IAEA Director General Elbaradei noted that Iran was operating only several hundred centrifuges and discounted claims of any big advance.[266] A letter sent by the IAEA deputy director general to the Iranian ambassador to the IAEA on April 18 2007, confirmed that eight separate centrifuge cascades, totaling 1,312 centrifuge machines, were operating in the underground facility at Natanz, but they were being fed only very limited quantities of uranium gas. This number of centrifuges was twice the four cascades reported by IAEA inspectors in February 2007 to have been assembled there but not enriching uranium. The letter also noted that Iran had recently agreed to install 24-hour monitoring cameras for the cascades at Natanz and allow unannounced inspections there but had revoked access by inspectors to the Arak heavy-water reactor after the March 2007 sanctions.[267]

On April 26, 2007, at the end of two days of talks in Ankara, Turkey between EU foreign policy chief Javier Solana and Iranian nuclear negotiator Ali Larijani, several new formulas were reported to have been put on the table, including redefining "enrichment suspension" to allow the building and testing of new centrifuges;[268] allowing less than one thousand centrifuges assembled and connected on cold standby under IAEA inspection;[269] and setting up an international consortium at Iran's behest to process uranium fuel inside Iran. The EU foreign ministers had gone one step beyond resolution 1747 by adding fifteen nuclear officials, scientists, and IRGC commanders and eight entities to the list in the sanction list along with a total arms embargo on Iran.[270]

## Dissent in Iran and Emerging U.S. Initiatives

John Negroponte testified on January 11, 2007, "Iran's influence is rising in ways that go beyond the menace of its nuclear program."[271] Negroponte, the outgoing U.S. director of national intelligence, noted that Iran had been "emboldened in the Middle East" by the demise of the Taliban and Saddam Hussein, increased oil prices, the election victory of Hamas, and the perceived recent success of Hizballah in fighting Israel. On January 30, 2007, Adm. William Fallon, slated to be the new head of the U.S. Central Command, including the Persian Gulf, stated that "Iranian support for terrorism and sectarian violence beyond its borders, and its pursuit of nuclear capability, is destabilizing and troubling."[272]

The Ahmadinejad regime suffered some political setbacks in December 2006 elections for the Assembly of Experts, the clerical board that oversees the choice of the supreme leader, and for local city councils nationwide. This reflected, in particular, dissatisfaction with rising inflation and unemployment. In the Assembly of Experts contest, reformist former president, Ayatollah Ali Akbar Hashemi Rafsanjani soundly defeated Ayatollah Taqi Mesbah-Yazdi, the reputed mentor of President Ahmadinejad. At the same time, clerics, former officials, and influential newspapers criticized Ahmadinejad for his inflammatory foreign policy rhetoric on uranium enrichment that lead to the UN sanctions.

An editorial in *Jomhouri Eslami*, a newspaper reflecting the views of the supreme leader Ayatollah Khamenei, said that Ahmadinejad was using the nuclear issue to distract the public from his failed policies and was lessening popular support for the nuclear program.[273] Ali Akbar Velayati, Ayatollah Khamenei's chief foreign policy advisor, said in an interview in mid-February 2007 that that the doors were open wide for negotiation on enrichment suspension with Mohammad ElBaradei. "There is no limitation," he said.[274]

An announcement in Iran that gasoline rationing would begin on June 27, 2007 due to growing demand and limited refinery capacity brought out strong protests in Tehran. There were some concerns that rationing would further aggravate an already faltering economy that could be further threatened by additional UN sanctions.[275] However, the worsening economic conditions brought on by Ahmadinejad's economic missteps, including a 17 percent inflation rate, were seen by some as enforcing his political agenda of isolation from the West. Oil revenues were being used to offset economic collapse and support the conservative ruling class dominated by the IRGC.[276]

The U.S. government began a concerted effort to accuse Iran of meddling in Iraq by assisting Shiite militias. In January 2007, American raids on Iranian offices in Iraq netted several Iranians, including one diplomat, identified as officers of the elite IRGC-Quds Force. Then, at a briefing in Baghdad on February 11, 2007, three U.S. military officials, speaking on the condition of anonymity, displayed an array of deadly weapons, including a shaped-charge, armor-piercing "explosively formed penetrator" (EFP), which the officials said was manufactured in Iran and smuggled into Iraq by the Quds force for use by Shiite militias in attacks on U.S. and Iraqi troops.[277]

In 2005, the United States sent a private diplomatic protest to Iran on training and bomb-making equipment supplied to Shiite insurgents by the IRGC and its Hizballah clients. The Bush administration's claimed that the EFP attacks were sanctioned at the "highest levels" of the Iranian government, but this was questioned by some critics.[278] Attacks on American-led forces in Iraq with EFP's supplied to Shiite militants reached a new monthly high in July 2007, according to military officials.[279]

In the wake of the sanctions voted by the Security Council, the United States indicated a more aggressive policy toward Iran, deploying a second aircraft carrier task force to the Persian Gulf and making public a Defense Department program to kill or capture Iranian operatives in Iraq.[280] The U.S. Treasury Department banned dollar dealings with two Iranian banks, and American pressure was put on European governments having extensive business dealings with Iran and its oil industry to curtail exports, block transactions, and freeze assets of some companies. The Bush administration warned foreign companies of possible sanctions for doing business with Iran in large-scale projects in the planning stage for producing oil and natural gas. [281]

Cut from the U.S. financial system and barred from obtaining dollars were Bank Saderat, cited as financing Hizballah, and Bank Sepah, cited as being involved in Iran's ballistic missile program. Three other Iranian banks with European branches were mentioned for future action: Bank Mellat, Bank Melli, and Bank Tejarat.[282] In part, this was a response to demands in Congress for sanctions on Iran because of its suspected nuclear weapons program and its support of terrorism.

In August 2007, the United States was reported to have made the decision to place the IRGC on the list of terrorist organizations, an unusual move against an organization within a government already cited for terrorism, but one that would further clamp down, it was hoped, on the IRGC's world wide financial activities.[283]

## The Centrifuges Keep Spinning

On May 22, 2007, the sixty-day deadline imposed by UN Security Council resolution 1747 of March 24, 2007 expired, and Iran for the third time failed to heed a Security Council call to suspend its activities related to uranium enrichment at Natanz and future plutonium production at Arak. The previous December, Security Council resolution 1737 invoked mild sanctions on Iran, and the March resolution increased them. After May, the U.S. continued to push in the UN Security Council for yet stronger sanctions. The U.S. Treasury Department encouraged steps by Asian and European banks to freeze Iranian assets. EU foreign policy chief, Javier

Solana, continued rounds of meetings with Tehran's chief nuclear negotiator, Ali Larijani, to discuss Iran's nuclear program and ways to get around the impasse on suspending enrichment.

In March 2007, Iran informed the IAEA that it would no longer adhere to a 2003 modification of its safeguards agreement ("modified Code 3.1") to provide the IAEA early design information about any planned construction of new nuclear facilities and permit design information verifications. This arose out of a confrontation over allowing inspectors onto the construction site of the IR-40 reactor at Arak. Iran said it would revert to the original requirement, which was to submit design information not later than 180 days before a new facility is scheduled to receive nuclear material for the first time, a time far in the future for the Arak reactor, Iran said.[284] This only added to the potential problems from Iran's disavowing the Additional Protocol that allowed short-notice inspections of undeclared nuclear sites, and threatened to further staunch the IAEA's access to information on matters such as centrifuge assembly, manufacture, and research and development.

Nevertheless, because of the growing number of centrifuges installed at the FEP, Iran agreed to let the IAEA carry out unannounced inspections there in addition to scheduled monthly inspections. The first unannounced inspection was on May 13, 2007 and the IAEA found eight 164-machine cascades (1,312) centrifuges operating simultaneously with $UF_6$ feed, two more being vacuum tested and three more under construction, for a total of 2,132 centrifuges–two-thirds of the stated near-term goal of 3,000 machine. Iran reported that enrichment levels were up to 4.8 percent U-235 and that 260 kilograms of $UF_6$ had been fed into FEP cascades over the previous three months. Additional talks on a final safeguards approach took place in late August 2007.[285]

Satellite images taken in June 2007 showed a complex tunnels being drilled in a mountain side adjacent to the Natanz centrifuge facility, raising concern at the IAEA about their possible use to hide nuclear activities.[286]

By July 2007, the number of operating centrifuges at the FEP appeared to be stabilizing at about 2,000 machines. Some saw this as a move to avoid a third round of UN sanctions. IAEA Director General ElBaradei said on July 9, 2007 that Iran had slowed down the expansion of its uranium enrichment program. In the previous week, IAEA inspectors observed that installation of new centrifuge machine cascades at Natanz had markedly slowed, calling into doubt Iran's stated goal of 3,000 operating centrifuges by the end of July. The number of operating centrifuges at the Natanz (FEP) had been increasing slowly and steadily as Iranian technicians gained know-how through trial and error, and earlier, IAEA Director General Elbaradei had told diplomats privately in Vienna in June 2007 to expect Iran to have 8,000 centrifuges running by December 2007 if it were able to maintain the current pace of installation.[287]

Russia continued to delay supplying the first fuel load for Bushehr, which was due in March 2007, ostensibly on the grounds that Iran had failed to make the regular 25 million dollar monthly payment. It became evident, however, that Russia actually was delaying completion of the reactor until the Iran heeded UN Security Council resolutions to suspend uranium enrichment, at a considerable financial penalty to itself and angering Iranian officials.[288] A Russian subcontractor to Atomstroiexport stated in late July 2007 that the nuclear power plant would not be finished before autumn 2008.[289] Russia's involvement in the construction at Bushehr has long strained relations with Washington, which has viewed the reactor as a factor in Iran's quest for nuclear weapons—for example, as a source of separated plutonium from discharged spent fuel. Russia's delaying actions possibly were taken to ensure its role as a key supplier in any plans that would require the international or multinational ownership of nuclear fuel cycle services as a diversion-proof alternative to countries acquiring enrichment and reprocessing facilities of their own.

In a turnabout, as part of an "action plan" to burnish its image, Iran agreed to allow IAEA inspectors again to have access to the Arak nuclear reactor site.[290] The visit took place on July 30, 2007, the first since April 2007.[291] In the interim, the IAEA had been forced to resort to analyzing satellite imagery in order to verify design information supplied by Iran on construction activities at the the IR-40 reactor. One concern of the IAEA was that hot cells were being built there to recover plutonium from fuel that would be irradiated during reactor operation.

Iran began discussions in July 2007 with the IAEA on resolving a number of outstanding issues that remained unexplained, namely, plutonium experiments, HEU particle contamination at military-related sites and the Green Salt Project.[292] This was seen as part of the attempt to hold off new sanctions by the Security Council. In June 2007, various proposals were being circulated to help Iran avoid a third set of sanctions. One entailed a "double suspension" involving a complete suspension of enrichment activities and a lifting of UN sanctions while negotiations continued. Another, identified with IAEA Director General ElBaradei, called for a "timeout" under which Iran would stop the *expansion* of uranium enrichment in return for a halt to further UN sanctions, thus freezing the number of operating centrifuges at about 2,000.[293]

A "transparency plan" emerged out of talks between Iran and the IAEA in late August 2007 in which Iran would explain, by the end of the year, its plutonium experiments, lift the veil on efforts to build P-2 centrifuges, and, thirdly, resolve the questions connected to HEU contamination, the machining of uranium into components suitable for bombs, and intelligence reports on design of a missile reentry vehicle for delivery of a nuclear warhead.[294] This was formalized by Ali Larijani and Mohamed Elbaradei on August 21, 2007 in an agreed-on timetable, subject to approval by the IAEA Board of Governors, under which Iran would answer all the IAEA's outstanding questions in stages during several months following. The general features of the agreement were as follows:[295]

Plutonium experiments:

- On August 20, 2007, the IAEA stated that its findings about plutonium experiments were now consistent with Iran's statements and that questions about the matter were resolved.

Natanz FEP safeguards:

- By end of September 2007, Iran would finalize the safeguards approach and facility attachment for the Natanz FEP in accordance with Iran's Comprehensive Safeguards Agreement. Lacking, however, was information relevant, for example, to ongoing advanced centrifuge research that would be required under the Additional Protocol from which Iran withdrew in early 1996.[296]

P-1, P-2 centrifuges:

- By November 2007, Iran would clarify and resolve all remaining questions about the "P1-P2 issue" on the acquisition of P-1 centrifuge technology in 1987 and P-1 and P-2 technology in the mid-1990s. The IAEA still sought a copy of the handwritten offer made by the Khan network in 1987.[297]

HEU contamination:

- Iran would address the IAEA's remaining questions about the source of HEU particle contamination found at a technical university in Tehran (the only outstanding contamination issue) and resolve the matter after the P1-P2 issue is closed.

15-Page (Uranium-Metal) Document:

- Iran would cooperate with the IAEA to close the issue concerning the this document describing the reduction of $UF_6$ to uranium metal and the casting of enriched and depleted uranium metal into hemispheres.[298]

Po-210:

- Once all the previously mentioned issues are resolved, Iran would enter into discussions and explanations regarding its Po-210 experiments.

Gchine Mine:

- Once the Po-210 file is closed, Iran would answer questions and provide explanations about operation of the Gchine mine and mill.

Green Salt Project—Alleged Studies:

- The IAEA would provide Iran with access to documentation in its possession regarding the Green Salt Project, including the conversion of $UO_2$ to $UF_4$, high explosive testing and the design of a missile reentry vehicle, and Iran would review the documents and provide its assessment.[299]
- Iran stated that in its view, the alleged studies were "politically motivated and baseless allegations."

General Understandings:

- Non-diversion at Natanz. An understanding was reached between Iran and the IAEA that it had verified the non-diversion of nuclear material at the enrichment facilities in Iran and concluded "that it remains in peaceful use."
- Questioning would end. The IAEA agreed that all remaining questions would be provided according to the work plan and that once received by Iran, no other questions would be left.

IAEA Director General Elbaradei looked to the agreement as a sign of hope. "This is the first time Iran is ready to discuss all the outstanding issues which triggered the crisis in confidence," he said. "Sanctions alone, I know for sure, are not going to lead to a durable solution," he stated.[300] Western goverments faulted the plan as having no real limitations and dragging out the whole process to avoid further Security Council sanctions.

As of August 19, 2007, twelve 164-machine cascades (1,968 centrifuges) were operating at the same time and being fed $UF_6$, one was operating without $UF_6$ feed, another was being vacuum tested, and two more were under construction, for a total of 2,624 machines in some stage of operation or construction. While this was on the path to the highly touted 3,000 machine goal, there was no strong indication that the earlier slowdown, planned or not, had changed, since the number of operating centrifuges stayed at about 2,000.[301]

New conclusions were reported on the plutonium experiments. Based on additional information provided by Iran on August 1, 2007, the IAEA reported its revised estimates of the expected Pu-240 content of plutonium separated in experiments at the TRR, and it found that new estimates were not inconistent with measurements taken ealier from samples, Added this to other information on dates and the quantities and types of materials involved, the IAEA declared all questions about the plutonium experiments resolved.[302]

Likewise, questions were resolved about the origin of HEU particle contamination found in spent fuel containers at the Karaj RWSF, due, Iran said, to leaking TRR fuel assemblies that were temporarily stored there. The IAEA calculated that the measured enrichment of the HEU contamination at Karaj was correlated both with leaking TRR fuel assemblies and with HEU contamination from the surface of the fuel cladding due to HEU contamination of the TRR cooling water.[303] This left open only the remaining questions about the source of the HEU and natural uranium contamination found on equipment at a technical university in Tehran and connected to the PHRC. These were yet to be resolved.

The Director General's report concluded by noting that Iran continuesd the operation of the PFEP and the construction and operation of the FEP, along with the construction of the IR-40 reactor and the operation of the HWPP, contrary to the Security Council's call for their suspension. It admonished Iran for not adhering to the safeguards and transparency measures required by the Additional Protocol.[304]

President Ahmadinejad seized on the mild and conciliatory tone of the report as an indication that Iran would be able to avoid another UN sanctions resolution, especially with the assistance of Russia and China. He declared on September 2, 2007 that Iran now had 3,000 running centrifuges, adding that a hardliner, Brig. Gen. Mohammed Ali Jafari, had been appointed as the new head of the IRGC to replace Gen. Yahya Rahim Safavi. Ahmadinejad's boasting about the state of centrifuge operations at Natanz did not seem to fit with the last report from IAEA inspectors on the lower than expected feed input. It was likely a defiant response to U.S. pressure on Iran to suspend its nuclear program and halt its support to insurgents in Iraq, as well as to threats by the Bush Administration to declare the IRGC (or its Quds Force unit) a terrorist organization subject to economic sanctions.[305]

## CONCLUSION

Iran presents an enigma. Its leaders are adamant about not giving up their centrifuge enrichment program regardless of any incentives to do so. The information already uncovered and made public about Iran's nuclear program still may only scratch the surface, and despite Iran's August 29, 2007 agreement with the IAEA to answer all outstanding questions. In one view,

> Virtually everything is for sale in today's Iran, especially in the intelligence arena. A wide array of Revolutionary Guards officers, top regime officials, defectors and exiles are peddling inside intelligence information from Iran. Some of the information is valuable, but active measures by the regime, as well as encounters with intelligence conmen and a notorious Marxist-Leninist opposition group [the MEK/NCRI] has jaded many U.S. intelligence professionals from seriously considering much of the potential intelligence take.[306]

There was frustration in Western countries over Iran's lack of transparency in explaining its nuclear programs and its unwillingness to suspend them. The responses of President Ahmadinejad and Ayatollah Khamenei to the sanctions voted by the Security Council in December 2006 and March 2007 were to assert Iran's "right" to enrichment and proclaim that it would not be denied its "great achievement." In late August 2007, French president, Nicholas Sarkozy, spoke of the urgency of a negotiated solution with with tougher sanctions and possible incentives. The catastrophic alternative, he bluntly said: was "an Iranian bomb or the bombing of Iran."[307]

## IRAN NUCLEAR SITES AND FACILITIES

| Activity | Facility | Location | Status |
|---|---|---|---|
| Centrifuge Uranium Enrichment | Pilot Fuel Enrichment Plant (PFEP) | Natanz | Operating |
| | Fuel Enrichment Plant (FEP) | Natanz | Construction complete |
| | Kalaye Electric Company | Tehran | Dismantled pilot enrichment facility |
| | Farayand Technique | Esfahan | Quality control, testing, assembly |
| | Pars Trash, Kalaye subsidiary | Tehran | Storage |
| Laser Uranium Enrichment | Lashkar Abad | Tehran | Dismantled |
| | Karaj Agricultural and Medical Center | Karaj, 20 km west of Tehran | Storage |
| Uranium Conversion | Uranium Conversion Facility (UCF) | Esfahan ENTC | Operating |
| Conversion & Reprocessing Experiments | Tehran Research Reactor (TRR) and Radiochemistry Laboratories | Tehran TNRC | Operating |
| | Jabr Ibn Hayan Multipurpose Laboratories (JHL) | Tehran TNRC | Operating |
| | Molybdenum, Iodine, Xenon (MIX) Radioisotope Production Facility | Tehran TNRC | Constructed, not operating |
| | Uranium Chemistry Laboratory (UCL) | Esfahan ENTC | Closed down |
| Fuel Fabrication | Fuel Fabrication Laboratory (FFL) | Esfahan ENTC | Operating |
| | Fuel Manufacturing Plant (FMP) | Esfahan ENTC | Under construction |

| | | | |
|---|---|---|---|
| | Zirconium Production Plant (ZPP) | Esfahan ENTC | Under construction |
| Uranium Mining & Milling | Gchine mine | Bandar Abbas | Operating |
| | Bandar Abbas Uranium Production Plant (BUP) | Bandar Abbas | Operating |
| | Saghand mine | Saghand, Yazd | Operating |
| | Yellowcake Production Plant (YPP) | Ardakhan,Yazd | Operating |
| Heavy Water Reactor & Facilities | Heavy Water Production Plant (HWPP) | Khondab, near Arak | Operating |
| | IR-40 Iran Nuclear Research Reactor | Arak | Operation 2011 |
| | Hot cells | Arak | In design stage |
| Nuclear Power | Bushehr Nuclear Power Plant (BNPP) | near Bushehr | Operation 2007 |
| Waste Storage | Anarak | near Esfahan | Operating |
| | Qom | near Qom | Operating |
| | Karaj Radioactive Waste Storage Facility (RWSF) | Karaj, west of Tehran | Operating |
| Suspect Sites | Physics Research Center (PHRC) at Lavizan-Shian (Tehran). Suspected nuclear activities; centrifuge, laser enrichment. | Operated by Ministry of Defense, 1989–1998. Site razed 2003 and equipment moved to a technical university in Tehran | |

## GLOSSARY OF TERMS

**Additional Protocol.** See Safeguards.

**Atomic Energy Organization of Iran (AEOI).** An organization established by Iran in 1973 to oversee its nuclear program. AEOI currently is headed by Gholam Reza Aghazadeh, the vice president of Iran.

**Bushehr Nuclear Power Plant (BNPP-1).** Iran's first civil nuclear power plant, a 1000 MWe reactor under construction on the Persian Gulf, 12 km south of city of Bushehr, and owned and operated by the AEOI. Construction was begun in 1975 by Germany's Kraftwerk Union but was halted by the revolution, and the plant sustained damage in the Iran-Iraq war. Subsequently, Iran contracted with the Ministry of Atomic Energy of the Russian Federation (MinAtom) and its successor, the Federal Atomic Energy Agency (RosAtom) to complete the plant based on the VVER-1000 design. BNNP-1 is expected to be operational by late

2007. The core holds 126 tons of 4 percent enriched fuel to be supplied by Russia. Spent fuel will be returned to Russia after cooling.

**Centrifuge Cascade.** See Uranium Centrifuge.

**Depleted Uranium.** Uranium with less of the isotope U-235 than in natural uranium, which contains about 0.7 percent U-235. Depleted uranium is created in the waste stream of a uranium enrichment plant and in the spent fuel discharged from a nuclear reactor that is fueled with natural uranium.

**Enrichment.** For uranium, a process that increases the concentration of the isotope U-235 relative to U-238 over what it is in the feed. Demonstrated enrichment processes include gas centrifuge, gaseous diffusion, aerodynamic, and laser.

**Fission.** The process by which a heavy nucleus, such as uranium or plutonium, is split into two lighter nuclei by the absorption of a neutron, with the release of a large amount of energy.

**Heavy Water.** Water enriched in the proportion of deuterium oxide ($D_2O$) to ordinary water ($H_2O$), which occurs naturally as 1 part in 6500, so that the product is mainly $D_2O$. Heavy water is used as the moderator in nuclear power and research reactors fueled with natural uranium.

**Highly Enriched Uranium (HEU).** Uranium enriched to 20 percent or greater in the isotope U-235.

**Hot Cell.** A lead-shielded box with protected view windows and using remote manipulators, designed for remote handling radioactive materials. Also, a small reprocessing plant that uses a hot cell to recover radioactive isotopes from irradiated targets or separate plutonium from irradiated nuclear reactor fuel.

**International Atomic Energy Agency (IAEA).** An organization established in 1957 under the United Nations to carry out programs to verify and promote the peaceful use of nuclear energy. It is headquartered in Vienna, Austria.

**Isotopes.** Atoms of the same element having different numbers of neutrons in their nuclei.

**Laser Enrichment.** The enrichment of uranium using finely tuned optical or infrared lasers to selectively excite and ionize atoms or molecules in a metal vapor or gas ($UF_6$) to permit the removal of the desired isotope (U-235). Two processes under development for uranium enrichment are atomic vapor laser isotope separation (AVLIS) and molecular vapor laser isotope separation (MLIS).

**Light Water.** Ordinary water, $H_2O$.

**Light-Water Reactor.** A nuclear power reactor using ordinary water as moderator and coolant and LEU fuel.

**Low-Enriched Uranium (LEU).** Uranium enriched to greater than natural (0.7% U-235) and less than 20 percent U-235.

**Milling.** A process in the uranium fuel cycle in which ore containing only a very small percentage of uranium oxide ($U_3O_8$) is converted into a product containing a high percentage (80%) of the oxide, $U_3O_8$, referred to as uranium ore concentrate (UOC) or yellowcake.

**Moderator.** A material, usually water, heavy water, or graphite, surrounding the fuel in a nuclear reactor and slowing the speed of neutrons produced from fissions in the fuel in order to increase the probability of producing subsequent fissions.

**Mujahedin-e Khalq Organization (MEK).** An Islamic-Marxist organization, formed in the 1960s and expelled from Iran in 1979, that seeks to overthrow the Iranian regime. Beginning in the late 1980s, it obtained support from Saddam Hussein and conducted terrorist attacks within Iran and abroad. On the U.S. State Department list of terrorist groups. Military arm of National Council of Resistance of Iran (NCRI).

**Natural Uranium.** Uranium as found in nature, containing 0.7 percent of uranium-235, 99.3 percent of uranium-238, and a trace of uranium-234.

**Neutron.** An electrically neutral subatomic particle, having a mass 1,839 times the electron. The neutron is one of the two basic building blocks of atomic nuclei.

**Nuclear Fuel.** Material that undergoes a fission chain reaction in the nuclear reactor core, releasing energy and heating the surrounding coolant. Commonly used fissionable materials employed in electricity-generating power reactors are natural and LEU. Plutonium is also used in the fuel of some power reactors and HEU is used to fuel some research reactors.

**Nuclear Fuel Fabrication Plant.** A facility for mechanically fabricating nuclear fuel into rod, tube, plate, or other shape for insertion into a reactor core.

**Nuclear Material.** In the terminology of the IAEA, includes natural uranium, depleted uranium, uranium enriched in the isotope uranium-235, and plutonium-239. Excludes uranium ore and yellowcake.

**Nuclear Non-Proliferation Treaty (NPT).** A treaty created in 1968 that obligates the five nuclear-weapon states not to transfer nuclear weapons or technologies to nonnuclear-weapon states and obligates non-weapon states, as treaty signatories, not to produce or acquire nuclear weapons or nuclear explosive devices. Additionally, countries must accept IAEA safeguards, which include declaring all peaceful civil nuclear facilities to the IAEA and permitting routine inspections.

**Nuclear Power Plant.** A facility using the controlled production of nuclear energy to produce heat and electrical power.

**Nuclear Reactor.** A facility using the controlled production of nuclear energy for producing heat or electricity or for creating radioactive isotopes, or testing materials by neutron irradiation.

**Reprocessing.** Chemical treatment of spent reactor fuel to separate the plutonium and uranium from radioactive fission by-products.

**Research Reactor.** A reactor designed primarily to supply neutrons for experimental purposes, such as materials testing and isotope production.

**Safeguards.** Activities implemented by the IAEA under the NPT to verify that states are living up to international commitments not to use nuclear programs for nuclear weapons purposes. IAEA safeguards, as applied to a nonnuclear-weapon state, consist of a comprehensive safeguards agreement augmented by the Additional Protocol. Comprehensive safeguards are based largely on nuclear material accountancy, complemented by containment and surveillance techniques, such as cameras and tamper proof seals installed by the IAEA at nuclear facilities. Their scope of safeguards includes any nuclear material that should have been declared to the IAEA.

The **Additional Protocol**, stemming from the development of strengthened safeguards in the decade of the 1990s to increase the likelihood of detecting a clandestine nuclear weapons program, adds to and complements the comprehensive safeguards agreement. The Additional Protocol gives the IAEA access to both declared and possible undeclared nuclear activities and to all aspects of the nuclear fuel cycle. It grants expanded rights of access to information and sites, including unannounced inspections, and provides the IAEA enhanced authority for using advanced technologies, such as environmental sampling, in the verification process.

Iran ratified the NPT on Feburary 2, 1970, as one of the original signatory states, and concluded a comprehensive safeguards agreement with the IAEA on May 15, 1974. Iran signed an Additional Protocol on December 18, 2003 but has not ratified it.

**Separative Work Unit (SWU).** A measure of the effort required to enrich uranium, starting with feed of a given enrichment and obtaining product of higher enrichment along with waste (or tails) of lower enrichment. Commercial uranium enrichment services are priced in dollars per separative work to produce a kilogram of enriched product (kgSWU).

**Spent fuel.** Fuel elements that have been discharged from a nuclear reactor after use because they contain too little fissile and too high a concentration of unwanted radioactive by-products to sustain reactor operation.

**Tehran Nuclear Research Center (TNRC).** Nuclear complex located at the University of Tehran, operational since 1965 and currently under the management of AEOI. The TNRC is the site of the TRR and a TRIGA research reactor supplied by the United States in 1967 along with hot cells. The TRR core was converted to less than 20 percent U-235 enrichment with fuel fabricated in Argentina using uranium enriched in Russia. Secret activities at the site have included laser enrichment and plutonium reprocessing, which some believe indicates attempts at weapons design.

**Uranium.** An element with the atomic number 92. The two principal natural occurring isotopes are uranium-235 (0.7% in natural uranium), which is fissile, i.e. capable of being fissioned by slow neutrons, and uranium 238 (99.8% in natural uranium), which is fertile, meaning that it absorbs slow neutrons to create plutonium-239.

**Uranium Centrifuge.** A machine for enriching uranium feed in the fissile isotope U-235. A tall, stationary thin-walled cylinder is fed uranium hexafluoride ($UF_6$) gas that is set in rotation at high speeds by the action of a central rotor, thus enriching gas near the center (and at the top of the cylinder) in the isotope U-235 by concentrating the heavier U-238 isotope near the outer wall (and at the bottom).

The central rotor is made of high strength materials, e.g. special aluminum alloys, "maraging" steel, and carbon fiber-resin composites to withstand acceleration to ~50,000 rpm without being torn apart by lengthwise resonant vibrations. The weight of the centrifuge rotor is supported at the bottom by a frictionless bearing and is secured at the top without friction by a small magnet.

*Centrifugal force* causes a difference in the concentration of U-235 between the inner and outer regions of the cylinder, but an even greater concentration difference between the cylinder top and bottom is due to *countercurrent flow* of $UF_6$ streams along the cylinder axis. The capacity of a centrifuge machine to separate light from heavy isotopes is measured in kilogram separative work units (kgSWU). Practically, a centrifuge's separative capacity is proportional to the product of its length and the square of the speed of the cylinder at the outer radius.

The machine types of interest in Europe, Pakistan, Iran, and Libya are P-1 (L-1, G-1) and P-2 (L-2, G-2). Their properties are as follows. P-1: aluminum, length ~2m, diameter ~10cm, peripheral speed ~350m/sec, separative capacity ~2.3 SWU/yr; P-2: maraging steel, length ~1 m, diameter ~10 cm, peripheral speed ~350 m/sec, separative capacity ~5 SWU/yr. Associated equipment includes vacuum systems, mass spectrometers, and frequency converters.

Centrifuges in an enrichment plant are configured in multistage *cascades* for the desired product enrichment. Machines in an LEU plant (where many machines are connected in parallel to produce a large quantity of LEU may be rearranged, connecting them in series to produce a small amount of highly enriched, weapons grade uranium. Also HEU may be produced by "batch recycle" from repeated passes of enriched product through an LEU cascade.

**UOC.** Uranium Ore Concentrate, yellowcake. UOC is predominantly the uranium oxide $U_3O_8$.

**Weapons Grade.** Nuclear material of the type most suitable for nuclear weapons. Uranium enriched to 90 percent or greater U-235 and plutonium that is primarily plutonium-239, with no more than 6 percent $Pu_24_0$.

**Yellowcake.** A product of the milling of uranium ore that contains 80 percent $U_3O_8$.

# 7

# Iran's Ballistic Missile, Chemical, and Biological Capabilities

## IRAN'S BALLISTIC MISSILES

Iran possesses or is developing an array of missiles of many types and ranges. Evidence of its short-range capabilities was seen in the rocket launches by its client Hizballah from Lebanon into Israel during the brief 2006 Israel-Hizballah war. Yet, only ballistic missiles with ranges on the order of 1000 km or more and falling into the medium-range ballistic missile (MRBM) category would serve Iran against strategic targets in a direct confrontation with countries in the Middle East. The distance from Tehran to Riyadh is about 1300 km, to Tel Aviv, about 1600 km, and to Istanbul, about 2000 km.

Iran has a variety of short- and medium-range ballistic missiles, and some have the capability to reach Tel Aviv and other potential targets in the Middle East. With origins traced back to China, Russia, or North Korea, Iran's models go mainly under the name "Shahab," Persian for "meteor" or "shooting star." Director of National Intelligence John Negroponte testified on January 11, 2006,

> Iran is enhancing its ability to project its military power, primarily with ballistic missiles and naval power with the goal of dominating the Gulf region and deterring potential adversaries.... Tehran views its growing inventory of ballistic missiles (it already has the largest inventory of these missiles in the Middle East), as an integral part of its strategy to deter and if necessary retaliate against forces in the region, including U.S. forces.[1]

Missiles are projectiles, which, after firing, have some form of internal guidance. They encompass long-range artillery projectiles, guided rockets, cruise missiles, and ballistic missiles. A rocket is propelled by the exhaust from an internal jet engine throughout its trajectory. Guided missiles are rockets with internal postlaunch guidance systems that direct the missile to its target. Cruise missiles, using jet-engine propulsion, fly in low altitude trajectories, and they may employ terrain contour guidance from a stored map. Ballistic missiles are powered by one or more rocket stages upon launch but shortly move into ballistic trajectories governed only by gravity toward selected targets, making use of inertial guidance systems.

The ranges of missiles vary from short for rockets and guided missiles to short, medium, intermediate, and long-range/intercontinental for ballistic missiles, which may be launched from fixed sites, mobile launchers, aircraft, ships, and submarines.[2] Missile payloads may be almost anything deliverable—conventional explosives, chemical and biological materials, and nuclear warheads—that meets limitations on size and weight imposed by the design of the nose cone.

Iran's acknowledged development of an indigenous missile production industry may have several motivations—as a display of its technological achievement, as a threat to Israel and a deterrent against other countries in the region, and to eliminate its dependence on uncertain foreign supply, particularly from North Korea. In 1997 Iran was already buying missile design and production components from Russia and constructing missile production facilities in two tunnels at Kuh-e-Padri, on the Persian Gulf between Bandar Abbas and Bushehr.[3] Most of the missile-development industry is located in Karaj. The missile infrastructure includes a Chinese-built missile plant near Semnan, North Korean-built plants at Esfahan and Sirjan for liquid fuels and some structural components, and missile test facilities at Shahroud and at the Shahid Hemat Industrial Group research facility just south of Tehran.[4] Other centers are at Sultanatabad, Lavizan, and Kuh-e Bagh-e-Melli on the outskirts of Tehran.[5]

Russia has always insisted that that its dealings with Iran have adhered to its obligations under the Missile Technology Control Regime (MTCR). However, it has acknowledged the role of individual organizations in transferring technology to Iran's missile projects. In July 1998, President Clinton announced that seven Russian companies and organizations were being economically sanctioned by the U.S. government, after an investigation revealed that the Russian government was supplying Iran's missile program with items, such as guidance systems, electronics, high-strength composite materials for nose cones, and special alloys.[6]

On December 23, 2006, the UN Security Council voted economic sanctions against Iran for its refusal to halt its uranium centrifuge enrichment program and other nuclear activities. Individuals and organizations in both the nuclear and ballistic missile programs were cited. These included affiliates of the Aerospace Industries Organization (AIO), Iran's missile producing entity, and the head of the AIO and other AIO officials and Gen Hosein Salimi, Commander of the Iran Revolutionary Guard Corps (IRGC) Air Force.[7]

## BALLISTIC MISSILE DELIVERY SYSTEMS

The 1998 report of the Commission to Assess the Ballistic Missile Threat to The United States ("Rumsfeld Report") noted Iran's severe systems integration problems in the management of large science and technology programs. The report states that Iran had yet to fully develop an indigenous missile production system and was unlikely to develop one without considerable external help via education, training, and technology transfer.[8] Therefore its pursuit of medium and long-range ballistic missiles will continue to depend on the transfer of technology, particularly from North Korea. Almost invariably, a long-range ballistic missile capability is synonymous with the ability to deliver a nuclear payload, so Iran might be looking into designing a compact nuclear warhead to fit inside such a missile's nose cone.

### Shahab-1/Scud B

In 1985, during the Iran-Iraq war, Iran acquired Soviet-era Scud-B missiles and launchers from Libya and Syria to counter the use of ballistic missiles by Iraq. The range of the Scud-B permitted strikes around Baghdad starting in March 1985.[9] Later, Iran began the acquisition of Scud-B missiles from North Korea, which would eventually become its primary supplier.[10] The war experience would contribute to the beginnings of Iran's indigenous missile production capability using reverse engineering techniques, and it would instill within Iran's ruling elite the strategic, political, and military importance of a ballistic missile capability.[11]

Iran has an estimated inventory of up to 300 Shahab-1 short-range ballistic missiles (SRBMs) that constitutes the core of its ballistic missile force.[12] Analysts of the1998 Rumsfeld Commission estimated that Iran bought 200–300 Scud-Bs from North Korea between 1987 and 1992.[13] An Israeli analysis estimated that Iran had at least 250–300 missiles and 8–15 launchers in 1997 and recent estimates are that Iran has between 6 and 12 launchers and up to 200 missiles.[14] It is believed by U.S. officials that Iran has a nearly independent Shahab-1/Scud-B production capability with possible exceptions for its more complex guidance packages and rocket motors.[15] Production sites have been reported at Shiraz, Khorrambad, Parchin, and Semnan.[16]

Shahab-1 technical capabilities are as follows: a single stage liquid fueled SRBM, range of 290–300 km (180–186 miles), conventional explosive payload of 987–1000 kg, and Circular Error Probability (CEP)[17] of 450 m.[18]

### Shahab-2/Scud-C

The Shahab-2/Scud-C missile is a variant of the Shahab-1 with an extended range and upgraded inertial guidance.[19] The Shahab-2 was first introduced into the

Iranian ballistic missile fleet in 1990.[20] North Korea began full-scale production of the Scud-C in 1987 and began shipments to Iran in 1990. It is believed Iran stopped purchasing the Scud-B from North Korea around the time of the Gulf War and then began buying the more advanced Scud-C system. In May 1991, Iran's first test firing of a North Korean Scud-C impacted near Sharoud, 310 miles to the west of the launch center near the city of Qom.[21] By 1994, Iran had purchased 150–200 Scud-Cs from North Korea. In addition, Iran sent 21 missile specialists led by Brigadier General Manteghi to North Korea in 1993 for training in missile technology, and this lead directly to the beginning of Iran's autonomous production of Scud-Cs in 1997.[22]

Iran's arsenal by 1998 is estimated to have contained more than 60, and as many as 170, Shahab-2/Scud-Cs. Iran may have 5–10 launchers, including four North Korean Transporter-Erector Launchers (TELs) acquired in 1995.[23] Iran has deployed the missiles and launchers in a dispersed manner to minimize the success of any attack. Other defensive measures include shelters and tunnels constructed in Iran's coastal areas in which missiles are stored in hardened sites to reduce their vulnerability to attack.[24]

The Shahab-2/Scud-C system is reported to have sufficient range and payload capability to strike as far as the southern coast of the Gulf, nearly all populated areas of Iraq, parts of eastern Syria, eastern Turkey, as well as western Afghanistan and Pakistan.[25]

Many technical aspects of Iran's Shahab-2/Scud-C are uncertain. It appears to differ substantially in detail from the original Soviet Scud-C, perhaps based more on the Chinese DF-61 missile than a direct copy of the Soviet weapon.[26] Accuracy and reliability also remain major uncertainties. The missiles estimated capabilities are as follows: a single stage liquid fueled SRBM, a range of 300–700 km (190–430 miles), CEP of 50 m, and a 700–989 kg conventional high-explosive warhead payload.[27] It is believed that Iran can now assemble these missiles using foreign-made components and may soon have an autonomous capability for missile system and warhead package production.[28]

## Shahab-3/Zelzal-3

The Shahab-3, or alternatively Zelzal-3 ("Earthquake"), is a road-mobile MRBM, based on the North Korean No-dong-1/A and No-dong-B missiles, which some analysts say were developed with Soviet technical participation, and Chinese and Iranian financial assistance.[29,30] Various Shahab-3 upgrades and variants appear to have been spurred by Iran's desire for a missile that could reach Israeli targets,[31] possibly even with a nuclear warhead.

The Shahab-3 series has been developed and largely produced domestically with some Chinese and Russian help[32] under the control of the IRGC. In October 1997, Iranian missile experts traveled to Russia to train in missile production for the Shahab-3 program. Iran perfected and tested its Shahab-3 designs throughout the 1990s. Its first (abortive) test flight was in July 1998 from the Qom launching site.[33] Iran's first successful test of a Shahab-3 was on July 15, 2000, and production began shortly thereafter.[34] The Shahab-3 underwent only nine tests through 2003, and only four of them could be considered successful in terms of basic system performance.[35] By early 2006, Iran had test launched some ten Shahab-3s, with roughly 30 percent of them completely malfunctioning and another six only partially successful.[36]

The Great Prophet 2 war games started on November 2, 2006, with the IRGC firing dozens of missiles with ranges 300–2000 km including a Shahab-3 variant having a 2,000 km range and modified to carry a cluster warhead with 1,400 bombs.[37]

There is some debate within the scientific and intelligence community on the Shahab-3 system's true operational capability. Some reports claim that the system was operational as early as 1999, while others state it underwent "final" tests in July 2003.[38] Also, some experts believe Iran possesses between 25 and 100 operational missiles in its inventory while others claim that in Spring 2006, the IRGC was operating only six batteries and was redeploying them every 24 hours due to the risk of U.S. or Israeli attack.[39] Iran's credible threat may be embodied in Shahab-3—mobile and silo-deployable with a range of 1,350–1,500 km carrying a 760–1000 kg warhead—but it is noted that the missile requires large and identifiable logistic support, which opens it to identification and elimination.[40]

The technical specifications and performance characteristics of the Shahab-3 system remain uncertain. The range, payload, and accuracy of the Shahab-3 are rough engineering estimates given the lack of sufficient testing in its final configuration.[41] Shahab-3 specifications are as follows: a single stage liquid fueled MRBM, and a range of 820 km with a 1,300 kg and 1,100 km with a 700 kg payload.[42] Another source specifies a range of 1,289 km.[43] Longer-range estimates up to 2,000 km come from Iranian sources that may not be completely accurate or may refer to an improved version of the system.[44] The Shahab-3 or one of its variants is thought to be capable of carrying a compact nuclear warhead well over 1,000 km in addition to carrying standard high-explosive airburst warheads, or chemical or biological dispersion agents.[45] The design of the compact nuclear warhead and its missile reentry vehicle present substantial challenges.

## Shahab-3D, IRIS, and Shahab-3M

The missile test launch on September 21, 2000, from Emamshahr was described by Iran as the first test of the liquid and solid-fueled Shahab-3D MRBM, derived by adding a second, solid stage to the No-dong-derived Shahab-3 and possibly giving the missile the extra range needed to reach Israel.

Another explanation of the test is that the two-stage missile was actually the IRIS space booster, first shown by Iran at a 1998 aerospace show. While the IRIS is considered to be adequate as a sounding rocket for research or for launching a scientific payload, it could not alone launch a satellite of appreciable mass for Iran's space program, so the test may only have been of the second and third stages of the larger Taep'o-dong-2 (TD-2)/Shahab-5 space booster.[46] Iran's tests of the two-stage Shahab-3D/IRIS system are reported to have been successful in five out of eight tries in the July 1998–October 2004 period.[47]

In August 2004, Iran announced the test firing of the Shahab-3M, a Shahab-3 variant with a purported 2,000-km range and featuring a "bottleneck"-shaped nose cone. This modified design would allow for greater range and accuracy, but at the price of a decreased payload space, best suited for a compact nuclear, chemical, or biological warhead.[48]

## Shahab-4

Iran's Shahab-3 and Shahab-4 missiles were first publicly identified in 1997.[49] Both were said to be derivatives of North Korea's No-dong missile, with ranges of up to 1,496 km (930 miles) and 1,995 km (1,240 miles), respectively. At the time, some identified the Shahab-4 with the No-dong-B, while other sources, such as the working papers of the 1998 Rumsfeld Commission, held that the Shahab-4 was based on the design of the Soviet SS-4 as expressed in the Taep'o-dong-1.[50]

The bulk of evidence strongly suggests that the Shahab 4 is the North Korean three-stage Taep'o-dong-1 (TD-1), which was flown initially by North Korea as a space launch vehicle.[51] As of early 2006, the Shahab-4 had not been flight-tested and the precise configuration remained somewhat conjectural.[52] In 2004, it was reported that President Khatami had halted work on both the Shahab-4 (range 2,800 km) and the Shahab 5 (range 4,900–5,300 km) because the projects were incompatible with Iran's strategic interests and defense needs.[53] Alternatively, North Korea and Iran temporarily stopped the development of the Taep'o-dong-1/Shahab-4 and continued only with the Taep'o-dong-2/Shahab-5 in looking to the deployment of a full-range ICBM.[54] The Taep'o-dongs are large liquid and solid-fueled missiles not designed to be deployed in missile silos or on road mobile launchers, making them easy targets for detection during fueling and assembly.[55] Another conjecture is that Iran's flight test on January 17, 2006, of the North Korean mobile and liquid propellant No-dong-2, a derivative of the Soviet SS-N-6 submarine-launched missile, was indeed a test of the new Shahab-4 space booster. The performance data showed a range capability of 4,000 km. The flight test was terminated, but only after a successful separation of a reentry vehicle with its "baby-bottleneck" nose cone.[56]

## Shahab-5, Shahab-6 Long-Range Ballistic Missiles

Iran is reported to have begun efforts to design intercontinental ballistic missiles with extended range and payload using a mix of Russian, Chinese North

Korean, and indigenous technologies. As of 2006, none were being produced and the exact nature of the programs remained a matter of speculation.

The Shahab-5 and Shahab-6 ICBM designs are taken to be variants of the Taep'o-dong-2. Their first stage may be based on the RD-216 liquid propellant Energomash engines of the Soviet-era SS-5 missile. It is uncertain whether Iran is capable of producing the first-stage engines, meaning that Iran would have to rely on North Korean missile technology. The second and third Taep'o-dong stages probably would be based on No-dong missile. The Shahab-5 is expected to have a range of 3,500–3750 km with a 1,000 kg warhead and 4,000–4,300 km with a 750 kg warhead. The Shahab-6 would be capable of reaching Europe. But, to meet Shahab-6 expectations, the upper two stages of the Shahab-5 would need to be redesigned to improve performance. That would take considerable time and investment. North Korea finally conducted a test flight of its Taep'o-dong-2 on July 4, 2006, that apparently failed or was aborted 42 seconds after it was launched.[57]

Iranian Ballistic Missile System Characteristics[a]

| Name | Stages | Propellant | Range (km) | CEP (m) | Inventory | Type | North Korean-Related |
|---|---|---|---|---|---|---|---|
| Shahab-1 | 1 | Liquid | 285–330 | 450 | 250–300 | SRBM | Scud-B |
| Shahab-2 | 1 | Liquid | 500–700 | 50 | 200–450 | SRBM | Scud-C |
| Shahab-3/ Zelzal-3 | 1 | Liquid | 1,000– 1,350– 1,500 | 190 | 50–450 | IRBM | No-dong |
| Shahab-3D, IRIS | 2 | Liquid, Solid | 1,500+ | – | – | IRBM | No-dong |
| Shahab-4 | 3 | Liquid, Solid | 1,800– 2,000 | – | – | IRBM | Taep'o-dong-1, Soviet SS-4 |
| Shahab-5/ Kosar | 2 and 3 | Liquid, Solid | 3,500– 3,750 (2-stage) 4,000– 4,300 (3-stage) | – | – | ICBM | Taep'o-dong-2, Soviet SS-5 |
| Shahab-6/ Kosar | 3 | Liquid, Solid | 5,470– 6,700; >8,000 | – | – | ICBM | TD-2/NKSL-X-2, Soviet SS-5 |

[a]Federation of American Scientists, Iran Missile Overview, December 1, 2005. <http://www.fas.org/nuke/guide/iran/missile/index.html>; Federation of American Scientists, "Shahab-3/Zelzal-3," December 14, 2006. <http://www.fas.org/nuke/guide/iran/missile/shahab-3.htm>

## IRAN'S CHEMICAL WEAPONS CAPABILITY

In May 1998, Iran acknowledged for the first time the existence of a past chemical weapons program, admitting that it had developed one during the latter stages of the Iran-Iraq war as a deterrent to Iraq's use of chemical agents. But Iran also claimed that it had terminated the program after the 1988 cease-fire. Despite these statements, Iran has never admitted to actually possessing chemical weapons.[58]

The United States alleges in the State Department's 2005 Noncompliance Report that Iran is retaining and modernizing three key elements of its chemical weapons infrastructure: offensive research and development, an offensive production capability, and a possible undeclared chemical weapons stockpile.[59] This concern has persisted, ever since doubts were raised about the completeness of Iran's initial declaration when it became a party to the Chemical Weapons Convention (CWC) on December 3, 1997.[60] However, the size and composition of any Iranian chemical weapons stockpile remain uncertain.[61]

Iran maintains a very public stance against the use of chemical weapons, referring to its claim of over 10,000 casualties suffered as a result of Iraq's use of chemical weapons in the Iran-Iraq war.[62] Iran has openly declared a no-use policy, maintaining that chemical weapons are unethical and contrary to Muslim beliefs because they harm the environment.[63] It has actively lobbied on behalf of the Organization for the Prohibition of Chemical Weapons (OPCW), which verifies adherence to the CWC.

## CHEMICAL WEAPONS CONVENTION

The Chemical Weapons Convention (CWC) imposes a number of basic obligations on states that are parties. Under Article I, the parties agree not to develop, produce, otherwise acquire, stockpile, or retain chemical weapons, or to transfer them to anyone, directly or indirectly. Article I also obligates parties to "never, under any circumstances" use chemical weapons, undertake "military preparations" for their use, or "assist, encourage or induce, in any way, anyone to engage in any activity prohibited" to a party to the Convention. In addition, each state party must destroy all the chemical weapons in its possession or control, or even abandoned in another country, and a party must destroy all its chemical weapons production facilities.

Article III requires the submission of detailed declarations of chemical weapons stockpiles, production facilities, other related facilities, including laboratories and test and evaluation sites, going back to January 1, 1946, including the types of riot control agents it owns. Article VI guarantees to each party "the right, subject to the provisions of this Convention, to develop, produce, otherwise acquire, retain, transfer and use toxic chemicals and their precursors for purposes not prohibited under this Convention."[64]

The Organization for the Prohibition of Chemical Weapons (OPCW), which is established under the CWC, oversees and ensures implementation, compliance, and verification. Article VIII authorizes the Conference of States Parties to review compliance and bring "cases of particular gravity" to the attention of the UN Security Council and the General Assembly.

## THE U.S. ASSESSMENT PROCESS

The U.S. State Department's 2005 Noncompliance Report provides an independent review of the adherence by individual states to the CWC, based on intelligence and other available information. Its compliance assessments focus on the degree to which states fulfill not only their detailed declaration and destruction/conversion obligations under Articles III, IV, and V, but also their general obligations under Article I.[65]

The U.S. assessment process takes into account a range of factors: the state's record of CWC compliance; the accuracy and completeness of its declarations; its history of chemical weapons-related activity; the legitimate economic or commercial need for the chemicals if the processes required are easily adaptable for chemical weapons production; the degree to which production methods adopted diverge in unexplained ways from industry practice, or are uneconomical or implausibly inefficient for peaceful applications; and whether the possession of chemical agents is for protective purposes, as permitted by Article II.

Under Article V, a state may not "construct any new chemical weapons production facilities or modify any existing facilities for the purpose of chemical weapons production or for any other activity" prohibited by the CWC. From the U.S. viewpoint, this focus on "purpose" indicates that merely the development of a potential chemical weapons capability would amount to noncompliance with the CWC, if it were undertaken with prohibited chemical weapons applications in mind, whether or not prohibited quantities of banned or controlled chemicals are actually present.[66]

## IRAN'S CHEMICAL WEAPONS PRODUCTION AND DELIVERY CAPABILITY

According to the 2005 Noncompliance Report, the United States believes that Iran has not revealed the full extent of its chemical weapons program. The assertion is that Iran has manufactured and stockpiled first-generation chemical weapon agents—blister, blood, and choking chemical agents—and has weaponized some of these into artillery shells, mortars, rockets, and aerial bombs. Iran also has the capability to produce traditional nerve agents.[67] The United States finds Iran in violation of its CWC obligations because it is acting to retain and modernize key elements of its chemical weapons' infrastructure to include an offensive chemical weapons' research and development (R&D) capability and dispersed mobilization facilities.[68]

Similarly, the November 2004 "721 Report" to Congress by the Director of Central Intelligence states that over the July–December 2003 period, Iran "continued to seek production technology, training, and expertise from foreign entities that could further Tehran's efforts to achieve an indigenous capability to produce nerve agents." Moreover, the report says, "Iran may have already stockpiled blister, blood, choking, and possibly nerve agents-and the bombs and artillery shells to deliver them-which it previously had manufactured."[69] The table below lists the chemical agents Iran is known to possess.[70]

Known Chemical Agents in Iran's Possession

| CW Agent | Type | Quantity | Weaponization |
|---|---|---|---|
| CS | Riot control agent | Unknown | Unknown |
| Mustard Gas | Blister agent | Unknown | Unknown |
| Hydrogen Cyanide, Cyanogen Chloride | Blood agents | Unknown | Unknown |
| Phosgene | Choking agent | Unknown | Unknown |
| Chlorine Gas | Choking agent | Unknown | Unknown |
| Sarin | Nerve agent | Unknown | – |
| Tabun | Nerve agent | Unknown | Unknown |
| V-Series Nerve Agents (VX, VG, VM, VE) | Nerve agents | Unknown | Unknown |

## Foreign Suppliers

A 2001 CIA report asserted that Iran sought production technology, machinery, instruction, and expertise along with particular chemicals, from both Russian and Chinese entities.[71] Iran also depends heavily on the support of India for supplies of chemical equipment and precursor chemicals, and, at times, companies in Germany, Israel, and the U.S. have also been implicated in selling chemical weapon supplies and technology to Iran.[72]

> *China*: Provided precursor chemicals, glass-lined vessels, special air filtration equipment, and production technology for manufacture of chemical weapon production equipment.[73]
>
> *Russia*: Provided dual-use chemicals, equipment, and chemical production technology that can be converted into an offensive chemical weapon program; also provided technology, training, and expertise.[74]
>
> *India*: Sold thionyl chloride, a specific precursor chemical used to produce mustard gas. India was identified among Iran's primary suppliers of chemical weapons-related material during the second half of 1996. It has not been singled out as a country of concern regarding Iran's chemical weapons program since 1996.[75]

Iranian Chemical Warfare Milestones[a]

| | |
|---|---|
| November 1929 | Iran consents to the Geneva Protocol for the prohibition of the use of asphyxiating, poisonous, or other gases, and of bacteriological methods of warfare. |
| September 1980 | Iraqi troops invade Iran signaling the beginning of the Iran-Iraq war. Spiritual leader Ayatollah Ruhollah Khomeini objects to chemical weapons use. |
| November 1983 | Iran accuses Iraq at the United Nations of chemical weapon use. |
| 1983 | Iran initiates a chemical weapon development program "in response to Iraqi use of riot control and toxic chemical agents" during the Iran-Iraq war. |
| April 1984 | Iranian representative to the UN, Rajai Khorassani, states at a London news conference that Iran is "capable of manufacturing chemical weapons . . . [and would] consider using them." |
| April 1984 | UN Security Council report confirms that aerial bombs containing mustard gas and the nerve agent, tabun, were used against Iran. |
| 1985 | The Australia Group is formed to require and enforce licensing for export of certain chemicals. |
| May 1988 | UN Security Council Resolution 612 is unanimously adopted; which condemns the use of chemical weapons in the Iran-Iraq war, and calls on both sides to adhere to Geneva Protocol. |
| February 1997 | CIA Director George Tenet names Iran as one of twenty countries that has or currently is developing chemical and biological weapons. Iran's chemical weapon program at the time is described as "increasingly active." |
| December 3, 1997 | Iran becomes a party to the CWC, prohibiting them from developing, producing, or stockpiling chemical weapons. |
| 1998 | Iran publicly acknowledges that it began a chemical weapon program during the Iran-Iraq war. |
| September 2000 | CIA assessment states Iran is "rapidly approaching self-sufficiency and could become a supplier of chemical weapon-related materials to other nations." |
| November 2004 | CIA assessment of Iran's chemical weapon development concludes "Iran may have already stockpiled blister, blood, choking, and possible nerve agents—and the bombs and artillery shells to deliver them." |
| February 2005 | ZKA (German Customs Office of Criminal Investigations) assessment states that Iran is believed to have secretly carried out chemical weapon research and development in small, well-guarded university laboratories. ZKA alleges that Iran likely controls sulfur mustard, tabun, and prussic acid (hydrogen cyanide) and may possess sarin and VA nerve agents. |

[a]Michael R. Gordon with Stephen Engelberg, "Iran is Said to Try to Obtain Toxins." *New York Times*, August 13, 1989, p. 11; "Says Iran Made Two Attempts to Buy Hazardous Fungi in Netherlands." *Associated Press*, August 15, 1989.

## Chemical Weaponization and Delivery

A variety of technologies may be used to weaponize toxic chemical agents.[76] Munitions include bombs (explosives), missile warheads, sub-munitions, projectiles, and spray tanks. A key factor in the use of chemical weapons is the efficiency of dissemination. The techniques by which chemical weapons are stored and filled are also important to their effectiveness.[77]

Countries capable of developing chemical agents could most likely also adapt their standard munitions to carry the agents. It is much more difficult, however, to achieve success in effective dispersal and dissemination. Weather observation and forecasting are essential factors for increasing the probability of effective chemical weapon dissemination and to reduce the risk of injuring friendly forces.[78]

The use of explosives in disseminating chemical agents is usually achieved with a central burster expelling the agent laterally. Efficiency is not particularly high since a good deal of the agent is incinerated in the blast or directed into the ground. The flammable nature of the agents means that they may be ignited by the disseminating explosive and consumed before delivery to the target.

Nonexplosive methods for delivery of chemical weapons include *aerodynamic dissemination* from a line source and *thermal dissemination*, in which the agent is heated to form a fine mist carried by an inhalable cloud. The majority of the most potent chemical agents are not very volatile, meaning they are not apt to evaporate easily at room temperatures. The most volatile of the G-series nerve agents is GB (sarin), which has volatility near that of water. To effectively employ a line source, the altitude of dissemination must be controlled and the wind direction and velocity known. The chemical agent must be dispersed at high enough altitudes (<200–300 ft above the ground) to allow effective dispersal of the agent. Inaccurate weather observations can cause the chemical weapon deployment to backfire, as was the case with Iraq's use of chemical weapons in the Iran-Iraq war.[79] Short and intermediate range ballistic missiles also may carry chemical warheads.

Most first and second world countries have the capability to develop chemical weapons. Those with a well-developed military infrastructure could readily adapt existing munitions for chemical warfare. Any nation with substantial foreign military purchases or an indigenous capability in conventional weapons would have access to the technology and components required to implement at least a moderate chemical weapon capability.[80] For example, by the late 1980s, Syria is alleged to have armed some of its latest missiles, including Scuds, with chemical warheads.[81]

## Iran's Missile Arsenal

The use of ballistic or cruise missiles as a means for delivery of chemical or biological warheads, as cited here, is based on U.S. intelligence reports indicating that the delivery system could be used in such a capacity.[82] Potential delivery vehicles of biological weapons include short-range cruise missiles; short-range, air-launched tactical missiles; fighter aircraft; artillery shells; and rockets.[83,84] Potential delivery vehicles for chemical weapons also include artillery shells, mortars, rockets, and aerial bombs.[85]

For over two decades Iran has pursued an aggressive ballistic missile and long-range artillery rocket development program.[86] Iran's ballistic missile development program receives a significant amount of Iranian financial and material resources and will likely continue to do so.[87] As this support continues during a time of low economic growth and high unemployment in Iran, it can be deduced that Iran's missile program is of high priority and will likely remain so.[88]

Iran currently has the second largest ballistic missile force in the third world, possessing ballistic missiles and/or long-range artillery rockets that could reach Iran's regional neighbors and potentially Israel.[89] Iran's ballistic missile force is second to North Korea; it has the largest ballistic missile force in the Middle East.[90] Among these ballistic missiles are several that could deliver chemical, biological and radiological dispersion warheads, as well as conventional high explosives and submunitions. Iran's missile sheltering, dispersal, and hardening programs are estimated to have the ability to survive a number of air strikes.[91] Iran may also be on the verge of developing a space launch vehicle and medium-range and intercontinental ballistic missiles, which could reach Europe and the United States.

## IRAN'S BIOLOGICAL WEAPONS CAPABILITY

Iran began an offensive biological weapons (BW) program in the early 1980s during the Iran-Iraq war.[92] The full extent of its biological weapons capability remains uncertain. The November 2004 "721 Report" of the Director of Central Intelligence gave this assessment,

> Even though Iran is part of the Biological Weapons Convention (BWC), Tehran probably maintained an offensive BW program.[93] Iran continued to seek dual-use biotechnical materials, equipment, and expertise that could be used in Tehran's BW program. Iran probably has the capability to produce at least small quantities of BW agents,[94]

and the 2005 U.S. State Department Noncompliance Report concurred, noting that "Iran's capabilities and activities continue to raise concerns about the nature of its BW-related activities."[95]

The 2005 Noncompliance Report reiterated the concern over the nature of Iran's BW-related activities, stating, "Iran is technically capable of producing at least rudimentary biological warheads for a variety of delivery systems, including missiles."[96] Director of National Intelligence (DNI) John Negroponte said in February 2006 testimony that the threat from biological agents or even chemical ones "would have psychological and possibly political effects far greater than their actual magnitude."[97]

## A Growing Biotechnology Base

Iran's biotechnology technical base has grown since the mid-1980s, and its bioproduction capabilities have greatly improved over the past decade. Iran possesses a sophisticated biological and genetic engineering program, including the technology to mass-produce well-developed vaccines.[98] Iran continues to aggressively seek foreign technology, training, and expertise. The 2005 Noncompliance Report concludes, "The scope and nature of Iranian activities demonstrate an expanding legitimate biotechnology industry, which could house an offensive biological weapons program."[99] Iran is believed to be building large, state-of-the-art research and pharmaceutical production facilities that could hide pilot to industrial-scale production capabilities for a potential biological weapons program and could mask procurement of biological weapons-related process equipment.[100] Moreover, the Iranian military has used medical, education, and scientific research organizations for biological weapons-related agent procurement, research, and development.[101] It has been alleged by both British and American intelligence that Iran employs several former Soviet biological engineers to work on Iran's biological weapon arsenal.[102]

## A Developing Delivery Capability

The 2005 Noncompliance Report judges from available information that Iran's offensive program appears to be maturing, with a rapidly evolving capability for the delivery of nuclear, chemical, and biological weapons in a variety of ways. "Iran is technically capable of producing at least rudimentary, bulk-fill biological warheads for a variety of delivery systems, including missiles," the report states.[103] Iran's medium-range Shahab-3 missile is reported to be capable of carrying a biological warhead.[104]

Iran's Biological Warfare Imports and Milestones[a]

| Year/Date | Exporter | Item(s) | Remarks |
|---|---|---|---|
| 4July 4, 1929 | – | – | Iran accedes to the Geneva Protocol. |
| 1955–1960 | United States | Training | Eleven Iranian officials attend U.S. Army chemical and biological weapons training courses. |
| August 22, 1973 | – | – | Iran ratifies the Biological Weapons Convention.[b] |
| Early 1980s | – | – | Iran Research Organization for Science and Biotechnology begins the possession and study of the 600-strain Persian-type culture collection. The cultures are supplied to Iran's private biotechnology industry. |
| Early Mid-1980s | – | – | Iran begins its offensive biological warfare program. |
| 1980s | Canada, the Netherlands | Toxin-producing fungus | Iranian scientist reportedly makes repeated efforts to acquire different strains of a fungus that produces mycotoxins from Canadian and Dutch facilities. |
| July 2, 1987 | – | – | Islamic Republic News Agency (IRNA) claims Iraq used bio weapons during bomb raid on the Iranian town of Sardasht. |
| Mid-1980s | Polish company | NBC protective suits | Mana International Investments, a company registered in Poland and controlled by Israeli businessman Nachum Manbar, supplies Iran with nuclear, biological, and chemical (NBC) protective suits. |
| October 18, 1988 | – | – | Speaker of Iranian Parliament, Hashemi Rafsanjani, suggests considering chemical and bio weapons for Iranian defense. He claims that while inhuman, such weapons may be necessary when "international laws are only scraps of paper" (IRNA, October 19, 1998; FBIS Document).[c] |
| December 1988 | – | – | An Iranian national attempts to buy toxigenic strains of fungi from a Canadian scientist. The Canadian government refuses.[d] |
| 1989 | Germany | Growth media | Iran reportedly purchased growth media for producing mycotoxins. |

| | | | |
|---|---|---|---|
| February 21, 1989 | – | – | U.S. Intelligence reports that Iran is attempting to purchase new strains of fungi from Canada and the Netherlands to produce mycotoxins. This could be for defense-related purposes, such as in the testing of gas masks.[e] |
| August 1989 | – | – | Iran attempts again to purchase fungi, which can be used to produce mycotoxins, from the Netherlands' Central Bureau for Fungus Cultures. The Dutch reject the order.[f] |
| Early 1990s | Unknown | Castor beans | Iran reportedly acquires 120 tons of castor beans, used in the production of toxin, ricin. |
| Spring 1993 | Switzerland, Germany | Technology from Switzerland; equipment from Germany | Reports suggest that Iran has succeeded in obtaining advanced technology that can be applied to biological weapons (BW) from companies in Switzerland as well as containment equipment and technology from Germany. |
| Feb 1997 | China (National Chemical Import-Export Corporation Sinochem) and Poly Group, or Polytechnologies, or the Chinese Commission of Science Technology and Industry for National Defense (or affiliates) | BW-related equipment and technology | Chinese companies are suspected of illicitly transferring BW-related materials and technology to Iran. |
| December 8, 1998 | Russia | Scientific personnel | According to a *New York Times*, Iran has allegedly succeeded in recruiting at least five scientists from the former Soviet Union who once worked in the germ warfare program. This claim is refuted by Russian scientists. |
| 2001 | Cuba | Vaccine-related equipment | The Center for Genetic Engineering and Biotechnology (CIGB) in Cuba states that it sold Iran the "production technology for three of the CIGB's most significant accomplishments: a recombinant hepatitis B vaccine, IFN-$\alpha$IIb, and streptokinase." |

(*continued*)

*(continued)*

| Year/Date | Exporter | Item(s) | Remarks |
| --- | --- | --- | --- |
| 2001 | Chinese entities | CBW equipment | The United States sanctions three Chinese entities for selling materials to Iran: Liyang Chemical Equipment, the China Machinery and Electric Equipment Import and Export Company, and Mr. Q.C. Chen. One of the firms produces glass-lined equipment, but reports did not mention if such equipment was transferred to Iran. State Dept. statement goes on to say that "Q.C. Chen is already subject to U.S. sanctions. In May 1997, he was among seven Chinese entities sanctioned, pursuant to the Chemical and Biological Weapons Control and Warfare Elimination Act of 1991, for knowingly and materially assisting Iran's chemical weapons program through the transfer of chemical weapons, precursor chemicals and/or chemical weapons-related production equipment and technology." These sanctions currently remain in place. |

[a] Nuclear Threat Initiative, Iran Profile: Biological Imports (Updated January. 2004). <http://www.nti.org/e_research/profiles/Iran/Biological/3408.html>; NTI, Country Overviews: Iran Biological Capabilities. <http://www.nti.org/e_research/profiles/Iran/Biological/2302.html>

[b] Signatories of the Biological Weapons Convention. <http://www.opbw.org/convention/status.html>

[c] *IRNA*, October 19, 1998; FBIS Document, FBIS-NES, October 19, 1998; Paula DeSutter, *Denial and Jeopardy: Deterring Iranian Use of NBC Weapons*, National Defense University, <http://www.ndu.edu/ ndu/inss/books/dajd/ch5.html>; Michael Eisenstadt, *Iranian Military Power: Capabilities and Intentions*, The Washington Institute for Near East Policy, Policy Paper No. 42, 1996, pp. 25–26.

[d] Michael R. Gordon with Stephen Engelberg, "Iran is Said to Try to Obtain Toxins." *New York Times*, August 13, 1989, p. 11.

[e] Anthony H. Cordesman and Ahmed S. Hashim, *Iran: Dilemmas of Dual Containment* (Westview Press, 1997), p. 293; Anthony H. Cordesman, "Iranian Chemical and Biological Weapons," CSIS Middle East Dynamic Net Assessment, July 30, 1997, p. 32; Michael Eisenstadt, *Deterrence Series: Chemical and Biological Weapons and Deterrence, Case Study 4: Iran*, Chemical and Biological Arms Control Institute, 1998, p. 2.

[f] Michael R. Gordon with Stephen Engelberg, "Iran is Said to Try to Obtain Toxins." *New York Times*, August 13, 1989, p. 11; "Says Iran Made Two Attempts to Buy Hazardous Fungi in Netherlands." *Associated Press*, August 15, 1989.

# Appendix I: Iran's Policies and International Reaction

## POLICY PRONOUNCEMENTS BY IRAN'S LEADERSHIP

### Mahmoud Ahmadinejad, President of Iran

#### *The Holocaust*

"Their (Zionist's) methods resemble Hitler's. When Hitler wanted to launch an attack, he came up with a pretext, Zionists say they are Hitler's victims, but they have the same nature as Hitler."[1]

"Who actually counted all the victims?"[2]

"They (Zionists) have invented a myth that Jews were massacred and place this above God, religions and the prophets."[3]

"The West claims that more than six million Jews were killed in World War II and to compensate for that they established and support Israel. If it is true that the Jews were killed in Europe, why should Israel be established in the East, in Palestine?"[4]

"If you have burned the Jews, why don't you give a piece of Europe, the United States, Canada or Alaska to Israel. Our question is, if you have committed this huge crime, why should the innocent nation of Palestine pay for this crime? . . . Some European countries are insisting on saying that Hitler burned millions of oppressed Jews in crematoria . . . Although we do not accept this claim [about the annihilation of European Jewry], let's assume that it is true, and we ask the Europeans: Does the killing of oppressed Jews by Hitler [justify] their support for the regime that is occupying Jerusalem? . . . Please, give a part of Europe, and we too will support this. . . .

"Those who support freedom of expression, democracy, and human rights are exploiting the propagandist media [in order to protest] against my clear and documented claims and to criticize me and say that the Iranian president is not capable of living in the civilized world. . . . If your civilization is made up of aggression, of transferring the oppressed nations [from their territory], of repressing the voices of the seekers of justice, and of spreading injustice and poverty among most of the people on Earth, then we say this loud and clear: We scorn your hollow civilization."[5]

### *Israel*

"This is what God has promised and what all nations want. Just as the Soviet Union was wiped out and today does not exist, so will the Zionist regime soon be wiped out."[6]

"Thanks to people's wishes and God's will the trend for the existence of the Zionist regime is downwards and this is what God has promised and what all nations want."[7]

"The Islamic *umma* [community] will not allow its historic enemy to live in its heartland."[8]

"Any leaders in the Islamic *umma* who recognize Israel face the wrath of their own people."[9]

"There is no doubt that the new wave [of attacks] in Palestine will soon wipe off this disgraceful blot [Israel] from the face of the Islamic world."[10]

"Our dear Imam [Ruhollah Khomeini] ordered that the occupying regime in Jerusalem be wiped off the face of the earth. This was a very wise statement. The issue of Palestine is not one which we could compromise on. . . . This would mean the defeat of the Islamic world."[11]

"The issue in Palestine is by no means finished. The Palestinian issue will only be resolved when all of Palestine comes under stringent Palestinian rule."[12]

"I am hopeful that just as the Palestinian nation continued its struggle for the past ten years, they will continue to keep their awareness and vigilance. This period is going to be short-lived. If we put it behind us successfully, god willing, it will pave the way for the destruction and the downfall of the Zionist regime."[13]

"Anybody who recognizes Israel will burn in the fire of the Islamic nation's fury."[14]

"The skirmishes in the occupied land are part of a war of destiny. The outcome of hundreds of years of war will be defined in Palestinian land. As the Imam said, Israel must be wiped off the map."[15]

"Israel is a tyrannical regime that will one day be destroyed."[16]

"Like it or not, the Zionist regime is heading toward annihilation. The Zionist regime is a rotten, dried tree that will be eliminated by one storm."[17]

"We say that this fake regime Israel cannot logically continue to exist."[18]

"Once its [the Muslim world's] storm begins blowing, it will go beyond the borders of Lebanon and Palestine, and it will hurt European countries."[19]

[through translator]: ". . . These Zionists, I want tell you, are not Jews. That's the biggest deception we've ever faced. Zionists are Zionists, period. They are not Jews, they are not Christians and they are not Muslims. They are a power group, a power party and we oppose the oppression and the aggression that any party that seeks pure power, raw power, goes after and we announce and declare loudly that if you support that, you will be condemned by the rest of the world . . . "[20]

"The Zionist regime has deprived the Palestinian nation and other nations of the region of a single day of peace. In the past 60 years it has imposed dozens of wars on the Palestinian nation and others."[21]

"The final point of liberal civilization is the false and corrupt state that has occupied Jerusalem. That's the bottom line. That's what all those who talk about liberalism and support it have in common. In my opinion, if we unmask the liberal order, and present it to humanity bare and without any mask, we will see that its role model is a bunch of shameless Zionists, perpetrating crimes in Palestine. They should know that the volcano of rage of the peoples of the region is boiling. I'm telling you if this volcano erupts—and we are on the brink of eruption and if this ocean rages, its waves will not be limited to the region."[22]

"Israel should be removed from the pages of history."[23]

"The real cure for the conflict is elimination of the Zionist regime."[24]

"With God's blessing, the countdown is now going ahead for the disintegration of Israel, and that is the will of all nations of the world."[25]

"The Zionist regime is counterfeit and illegitimate and cannot survive. The big powers have created this fraud regime and allowed it to commit all kind of crimes to guarantee their interests."[26]

"We ask the West to remove what they created sixty years ago and if they do not listen to our recommendations, then the Palestinian nation and other nations will eventually do this for them."[27]

"If the West does not support Israel, this regime will be toppled. As it has lost its raison d'etre, Israel will be annihilated."[28]

### *Israel During 2006 Lebanon War*

"If the Zionist regime committed the stupidity of attacking Syria, then this would be regarded as an attack against the whole Islamic world and lead to a ferocious reply."[29]

"They (British soldiers) have no boundaries, limits, or taboos when it comes to killing human beings. Who are they? Where did they come from? Are they human beings? 'They are like cattle, nay, more misguided.' A bunch of bloodthirsty barbarians. Next to them, all the criminals of the world seem righteous." "Sixty years ago, by means of a highly complex plan involving psychology, politics, and propaganda, and by means of weapons, they managed to establish a false regime in the heart of the Middle East.... I hereby declare: The world must know that America and England are accomplices to each and every one of the crimes of the regime that has occupied Jerusalem. They must be held accountable.

"Today, Hizbullah in Lebanon is the standard-bearer of the resistance of all the monotheistic peoples, of the seekers of justice, and of the free people. Hassan Nasrallah is shouting the loud cry of the vigilant human consciences. Today, Hizbullah stands tall as the representative of all the peoples, all the vigilant consciences, all the monotheistic people, all the seekers of justice, and all free people of the world, against the rule of hegemony. Until now, with the help of Allah, [Hizbullah] is winning, and, Allah willing, it will reach the ultimate victory in the near future."[30]

In my opinion, Lebanon is the scene of an historic test, which will determine the future of humanity. Everyone must be put to the test. Everyone. It is inconceivable for anyone who calls himself a Muslim and who heads an Islamic state to maintain relations under the table with the regime that occupied Jerusalem. He cannot take pleasure in the [Israeli] killing of Muslims yet present himself as a Muslim. This is inconceivable, and must be exposed. Allah willing, it will. You will see.[31]

### *Western/U.S. Support for Israel and West*

"They (Westerners) did two ugly things. First, they attacked Lebanon in order to extract concessions from us [i.e. Iran]. Second, they took the [nuclear] issue to the [U.N.] Security Council... We, for our part, did not retreat one millimeter.... I say that now, by the grace of God, we have gone most of the way; be confident that they will not dare to attack us." ".... The president of America is like us.

That is, he too is inspired . . . but [his] inspiration is of the satanic kind. Satan gives inspiration to the president of America. . . . ”[32]

“The war that is presently going on in Palestine is the frontline of the war of destiny between the Islamic world and the World Arrogance, which will determine the outcome of hundreds of years [of war] in Palestine.”[33]

“What have the Zionists done for the American people that the US administration considers itself obliged to blindly support these infamous aggressors? Is it not because they have imposed themselves on a substantial portion of the banking, financial, cultural and media sectors?”[34]

“When we protest to the [Europeans, about Israeli foreign policy], they say: ‘There is freedom in our country.’ They are lying when they claim they have freedom. They are hostages in the hands of the Zionists. The people of Europe and America are the ones that should be paying the heavy price of this hostage-taking.”[35]

“. . . . The US Government used the pretext of the existence of weapons of mass destruction in Iraq, but later it became clear that that was just a lie and a deception. . . . ”[36]

“His (George W. Bush) arms . . . ‘are smeared up to the elbow in the blood of other nations.’ ”[37]

### *Iranian Nuclear Crisis*

“Today, the Iranian people are the owner of nuclear technology. Those who want to talk with our people should know what people they are talking to. If some believe they can keep talking to the Iranian people in the language of threats and aggressiveness, they should know that they are making a bitter mistake. If they have not realized this by now, they soon will, but then it will be too late. Then they will realize that they are facing a vigilant, proud people.”[38]

“There are no limits to our dialogue.”[39]

“Anyone who wants to attack our country will be seriously punished.”[40]

“Do you think you are dealing with a 4-year-old child to whom you can give some walnuts and chocolates and get gold from him?”[41]

“Obtaining this technology is very important for our country’s development and honour. It is worth it to stop other activities for 10 years and focus only on the nuclear issue.”[42]

“It is a piece of torn paper . . . by which they aim to scare Iranians . . . It is in the Westerners’ interest to live with a nuclear Iran.”[43]

"Give up this Muppet game. You (the backers of the resolution) cannot send secret friendly messages to us and at the same time show your teeth and claws. End this dual game."[44]

"[Western countries] know that they are not capable of inflicting the slightest blow on the Iranian nation because they need the Iranian nation. . . . They will suffer more and they are vulnerable."[45]

"Even if they adopt 10 other resolutions it will not have any effect."[46]

"Becoming a nuclear state is a high aspiration and a holy goal for Iran."[47]

"Thank God today the train of Iran's nuclear technology has already started and is speeding up day after day and no one is going to stop this train from moving."[48]

"That . . . we shut down our nuclear fuel cycle program to let talks begin. It's no problem. But justice demands that those who want to hold talks with us shut down their nuclear fuel cycle program too. Then, we can hold dialogue under a fair atmosphere."[49]

## Mostafa Mohammed Najjar, Iranian Minister of Defense

### *Persian Gulf Security*

"The volatile situation in the region and the lack of a joint security system between Iran and those Arab states which are situated on the other side of the Persian Gulf have given rise to the presence of foreign forces in the region."[50]

## Major General Yahya Safavi, Head of IRGC

### *U.S., Israeli, and British Regional Involvement*

"Americans, British and Zionists are the root cause of all atrocities in the world . . . Americans' hands are stained with bloods of Iraqi, Palestinian and Afghan people."[51]

### *Arab Sentiment Toward U.S. and Israeli Involvement in the Region*

"I hope that our courageous and great nation will succeed one day in taking revenge against Israel and America, avenging the blood of the oppressed Muslims and the martyrs."[52]

"In light of the Zionists' crimes and oppression, I ask God to hasten the years when this regime will no longer exist. . . . The Zionists are hastening their own death. . . . "[53]

## Ali Larijani, Head of Supreme National Security Council

### *2006 Israel-Hizballah War*

"Israel, which has built up a strong army during the past 60 years, had planned to show its control over Islamic states, but to no avail."[54]

### *U.S. Actions During 2006 Israel-Hizballah War*

"The United States and Britain are responsible for blood of all martyrs of Lebanon and destructions of its civilian infrastructure as they prevented an earlier resolution of the UN Security Council calling for a ceasefire between Israel and Lebanon, Secretary of Supreme National Security Council . . . this shows that the US administration has a liberal appearance but there is a fascist will behind liberalism."[55]

*When asked about possibility of direct negotiations with United States and Israel over terrorism/Iraq/2006 Israel-Hizballah war:*

"The problem with the US is not an emotional problem. The problem is related to the behavior of Americans. Americans should change their views."[56]

### *Iranian Nuclear Ambitions*

"We will start our installation activities (of 3,000 centrifuges) at the Natanz facility from Sunday. . . . It is our immediate answer to the resolution and we will go ahead with full speed."[57]

## Ali Akbar Hashemi Rafsanjani, Head of Iranian Expediency Council

### *Nuclear Issue*

"I have always been hostile to the manufacture of weapons of mass destruction and nuclear weapons. But it is not acceptable for us to renounce (uranium) enrichment."[58]

"The sound strategy is that we should continue talks with the Europeans, and the Europeans and we should be patient to build a sort of confidence which can enable us to carry out enrichment."[59]

"The use of a nuclear bomb in Israel will leave nothing on the ground, whereas it will only damage the world of Islam."[60]

"The United States is the most important country in the world and Iran is the most important country in the region, so it is logical that they solve their problems."[61]

### *Middle East*

"Peace and development in the Middle East cannot materialize [sic.] without the presence of a powerful, independent, free and developed Iran. The vast and powerful Iran is the gateway of peace and stability in the Middle East region and a bridge which links East, West, North and South."[62]

### *His Presidential Term*

"The country must be managed in a non-partisan way. Decision-makers must ignore factional interests. . . . I have never limited myself to a specific staff. During my presidency . . . my administration consisted of rightists, leftists and independents. In selecting my ministers, I chose on the basis of merit."[63]

### *Iranian Government and Civil Liberties*

"At the present time, we must do something for the segment under the poverty line to have a dignified life. This goal can be achieved by creating complete social security and creating employment in the country, without harming economic prosperity. The issue of social safety is also important. The people should not have concerns about improper interference in their lives. Of course, there is the rule of law, and everyone must observe the law. When we go beyond this, we must allow all the people to be comfortable. At the present time, the conditions in the world are such that with the existence of telecommunications, satellites, the Internet, and the media, the people cannot be deprived of information or act without any control."[64]

### *The Islamic Revolution*

"The Islamic revolution does not confine its true and noble nature to geographical borders."[65]

### *Regarding the Possibility of Sending Iran's Nuclear Case to UN Security Council (Addressing Europeans)*

"If you are really honest and worried that Iran may obtain nuclear weapons, there are better ways to gain confidence."[66]

### *Prior to IAEA Referral of Iran's Nuclear Case to UNSC*

"It will be a matter of disgrace if five big countries, enjoying the veto right, show injustice and cruelty and record such an unfair measure in the history."[67]

### Karimi-Rad, Head of Judiciary

#### *Britain*

"[Great Britain's] actions in Iraq, Afghanistan, the way it deals with Muslims and the recent events in London are clear. This country's human rights record is clear and it is the leader of human rights violators in the world and now wants to undermine a populist regime based on the best religion of God with all this propaganda about human rights violations. These issues are all to put more pressure on us over the nuclear energy issue."[68]

#### *Iranian Prison Conditions*

"There is no solitary confinement in Iranian prisons. However, in very few cases, only on the order of a judge and according to the law, some comfortable suites have been built to keep some accused people separate from each other for a limited time."[69]

### Gholam-Ali Haddad-Adel, Iranian Majlis Speaker

"The bill gives a free hand to the government to decide on a range of reactions—from leaving the Nuclear Non-proliferation Treaty to remaining in the International Atomic Energy Agency and negotiating"[70] (speaking about bill passed in Iran which obliges Iranian government to review its cooperation with IAEA).

*Iran's foreign ministry spokesman, Mohammad Ali Hosseini, condemning the resolution as illegal:*

"The decision . . . 'cannot affect or limit Iran's peaceful nuclear activities but will discredit the decisions of the Security Council, whose power is deteriorating.'"[71]

### Javad Zarif, Iranian Ambassador to the United Nations

"Today is a sad day for the non-proliferation regime. . . . The same governments which have pushed this council to take groundless punitive measures against Iran's peaceful nuclear programme have systematically prevented it from taking any action to nudge the Israeli regime towards submitting itself to the rules governing the nuclear non-proliferation regime."[72]

"'A nation is being punished for exercising its inalienable rights' to develop nuclear energy, primarily at the behest of the United States."[73]

### Manouchehr Mottaki, Iranian Foreign Minister

"George Bush is trying to 'cover up' his setbacks in the region, particularly in Iraq."[74]

"Iran's nuclear programme is non-negotiable and we are ready to answer any ambiguities . . . we do not recognise the resolution."[75]

### *Mohsen Rezai, Secretary of the Expediency Council*

". . . the United States was inciting Iranians to rise up against the Islamic regime and to 'promote a sectarian war'."[76]

## INTERNATIONAL REACTIONS TO UNITED NATIONS NUCLEAR SANCTIONS AGAINST IRAN

### Arab and Muslim Responses

### *Khaled Mahmud Arif, Vice Chief of the Pakistani Army General Staff (Ret.)*

"The sanctions the United States had imposed on Iran could not be implemented and were unjust, given the perspectives of the prevailing situation. It was a wrong against Iran, and it was not possible for the United States to implement its sanctions against it."[77]

### *Riaz Muhammad Khan, Foreign Secretary of Pakistan*

"Iran has right to have access to peaceful nuclear technology under the IAEA (International Atomic Energy Agency) safeguards and it should also abide by its obligations under the NPT (Nuclear Non- Proliferation Treaty)."[78]

Text of "Exclusive" Report Entitled: "Press statement by Palestinian Islamic Jihad on UNSC [United Nations Security Council] Resolution Imposing Economic Sanctions on Iran," Posted on Islamic Jihad Movement Web site on December 24, 2006;

> During its 23 December session, the UNSC decided to impose sanctions on the Islamic Republic of Iran for its pursuit of its right to acquire nuclear technology. We in the Palestinian Islamic Jihad [PIJ] strongly condemn this unjust decision against Iran and stress the following:
>
> 1. The UNSC proves time and again its bias in favour of the USA, which monopolizes technological, scientific and nuclear advances for itself and its allies while constraining any attempts at such advancement in our Arab and Islamic world.

Therefore, the UNSC has lost its claim to be defending peace and security in the world.

2. The UNSC turns a blind eye to the numerous violations of international law carried out by the occupation and Zionist aggression state as it continues its nuclear production programme, crowned by a clear admission to this effect by the enemy's prime minister a few days ago.
3. The USA entangles the countries of the world in wars and crimes by producing bogus and misleading reports that meet with silence on the part of the UNSC, which covers up the said reports, despite compelling evidence of the US administration's lies and its concealing of facts related to many of the destructive wars it has launched under an international guise.
4. We hereby express our complete solidarity with the Islamic Republic of Iran, its leadership and its people.[79]

### *Ahmed Abul Gheit, Foreign Minister of Egypt*

"The negligence of certain Western countries over questions of non-proliferation, and the fact that they permit some states to acquire a nuclear capacity while preventing others from doing so, is nothing but double standards.... That must stop. It is known that Israel has a nuclear capability that is not subject to any control by the International Atomic Energy Agency."[80]

### *Bashar Al-Assad, President of Syria*

"Sanctions won't do anything, from the experience in Iraq, in many different countries. Sanctions won't do anything. But the consequences of destabilizing the region by sanctions, by military actions, by any kind of means, will lead to destabilizing the whole Middle East."[81]

### *King Abdullah II, Monarch of Jordan*

"We would like to see a balanced and positive relationship between Iraq and Iran and between Arab states and Iran. We also see that Iran should stop seeking to destabilize Palestine, Lebanon and Iraq or any other country of the region so that we can build constructive relations."[82]

### *Aliyev Baku, President of Azerbaijan*

*Reference to U.S. launch of Iraq war over WMD's and the consequences of speculation over their existence:*

"We have witnessed in the past that such speculations have led to mistakes, so a country should not be punished based on them."[83]

## Non-Arab Responses

### *Condoleezza Rice, U.S. Secretary of State*

"[We] agree that the removal of seals by the Iranian Government, in defiance of numerous IAEA Board resolutions, demonstrates that it has chosen confrontation with the international community over cooperation and negotiation. As the EU-3 and EU have declared, these provocative actions by the Iranian regime have shattered the basis for negotiation."

"We join the European Union and many other members of the international community in condemning the Iranian Government's deliberate escalation of this issue. There is simply no peaceful rationale for the Iranian regime to resume uranium enrichment. We're gravely concerned by Iran's long history of hiding sensitive nuclear activities from the IAEA, in violation of its obligations, its refusal to co-operate with the IAEA's investigation, its rejection of diplomatic initiatives offered by the EU and Russia and now its dangerous defiance of the entire international community."[84]

### *Nicholas Burns, U.S. Under-Secretary of State*

"We don't think this resolution is enough in itself. We want the international community to take further action. . . . We would like to see countries to stop doing business as usual with Iran."[85]

### *Alejandro D. Wolff, Acting U.S. Ambassador to the United Nations*

"If necessary, we will not hesitate to return to this body if Iran does not take further steps to comply."[86]

### *Tony Blair, Former Prime Minister of the United Kingdom*

"Iran is deliberately at the present time causing maximum problems for moderate governments and for ourselves in the region—in Palestine, in Lebanon and in Iraq, . . . there is no point in hiding the fact that Iran poses a major strategic threat to the cohesion of the entire region . . . I think there is a very clear sense in the region now that Iran poses a significant strategic threat and how we deal with that is a major challenge."[87]

### *Margaret Beckett, Former Foreign Secretary of the United Kingdom*

". . . Enforcement of the sanctions was important . . . to keep pressure on Iran to accept the offer of the international community to come back to the negotiating table."[88]

### *Emyr Jones-Parry, British Ambassador to the United Nations*

"Iran has simply thumbed its nose at the council and defied international law.

"Iran . . . faces a choice—the vote today illustrates the gravity of that choice and the seriousness with which we as a council view Iran's behaviour.

"We hope Iran will heed the decision of the council and return to negotiation to resolve the nuclear dossier."[89]

"Iran is deliberately at the present time causing maximum problems for moderate governments and for ourselves in the region—in Palestine, in Lebanon and in Iraq.

" . . . there is no point in hiding the fact that Iran poses a major strategic threat to the cohesion of the entire region . . . I think there is a very clear sense in the region now that Iran poses a significant strategic threat and how we deal with that is a major challenge."[90]

### *Ehud Olmert, Prime Minister of Israel*

"The statements of the Iranian leadership at the conference underline once again the unacceptable character of the Iranian policy and underline the danger to Western civilisation as a whole from such a state."[91]

### *Mark Regev, Israeli Foreign Ministry Spokesman*

"[The resolution sends] a clear message to the Iranian leadership that Iran's nuclear program is total unacceptable and the community of nations will act to prevent the Iranian regime from obtaining nuclear weapons."[92]

### *Amir Peretz, Former Minister of Defense of Israel*

"Pressure should continue to be applied on the international community to impose even more significant sanctions on Iran."[93]

### *Philippe Douste-Blazy, Former Foreign Minister of France*

"Today, more than ever, our objective remains convincing Iran to conform with its international commitments."[94]

### *Kenzo Oshima, Japanese Ambassador to the United Nations*

"In adopting this resolution we earnestly hope and make an appeal to Iran that the country will seek to resolve this issue at the earliest possible time through diplomatic negotiations in full respect of the international obligations."[95]

### *Hu Jintao, President of China*

"The UN Security Council unanimously adopted Resolution 1737, which reflects the shared concerns of the international community over the Iranian nuclear issue, and we hope Iran will make a serious response to the resolution. . . . "[96]

## INTERNATIONAL REACTIONS TO THE IRANIAN NUCLEAR CRISIS

### Angela Merkel, Chancellor of Germany

"We want to prevent the production of Iranian nuclear weapons, and we must. Iran's nuclear programme prompts the justified suspicion, the justified concern, the justified fear that its goal is not the peaceful utilization of nuclear energy, but that military considerations are also in play. Iran has willfully—I am afraid I have to say this—and knowingly overstepped the mark. I must add that we are, of course, compelled to respond to the totally unacceptable provocations of the Iranian President."[97]

### Frank-Walter Steinmeier, Foreign Minister of Germany

"It is clear that this does not mean the end of diplomacy. On the contrary—the Security Council should add weight to the already existing efforts and decisions of the IAEA. We remain committed to a diplomatic solution."[98]

### Vladimir Putin, President of Russia

"We stand unambiguously for strengthening the [nuclear] nonproliferation regime with no exceptions, on the basis of international law. . . . It is known that methods of force rarely give the desired result and their consequences are sometimes more terrible than the original threat."[99]

"I have already mentioned that we will not participate in any crusades, in any holy alliances. This is true, I reaffirm our position in this matter, but our common goal is to make the world a more secure place. . . . The approach has to be balanced and has to take into account the interest of the Iranian people in their desire to develop state-of-the-art high-tech industries, including nuclear ones."[100]

### Sergei Lavrov, Russian Foreign Minister

"We are convinced that there is no military solution to this crisis. The same, I believe, is the position of the UK and Germany as publicly stated by their ministers. And I don't think sanctions as a means to solve a crisis have ever achieved their goal."[101]

### Peter Jenkins, Former United Kingdom Ambassador to the IAEA

"It seems to me that the Iranians are being over-confident in some of the assumptions that they're making about the possible consequences of persisting on their current course. I can think of potential consequences that would cause the current regime to rue their failure to understand the need for confidence building—and in particular, the full suspension of all enrichment activities."[102]

### Philippe Douste-Blazy, Former French Foreign Minister

"A crisis of confidence over the nature and aims of the Iranian programme remains. Once again Iran has not taken up the hand extended by the Europeans and their principal partners, including Russia."[103]

### Jean Marc De La, French Ambassador to the United Nations

"The actions of the council and the work of the council should be gradual and we would be following a gradual approach. . . . Because we want Iran to go back to suspension, so the actions would be gradual and reversible if Iran goes back to suspension."[104]

### Zhang Yan, Director of the Department of Arms Control, Foreign Ministry of China

"China believes that the continuation of the diplomatic efforts remains the wise option for the solution of the Iranian nuclear issue, . . . China appreciates and supports the diplomatic efforts of all parties and call on the international community to exercise patience and restraint in order to give more time to diplomatic efforts."[105]

### Mark Malloch Brown, Deputy Secretary General of the United Nations

"There's been very close collaboration between . . . the five permanent members of the council—that's the US, Britain, France, Russia and China. . . . There's going to be a lot of debate, nevertheless, because this is not an easy issue to handle. But I think everybody wants to avoid another Iraq."[106]

### Mohammed ElBaradei, Director General of the IAEA

"...Everybody will benefit from a political settlement of the Iranian issue. It would be a positive implication on an already a volatile area which is the Middle East."[107]

## INTERNATIONAL REACTIONS TO IRAN'S DIPLOMATIC AND POLITICAL BEHAVIOR

### George W. Bush, President of the United States

"The threat from Iran is, of course, their stated objective to destroy our strong ally Israel. That's a threat, a serious threat. It's a threat to world peace."[108]

"If we catch your people inside [Iraq] harming US citizens or Iraqi citizens you know we will deal with them."[109]

"The message to the Iranian people is that your leaders are making decisions that are isolating you in the world, thereby denying you a brighter future."[110]

### Condoleezza Rice, U.S. Secretary of State

"The government of President Ahmadinejad has done nothing but confront the international system ever since he came into power, confront the international system and their behavior on the nuclear issue, confront the international issue with outrageous statements that I don't think have been made in polite company in many, many, many years.... And so this is about the Iranian regime, and it is the Iranian regime that is isolating Iran."[111]

"We may face no greater challenge from a single country than from Iran, whose policies are directed at developing a Middle East that would be 180 degrees different from the Middle East that we would like to see develop. This is a country that is determined, it seems, to develop a nuclear weapon in defiance of the international community...."[112]

### Nicholas Burns, U.S. Under-Secretary of State

"If Iran takes this step, it is going to confront universal international opposition. If they think they can get away with 3,000 centrifuges without another Security Council resolution and additional international pressure, then they are very badly mistaken."[113]

### Tony Snow, White House Spokesman

"There is a statement of intent and we will see how they follow through on it. We would certainly welcome Iran to start playing a constructive role in the region. And among other things, they could stop smuggling arms—or at least contributing arms. They could stop contributing to terrorist organizations. They could stop supporting Hezbollah."[114]

### Igor Ivanov, Russia's National Security Advisor

"The situation of Iran's nuclear case is critical. Reducing its intensity is our aim. We are currently discussing to remove obstacles from the way of negotiations. All sides should show flexibility and avoid statements that worsen the situation."[115]

### Sergei Lavrov, Foreign Minister of Russia

*Following Iranian President Mahmoud Ahmadinejad's public declaration that Israel should be "wiped off the map":*

"Those who insist on transferring the Iranian nuclear dossier to the UN Security Council have received an additional argument for doing so."[116]

### Sergei Kislyak, Deputy Foreign Minister of Russia

"IAEA inspectors must under all circumstances have an opportunity to fulfill their functions in line with Iran's agreement with this international agency."[117]

## INTERNATIONAL RESPONSES TO IRAN'S HOLOCAUST CONFERENCE

### Ehud Olmert, Prime Minister of Israel

"The conference in Iran was sickening and shows the depths of the hatred."[118]

### Angela Merkel, Chancellor of Germany

"I would like to make clear that we reject with all our strength the conference taking place in Iran about the supposed nonexistence of the Holocaust, . . . Germany will never accept this and will use all possibilities at its disposal to oppose it."[119]

### Tony Blair, Former Prime Minister of the United Kingdom

"I think it is such a symbol of sectarianism and hatred towards people of another religion, I find it just unbelievable. . . . I mean to go and invite the former head of the Ku Klux Klan to a conference in Tehran which disputes the millions of people who died in the Holocaust . . . what further evidence do you need that this regime is extreme?"[120]

### Stephen Harper, Prime Minister of Canada

"On behalf of the Government of Canada, I want to condemn, in the strongest terms, this latest example of anti-Israeli and racist statements from the President of Iran. In addition, the conference hosted by President Mahmoud Ahmadinejad with the sole purpose of denying the Holocaust is an offence to all Canadians."[121]

### White House Statement

"The United States condemns the conference on the Holocaust convoked by the Iranian regime on Monday in Tehran. While people around the world mark International Human Rights Week and renew the solemn pledges of the Universal Declaration on Human Rights . . . the Iranian regime perversely seeks to call the historical fact of those atrocities into question and provide a platform for hatred. The gathering of Holocaust deniers in Tehran is an affront to the entire civilized world, as well as to the traditional Iranian values of tolerance and mutual respect."[122]

### Franco Frattini, European Union Justice Commissioner

"I want to express publicly my shock and indignation [at the Holocaust Conference]. In the face of this event, I want to state my firm condemnation of any attempt to deny, trivialise or minimise the Shoah (Holocaust) war crimes and crimes against humanity. . . . Anti-Semitism has no place in Europe; nor should it in any other part of the world. Dialogue and understanding should overcome hatred and provocation."[123]

# Appendix II: Nuclear Chronology

## 2002

### August 14: MEK/NCRI Reveals Secret Centrifuge Enrichment Plants at Natanz

The Mujaheddin-al-Khalq/National Council of Resistance of Iran (MEK/NCRI) reveals Iran is building two centrifuge plants at Natanz, the Pilot Fuel Enrichment Plant (PFEP), the commercial-scale Fuel Enrichment Plant (FEP), as well as a heavy-water production plant at Arak. The group also says Kalaye Electric Company in Teheran is a front for the project.[1]

## 2003

### February 9: Iran President Khatami Unveils Complete Nuclear Fuel Cycle Plan

President Khatami announces Iran's complete nuclear fuel cycle program to consist of uranium mining at Saghand in Yazd province, yellowcake preparation in a plant under construction in Ardakan near Yazd, uranium conversion at the Uranium Conversion Facility (UCF) under construction in Esfahan, and uranium centrifuge enrichment in plants under construction at Natanz.[2]

### February 21–22: Iran Declares Natanz Centrifuge Facilities, Arak Heavy-Water Plant

International Atomic Energy Agency (IAEA) Director General Mohamed El-Baradei makes the first IAEA visit to Natanz PFEP and FEP centrifuge enrichment plants that Iran had failed to report under comprehensive safeguards agreement. Iran declares enrichment plants, puts maximum enrichment level at 5 percent U-235, and confirms heavy-water plant at Arak.[3]

Iran admits that the Kalaye Electric Company workshop in Tehran was used to produce centrifuge components, but asserts no testing there with $UF_6$ feed or at Natanz.[4]

Iran Vice President Aghazadeh informs IAEA Director General ElBaradei that 100 of the planned 1,000 centrifuges have been installed at PFEP, which is scheduled to start operating in June 2003, and that the commercial-scale FEP is scheduled to receive 50,000 centrifuges when completed.[5]

### February 21–22: Iran Admits Importing Uranium from China in 1991

Iran acknowledges receiving natural uranium from China in 1991: $UF_6$ (1,000 kg), $UF_4$ (400 kg), and $UO_2$ (400 kg), all previously unreported to the IAEA. Material put in storage at the undeclared Jabr Ibn Hayan Multipurpose Laboratories (JHL) at the Tehran Nuclear Research Center (TNRC); most of the $UF_4$ was converted to metal at JHL in 2000.[6] Some of the $UO_2$ was used to test uranium purification and conversion processes intended for planned UCF in Esfahan; other amounts of $UO_2$ were fabricated into targets at the JHL and irradiated in the Tehran Research Reactor (TRR) in undeclared isotope production experiments,[7] wastes were transferred to the waste disposal site at Anarak.[8]

Iran's use of undeclared uranium may have allowed it to experiment with nuclear weapon-related processes that would have been closely scrutinized had they been subject to safeguards.[9]

### March: 1.9 Kilograms of $UF_6$ Found Missing

The IAEA inspectors note that 1.9 kg of $UF_6$ stored in cylinders containing the material imported in 1991 and stored at JHL is missing from leaking cylinder.[10]

### March: MEK/NCRI Charges Secret Activities at Lavizan-Shian

The MEK/NCRI group discloses secret nuclear activities under the Ministry of Defense (MOD) at the Lavizan–Shian site's Physics Research Center (PHRC) in northeastern Tehran. The sensitive equipment at the site is subsequently removed and after November 2003 the site is razed, as revealed in satellite images released in March 2004, to eliminate any trace of the secret activities.[11]

## May 5: Iran Admits Heavy-Water Reactor Program

Iran informs the IAEA that its heavy water reactor program will consist of the heavy-water production plant (HWPP) under construction at Arak (in Khondab); the 40 MW IR-40 heavy-water moderated and cooled research reactor at Arak, with startup planned in 2004; and the Fuel Manufacturing Plant (FMP) at Esfahan, with construction planned for 2003 and operation in 2007, to provide fuel assemblies for the IR-40 and the Bushehr Nuclear Power Plant (BNPP).[12]

The IR-40 is of indigenous design and intended, Iran says, for medical and industrial isotope production and research and development (R&D). Due to restrictions on importing a reactor, the decision was made in the 1980s to build a heavy-water reactor using natural $UO_2$ fuel produced in the UCF, the Zirconium Production Plant (ZPP), and the FMP.[13]

## May 27: MEK/NCRI Claims Enrichment Activities at Lashkar-Abad and Ramandeh

MEK/NCRI alleges additional Iranian centrifuge enrichment sites in AEOI facilities at Lashkar-Abad and Ramandeh, a part of the Karaj Agricultural and Medical Center. Both are in the Hashtgerd region near Karaj about 40 km east of Tehran.[14]

In a visit to Lashkar-Abad on August 12, the IAEA confirms that it was actually a laser laboratory and is told that the Ramandeh site is involved in agricultural studies unrelated to nuclear activities.[15]

## June: Experts Say Centrifuge Development at Natanz Not Possible Without $UF_6$

After visiting the Natanz site, IAEA experts report centrifuges in the PFEP are early European design P-1s. Say observed level of development could not have been based solely on open source information and computer simulations, as claimed, without testing using $UF_6$. Inspectors seek to clarify earlier statement by Iran that design and development started only in 1997.[16]

### June 11: Sampling at Natanz Reveals HEU Particle Contamination

Results from routine samples taken by IAEA in March–June at Natanz PFEP, in preparation for introducing $UF_6$ feed, reveal presence of HEU particles. Material is not in Iran's inventory declared to the IAEA. Iran asserts that HEU particles were carried by centrifuge components obtained from foreign suppliers of the A.Q. Khan network.[17]

### June 25: Iran First Feeds $UF_6$ Gas into a Centrifuge at Natanz PFEP

Iran introduces $UF_6$ gas into one centrifuge at the completed PFEP facility in Natanz; on August 19 begins testing 10-machine cascade.[18]

### July 8: MEK/NCRI Claims Kolahdouz Suspect Nuclear Site

MEK/NCRI identifies a new site in the Kolahdouz industrial complex in west Teheran as a pilot centrifuge test facility operated by the Defense Industry Organization.[19] On October 5, IAEA inspectors take environmental samples at Kolahdouz.[20]

### August 4: IAEA Questions Absence of Plans for IR-40 Hot Cells; Iran Says Nine Planned

The IAEA voices concern that the plans filed for the IR-40 research reactor do not contain any references to hot cells, contrary to what would be expected. It cites reports of alleged efforts by Iran to import remote manipulators and shielded lead glass windows that would be suitable for use in hot cells.[21]

Iran informs the IAEA of an abandoned project to recover long-lived radioisotopes, presenting detailed drawings from a foreign company in 1977 for hot cells to have been constructed at Esfahan. Iran says it used these drawings as basis to its efforts to procure manipulators for hot cells intended for the production of cobalt and iridium isotopes.

On August 19, Iran states that project at Arak includes of nine hot cells: four for the "production of radioisotopes," two for the production of cobalt-60 and iridium-192, and three for waste management processing, requiring ten backup manipulators.[22]

### August 9–12: Iran Now Says Centrifuge Program Launched in 1985, Admits Foreign Aid

Atomic Energy Organization of Iran (AEOI) officials, revising claims that centrifuge program was indigenous and launched in 1997, admit to starting it in

1985; reveal that centrifuge drawings and components were received through a foreign intermediary (the Khan network) around 1987.

AEOI officials describe three-program phases: 1985–1997, mainly at AEOI in Teheran; 1997–2002, concentrated at Kalaye Electric Company in Teheran; since 2002, R&D and assembly at Natanz.[23] AEOI states that in first phase, components were obtained from abroad through foreign intermediaries or directly by Iranian entities; no help was received to assemble centrifuges or provide training; there were many difficulties and machine crashes due to poor quality components; no tests were made with inert or $UF_6$ gas.[24]

### August 9–12: Inspectors Take Samples at Kalaye Centrifuge Facility, Note Changes

IAEA inspectors, after being refused access in March, are allowed to take environmental samples at Kalaye Electric Company workshop to assess enrichment program R&D and note considerable modification of premises since March and May visits.[25]

### August 9–12: Sampling Shows Two Types of HEU Particles at Natanz PFEP

Tests indicate HEU particles of different enrichments taken from two different test centrifuges. IAEA inspectors say this was due to the possibility that one centrifuge was imported, and the other was produced domestically.[26]

### August 12: Inspectors Make First Visits to Lashkar-Abad and Ramandeh Sites

IAEA inspectors visit Lashkar Abad and Ramandeh, earlier identified by MEK/NCRI as sites for centrifuge enrichment. Lashkar-Abad is found to be a laser laboratory; inspectors see current work on the production and testing of copper vapor lasers. No activities observed connected directly to laser spectroscopy or enrichment. Iran says Lashkar-Abad research was originally in laser fusion and spectroscopy.[27]

### August 19: Iran Admits Undeclared Uranium Conversion Experiments in 1990s

After repeated denials, Iran acknowledges undeclared "bench scale" uranium conversion experiments in the 1990s in violation of safeguards; their purpose, presumably, was to design processes for the UCF.[28]

### September 12: IAEA Board Adopts Resolution on Iran Nuclear Activities

The IAEA Board of Governors calls on Iran to "provide accelerated cooperation and full transparency," to ensure no further failures to report materials, facilities, and activities as required under its safeguards agreement; to suspend all reprocessing and enrichment-related activities; and to resolve questions regarding HEU particle contamination, the correctness and completeness of its declarations, the expert view that its centrifuges must have required testing to reach the current state of development, and the completeness of its information on the conduct of conversion experiments.[29]

### September 16: Tests Show Unexplained HEU and LEU Particles at Kalaye Centrifuge Plant

IAEA analysis of sampling at Kalaye Electric Company in August shows presence of HEU and LEU particles; not consistent with Iran's declared nuclear materials inventory.[30]

### September: Records Show Attempts by Iran to Produce Polonium-210

IAEA inspectors find records at TRR indicating irradiation of bismuth metal during 1989–1993. Bismuth is not a safeguarded material, but its irradiation produces polonium-210 (Po-210), an intensely radioactive, alpha particle-emitting isotope that was used in alloyed with beryllium as the neutron initiator of early nuclear weapons designs. Iran says Po-210 was to power thermoelectric generators (RTG's) for satellites.[31]

In February 2004, Iranian officials admit that Po-210 was intended for experiments to study neutron sources. Two targets were irradiated; an unsuccessful attempt was made to extract polonium from one, and the other was discarded.[32]

### October 9: AEOI Admits Undeclared Uranium Conversion Experiments in 1981–1993

The AEOI concedes doing undeclared bench-scale uranium conversion experiments in 1981–1993 on $UO_2$ preparation at the Esfahan ENTC and on preparation of ammonium uranyl carbonate, $UO_3$, $UF_4$, and $UF_6$ at the TNRC.[33]

### October 16: ElBaradei Meets Rohani to Discuss Urgent Nuclear Issues

Chief nuclear negotiator Hassan Rohani and IAEA Director General ElBaradei meet in Tehran to discuss issues related to the HEU and LEU particles found at Kalaye and Natanz, conversion experiments, uranium metal production, the existence of laser isotope enrichment, and the heavy water program.[34]

### October 21: Aghazadeh Admits Centrifuge Tests, Laser Enrichment, Plutonium Experiments

In a sweeping letter to the IAEA, Iran vice president and AEOI head Gholam-Reza Aghazadeh reverses earlier denials and admits testing centrifuges in 1998–2002 at the Kalaye Electric Company, using small amount of $UF_6$ feed imported in 1991. He admits that Iran had a laser enrichment program in 1991–2003 that used 30 kg of undeclared uranium metal. He confirms irradiating 7 kg of $UO_2$ targets (prepared at the Esfahan ENTC) during 1988–1992 at the TNR and processing 3 kg of that in glove boxes at TNRC, separating small quantities of plutonium (Iran estimates 200 micrograms) stored in solution at JHL.[35]

He says that 1.9 kg of imported $UF_6$ was used in the experiments at Kalaye, which contradicted earlier explanation that missing $UF_6$ had leaked from storage.[36]

He acknowledges that Iran had contacts related to laser enrichment starting in 1970 with sources in four foreign countries, related to both Atomic Vapor Laser Isotope Separation (AVLIS) and Molecular Vapor Laser Isotope Separation (MLIS) processes.

### October 21: Iran Admits Plans to Produce Uranium Metal for Laser Enrichment Program

Iran tells the IAEA that a line at the UCF under construction at Esfahan was intended to convert $UF_6$ natural uranium metal for the laser enrichment program, contradicting earlier statement that the line would produce depleted uranium metal for shielding.[37]

### October 21: Iran in Joint Statement with EU-3 Ministers Says Will Halt Nuclear Program

Iran, in a joint statement with foreign ministers of France, Germany, and Britain (EU-3), agrees to suspend all uranium enrichment and reprocessing and to sign and ratify an Additional Protocol to its safeguards agreement; would meet an October 31 deadline set in September by the IAEA Board of Governors in return for recognition of Iran's right to pursue peaceful nuclear energy.[38]

### October 27–November 1: Iran Admits Lashkar Abad Was Laser Enrichment Plant

Iran acknowledges, during October 27–November 1 inspections, that a pilot plant for laser enrichment was set up at Lashkar Abad in 2000; enrichment experiments using undeclared uranium were conducted there in October 2002–January 2003; the equipment was dismantled in May 2003 and transferred with the uranium metal to Karaj for storage; it is observed there by inspectors on October 28.[39]

### October 30: 164-Centrifuge Cascade Installation Nearing Completion at PFEP

IAEA inspectors visiting Natanz PFEP note installation of 164-centrifuge cascade being completed; construction and installation work at the site continue.[40]

### November 1: Iran Says It Has Not Enriched Uranium Beyond 1.2 Percent

Iran tells the IAEA that it had not enriched uranium beyond 1.2 percent U-235 in centrifuges at Kalaye, asserting that HEU contamination was on centrifuge components of foreign origin and not due to indigenous activities.[41]

### November 1: Iran Confirms Hot Cells Planned on Arak Reactor Site

Iran confirms plans to build a facility with two hot cells at Arak, the site of the planned IR-40 heavy water.[42]

### November 10: Iran Announces Suspension of Uranium Enrichment And Reprocessing

Iran informs IAEA Director General ElBaradei of its decision to suspend all enrichment-related and reprocessing activities, meaning activities at Natanz and the production and import of feed materials for enrichment.[43]

### December: Razing of Lavizan-Shian Site Begun

Razing of Lavizan-Shian, a suspect military nuclear site, has begun, according to Iran, by the municipality of Tehran after a decision ordering the sites return to the municipality for use as a park. Analysis of the vegetation and soil samples shows no evidence of nuclear material, but razing of the site makes the detection of nuclear material in soil samples very difficult. Removal of buildings makes it impossible to verify what activities had taken place.[44]

### December 18: Iran Signs Additional Protocol to Safeguards Agreement

Iran signs the Additional Protocol to its comprehensive safeguards agreement with the IAEA, allowing broader inspections.[45]

### December 29: Iran Augments November 10 Enrichment, Reprocessing Suspension

Iran informs the IAEA that the uranium enrichment and fuel reprocessing suspension announced on November 10 will be expanded to cover installation of centrifuges at FEP and new centrifuges at PFEP, operation and testing of centrifuges, introduction of nuclear material into centrifuges, and the withdrawal of nuclear material from any centrifuge enrichment facility.[46]

## 2004

### January 20: Iran Says Received Only P-2 Centrifuge Drawings from Abroad

Iran acknowledges receiving P-2 centrifuge drawings from foreign sources (the Khan network) in 1994 and says that it conducted tests on domestically manufactured rotors without nuclear material. IAEA experts say drawings are similar to early advanced European design that use maraging steel rotors with bellows; Iran says that in 1999 or 2000, AEOI contracted with a private company in Teheran to develop and test carbon composite rotors based on a modified P-2 design.[47]

### January: IAEA Questions Why P-2 Design Omitted from Extensive October 21 Declaration

The IAEA criticizes Iran for omitting mention of P-2 centrifuge equipment stored at Par Trash after June 2003 from its declaration on October 21, 2003, especially since P-1 centrifuge components from Kalaye, secretly stored at Pars Trash in the Spring of 2003, were declared in October.[48]

### January 28: Tehran P-2 Contractor Developed Rotors for Modified Design

The owner of a Tehran company that was under contract to AEOI to develop the P-2 centrifuge explains to IAEA experts that the decision to develop a shorter subcritical carbon composite rotor was made because Iran was not capable of manufacturing the advanced European design. His company produced seven rotors of various dimensions, did mechanical tests without nuclear material. Work was terminated after June 2003 and the equipment was moved to Pars Trash Company in Tehran.[49]

### February 24: IAEA Suggests Maybe More Hidden Nuclear Material in Iran

An IAEA report to the Board of Governors notes that "given the size and capacity of the equipment used, the possibility cannot be excluded that larger quantities of nuclear material could have been involved than those declared" by Iran.[50]

### February 24: Iran Expands Suspension to Cover Manufacture of Centrifuge Components

Iran informs the IAEA that its enrichment and reprocessing suspension announced on November 10, 2003 will include assembly and testing of centrifuges and the domestic manufacture of centrifuge components.[51]

### April: Iran Admits Some P-2-Related Components Were Imported

Iran informs the IAEA that it had in fact imported some components relevant to its P-2 enrichment activities, but gives no additional information.[52]

### May 4: Iran Provides Information about Transfer of P-1s, But Not Source

Iran provides additional information on the transfer of imported P-1 centrifuge components, but gives no information about the origin of the P-1 components, which it claims it does not know.[53]

### May 30: Iran Acknowledges Importing Magnets for P-2 Centrifuges

Iran admits to importing magnets for P-2 centrifuges from Asian suppliers, contrary to earlier assertion that all P-2 components manufactured in workshop of private company in Tehran. Company also had inquired about procuring 4,000 or more P-2 magnets from a European supplier, but no deliveries had occurred.[54]

### Late May: IAEA Concludes Some Rotors for P-2 Manufactured in Tehran Workshop

In a visit to the workshop of the private company in Tehran under contract to the AEOI for the P-2 centrifuge program, the IAEA concludes that the carbon composite rotors for the modified P-2 design "had in fact been manufactured" there.[55]

### May-June: Iran Conducts Hot Tests at UCF to Produce $UF_6$

After informing the IAEA, Iran conducts hot tests at the UCF between May and June, generating about 30–35 kg $UF_6$. A larger test is planned for August–September 2004 with thirty-seven metric tons of yellowcake.[56] Iran's enrichment suspension did not include $UF_6$ production.[57]

### June 1: IAEA Questions Iran's Assertions on Timetable of P-2 Centrifuge Work

In a report to the Board of Governors, the IAEA questions Iran's statements that no work was begun on P-2 centrifuges until 2001 and that mechanical testing of rotors began only in 2002, even though design drawings were acquired in 1995. IAEA experts express doubt that Iran could have acquired and manufactured parts and components and carried out tests in the stated period of less than a year.[58]

### June 1: IAEA Experts Say Same P-2 Centrifuge Drawings Provided to Iran and Libya

The technical drawings of P-2 centrifuge that Iran says it received from foreign intermediaries around 1995 are determined by IAEA experts to be of the same origin as the drawings provided to Libya.[59]

### June 1: IAEA Says Iran Understated Plutonium Production by Factor of 5–10

According to earlier statements by Iran, two hundred micrograms of plutonium had been separated in glove boxes at TNRC from depleted $UO_2$ targets irradiated in the TRR reactor in the 1990s. From samples, IAEA experts conclude that the amount of plutonium separated is in the milligram range, a factor of 5–10 greater; Iran agrees.[60]

### June 1: LEU, HEU Particles Found at Natanz, Kalaye, Farayand Technique

The completeness of Iran's declarations of enrichment activities is called into question by uranium particle contamination found in environmental samples taken from Natanz and the Kalaye Electric Company workshop. The IAEA reports that the current accounting leaves a number of discrepancies and questions:

- Domestically manufactured centrifuge components show mainly LEU contamination, while imported components show both LEU and HEU particles; in conflict with Iran's explanation that domestic components were contaminated solely by imported ones.
- The 36 percent U-235 contamination found at Kalaye and Farayand Technique differs from that at Natanz; in conflict with Iran's statement that all the contamination sites are from the same source—imported P-1 components. Imported P-1 components may contain negligible traces of 36 percent U-235, but more than trace quantities in one room of Building 3 at Kalaye and on a balancing machine at Farayand, relocated from Kalaye. Thirty-six percent enriched U-235 is characteristically used in some research reactors outside Iran.
- Analytical results provided by Pakistan, the country of origin of the imported P-1 centrifuges, make it implausible as a source of the 36 percent U-235 contamination because of the very high U-236 content in the material found in Iran. [61]

### June 23: Iran to Remove Seals, Resume Manufacturing and Testing P-1 Centrifuges

Iran informs the IAEA of its intention, despite suspension declarations, to resume manufacturing P-1 centrifuge components and assembling and testing of P-1 centrifuges. Seals at Natanz, Pars Trash and Farayand Technique are removed and returned to the IAEA during July 6–18 visit. In mid-August, the IAEA is shown seventy new rotors assembled and tested. However, as of September 1, suspension of enrichment continues at Natanz PFEP and FEP and there is no reprocessing at JHL.[62]

### June 28: IAEA Visits Lavizan-Shian Site and Takes Environmental Samples

Iran permits IAEA inspectors to take environmental samples at suspect Lavizan-Shian and provides access to two whole body counters.[63]

### July 17: Inspections Conducted at Saghand and Gchine Uranium Mines and Mills

The IAEA conducts inspections at the Gchine mine on July 17, at the Saghand mine on October 6, and at the Ardakan Yellowcake Production Plant on October 7 to confirm the status of these operations in accord with Additional Protocol declarations of May 21.[64]

### August 3–8: Iran Says P-2 Not Discussed In 1995–1999 Meetings Khan Network

Iran officials tell the IAEA that despite frequent meetings and other contacts in 1995–1999 with Khan network intermediaries, the topic of P-2 centrifuges was never addressed, once the network had provided Iran with P-2 drawings in 1995.[65]

### August: State Department Issues 43-Page Briefing on Natanz Briefing

The U.S. State Department distributes a 43-page unclassified briefing on Iran's nuclear program to the IAEA Board members in preparation for their September 24 vote on Iran. The paper shows commercial satellite photos, states that a dummy building at the Natanz centrifuge facility hides a secret entrance ramp to an underground factory, and provides analysis to argue that Iran has uranium for a significant number of nuclear weapons, but that its proven uranium reserves cannot fuel a nuclear power program beyond 2010.[66]

### August 11: Iran Tests Upgraded Version of Shahab-3, May Be Geared to Nuclear Payload

Iran Defense Ministry announces that it has test-fired an upgraded version of the Shahab-3 missile. The test marked the appearance of an advanced nose cone with greater range, accuracy, and stability, but with less payload space in a configuration typically suited to a compact nuclear warhead.[67]

### September 1: IAEA Says Unanswered Questions Remain on LEU and HEU Contamination

The IAEA gives a report to the Board of Governors on the status of LEU and HEU particles found at Natanz, Kalaye Electric Company workshop, Farayand Technique, and Pars Trash. Iran continues to say the contamination is from imported P-1 components. It has identified intermediaries but denies knowing the origin of components.

Questions remaining to be answered:[68]

- why contamination found at Natanz PFEP is different from that at Kalaye,
- why 36 percent U-235 particles only at three locations with imported components, not at others,
- why at Kalaye the number of 36 percent U-235 particles is large compared to other enrichments,
- why domestic components showed predominantly LEU contamination, while imported ones showed both LEU and HEU contamination, if the contamination of the domestic components was due solely to contamination from the imported ones.

The IAEA analysis shows that "most of the HEU contamination found at the Kalaye Electric Company workshop and Natanz correlates reasonably with the HEU contamination found on imported components" and "it appears plausible that the HEU contamination found at the Kalaye Electric Company workshop and Natanz may not have resulted from enrichment of uranium by Iran at those locations."

### September 1: IAEA Not Convinced That No P-2 Work Done by Iran In 1995–2002

The IAEA reports to the IAEA Board on September 1 its suspicion that Iran's assurance of no P-2-related work being done in 1995–2002 is insufficient.[69] On August 3–8, Iran stated that the P-2 rotor manufacturing and testing took place in the period 2002–2003.[70]

### September 1: Iran Laser Enrichment Facility Could Have Produced HEU

In its report of September 1 to the Board of Governors, the IAEA says that an examination of the contract for the AVLIS facility at Lashkar-Abad and the specified design parameters for the production of uranium enriched from 3.5 to 7 percent indicates the facility could have produced HEU in gram quantities. Iran scientists said they were not aware of these features.[71]

### September 24: IAEA Board Passes Resolution Citing History of Concealment and Deception

The IAEA Board of Governors passes a resolution by a vote of 22 to 1 with 12 abstentions, citing Iran for a long history of concealment and deception and repeated failure to live up to its obligations under the NPT. The resolution sets up Iran for possible future referral to the UN Security Council.

### November 15: In Paris Agreement Iran Extends, Expands Nuclear Suspension

Paris Agreement between Iran, France, Britain, and Germany extends October 2003 agreement to include suspension of all enrichment related and reprocessing activities: specifically, the manufacture and import of gas centrifuges and components; the assembly, installation, testing, or operation of gas centrifuges; any plutonium separation, or work to construct or operate any plutonium separation installation; and all tests or production at any uranium conversion installation. In return, the EU will resume negotiations on a trade agreement and support Iran's entry into the World Trade Organization (WTO).[72, 73]

### November 19: U.S. Intelligence Obtains Iranian Documents on Nuclear Warhead Delivery

U.S. Secretary of State Colin Powell and U.S. officials brief reporters on over 1,000 pages of Farsi-language computer files, diagrams, and test results obtained by U.S. intelligence from a single unvetted "walk-in" source that are purported to be Iranian drawings and technical documents on modifications of a ballistic missile to carry a nuclear warhead. U.S. officials say the materials reveal efforts in 2001–2002 by Iran to adapt the Shahab missile for the delivery of a "black box" that is said to be a nuclear warhead from specifications of its size, shape, weight, and height of detonation.[74]

## 2005

### January: IAEA Takes Samples, Seeking to Explain Source of LEU and HEU Particles

Seeking to verify source of LEU and HEU particles found at centrifuge enrichment sites in Iran, IAEA revisits facilities in member state (Dubai) where Iran says P-1 centrifuge components were manufactured, used, or stored by the supply network prior to shipment to Iran. Additional samples are taken in March.[75]

### January: Iran Documents Show First Deliveries of P-1 Centrifuges in January 1994

Shipping documents supplied by Iran to the IAEA indicate that deliveries of P-1 centrifuge components started in January 1994, before Iran's previously declared date of the first meeting between AEOI and representatives of the Khan network.[76]

### January 12: Iran Lets IAEA See "1987 Offer" for Centrifuge Equipment

Iran shows the IAEA a one-page handwritten document reflecting an offer in 1987 by Pakistani scientist A.Q. Khan to deliver a centrifuge enrichment kit, including a disassembled centrifuge, blueprints for the production of P-1 centrifuges, specifications for a complete plant, and materials for 2,000 machines. The offer also includes uranium reconversion and casting equipment, the latter having a nuclear weapons connotation. Iran maintains that only some components of 1 or 2 disassembled centrifuges were delivered, that items delivered were declared, and that the reconversion unit with casting equipment was not received. It claims the one-pager is the only document in its possession relating to the 1987 offer. Iran tells the IAEA that the offer was not solicited.[77]

### February 27: Russia to Supply LEU Fuel for Bushehr-1 and Take Back Spent Fuel

On February 27, 2005, Iranian Vice President Gholam-Reza Aghazadeh, who also heads the AEOI, and Russian Federal Atomic Energy Agency chief Alexander Rumyantsev signed a ten-year agreement for Russia to supply fresh LEU fuel for the Bushehr-1 reactor and take back the spent fuel after a several years' cooling.[78]

### April 6: Iran Documents Show Contacts on P-1 Centrifuges in 1993

Iran provides documents showing trips relevant to P-1 centrifuge procurement made by AEOI representatives in August and December 1993. Shipping documents supplied in January by Iran to the IAEA indicated that deliveries of P-1 centrifuge components started in 1994, before Iran's previously declared date of the first meeting between AEOI and Khan network representatives.[79]

### July 18: U.S. Intelligence Briefs IAEA on Stolen Iran Laptop with Nuclear Data

U.S. intelligence officials secretly brief Director General ElBaradei and other IAEA officials on the reputedly stolen Iranian laptop computer, obtained in mid-2004 and said to contain over 1,000 pages of documents on computer simulations, calculations, and experiments related to the design modifications of a Shahab-3 missile nose cone for carrying a compact nuclear warhead. The classified briefing is provided in preparation for a vote at the upcoming IAEA board meeting on September 24 to recommend action by the UN Security Council against Iran. Britain, France, and Germany already have been briefed.

The laptop's documents do not contain the word "nuclear" but make references that could only apply to the design and delivery of a nuclear warhead; specifically, the symmetric placement of detonators to trigger a warhead's chemical explosive; the choice of 2,000 feet as the prime altitude for an explosion; and a study of how to secure a "black box" core in the nose cone during delivery of a weapon to its target.[80]

### August 1: Iran Resumes Uranium Conversion Activities at Esfahan UCF

Iran announces it is resuming uranium conversion activities at the UCF in Esfahan, after nearly 20 months of suspension. On August 8–10, the IAEA installs additional surveillance equipment there. On August 8, Iran starts feed into the process line. By August 29, 8.5 metric tons of uranium in $UF_4$ from a previous campaign is fed into the $UF_4$ to $UF_6$ process line, producing 6.8 metric tons of uranium in $UF_6$.[81]

### Early August: Analysis Supports Iran on Foreign Origin of HEU Particles

Tests from swipe samples taken by the IAEA on May 21 from centrifuge components obtained through the Khan network by another member state (Libya) "tend on balance to support Iran's statement about the foreign origin of most of the observed HEU contamination."[82]

### August: Iran Provides Documentation on Razing the Lavizan-Shian Site

Iran provides the IAEA with documentation that the Lavizan-Shian site was razed starting in December 2003 following its return to the municipality of Tehran. The IAEA is still waiting for an explanation of why two whole body counters were located there and about efforts of the Physics Research Center (PHRC) located there to acquire dual-use equipment, with both civil and military applications, that could have been used in uranium enrichment and conversion.[83]

### August 31: Iran Rejects EU-3 Framework Proposal as "Insulting"

The Framework proposal of the EU-3 countries (Britain, France, and Germany) that would support Iran's pursuit of a civil nuclear power program in return for Iran giving up its quest for uranium enrichment and reprocessing is condemned by Iran as an "insult on the Iranian nation."[84]

## September 2: IAEA Again Questions Iran's Nuclear Activities in Report to Board

The IAEA reports to the Board of Governors that it is unable to conclude that there are no undeclared nuclear materials or activities in Iran. The two important outstanding issues are the origin of LEU and HEU particle contamination found at various locations in Iran and the extent of Iran's efforts to import, manufacture, and use centrifuges of both the P-1 and P-2 designs.[85]

## September 2: Iran Reports on Mid-1990s Offer to Supply Iran 500 P-1 Centrifuges

Iran tells the IAEA that it has no written documents reflecting an oral offer in the mid-1990s by the Khan network to an Iranian company to deliver components for 500 P-1 centrifuges. The head of AEOI was made aware of the offer, which resulted in renewed contacts in 1993 between the AEOI and network intermediaries.[86]

## September 2: IAEA Skeptical About Timeline for Development of Gchine Mine and Mill

The IAEA is attempting to understand the apparent rapid development of the Gchine uranium mine and mill in the 2000 to mid-2001 period by a newly founded company with only limited experience in uranium ore processing. It also would like to know why no work was carried out at the Gchine site in 1993–2000. Iran states that experiments with Gchine ore were done at a TNRC lab.[87]

## September 24: IAEA Board Adopts Resolution Finding Iran Not in Safeguards Compliance

IAEA Board of Governors adopts a resolution finding Iran in noncompliance with its NPT safeguards agreement.[88] The vote was not by consensus, and the Board did not refer the issue to the Security Council, even though the IAEA Statute, Article XII.C, states that a finding by the Board of noncompliance must be reported to the Security Council.[89]

## September: Speech of Former Negotiator Rohani Shows How Iran Used Delay Tactics

A speech given in late 2004 by then chief nuclear negotiator Hassan Rohani to the Supreme Council of Cultural Revolution is published in the Expediency Council quarterly.[90]

Rohani explains how prolonging negotiations with the EU-3 bought time to complete the Uranium Conversion Facility at Esfahan. The strategy was to delay referral of the resolution adopted in September 2003 by the IAEA Board of Governors to the UN Security Council, avoiding the possibility of economic sanctions and giving time for Iran to finish upgrading its nuclear capabilities, with the result that 500 centrifuges were then operational, an increase from 150 at the beginning of the EU-3 talks.

The speech may have been leaked in response to Ahmadinejad's hard line since becoming president and to justify the Khatami regime's decision to sign the Additional Protocol and suspend centrifuge enrichment and manufacture.[91]

### October 9: Start of Esfahan Fuel Manufacturing Plant Probably Delayed Until After Planned 2007

Inspectors visiting the Fuel Manufacturing Plant (FMP) in Esfahan see ongoing civil engineering construction, but are told that planned commissioning date of 2007 is likely to be postponed.[92]

### November 1: Sampling at Parchin Military Site Finds No Nuclear Material

IAEA inspectors are given access to the Parchin military site and take environmental samples. Results of analysis of samples do not indicate nuclear materials in the buildings visited.[93]

### November: IAEA Takes Samples at Network Storage Site, Finds No Nuclear Material

IAEA reports that the analysis of environmental samples collected in a country (Dubai) where centrifuge components being shipped by the Khan network in the mid-1990s to Iran were stored did not show any traces of nuclear material.[94]

### December 28: Iran Vacillates on Russian Plan for Nuclear Fuel

A senior Iranian official says that Iran would "seriously and enthusiastically" study the proposal made by Russia, under which Iran would enrich its uranium gas in Russia, where it would be processed into fuel and then returned to Iran. This would serve to break the deadlock on efforts to block Iran from enriching uranium. The same proposal was rejected in talks in Vienna between Iran and the EU-3 a week earlier.[95] On January 3, a foreign ministry spokesman rejects any proposal that involves Tehran enriching uranium exclusively in Russia.[96] Iran's true position on this issue remains unclear.

## 2006

### January: IAEA Samples Equipment Procured by Lavizan-Shian PHRC

The IAEA is allowed to take environmental samples from dual-use and enrichment-related equipment procured by the Lavizan-Shian PHRC and relocated to a nearby technical university.[97]

### January 3: Iran Revokes Suspension of Enrichment

Iran informs the IAEA that as of January 9 it will resume enrichment activities at Natanz, Farayand Technique, and Pars Trash. It asks the IAEA to remove the seals applied for monitoring the voluntary suspension.[98] Seals are removed on January 10 and 11, and the IAEA places the facilities under safeguards.[99]

Inspectors report that substantial renovation of the gas handling system is underway at the PFEP at Natanz, and quality control of components and some rotor testing is being conducted at Farayand Technique and Natanz.

The IAEA is effectively unable to monitor Iran's R&D activities except at the Natanz PFEP, where containment and surveillance safeguards measures are being applied to the enrichment process. The feeding of the 10-machine cascade was begun on February 15, 2006, and on February 22, 2006, a 20-machine cascade was subjected to vacuum testing. Installation of the first 3,000 P-1 machines at the Natanz FEP is planned for the fourth quarter of 2006.[100]

### January 26: IAEA Again Questions Dual-Use Equipment at Lavizan-Shian

Replying to the IAEA's requests since 2004 for additional information on efforts by the PHRC at Lavizan-Shian to acquire dual-use items, Iran gives the IAEA documentation on unsuccessful efforts to obtain specific dual-use items—electric drives, power supplies, and a dye laser. All of the items, Iran asserts, were intended for the technical university laboratory where the head of PHRC at that time was a professor.

Other equipment in question could be relevant for uranium enrichment: balancing machine, mass spectrometers, magnets, and fluorine handling equipment. The IAEA presents a list of high-vacuum equipment purchased by the PHRC and asks to see it. Iran again declines a request to interview the professor.[101]

### January 26: Iran Made Efforts to Buy Special Dual-Use Materials in 2000

To explain its efforts in 2000 to acquire high strength aluminum, special steels, titanium, and special oils, all items related to centrifuge development, Iran says that the aluminum was acquired but found unsuitable for aircraft manufacturing. The IAEA continues to investigate other items, including the acquisition of corrosion resistant steel, valves, and filters.[102]

### January 27: Iran Attempts to Clarify Document on the Green Salt Project

Iran meets with the IAEA on Green Salt Project, the alleged studies on developing indigenous conversion of $UO_2$ to $UF_4$ (or "Green Salt"), and on testing related to high explosives and the design of a missile reentry vehicle.[103]

Iran reiterates that the document is fabricated, that any allegations are baseless, and that all conversion efforts are devoted to the UCF project, which is based on blueprints acquired from abroad (China), so that it would be senseless to develop indigenous capabilities to produce $UF_4$. Iran refuses to supply the IAEA with a copy but agrees to place it under IAEA seal.[104] Article II of the NPT obligates Iran not to receive any assistance in the manufacture of nuclear explosives.[105]

### February 4: IAEA Board Votes Resolution to Report Iran Nuclear Activities to UN

The IAEA Board of Governors adopts a resolution calling on the Director General to report to the UN Security Council on steps required of Iran, including: reinstituting full suspension of all uranium enrichment-related and fuel-reprocessing activities; halting plans to construct the IR-40 research reactor; continuing to abide by the provisions of the safeguards Additional Protocol; and continuing transparency measures relating to access to individuals, documents, and facilities.

The Board expresses its lack of confidence in Iran's intentions related to developing a fissile material production capability in light of Iran's poor record on safeguards and (1) asks for clarification on certain activities that could have a "military nuclear dimension" and (2) expresses concern about Iran's possession of the Green Salt document on the production of uranium metal hemispheres, and asks that a copy be given to the IAEA.[106]

### February 19: Opening of IR-40 Reactor May Be Postponed to 2011

Iran continues civil engineering work at the IR-40 reactor, but commissioning date is likely to be postponed until 2011, IAEA inspectors are told.[107]

### February 6: Iran Suspends Additional Protocol to Safeguards

Iran suspends its voluntary adherence to the Additional Protocol, which it signed on December 18, 2005 but has not ratified, and informs the IAEA that henceforth safeguards measures and verification activities will be based only on its NPT safeguards agreement.

On February 12, the IAEA modifies containment and surveillance measures at the UCF.[108]

### February 12: Iran Reports Stockpiling 85 Metric Tons of $UF_6$

The uranium conversion campaign, which began at the UCF in August 2005 is expected to end in April 2006. Since September 2005, approximately 85 metric tons of uranium in $UF_6$ has been produced there.[109]

### February 12–14: Iran Reiterates Claim of No Delivery of P-2 Components in 1995–2002

Responding to information shared by the IAEA with Iran in November 2005 on possible delivery of P-2 components in 1995–2002, Iran reasserts that no deliveries of P-1 or P-2 components were made after 1995. Iran has said it had no contacts with the network from 1987 to mid-1993, and the IAEA continues to ask for documentation on the acquisition of five hundred sets of P-1 components in the mid-1990s.[110]

### February 22: Iran Restarts Feeding $UF_6$ Gas into Centrifuges at Natanz

Iran vacuum tests a 20-machine cascade at PFEP after feeding a single P-1 with $UF_6$ gas on February 11 and a 10-machine cascade on February 15.[111]

### February 26: IAEA Interviews Former Head of PHRC Lab at Lavizah-Shian Site

The IAEA meets with a technical university professor who formerly headed the PHRC at Lavizan-Shian. He repeats claim that a laser and other dual-use equipment, although procured through the PHRC, were for use in R&D at the university, but denies knowing details of research projects. Iran refuses to permit the IAEA to interview the other former head of the PHRC.[112]

### March 12: Iran Rejects Russian Offer for Enrichment

Iran rejects an offer by Russia to enrich Iran-origin uranium in Russia and return it to Iran to fuel its nuclear power reactors.[113]

### March 29: UN Security Council Issues Statement, Calls on Iran to Suspend Enrichment

UN Security Council issues presidential statement calling on Iran to resume suspension of uranium enrichment and interim application of Additional Protocol and asks for a report on compliance from the IAEA by April 28.[114]

### April 11: Ahmadinejad Announces Iran Has Enriched Uranium to 3.5 Percent

In a speech, Iran President Mahmoud Ahmadinejad announces that Iran has enriched uranium to 3.5 percent, the level required for civil nuclear reactor fuel, placing Iran among the nuclear states.[115] On the same day, former president Hashemi Rafsanjani, who heads the Supreme National Security Council, states that Iran had enriched the uranium using a cascade of 164 centrifuges.[116]

### April 11, 13: Aghazadeh Provides Information on Centrifuge Program

AEOI head Gholam-Reza Aghazadeh reveals details about Iran's nuclear project, describes resolving problems with unstable spinning centrifuge rotors, and confirms plans to develop the more advanced P-2 centrifuge in order to multiply production. Iran now has a stockpile of 110 metric tons of $UF_6$, he says. He also says that Iran is planning a 360 MW nuclear power reactor and will issue a tender for two additional 1,000 MW nuclear power reactors.[117]

In the interview, Aghazadeh says that the annualized output of the centrifuges in the cascade is low, with a maximum feed rate of 70 gm per hour and a product of 7 gm per hour of 3.5 percent enriched uranium. He further implies that he expects the output of each centrifuge to almost double in the main plant.[118]

### April 12: Ahmadinejad Says Iran Testing Advanced P-2 Centrifuges

President Ahmadinejad tells students that Iran was testing advanced P-2 centrifuges with "quadruple the capacity of the P-1," raising concerns over a secret P-2 program based on machines obtained through the Khan network.[119] On June 16, Iran informs the IAEA that it is doing R&D on different types of centrifuge machines, but without introducing nuclear material.[120]

### April 17: IAEA Finds Inconsistencies in Iran Plutonium Data

After completing its analysis of Iran's undeclared experiments involving the separation of milligram quantities of plutonium, the IAEA says that it cannot exclude the possibility that some was derived from sources not declared by Iran.[121]

### April 19: Former Nuclear Negotiator Rohani Criticizes Handling of Nuclear Negotiations

Apparently in response to President Ahmadinejad's announcement of achieving 3.5 percent U-235 enrichment, former chief nuclear negotiator Hassan Rohani criticizes his successor, Ali Larijani, calling for "more balance . . . more reason and less emotion" in Iran's approach to the nuclear crisis and advocating negotiations with the West.[122]

### April 28: ElBaradei Sends Report on Iran to UN Security Council

IAEA Director General ElBaradei releases a report requested on March 29 by the UN Security Council on the implementation of Iran's NPT safeguards agreement. The report reiterates the Board's demand that Iran suspend enrichment and reprocessing activities, reconsider construction of the IR-40 reactor, abide by the Additional Protocol, and provide transparency to support the IAEA ongoing investigations.[123]

### April 28: IAEA Says It Lacks Understanding of Military Role in Iran's Nuclear Activities

The IAEA states that all of Iran's declared nuclear material is accounted for and that it has found no undeclared material, but that gaps remain in its knowledge of the scope and content of Iran's centrifuge program, as well as other gaps, including the role of the military in Iran's nuclear program. Consequently, it states that "it is unable to make progress in its efforts to provide assurance about the absence of undeclared nuclear materials and activities in Iran."[124]

### May 16: Iran Cannot Explain Uranium Traces on Equipment at Technical University

Iran responds to an IAEA request to explain uranium particles found in samples taken in January at a technical university from equipment possibly moved there from the PHRC at Lavizan-Shian. Iran says the equipment had not been acquired for or used in nuclear activities. When questioned about actions of the PHRC to acquire dual-use equipment, Iran has claimed that the equipment was procured by the university where the former head of the PHRC was also a professor. Iran has not allowed sampling from other equipment associated with the PHRC, which was a military facility established in 1989 to develop responses to nuclear attack and accidents and to provide scientific support to the Ministry of Defense.[125]

### June 6: Iran Resumes Centrifuge Enrichment in 164 Machines After Brief Layoff

Iran restarts feeding uranium into the 164-centrifuge cascade at Natanz PFEP after completing a campaign with the 164-machine cascade in April.[126]

### June 6: Six Nations Offer Incentives Package to Iran to Halt Enrichment

EU foreign policy chief Javier Solana meets in Tehran with nuclear negotiator Larijani and Foreign Minister Manocher Mottaki to present package of incentives from the United States, Britain, France, Russia, China, and Germany to persuade Iran to halt nuclear program.

Package is said to include a commitment from the six nations to support Iran's plan for a civilian nuclear energy program, if Iran freezes its centrifuge enrichment and reprocessing activities; offers Iran membership in the World Trade Organization, and offers to open direct talks with the United States. The written proposal is said to contain only benefits, omitting punishments for not accepting them, which were transmitted orally.[127]

### June 8: IAEA Still Wants Copy of the Green Salt Report, Explanation of Plutonium Experiments

The IAEA is still seeking from Iran a copy of the so-called Green Salt report describing procedures for the reduction of $UF_6$ to metal and the casting and machining of enriched and depleted uranium metal into hemispheres that it needs to understand the scope of the offers made to Iran by Khan network intermediaries. References to high explosives testing and the design of a missile reentry are still unresolved. The IAEA also continues to seek clarification from Iran of inconsistencies in its explanation of plutonium separation experiments.[128]

### June 8: Production at UCF Is About 118 Metric Tons of $UF_6$

Iran reports that the Esfahan UCF produced approximately 118 metric tons of $UF_6$ in August 2005–April 2006. A new conversion campaign at UCF began on June 6.[129]

### June 8: Iran Continuing Installation Work at PFEP, Refuses Remote IAEA Monitoring

Iran starts feeding $UF_6$ into the 164-machine cascade at PFEP on June 6 and continues installation on other 164-machine cascades. Iran refuses to discuss installation of equipment for remote transmission of encrypted safeguards data to IAEA headquarters in Vienna.[130]

### June 9: Iran Given Deadline of June 29 to Accept Incentives Package

The United States, China, Russia, and the EU-3 set a deadline of June 29 for Iran to accept their package of incentives and suspend uranium enrichment.[131]

### June 12: Secret Military Enrichment Site, Zirzamin 27, Reported Outside Tehran

A secret military site outside Tehran, code named Zirzamin 27, thought to be under the control of the Iran Revolutionary Guard Corps (IRGC), is reported to be the location of a uranium enrichment program in underground laboratories. IAEA experts are said to be pressing Iran for full disclosure.[132]

### June 27: Iran Starts New Conversion Campaign at UCF

Iran informs the IAEA that a new uranium conversion campaign, involving approximately 160 tons of uranium ore concentrate (yellowcake), began at the UCF on June 6 and is expected to be completed by January 2007. As of August, approximately 26 tons of uranium in $UF_6$ had been produced.[133]

### July 9: Iran Bars IAEA Inspector Critical of Iran

Chris Charlier, leader of 15-inspector IAEA team in Iran since 2003, is confirmed to have been barred since April from traveling in Iran. In a *BBC-2* interview on March 3, 2005, Charlier complained about the lack of free movement for inspectors in Iran. "I believe they've tried to conceal their program and their activities. And maybe there are other things they're doing that we couldn't find. And that's why we're getting suspicious," he said. [134]

### July 12: Russia, China Join U.S. Move to Take Iran Before UN Security Council

Russia and China, after a meeting of foreign ministers in Paris, join the United States and European countries in agreeing to seek a UN Security Council resolution ordering Iran to freeze its nuclear activities or face the possibility of sanctions.[135]

### July 31: Security Council Resolution Sets Deadline on Iran Nuclear Suspension

The UN Security Council passes resolution 1696 demanding that Iran suspend all enrichment and reprocessing activities by August 31, with the possibility of economic sanctions if it does not comply. The resolution also calls on all states "to exercise vigilance" in preventing the transfer of all goods that could be used for Iran's enrichment and ballistic missile programs. The resolution finally worked out on July 28 by the five permanent members is a weakened version of earlier drafts that would have made the threat of sanctions immediate.[136]

### August 8: IAEA Samples Storage Container at Karaj, Finds HEU Particles

Samples taken from a container at the Karaj Waste Storage Facility used to store depleted uranium targets irradiated at the TRR indicate HEU particle contamination.[137]

### August 15: HEU Contamination Confirmed at Karaj Waste Storage Facility

Recent lab results from environmental samples taken by IAEA inspectors on August 8, 2005 at the Karaj Waste Storage Facility on containers storing depleted uranium targets irradiated during early plutonium experiments indicate the presence of HEU particles on one of the containers. The IAEA asks Iran for an explanation of the source of the contamination and the prior use of the containers.[138]

### August 21: Iran Refuses IAEA Inspectors' Access to Natanz Fuel Enrichment Plant

During an August visit, Iran turns away IAEA inspectors wanting to enter its underground Fuel Enrichment Plant (FEP) site at Natanz for routine design information verification, in an apparent violation of safeguards agreement.[139] In subsequent visit on August 26–30, Iran allows inspectors to do a design information verification at FEP and other facilities.[140]

### August 22: Iran Responds to UN Resolution 1696, Rejects Suspension, Calls for Talks

In an official 21-page response handed to foreign envoys in Tehran by chief nuclear negotiator Ali Larijani, Iran rejects UN Security Council resolution 1696, passed on July 31, that calls for it to suspend uranium enrichment by August 31 or face the possibility of sanctions. The resolution was based on an incentives package worked out in June by the five permanent Security Council members plus Germany. Iran says it is prepared to enter "serious talks" and is offering a "new formula" to resolve the crisis.[141]

### August 24: MEK/NCRI Says Iran Building P-2 Centrifuges at Secret Tehran Site

MEK/NCRI makes claim that Iran has built and is testing at least fifteen advanced P-2 centrifuges for uranium enrichment at a secret Tehran site run by the Iran Centrifuge Technology Company (Sherkate Technology Centrifuge Iran or "TSA") and would have hundreds more P-2s by next year. TSA is the successor to Pars Trash and Farayand Technique to produce P-1 and P-2 centrifuges. Centrifuge Technology is headed by Jafar Mohammadi, formerly of the AEOI, and headquartered in Tehran's Yousef Abad district. Centrifuges are assembled in three hangars on the Tehran–Damavand Highway, 3 km from the Tehran–Pars Junction.[142]

Iran has told the IAEA that work on the P-2 ended in 2003, but in April, President Ahmadinejad announced that Iran is "presently conducting research" on the P-2 that would quadruple Iran's enrichment powers.

### August 26: Ahmadinejad Inaugurates Heavy-Water Plant at Arak

Iranian President Ahmadinejad inaugurates Iran's heavy-water production plant (HWPP) at Khondab, near Arak, 120 miles southwest of Tehran. According to plant official Manouchehr Madadi, the capacity is 16 tons of heavy water per year. The heavy water is to be used as moderator and coolant in the IR-40 reactor under construction at the site and scheduled for completion in 2009.[143] The plant began operation in 2004 and its capacity was officially doubled on August 26.[144]

### August 31: Uranium Particles Found on Equipment at Technical University

IAEA reports that analysis of environmental samples taken in January 2006 from equipment procured by the PHRC and moved to a technical university shows the presence of a small number of particles of natural and highly-enriched uranium.[145]

### August 31: IAEA Reports Uranium Enrichment Continuing at Measured Pace

The IAEA reports to the Board that Iran continues limited centrifuge enrichment of uranium at the Natanz PFEP in defiance of Security Council resolution 1696, which calls for a suspension of enrichment by August 31. Activities include[146] (GOV/2006/53, para. 2):

- Since June 1, testing of single machine and 10 and 20-machine cascades;
- June 6–8, June 23–July 8, testing 164-machine cascade with approximately 6 kg $UF_6$ feed;
- August 24, resumes feeding $UF_6$ into 164-machine cascade.

The second 164-machine cascade is being installed and vacuum testing is expected in September 2006.[147] In June, Iran announced achieving 5 percent enrichment in the 164-centrifuge cascade, but has declined some operating information, e.g., tails assays.[148]

### September 26: Russia Signs Agreement to Supply Iran with Bushehr Fuel

In an agreement signed by Sergei Shmatko, head of Russia's Atomstroiexport, and Mahmoud Hanatian, vice president of the AEOI, Russia will supply about 80 tons of low enriched fuel for the Bushehr reactor by March 2007. According to the document signed, physical startup of Bushehr is scheduled in September 2007 and electricity generation by November 2007. An additional protocol set establishes a time frame for construction of an $800-million fuel plant in Bushehr.[149]

### October 1: Iran Completes and Tests Second 164-Machine Cascade

Iran begins testing a second 164-centrifuge cascade at the PFEP with $UF_6$ gas. Says it fed about 34 kg of $UF_6$ into centrifuges between August 13 and November 2, enriching it to levels below 5 percent U-235.[150]

### October 16: IAEA Finds PU Particles on Target Storage Containers at Karaj

Further IAEA analysis of samples from containers at Karaj, used to store irradiated depleted uranium from Iran's plutonium separation experiments, finds plutonium in the samples and confirms the presence of HEU particles found in August.[151]

### November 13: *Der Spiegel* Claims Secret Fund to Finance Iran Nuclear Weapons Program

The German weekly *Der Spiegel* reports that western intelligence has learned of a secret $418 million fund set aside by Iran to protect its nuclear sites from attack, build dozens of new uranium centrifuges, and construct a new nuclear power plant. It is hidden in the annual budget as a "special fund."[152] Iran strongly denies any secret nuclear fund.[153]

### November 14: Iran Won't Give Full Access to Centrifuge Operating Records at Natanz

Iran refuses to provide the IAEA full access to operating records of centrifuge enrichment product and tails assays needed to complete auditing activities at PFEP.[154]

### November 23: IAEA Board Suspends Technical Assistance to Iran for Arak Reactor

The IAEA Board of Governors by consensus blocks indefinitely Iran's request for "atoms for peace" technical assistance to the IR-40 reactor project in Arak due to its potential for producing plutonium for nuclear weapons as a byproduct. IR-40 is omitted from list of projects submitted for Board's final approval, but Board approves assistance for seven other Iranian nuclear projects. Iran's foreign minister says that the project will go on despite the denial of aid.[155] The Board has repeatedly requested Iran to abandon the IR-40 reactor project.

### November 23: In Reversal, Iran Gives Access to Natanz Records Lavizan–Shian Equipment

In the midst of negotiations with the IAEA Board over technical assistance, Iran says that it will provide IAEA inspectors with records of product and tails assays from recent Natanz PFEP operations and also will allow inspectors to take further environmental samples from research equipment at the PHRC at Lavizan–Shian to determine the origin of traces of HEU there.[156]

### December 6: Iraq Study Group Says Iran's Nuclear Programs Should Be Dealt with in UN

The report of the Iraq Study Group recommends that while diplomatic efforts should seek to persuade Iran to take specific steps to improve the situation in Iraq (Recommendation 10), Iran's nuclear programs should continue to be dealt with in the UN by the five permanent members of the UN Security Council plus Germany (Recommendation 11).[157]

## December 9: Ahmadinejad Says 3,000 Centrifuges Being Installed at Natanz

Iranian President Ahmadinejad announces that Iran has now begun installing 3,000 uranium enrichment centrifuges at the Natanz FEP. Iran started up its second 164-machine cascade at the PFEP in October. It plans to have all 3,000 machines operating at the underground FEP by March 2007.[158]

## December 15: Ahmadinejad Opponents Win Assembly of Experts, Local Council Elections

In elections held for local council across Iran on December 15, moderate conservatives opposed to President Ahmadinejad won a majority of the council seats, followed by reformists, with allies of Ahmadinejad winning less than 20 percent of the seats. A parallel election for the 86 senior clerics making up the Assembly of Experts showed similar anti-Ahmadinejad sentiment with former president Rafsanjani, who lost to Ahmadinejad in the 2005 presidential election, receiving the highest number of votes, and Hasan Rohani, the nuclear negotiator under former president Khatami, gaining reelection. The vote is seen as a reaction to Ahmadinejad's hard-line policies on uranium enrichment and Israel and his failure to deal with the economy.[159]

## December 23: Security Council Votes Sanctions on Iran's Nuclear and Missile Programs

By a 15–0 vote, the UN Security Council adopts resolution 1737, calling on Iran to halt activities related to uranium enrichment, reprocessing, and a heavy-water reactor and imposes a ban on the export and import of materials and technology that could contribute to these activities or to the development of nuclear weapon delivery systems. The resolution is the culmination of months of intense negotiation among the five permanent members and Germany. It follows Iran's failure to comply with resolution 1696 of July 31, calling on it to halt its centrifuge enrichment and reprocessing activities by August 31.[160] Enforcement is mandatory under Chapter 7 of the UN Charter, but military action is excluded. The IAEA director general is to report back within sixty days.

The sanctions freeze the foreign financial assets of 12 Iranians and 10 organizations involved in Iran's nuclear and ballistic missile programs. Equipment and fuel for light-water nuclear power plants, such as the one that Russia is constructing at Bushehr, are excluded. A mandatory travel ban was eliminated and replaced by a notification whenever sanctioned individuals and agency representatives cross state boundaries. As a last minute concession to Russia, the final draft was amended to delete sanctions on Iran's Aerospace Industries Organization

(AIO), although its subsidiaries are cited. Nevertheless, Ahmad Vahid Dastjerdi, head of the AIO, is put outside financial transactions, as are Maj. Gen. Yahya Rahim Safavi, commander of IRGC, and Gen. Hosein Salimi, in charge of the air force branch of the IRGC. Others named include the AEOI vice president for R&D, officials of the Arak reactor and the Natanz PFEP enrichment plant, and the rector of the Malek Ashtar University of Defense Technology.[161]

## 2007

### January 2: U.S. Pursuing Financial Pressure to Augment Sanctions

Believing that the sanctions voted on December 23 by the UN Security Council are alone too weak to cause Iran to give up its nuclear ambitions, the United States is pursuing a new strategy of financial pressure, with varying degrees of cooperation from Britain, Germany, France, and Japan, to persuade foreign governments and institutions to cut ties with Iranian companies and organizations involved in its nuclear and missile programs, extending to the IRGC, which also is increasingly involved in commercial activities. In 2006, the European Banks Credit Suisse First Boston and UBS said they would not do new business with Iran. In December, the Japan Bank for International Cooperation stopped new loans to Iran until the nuclear problem is resolved.[162]

### January 3: Second U.S. Carrier Group Dispatched to Persian Gulf

As a warning to Syria and Iran, the United States will send a second aircraft carrier strike group, the USS Stennis, to the Persian Gulf, joining the USS Dwight D. Eisenhower carrier group that entered the Gulf in December.[163] In a speech on January 10, President Bush announces the deployment of the second carrier group and Patriot air-defense systems.[164] The Stennis arrives in the Gulf on February 19.[165]

### January 5: Iran Announces 250 Tons of $UF_6$ Produced at UCF, Stored in Tunnels

Iran Vice President Aghazadeh announces that Iran has produced 250 metric tons of uranium in $UF_6$ gas at the Esfahan UCF for centrifuge feed and has stored it in underground tunnels there.[166]

### January 5: Larijani: Nuke Program Peaceful, But if Threatened, "Situation May Change"

On a visit to China, Ali Larijani, Iran's chief nuclear negotiator and secretary general of its Supreme National Security Council, warns that Iran's commitment to the peaceful use of nuclear technology would change if the country were threatened. "We oppose obtaining nuclear weapons and we will peacefully use nuclear technology under the framework of the Nonproliferation Treaty," he said. "But," he warned, "if we are threatened, the situation may change."[167]

### January 7: *Sunday Times* Says Israel Has Plans to Hit Iran Facilities with Tactical Nukes

*The Sunday Times* in London reports that two Israeli squadrons are secretly training to attack the Natanz centrifuge enrichment plant with one-kiloton nuclear "bunker busters" that would penetrate and detonate deep underground to reduce radioactive fallout. Prime targets are the partly underground Natanz centrifuge plants, the UCF at Esfahan and the IR-40 heavy-water reactor under construction at Arak. The Mossad's assessment is that Iran will have enough enriched uranium for nuclear weapons within two years.[168]

### January 10: Former Officials, Cleric, Newspapers Criticize Ahmadinejad Nuclear Stance

On January 3, Hossein Moussavian, a former Iranian nuclear negotiator, calls for renewed diplomacy in the nuclear standoff with the West. Although, following the vote of UN sanctions, the Iranian parliament passed a bill requiring a review of relations with the IAEA, some reformist legislators have blamed Ahmadinejad for failing to prevent the sanctions. The Islamist Participation Front (Mosharekat), the largest reformist party, calls for return to less confrontational nuclear policies.[169]

Two leading conservative newspapers, the daily *Jomhouri-Elsami*, once owned by Ayatollah Khamenei and reflecting his views, and *Hamhahri*, run by Ahmadinejad when he was mayor of Tehran, have editorially criticized Ahmadinejad for his rhetoric pushing Iran's nuclear goals too strongly with negative consequences, leading to the UN resolution. "The resolution is certainly harmful for the country," *Jomhouri-Elsami* said, but criticized Ahmadinejad for calling it 'a piece of torn paper."[170,171] In a speech on January 19, Grand Ayatollah Hossein Ali Montazeri, Iran's most senior dissident cleric, criticizes Ahmadinejad's defiant stance against the West on the nuclear issue, calling it provocative. His comments were the first direct public attack on the president's nuclear policy by such a senior cleric.[172]

### January 11: IAEA Inspectors Find No Increased Activity at Natanz

According to diplomatic sources, IAEA inspectors visiting Natanz on January 10 found no change there in the number of centrifuges installed beyond the 328 machines seen two months ago and sporadic efforts to produce small quantities of low-enriched uranium, despite President Ahmadinejad's announcement of intentions to assemble, install, and operate 3,000 machines at Natanz by March 2007. Various explanations offered are (a) Iran is having technical problems operating the centrifuges, (b) Iran is using Natanz to divert attention from a secret military enrichment program, (c) Iran does not want to provoke stronger sanctions than already imposed by the UN Security Council on December 23, and (d) activity at Natanz is stopped because it is a possible Israeli or U.S. target.[173]

### January 15: Russia Delivers 29 Tor M-1 Air Defense Systems to Iran

Russian Defense Minister Sergei Ivanov announces that Russia has completed delivery of Tor M-1 antiaircraft missile systems to Iran. The delivery of 29 Tor M-1s was made, despite U.S. objections, under a $700-million contract signed at the end of 2005. At Russian insistence, the delivery of the Tor M-1 and S-300 air defense systems was excluded from the December 23 UN sanctions, as was construction of the Bushehr reactor. The Tor M-1 is designed to protect against aircraft and cruise missiles at altitudes of up to 10 km (6 miles). Each system has 8 short-range missiles and associated radars.[174]

### January 22: Iran Refuses Entry to 38 IAEA Inspectors in Response to UN Sanctions

Iran takes first step in limiting cooperation with the IAEA, after sanctions were voted by UN Security on December 23 for its refusal to end uranium enrichment, by informing the IAEA that 38 of its over 200 international nuclear safeguard inspectors will not be allowed to enter the country to carry out inspections at Iranian nuclear facilities. The entry ban, which was imposed by the Iranian parliament's Foreign Affairs and National Security Commission, is not expected to hinder inspection activities.[175] The barred inspectors are reported to be French, British, German, and Canadian nationals.[176] Iran said that it would not allow 10 inspectors, proposed by the IAEA, as replacements for inspectors who had left.[177]

### January 26: ElBaradei Calls for "Timeout" on Iran Nuclear Program, Sanctions

At the World Economic Forum in Davos, Switzerland, IAEA Director General ElBaradei calls for a "timeout" on the Iran nuclear issue during which Iran would suspend its enrichment activities, the international community would lift sanctions on Iran, and the parties would "go immediately to the negotiating table."[178]

### February 5: Iran Installs Two 164-Machine Cascades at Natanz FEP

Iran has installed two 164-centrifuge cascades in the underground FEP at Natanz, according to diplomats in Vienna as the first step in the planned installation of six cascades by Spring and 3,000 machines there by June. Testing is to be "dry," without $UF_6$. This adds to the two 164-machine cascades operating intermittently in the pilot PFEP and enriching only small amounts of $UF_6$ feed. The subterranean facility is ringed by antiaircraft systems.[179]

### February 8: Khamenei Warns that Iran Will Retaliate If Attacked By U.S.

Iran's Supreme Leader, Ayatollah Ali Khamenei, says that Iran would attack American interests world wide if it was attacked by the United States.[180]

### February 9: IAEA Cancels 18 More Technical Assistance Projects with Iran

The IAEA reports the suspension of 18 technical assistance projects with Iran, adding to 5 suspended in January out of a total of 55 projects involving Iran, following sanctions imposed on Iran by the UN Security Council on December 23 for not halting its uranium enrichment activities. The suspensions will be submitted to the March meeting of the IAEA Board for approval. They follow the November cutoff of IAEA aid to construction of Iran's heavy-water reactor.[181]

### February 12: EU Ministers Approve Limited Sanctions on Iran

European Union (EU) ministers meeting in Brussels approve plans to implement the sanctions against Iran voted by the UN Security Council in December to pressure Iran to halt its uranium enrichment program. The sanctions include banning the sale of materials and technology that could be used in Iran's nuclear and missile programs. They also include freezing the financial assets of ten companies and twelve individuals said to be involved with Iran's nuclear program. The EU adopted the limited sanctions under pressure from the United States to sever all economic ties with Tehran.[182]

### February 19: Russia to Delay Construction Work on Bushehr Reactor

The Russian nuclear power agency Rosatom says that start up of the Bushehr nuclear power plant will be delayed because Iran has failed to make the monthly $25 million payment for January and paid only a quarter of the amount for January. Over 2,000 specialists from Russia, Ukraine, and other countries are currently employed. The contract requires payment in dollars, and Iran has offered euros. Fuel deliveries from Russia were scheduled to start in March 2007 with planned start of operation in September. Atomstroiexport, the Russian company in charge of exports, said that a trading ban on certain equipment due to UN sanctions on Iran also contributed to the delay. The dispute may put off startup until mid-2008.[183]

### February 22: IAEA Reports Iran Ignoring Security Council Resolution to Halt Enrichment

The IAEA reports to the UN Security Council that in defiance of the sixty-day deadline to halt uranium enrichment and heavy water-related activities, Iran is steadily increasing its uranium enrichment activities at Natanz. This is likely to trigger U.S. efforts for harsher sanctions than imposed by the Security Council on December 23 on Iran's nuclear and missile programs.[184] The five permanent members of the Security Council and Germany will meet on February 26 in London to discuss increased international pressure on Iran to halt enrichment.[185]

### February 22: Brazil, India Implement UN Sanctions against Iran

India has banned the export of all material, equipment, and technology that could contribute to Iran's nuclear program in compliance with sanction voted in the UN Security Council resolution of December 23, 2006. India is an ally and longtime trading partner of Iran.[186] Likewise, the president of Brazil has signed a decree banning the sale and transfer of nuclear equipment and technology to Iran.[187]

### February 24: Israel Seeking Air Corridor through Iraq, Should It Decide to Strike Iran

The *Daily Telegraph* says that Israel is negotiating with U.S. commanders in Iraq for permission to fly through U.S.-controlled air space to attack Iranian nuclear facilities should current diplomatic efforts in the UN to halt Tehran's uranium enrichment program fail.[188]

### March 19: Russia Will Deny Iran Fuel for Bushehr Unless It Suspends Enrichment

In the past week, Russia has informed Iran, according to a *New York Times* report, that it will withhold delivery of the initial fuel loading for the Bushehr nuclear power reactor, scheduled for delivery in March, unless Iran suspends its uranium enrichment activities as demanded by UN Security Council resolution 1737 of December 23, 2006.[189]

## March 24: UN Security Council Votes to Broaden Sanctions on Iran

The UN Security Council votes unanimously to adopt resolution 1747, imposing new and toughened sanctions on Iran for failure to suspend its uranium enrichment program, adding to the sanctions voted December 23. The sanctions prohibit arms sales and transfers by Iran to any nation or organization; call on nations to voluntarily exercise vigilance and restraint in exporting heavy weapons to Iran; call on nations and organizations voluntarily not to enter into new commitments for export credit, grants, or loans to Iran except for humanitarian purposes; and extend resolution 1737 by freezing assets of an additional 15 individuals and 13 organizations who are involved with the nuclear and missile programs or are key persons in IRGC. The resolution calls for voluntary restrictions on travel by individuals subject to sanctions. In particular, it freezes the assets abroad of Bank Sepah, Iran's fourth largest bank, which was already sanctioned by the U.S. Treasury Department, to isolate it from international financing of Iran's programs. The IAEA is to report back in 60 days.

The resolution, by invoking Chapter 7 of the UN charter, is mandatory but excludes military action. Although weaker than sought by the United States, the resolution involved intense negotiations by the five permanent members of the Security Council plus Germany, along with South Africa, Indonesia, and Qatar. At the insistence of South Africa, one provision stresses the goal of a making the Middle East weapons-of-mass-destruction free zone. [190]

## March 25: Iran to Keep Information from IAEA Due to Sanctions, Fear of Bombing

In retaliation to the new sanctions voted by the UN Security Council, Iran says that it will suspend provisions of its safeguards agreement, which it agreed voluntarily in 2002 under the Additional Protocol, that require providing the IAEA with early design information on new nuclear facilities. This provision was already violated in 2004, when Iran failed to inform the IAEA of construction of underground tunnels at the Esfahan Uranium Conversion Facility. Iran, however, will continue, as required, to inform the IAEA six months before introducing nuclear material into any facility. The suspension will last until its nuclear case is referred back from the Security Council to the IAEA, according to government spokesman, Gholam Hossein Elham. The decision was expanded on as a security measure against the use of force by the United States and Israel in a letter to the IAEA from Iran's chief representative to the IAEA, Ali Ashgar Soltanieh, dated March 29.[191]

### March 30: IAEA Pushing Iran to Accept Remote Monitoring Cameras at Natanz FEP

The IAEA is reported to be pressuring Iran to install cameras in the underground FEP centrifuge facility at Natanz to provide remote monitoring. Earlier the IAEA had informed Iran that remote monitoring would be required once the number of centrifuges exceeded five hundred. A wall is reported to block the view of centrifuges in the lower level of the three-tiered Natanz facility.[192]

### April 4: Talks Between Iran and EU Resume After Release of British Crew

On March 26, two days after the UN Security Council imposed additional sanctions on Iran, Iran's chief nuclear negotiator Ali Larijani told the *IRNA* news agency that EU foreign policy chief Javier Solana expressed the desire in a telephone conversation to resolve the Iranian nuclear issue through negotiations. Solana negotiates on behalf of permanent UN Security Council members, the United States, France, Britain, Russia, and China, plus Germany.[193] Talks between Solana and Larijani resume just hours after Ahmadinejad announces the release of the British navy crew seized by Iran on March 23.[194]

### April 9–13: Ahmadinejad Says Iran Can Enrich Uranium on "Industrial Scale"

President Ahmadinejad announces at a National Day of Nuclear Technology ceremony at the Natanz centrifuge plant that Iran "is among the countries of the world that produce nuclear fuel on an industrial scale." This is the first anniversary of his announcing Iran's production of enriched uranium at the Natanz PFEP. Ali Larijani, Iran's chief nuclear negotiator, when asked whether uranium gas had been injected into the centrifuges being installed in the larger FEP at Natanz, said, "Yes we have injected gas."[195] Russia and France voice skepticism about any dramatic expansion of Iran's enrichment program. IAEA inspectors going to Natanz are reported to have arrived in Iran.[196] IAEA Director General ElBaradei says Iran is only operating several hundred centrifuges at Natanz, discounting claims of a big advance.[197]

### April 9: $UF_6$ Produced at Esfahan Conversion Facility Rises to 270 Metric Tons

During the National Day of Nuclear Technology ceremony at Natanz, Iranian Vice President and AEOI head Reza Aghazadeh announces that 270 metric tons of $UF_6$ have been produced at the Esfahan UCF over the past year.[198]

### April 15: Iran Seeks Bids on Two More Nuclear Power Plants

Iran announces that it is seeking bids for two additional light-water nuclear power reactors to be built near the 1,000 MW Bushehr nuclear reactor. According to Ahmad Fayyazbakhsh, deputy head of the AEOI, each would have an electricity generating capacity of up to 1,600 MW and would take up to 11 years to construct at a cost of up to $1.7 billion. Under Iranian law, AEOI has been tasked with providing 20,000 MW of nuclear power in the next 20 years.[199]

### April 18: IAEA Confirms Over 1,300 Centrifuges Operating at Natanz FEP

IAEA deputy director general Olli Heinonen, in a letter from to the Iranian ambassador to the IAEA, Ali Asgar Soltaneih, confirms Iran's claim of increased centrifuge capacity at Natanz FEP. Eight separate centrifuge cascades totaling 1,312 machines are operating in the underground facility at Natanz but are being fed only very limited quantities of uranium gas. This is twice the 4 cascades reported by IAEA inspectors in February to be assembled there but not enriching uranium.[200]

The letter also noted that, after several months of negotiation, Iran had recently agreed to install tamper-proof 24-hour monitoring cameras at the Natanz cascades and allow unannounced inspections there but had revoked inspectors' access to the IR-40 heavy-water reactor under construction at Arak after the UN imposed sanctions in March.

### April 23: EU Adds to UN Sanctions on Iran

European Union foreign ministers adopt a regulation implementing UN sanctions on individuals and organizations involved in Iran's nuclear and missile programs and add to the list banning visas and freezing assets and imposing a total arms embargo on Iran. The added list contains 15 nuclear officials, scientists, and Revolutionary Guard commanders and 8 entities including subsidiaries of defense and aerospace companies and the state-owned Bank Sepah.[201]

### April 26: Talks Between Iranian and EU Negotiators End Without Breakthrough

Two days of talks in Ankara, Turkey between EU foreign policy chief Javier Solana and Iran's chief nuclear negotiator Ali Larijani end without any breakthrough needed to restart formal negotiations on Iran's nuclear program.[202] They are to meet again in two weeks. There are unconfirmed reports of new formulas being considered: redefining "enrichment suspension" to allow the building and testing of new centrifuges;[203] allowing less than 1,000 centrifuges assembled and connected on cold standby under IAEA inspection;[204] and setting up an international consortium at Iran's behest to process uranium fuel inside Iran.[205]

### April 30: Former Nuclear Negotiator, Hossein Mousavian, Arrested on Spying Charges

Iranian authorities reportedly arrest former nuclear negotiator Hossein Mousavian on charges of espionage and are holding him in Tehran's Evin prison.[206]

### May 13: IAEA Carries Out Unannounced Inspection at Natanz FEP

While no longer honoring its Additional Protocol, Iran agrees on March 22, 2007 to allow unannounced inspections at the FEP in addition to scheduled inspections because of the growing number of centrifuges there. The first unannounced inspection is on May 13.[207]

### May 22: Deadline Set in Security Council Resolution 1747 Passes Without Iran Action

The sixty-day deadline imposed by UN Security Council resolution 1747 of March 24, 2007 expired with Iran (for the third time) failing to heed a Security Council call to suspend its activities related to uranium enrichment and plutonium production.

### June: Satellite Pictures Show Tunnels Being Drilled at Natanz

Satellite images taken in June 2007 showed complex tunnels being drilled in a mountain side adjacent to the Natanz centrifuge facility, raising concern at the IAEA about their possible use to hide nuclear activities.[208]

### June 27: Iran Announces Gas Rationing

An announcement that Iran would begin gasoline rationing on June 27, 2007 due to growing demand and limited refinery capacity brings out strong protests in Tehran with long lines and gas stations set afire.[209]

### July 9: ElBaredei Says Iran Slowing Expansion of Uranium Enrichment Program

IAEA Director General ElBaradei states that IAEA inspectors observed that installation of new centrifuge machine cascades at Natanz had markedly slowed, calling into doubt Iran's stated goal of 3,000 operating centrifuges by the end of July.[210]

### July 25: Fuel Materials Plant (FMP) at Arak in Advanced Stage

IAEA carries out a physical inventory verification (PIV) at the FMP and found the installation of process equipment there to be in an advanced stage. The plant will fabricate natural uranium fuel for the Arak reactor.[211]

### July 25: Russia to Delay Fuel for Bushehr Nuclear Power Reactor until 2008

A Russian subcontractor to Atomstroiexport says that the nuclear power plant would not be finished before autumn 2008. Russia is delaying completion of the reactor until the Iran heeds UN Security Council resolutions to suspend uranium enrichment, although the ostensible reason is Iran's default on its monthly $25 million payment in U.S. dollars. [212]

### July 30: IAEA Inspectors Readmitted to Arak Reactor Site

After having to rely since April 2007 on satellite images to verify construction progress at the IR-40 reactor at Arak, IAEA inspectors once again visit the nuclear reactor site.[213]

### August: United States Said Planning to Put Iran Revolutionary Guard on Terrorist List

The Bush Administration is reported to have decided to place the IRGC on the list of terrorist organizations, an unusual move in singling out a government organization, but one that would further clamp down on the IRGC's world wide financial activities.[214]

### August 20: IAEA Says That Findings Consistent with Iran's Statements about Plutonium

The IAEA says that its findings about Iran's plutonium experiments were now consistent with Iran's statements and that questions about the experiments were resolved. [215]

### August 19: At Natanz, 2,624 Centrifuges in Operation or Construction, IAEA Says

According to IAEA inspectors, at Natanz, 2,624 centrifuge machines were in some stage of operation or construction, with 1,968 machines operating at the same time and being fed $UF^6$ gas.[216]

### August 21: Iran Agrees on Timetable to Answer All IAEA's Outstanding Nuclear Questions

On August 21, IAEA Director General ElBaredei and Iranian chief nuclear negotiator, Ali Larijani, conclude a multi-stage agreement by which will give final answers to all outstanding questions on its nuclear program over the next several months. The questions to be resolved concern the acquisition of P-1 and P-2 centrifuge technology and designs from the Khan Network, the 15-page document and the Green Salt Project studies on the fabrication of nuclear warhead from uranium and the design of a missile reentry vehicle for a nuclear warhead, HEU particle contamination on equipment moved to a technical university from the PHRC, the Po-210 experiments, and operations at the Gchine uranium mine and mill.[217]

### August 28: French President Sarkozy Says Negotiate or Face "Catastrophic Alternative"

French president, Nicholas Sarkozy, addresses the urgency of a negotiated solution with tougher sanctions and possible incentives to suspend Iran's nuclear program, he bluntly says, the catastrophic alternative: "an Iranian bomb or bombing of Iran."[218]

### August 30: Elbaradei Says $UF_6$ Feed into Centrifuges since February Lower Than Expected

In the August 30, 2007 report to the IAEA Board of Governors, Director General ElBaradei notes that since February 2007, Iran had fed approximately

690 kilograms of $UF_6$ into the centrifuges at the Natanz FEP, "well below the expected quantity for a facility of this design" to support view that centrifuges are not fully operational. [219]

### September 2: Ahmadinejad Announces 3,000 Centrifuges Now Operating at Natanz

President Ahmadinejad, speaking defiantly against U.S. demands for Iran to halt its nuclear program, announces that Iran has reached its goal of 3,000 centrifuges operating at Natanz. He says that agreement to answer IAEA questions and conciliatory report submitted by IAEA Director General ElBaradei for the September 2007 IAEA Board of Governors meeting show that Iran's program is "peaceful."[220]

# Acronyms

| | |
|---|---|
| AEOI | Atomic Energy Organization of Iran |
| AIO | Aerospace Industries Organization |
| AMIG | Ammunition and Metallurgy Industries Group |
| AUC | ammonium uranyl carbonate |
| AVLIS | atomic vapor laser isotope separation |
| BNNP-1 | Bushehr Nuclear Power Plant |
| BUP | Bandar Abbas Uranium Production Plant |
| CEP | circular error probability |
| CNNC | China National Nuclear Corporation |
| CSL | Comprehensive Separation Laboratory |
| CWC | Chemical Weapons Convention |
| DIO | Defense Industries Organization |
| EFP | explosively formed penetrator |
| ENFRPC | Esfahan Nuclear Research and Production Center |
| ENTC | Esfahan Nuclear Technology Center |
| FEP | Fuel Enrichment Plant |
| FMP | Fuel Manufacturing Plant |
| HEU | Highly Enriched Uranium |
| HWPP | Heavy-water Production Plant |
| IAEA | International Atomic Energy Agency |
| IR-40 | Iran Nuclear Research Reactor |
| IRGC | Iranian Revolutionary Guard Corps |
| IRIB | Islamic Republic of Iran Broadcasting |
| JHL | Jabr Ibn Hayan Multipurpose Laboratories |
| LEU | low-enriched uranium |

| | |
|---|---|
| LSL | Laser Spectroscopy Laboratory |
| MEK | Mujahedin-e-Khalq |
| MIX | Molybdenum, Iodine, and Xenon radioisotope production facility |
| MLIS | molecular laser isotope separation |
| MOD | Ministry of Defense |
| MODAFL | Ministry of Defense and Armed Forces Logistics |
| MRBM | medium-range ballistic missile |
| NCRI | National Council of Resistance of Iran |
| NPT | Nuclear Non-Proliferation Treaty |
| NRCAM | Nuclear Research Centre for Agriculture and Medicine |
| OPCW | Organization for the Prohibition of Chemical Weapons |
| OPEC | Organization of Petroleum Exporting Countries |
| OPM | (State) Organization for Management and Planning |
| PFEP | Pilot Fuel Enrichment Plant |
| PHRC | Physics Research Center |
| PIV | Physical Inventory Verification |
| PLO | Palestine Liberation Organisation |
| R&D | Research and Development |
| RosAtom | Russian Federal Atomic Energy Agency |
| RTG | radioisotope thermoelectric generator |
| RWSF | Radioactive Waste Storage Facility |
| SHIG | Shahib Hemmat Industrial Group |
| TNRC | Tehran Nuclear Research Center |
| TRR | Tehran Research Reactor |
| TSA | Sherkate Technology Centrifuge Iran |
| UCF | Uranium Conversion Facility |
| UNCHR | United Nations Commission on Human Rights |
| UNIFIL | United Nations Interim Force in Lebanon |
| UOC | uranium ore concentrate |
| WMD | Weapons of Mass Destruction |
| YPP | Yellowcake Production Plant |
| ZPP | Zirconium Production Plant |

# Notes

## Preface

1. Among the latest reports and studies published in 2007, see for example, "Iran's 'Unacceptable' Bomb: Deterrence and Prevention in the Age of Terror," *Proceedings for the 2007 Soref Symposium* (Washington, DC: The Washington Institute for Near East Policy, May 9–11, 2007), and Barbara Slavin, *Bitter Friends, Bosom Enemies: Iran, the U.S., and the Twisted Path to Confrontation* (New York: St. Martin's Press, 2007).
2. Reuters, http://www.reuters.com/article/worldNews/idUSBLA23828120070902.
3. Reuters, http://www.reuters.com/article/worldNews/idUSBLA22629420070902.
4. BBC News, http://news.bbc.co.uk/go/pr/fr/-/2/hi/middle_east/6975983.stm.
5. Haaretz, http://www.haaretz.com/hasen/spages/903727.html.
6. Al-Jazeera, http://english.aljazeera.net/NR/exeres/74BCA3F6-20B9-4478-947C-31964B404273.htm.
7. Haaretz, http://www.haaretz.com/hasen/spages/904404.html.
8. *The New York Times*, http://www.nytimes.com/2007/09/26/world/26nations.html?ref=middleeast.
9. BBC News, http://news.bbc.co.uk/2/hi/middle_east/7055042.stm and http://news.bbc.co.uk/2/hi/middle_east/7054548.stm.
10. UPI, http://www.upi.com/NewsTrack/Top_News/2007/09/07/judge_iran_owes_billions_for_1983_bombing/7192/.
11. General David H. Petraeus, *Report to Congress on the Situation in Iraq* (September 10–11, 2007), pp. 1, 2, and 4.
12. Cited in *Near East Report*, October 1–15, 2007, p. 1.
13. Cited in *The Washington Post*, October 19, 2007.
14. Ann Gearan, "U.S. Levies Harsh Sanctions against Iran," *The Associated Press*, October 25, 2007, http://ap.google.com/article/ALeqM5iVp6OcsznLJpeFv8SenE_EhxIpmg.

15. BBC News, http://news.bbc.co.uk/go/pr/fr/-/2/hi/americas/7052080.stm.

16. UPI, http://www.upi.com/NewsTrack/Top_News/2007/09/16/france_war_may_be_called_for_in_iran/7346/.

17. UPI, http://www.upi.com/NewsTrack/Top_News/2007/09/22/sarkozy_says_iran_bomb_unacceptable/3320/.

18. BBC News, http://news.bbc.co.uk/2/hi/middle_east/7046258.stm.

19. BBC News, http://news.bbc.co.uk/2/hi/middle_east/7018672.stm.

20. Cited in *The Washington Times*, October 29, 2007.

## Chapter 1

1. Mehran Kamrava. *The Political History of Modern Iran*. London: Praeger, 1992, pp. 18, 33–35.

2. Ibid. pp. 20–21.

3. Mansour Bonakdarian. "Iranian Constitutional Exiles and British Foreign-Policy Dissenters, 1908–1909." *International Journal of Middle East Studies*, 27(2) (1995): pp. 175–191.

4. Ali M. Ansari. *Modern Iran Since 1921: The Pahlavis and After*. London: Longman, 2003, pp. 20–24, 54, 72–73.

5. Elton L. Daniel. *The History of Iran*. Westport, CT: Greenwood Press, 2000, p. 150.

6. Nikki R. Keddie. *Modern Iran: Roots and Results of Revolution*. New Haven, Conn.: Yale University Press, 2003, pp. 131–135, 153–154.

7. Rouhollah K. Ramazani. "Iran's 'White Revolution': A Study in Political Development." *International Journal of Middle East Studies*, Cambridge University Press, 1974.

8. Ervand Abrahamian. "The Guerrilla Movement in Iran, 1963–1977." *MERIP Reports*. 1980 Middle East Research and Information Project.

9. Keddie, op. cit. pp. 163, 167–169.

10. Daniel, op. cit, pp. 160, 166–172.

11. C.M. Lake. "The Problems Encountered in Establishing an Islamic Republic in Iran 1979–1981." *Bulletin (British Society for Middle Eastern Studies)*. 1982 British Society for Middle Eastern Studies. Published by Taylor & Francis Ltd., p. 153.

12. Chris Hedges. "Rafsanjani Re-elected in Iran, But Without a Huge Mandate." *The New York Times*, June 14, 1993, p. 8.

13. Scott Harrop. "Clinton Team Should Heed Iranian President's Signals." *Christian Science Monitor*, June 29, 1994, p. 19.

14. Rashid Ahmed. "A friend indeed." *Far Eastern Economic Review*, Hong Kong, June 15, 1995.

15. Elaine Sciolino. "C.I.A. Says Iran Makes Progress on Atom Arms." *The New York Times*. November 30, 1992.

16. Matthew C. Wells. "Thermidor in the Islamic Republic of Iran: The Rise of Muhammad Khatami." *British Journal of Middle Eastern Studies* (1999), p. 31.

17. Kenneth M. Pollack. *The Persian Puzzle: The Conflict Between Iran and America*. New York: Random House, 2004, pp. 310–311.

18. Ibid. p. 326.

19. Ibid. pp. 328, 332.

20. Ibid. pp. 333, 338.

21. Kenneth Katzman. "Iran Current Developments and U.S. Policy." *Congressional Research Service*. July 2003.

22. "U.S. 'Evil Axis' Charge Enrages Iran." *China Daily*. New York, June 5, 2002.

23. Michael Slackman. "Front-Runner in Iran Finds Students to Be a Tough Audience." *The New York Times*, June 22, 2005; and "Victory for a religious hardliner in Iran." *The Economist*, June 27, 2005.

24. "The Non-Music Man." *The Wall Street Journal*, December 21, 2005.

25. Kimia Sanati. "Media-Iran: Criticizing Regime Gets Reformist Paper Banned." *Global Information Network*, September 12, 2006, p. 1.

26. Nazila Fathi. "Iranian Leader Wants Purge Of Liberals From Universities." *The New York Times*, September 6, 2006.

27. Khamenei Speech: Excerpts. *BBC*, June 4, 2006, available at http://news.bbc.co.uk/o/pr/fr/-/2/hi/middle_east/5045990.stm

## Chapter 2

1. *Webster's International Dictionary* (Springfield, MA: G & C Merriam Corp., 1900) pp. 641, 1405.

2. Ruhollah Khomeini, *Islam and Revolution: Writings and Declarations of Imam Khomeini*. Berkeley Cal.: Muzan Press, 1981, pp. 60–61.

3. See, for instance, the position of the late Grand Ayatollah Abu-al Qassam Kho'i, in: Martin S. Kramer, "The Origins of Fundamentalism," in R. Scott Appleby, ed., *Spokesmen for the Despised: Fundamentalist Leaders of the Middle East*. Chicago: University of Chicago Press, p. 161.

4. He has, in fact, been openly belittled in terms of his practical expertise in running the theocracy. See Patrick Clawson, "Prospects for Dialogue with Iran: Implications for U.S. Policy." *PolicyWatch #289*, 1997.

5. "The Structure of Power in Iran." *Iran Chamber Society*, July 2006. Available at: http://www.iranchamber.com/government/articles/ structure_of_power.php

6. Article 115, Constitution of the Islamic Republic of Iran.

7. Two candidates were allowed to run only after the Supreme Leader intervened on their behalf to the Council of Guardians. Also, see, for example, "Iran Council Sets June 17 as Election Day." *The New York Times*, January 2, 2005; "Iran's Giant Question Mark: To Vote or Not?" *The New York Times*, June 14, 2005.

8. "The Structure of Power in Iran." *Iran Chamber Society*, July 2006.

9. "Details of Iran's terror HQ in Europe revealed." *The Jerusalem Post*, April 23, 1996.

10. Ibid.

11. http://www.rferl.org/featuresarticle/2006/11/8fedc969-a5b6-4cf8-ba8f-7ad878ae04a5.html

12. "The Structure of Power in Iran." *Iran Chamber Society*, July 2006: "The Supreme National Security Council"; "Governing Iran," *PBS Online News Hour* http://www.pbs.org/newshour/bb/middle_east/iran/structure.html; "The Structure of Power in Iran." *PBS*, http://www.pbs.org/wgbh/pages/frontline/shows/ tehran/inside/govt.html

13. Article 176, Constitution of the Islamic Republic of Iran.

14. Article 67, Constitution of the Islamic Republic of Iran.

15. Articles 69–70, Constitution of the Islamic Republic of Iran.

16. Nazila Fathi, "One-Third of Iranian Parliament Quits in Protest." *The New York Times*, February 2, 2004.

17. "The Structure of Power in Iran." *Iran Chamber Society*, July 2006; "Governing Iran," PBS Online News Hour.

18. Gasiorowski, Mark J. "The Power Struggle in Iran." *Middle East Policy*, 4:7, October 1, 2000, p. 22.

19. "The Structure of Power in Iran." *Iran Chamber Society*, July 2006; "Governing Iran." *PBS Online News Hour*; "The Structure of Power in Iran." *PBS*

20. Articles 167–168, Constitution of the Islamic Republic of Iran.

21. "The Structure of Power in Iran." *Iran Chamber Society*, July 2006; "Governing Iran." *PBS Online News Hour*; "The Structure of Power in Iran." *PBS*.

22. Patrick Devenny, "Iran's Most Radical Regime." *Front Page Magazine*, August 25, 2005.

23. "UK sailors captured at gunpoint." *BBC News*, March 23, 2007. http://news.bbc.co.uk/2/hi/uk_news/6484279.stm

24. "Former hostage-taker appointed chief of Iranian television" Associated Press, May 24, 2004. http://www.eurasianet.org/departments/insight/articles/eav051904a.shtml

25. Wilfried Buchta, "Iran's Security Sector: An Overview." *Geneva Centre for the Democratic Control of Armed Forces*, August 2004. http://www.dcaf.ch/_docs/WP146.pdf

26. "Iran student protests: Five years on," *BBC NewsOnline*, July 9, 2004. http://news.bbc.co.uk/2/hi/middle_east/3879535.stm

27. Michael Eisenstadt, *Statement Before the United States Senate Foreign Relations Committee, Subcommittee on Near East and South Asian Affairs*, May 14, 1998.

28. *Voice of the Islamic Republic Radio*, July 20, 2003.

29. Ely Karmon, "Counterterrorism Policy: Why Tehran Starts and Stops Terrorism." *Middle East Quarterly*, 5(4), December 1998. http://meforum.org/article/427

30. FAS (Federation of American Scientists), "Qods (Jerusalem) Force – Iranian Revolutionary Guard Corps (IRGC – Pasdaran-e Inquilab). http://fas.org/irp/world/iran/qods/

31. Magnus Ranstorp "Hizbollah's Command Leadership: Its Structure, Decision-Making and Relationship with Iranian Clergy and Institutions" *Terrorism and Political Violence*, Vol. 6, No. 3 (Autumn 1994), 311.

32. Con Coughlin. "Teheran Fund Pays War Compensation to Hizbollah Families." *Telegraph*, August 4, 2006. http://www.telegraph.co.uk/news/main.jhtml?xml=/news/2006/08/04/wmid404.xml

33. Ibid.

35. Ramit Plushnick-Masti, "Israel: Iran Aided Hezbollah Ship Attack," *Associated Press*, July 15, 2006. Available at: http://www.comcast.net/news/international/middleeast/index.jsp?cat=MIDDLEEAST&fn=/2006/07/15/434861.html&cookieattempt=1

36. Ibid.

37. "History: Ministry of Intelligence and Security [MOIS] Vezarat-e Ettela'at va Amniat-e Keshvar VEVAK." *Global Security*. Available online at: http://www.globalsecurity.org/intell/world/iran/vevak-history.htm

38. "Operations: Ministry of Intelligence and Security (MOIS), Vezarat-e Ettela'at va Amniat-e Keshvar VEVAK." *Global Security*. Available online at: http://globalsecurity.org/intell/world/iran/vevak-ops.htm

39. Ibid.

40. Ibid.

41. Ibid.

42. Ben-Yishai, Ron, "The Iranian Hand on the Plunger," *Yediot Ahraniot*, July 29, 1994 (pp. 6–7, 26).

43. "Iran legal expert rips 'outrageous defamation' in HRW report," *Iran Focus*, May 19, 2005. Available at: http://www.iranfocus.com/modules/news/article.php?storyid=2138.

44. Karim Haqi is a former MEK member who left the organization in 1993. The group funded his family's relocation to France. Haqi and his family later relocated to the Netherlands where he was recruited by the MOIS, apparently for financial remuneration, and he has actively participated in Mohammad Hossein Sobhani's European MOIS disinformation ring ever since.

45. "Iran legal expert rips 'outrageous defamation' in HRW report," *Iran Focus*, May 19, 2005. Available at: http://www.iranfocus.com/modules/news/article.php?storyid=2138.

46. "Iranian intelligence gaining foothold in US?" *Iran Focus*, June 1, 2005. Available at: http://www.iranfocus.com/modules/news/print.php?storyid=2259.

47. "U.S. Expels Two From Iran's U.N. Mission." *Reuters*, June 29, 2004.

## Chapter 3

1. "Quotes from Ayatollah I Khomeini." *Iran-Heritage*, July 25, 2003. http://www.iran-heritage.org/interestgroups/government-article2.htm

2. "Quotes from Ayatollah I Khomeini." *Iran-Heritage*, July 25, 2003. http://www.iran-heritage.org/interestgroups/government-article2.htm

3. "Khomeini Backs Iranians Holding U.S. Hostages; U.N. Panel Leaves after Failing to See Captives U.S. Says Teheran Breaks Pledge." *Facts on File Inc.: 1980*, March 14, 1980, p. 177

4. Jonathon Randal "Khomeini Endorses Threat to Kill Hostages; Khomeini Backs Death Threat In Warning to U.S. Military; Militants Free Asian Captives." *The Washington Post*, November 23, 1979, p. 1A.

5. Jonathon Randal, "Exile Leader Shifts View on U.S.-Iran Ties; Iranian Exile Leader Shifts Stance on U.S." *The Washington Post*, January 2, 1979.

6. *Associated Press*. November 6, 1979

7. Elaine Sciolino, "Iran Will Not Rely on US or Soviets, Khomeini Declares." *New York Times*, October 5, 1988, p. 1A

8. Robert Spencer. *Front Page Magazine,* November 17, 2004. http://www.frontpagemag.com/ Articles/ReadArticle.asp?ID=15983

9. "Quotes from Ayatollah I Khomeini." *Iran-Heritage*, July 25, 2003. http://www.iran-heritage.org/interestgroups/government-article2.htm

10. Official Iranian biography of Ayatollah Sayyed Khamenei, available online at: http://www.leader.ir/langs/EN/index.php?p=bio

11. Notable among these are the assassinations of Abdul-Rahman Ghassemlou in Vienna in 1989 and Mohammad Hossein Naghdi in Italy in 1993. Both of the ensuing trials in these countries implicated individuals closely linked to the regime's security echelon.

12. "Leader's Address to the 3rd Intl. Conference on the Holy Quds and Support for the Palestinian People's Rights." April 14, 2006. http://www.khamenei.ir/EN/Speech/detail.jsp?id=20060414A

13. Ibid.

14. "Annan: 'Dismay' over Iranian comments on Israel." *CNN* http://edition.cnn.com/2005/WORLD/meast/10/27/ahmadinejad.reaction/index.html

15. "Iran Leader Encourages Destruction of "Cancerous" Israel." *CNN*, December 15, 2000. http://archives.cnn.com/2000/WORLD/meast/12/15/mideast.iran.reut/

16. "Iran Urges Muslim States to Retaliate Against Jerusalem Dig." *Haaretz*, February 7, 2007.

17. "Iran Mullahs Glorify Hezbollah's Terrorism Against Israel." *Iran News*, July 16, 2006. http://www.iranian.ws/iran_news/publish/article_16714.shtml

18. Ibid.

19. Islamic World Proud of Hezbollah, Says Iranian leader." *Deutsche Presse-Agentur*, July 16, 2006.

20. Ibid.

21. "Leaders Address to the 3rd Intl. Conference on the Holy Quds and Support for the Palestinian People's Rights." April 14, 2006 http://www.khamenei.ir/EN/Speech/detail.jsp?id=20060414A

22. "Iranian Leader, Khamenei: We Don't Need An Atomic Bomb. We've Been Defeating America For 25 Years Without It." The Middle East Media Research, June 24, 2004 http://memritv.org/Transcript.asp?P1=136

23. "One Day the US Too Will Be History." Middle East Media Research Institute, June 4, 2004. http://memri.org/bin/articles.cgi?Page=countries&Area=iran&ID=SP72704#_edn1

24. "Khamenei Speech: Exerpts." *BBC*, June 4, 2006. http://news.bbc.co.uk/go/pr/fr/-/2/hi/middle_east/5045990.stm

25. Ibid.

26. "Saudi Arabia Agrees to Aid U.S. Coalition, Iran Refuses." *CNN*, September 26, 2001. http://edition.cnn.com/2001/WORLD/meast/09/26/gen.mideast.eu/index.html

27. "One Day the U.S. Too Will Be History." Middle East Media Research, June 4, 2004. http://memri.org/bin/articles.cgi?Page=countries&Area=iran&ID=SP72704#_ednref4

28. "Khamenei Speech: Exerpts." *BBC*, June 4, 2006. http://news.bbc.co.uk/go/pr/fr/-/2/hi/middle_east/5045990.stm

29. Karimi, Nasser, "Iran–Ayatollah Ali Khamenei: U.S. Nuke Talks Not Needed." June 28, 2006. http://www.ncr-iran.org/content/view/1840/71/.

30. "Khamenei Speech: Exerpts." *BBC*, June 4, 2006. http://news.bbc.co.uk/go/pr/fr/-/2/hi/middle_east/5045990.stm

31. Ibid.

32. Ibid.

33. Nazilla Fathi, "Iran Won't Give Up Right to Use Atomic Technology, Leader Says." *New York Times*, June 28, 2006, p. 3A

34. "Iran Committed to Nuclear Programme Says Ayatollah Khamenei." *Deutsche Presse-Agentur*, October 21, 2005.

35. "Roundup: Iran "Not Intimidated" Ahead of Breaking Nuclear Seals." *Deutsche Presse-Agentur*, January 9, 2006.

36. "Khamenei Speech: Excerpts." *BBC*, June 4, 2006. http://news.bbc.co.uk/go/pr/fr/-/2/hi/middle_east/5045990.stm

37. Ibid.

38. "Profile: Mahmoud Ahmadinejad." http://news.bbc.co.uk/1/hi/world/middle_east/4107270.stm

39. Ibid.

40. Margaret Warner, "Iran's Presidential Winner." *Online News Hour*, June 27, 2005.

41. Iran and the Recent Escalation on Israel's Borders. MEMRI – No. 1204, July 13 2006

42. Iranian President, in Tajik Capital, Warns of MidEast Storm. *RFL/RL*, July 25, 2006. http://www.globalsecurity.org/wmd/library/news/iran/2006/iran-060725-rferl01.htm

43. Bill Samii, "Tehran Playing a Key Role in Israel-Lebanon Crisis." *RFL/RL*, July 17, 2006. http://www.globalsecurity.org/military/library/news/2006/07/mil-060717-rferl04.htm

44. Fathi Nazila, "Wipe Israel 'Off The Map' Iranian says." *International Herald Tribune*, October 27, 2005. http://www.iht.com/articles/2005/10/26/news/iran.php

45. "Ahmadinejad: Israel 'Will Be Removed'." *Bangkok Post*, February 11, 2006. http://www.bangkokpost.net/breaking_news/breakingnews.php?id=78985

46. "Iran's Ahmadinejad Calls for 'Removal of Zionist Regime'." *Yahoo! News*, July 8, 2006. http://uk.news.yahoo.com/08072006/323/iran-s-ahmadinejad-calls-removal-zionist-regime.html

47. Ibid.

48. Ibid.

49. Zionist Regime Bent on Countering the World of Islam. *IRNA—Islamic Republic News Agency*. October 26, 2006. http://www.globalsecurity.org/wmd/library/news/iran/2005/iran-051026-irna04.htm

50. Challiss McDonough, "Iran's President Warns Israel Over Gaza." *Voice of America*, July 7, 2006.

51. "Ahmadinejad: Israel 'Will Be Removed'." *Bangkok Post*, February 11, 2006, http://www.bangkokpost.net/breaking_news/breakingnews.php?id=78985

52. Farhad Pouladi, "Iran's Ahmadinejad Attacks Israel at Iraq Conference," *Agence-France Presse* via. *Middle East Times*, July 9, 2006. http://www.metimes.com/storyview.php?StoryID=20060709-014952-3804r

53. Ibid.

54. "Iran Denies Having Any Troops in Lebanon." *Fox News*, July 14, 2006. http://www.foxnews.com/story/0,2933,203829,00.html

55. Ibid.

56. "Ahmadinejad Says Israel Does Not Have Power to Harm Iran." *Fox News*, July 14, 2006. http://www.foxnews.com/story/0,2933,203568,00.html

57. The American Israel Public Affairs Committee—Op Cit.

58. Iranian Leaders: Statements and Positions (Part I). MEMRI—Middle East Media Research Institute, January 5, 2006, special report, 39. http://memri.org/bin/articles.cgi?Page=archives&Area=sr&ID=SR3906

59. Ibid.

60. Golnaz Esfandiari, "Iran/Syria: Increasingly Isolated Leaders Seek Mutual Support." *Radio Free Europe/Radio Liberty*, January 20, 2006. http://www.rferl.org/featuresarticle/2006/01/F1C63BCD-9432-41E4-A072-46D570DE011E.html

61. Iranian and Syrian Presidents Call for Expansion of Relations. *IRNA—Islamic Republic News Agency*, August 7, 2005. http://www.iranwatch.org/government/Iran/iran-irna-syria-080705.htm

62. Ibid.

63. "Iran's President on Nukes, Iraq, Terrorism." *MSNBC* interview, September 18, 2005.

64. "Ahmadinejad Says Israel Does Not Have Power To Harm Iran." *FoxNews*, July 14, 2006. http://www.foxnews.com/story/0,2933,203568,00.html

65. The American Israel Public Affairs Committee. October 26, 2005.

66. Breffini O'Rourke, "Ahmadinejad Seeks Support in Indonesia As Nuclear Crisis Sharpens." *RFE/RL*, http://www.globalsecurity.org/wmd/library/news/iran/2006/iran-060510-rferl01.htm

67. "Syria Says Willing for Talks with U.S. over Lebanon Ceasefire." *The Haaretz*, July 24, 2006. http://www.haaretz.com/hasen/spages/741719.html

68. "Ahmadinejad: Israeli Aggression on Lebanon Aim to Revive Dead Plan of Greater Middle East." August 1, 2006. http://www.irna.ir/en/news/view/line-17/0608016240201110.htm

69. Ahmadinejad, Chavez Reaffirm Brotherly Ties. *IRNA—Iran Republic News Agency*, August 11, 2006. http://www.irna.ir/en/news/view/line-17/0508123386001333.htm

70. Iran's President on Nukes, Iraq, Terrorism. *MSNBC* interview, September 18, 2005.

71. "Excerpts: Ahmadinejad Conference." *BBC News*, January 14, 2006. http://news.bbc.co.uk/1/hi/world/middle_east/4613644.stm

72. Iran Shrugs Off Security Council Referral. *FoxNews*, July 13, 2006. http://www.foxnews.com/story/0,2933,203285,00.html

73. The American Israel Public Affairs Committee. June 20, 2005. http://www.aipac.org/iran/in_their_own_words.html

74. Ibid., September 15, 2005.

75. "Ahmadinejad: Israel 'Will Be Removed'." *Bangkok Post*, February 11, 2006. http://www.bangkokpost.net/breaking_news/breakingnews.php?id=78985

76. "Ahmadinejad's letter to Bush." *Asia Times*, May 11, 2006. http://www.atimes.com/atimes/Middle_East/HE11Ak01.html

77. Iran and the Recent Escalation on Israel's Borders. *MEMRI—No.1204*, July 13, 2006.

78. "Iranian Leader: Israel Will Be Destroyed." *China Daily*, October 26, 2005. http://www.chinadaily.com.cn/english/doc/2005-10/26/content_488038.htm

79. Iran Manif. http://iranmanif.org/en/IRAN-PRESIDENT-AHMADINEJAD.htm

80. Ahmadinejad Says Enemies Will Fail to Prevent Iran Progress. *IRNA—Islamic Republic News Agency*, February 5, 2006. http://www.globalsecurity.org/wmd/library/news/iran/2006/iran-060205-irna06.htm

81. "Iranian Leaders: Statements and Positions (Part I)." *Middle East Media Research Institute*, Special Report No. 39, January 5, 2006. http://memri.org/bin/articles.cgi?Page=archives&Area=sr&ID=SR3906#_ednref28

82. Patrick Clawson, "Iran's Reaction to New Bush Policy Shows America-Bashing Is Out of Style." *The Washington Institute for Near East Policy*, 7 August, 2002. http://www.washingtoninstitute.org/ templateC05.php?CID=1525

83. "Iraq Unrest Will Spread Terrorism." *Iran Daily*, December 2, 2004. http://www.iran-daily.com/1383/2154/html/index.htm

84. Press Release-Heinrich Bol Stiftung. Accessed December 6, 2006. http://www.boell.de/downloads/nahost/IranAnalysis_PresidentialElection.pdf

85. Though the eventual indictment did not implicate any members of the regime. See Gary Sick, "Iran: Confronting Terrorism." *Washington Quarterly* 26:(4), 2003: pp. 87–88.

86. "Argentina Seeks Rafsanjani Arrest." *BBC World News*, November 9, 2006. Available at: http://news.bbc.co.uk/1/hi/world/americas/6134066.stm

87. Barbara Slavin, "Iran Looks, Again, to "Experienced Captain." *USA TODAY*, February 6, 2006. http://www.usatoday.com/news/world/2005-02-06-rafsanjani-interview_x.htm.

88. See, for example, "Iran: Rafsanjani's Second Shot At Reform." *Business Week Online*, June 27, 2005. Available at: http://www.businessweek.com/magazine/content/05_26/b3939098_mz015.htm

89. "Weekly Update." Foundation for Defense of Democracies, October 12, 2004. http://www.defenddemocracy.org/archive/archive_newsletter.htm?issue_id=1291

90. "Iran Election: Biography Of Ali Akbar Hashemi-Rafsanjani." *BBC Monitoring International Reports*, May 17, 2005.

91. Ibid.

92. "Iran's Presidential Contenders in Their Own Words." *Agence France Presse—English*, June 24, 2005.

93. "Iran Election: Biography of Ali Akbar Hashemi-Rafsanjani." *BBC Monitoring International Reports*, May 17, 2005.

94. "Rafsanjani Sketches Vision of a Moderate, Modern Iran." *The New York Times*, April 19, 1992.

95. "Rafsanjani-Iran-Council." *Islamic Republic News Agency*, February 3, 2006.

96. Iran Focus, "Iran's New Foreign Minister 'Was Involved in Terrorism'." *Iran Focus*. Available at: http://www.iranfocus.com/modules/news/article.php?storyid=3460

97. Iranian Briefing Material from BBC Monitoring in English September 7, 2005. Accessed December 6, 2006—*BBC Monitoring International Reports*, September 7, 2005, A200509072E-E5F8-GNW, 529 words.

98. "Biography of New Iranian Foreign Minister Manuchechr Mottaki." *BBC Monitoring International Reports*, September 7, 2005 via *Mehr News Agency*, July 19, 2005.

99. "Biography of New Iranian Foreign Minister Manuchechr Mottaki." *BBC Monitoring International Reports*, September 7, 2005 via *ISNA*, August 17, 2005.

100. *ISNA*, August 25, 2005 in "Biography of Foreign Minister Manucher Mottaki." *BBC-Monitoring International Reports*, September 7, 2005.

101. "Cabinet List Presented." *Iran Daily*, August 15, 2005. http://www.iran-daily.com/1384/2350/html/ index.htm

102. "Biography of Pour-Mohammadi, Nominee for Post of Interior Minister." *Global Security* http://www.globalsecurity.org/wmd/library/news/iran/2005/iran-050814-irna04.htm

103. Ibid.

104. Iranian Briefing Material from *BBC Monitoring in English*. BBC Monitoring International Reports, August 14, 2005.

105. Ibid.

106. Ibid.

107. "A Weekly Review of Developments in and Pertaining to Iran." *Radio Free Europe/ Radio Liberty*, September 5, 2005.

108. "Biography of Iranian Defense Minister Brig- Gen Mostafa Mohammad Najjar." *BBC Monitoring Middle East*, November 7, 2005 via *IRNA*, September 24, 2005.

109. "Biography of Iranian Defense Minister Brig-Gen Mostafa Mohammad Najjar." *BBC Monitoring Middle East*, November 7, 2005 via *IRNA*, October 16, 2005.

100. Ibid.

111. "Biography of Iranian Defense Minister Brig-Gen Mostafa Mohammad Najjar." *BBC Monitoring Middle East*, November 7, 2005 via *IRNA*, September 24, 2005.

112. "Biography of Iranian Defense Minister Brig-Gen Mostafa Mohammad Najjar." *BBC Monitoring Middle East*, November 7, 2005 via *IRNA*, November 2, 2005.

113. "All the President's Men," *Asia Times*. http://www.atimes.com/atimes/Middle_East/GH16Ak01.html; "Cabinet List Presented." *Iran Daily*. http://www.iran-daily.com/1384/2350/html/index.htm; "Iran Unveils Hardline Cabinet, Warns US over Nuclear Threat." *Turkish Press*, *http://archive.turkishpress.com/news.asp?id=65370*

114. "Iran Elections Candidates: Ali Larijani." http://www.iranfocus.com/modules/news/article.php?storyid=2398 "Profile: Ali Larijani." *BBC News*. http://news.bbc.co.uk/2/hi/middle_east/3625019.stm.

115. Press Release-Heinrich Bol Stiftung- http://www.boell.de/downloads/nahost/IranAnalysis_PresidentialElection.pdf

116. Ibid.

117. Ibid.

118. American Iranian Council. http://www.american-iranian.org/pubs/aicupdate/03242005.html

119. "Iran Election Biography of Dr Ali Larijani." *BBC Monitoring International Reports*, May 17, 2005

120. Ibid.

121. "Iran, 'Swiftly Seeks Nuclear Goal.'" *BBC News*, February 21, 2007.

122. "Iran Election Biography of Dr Ali Larijani," *BBC Monitoring International Reports*, May 17, 2005

123. "Iran Urges Arab Countries to Eject U.S. Military." *The Associated Press*, December 5, 2006.

124. Profile: Ibid. Behnoud, Masoud, "Losses and Gains in the Void of US-Iran Relations." *Iran Press Service*, June 1, 2004. http://www.iran-press-service.com/ips/articles-2004/june/iran_us-relations_1604.shtml

125. "Majlis Urges Gov't to Revise Cooperation with IAEA." *IRNA*, December 27, 2006. http://www.irna.com/en/news/view/line-17/0612274790134716.htm

126. "Supreme Defense Council." *GlobalSecurity*. http://www.globalsecurity.org/military/world/iran/sdc.ht; "Fazli Named Deputy Secretary of SNSC." *Iran Daily* http://www.iribnews.ir/Full_en.asp?news_id=199425&n=34

127. Buchta Wilfried, "Iran's Security Sector: An Overview." Geneva Center for Democratic Control of Armed Forces.

128. *Intelligence Newsletter.* Accessed on December 6, 2006. *Intelligence Newsletter*, September 25, 1997. Who's Who N. 319

129. Ibid.

130. Ibid.

131. Ibid.

132. Ibid.

133. *IRNA News Agency*, Tehran, September 14, 1997; BBC Summary of World Broadcasts.

134. "Iran's Guard Commander Comments on Tehran's Missile Power." *BBC Monitoring Middle East*, November 13, 2006

135. "Iran Guards Chief Excoriates West's Double-Standards Towards Palestine." *BBC Monitoring Middle East*, October 20, 2006.

136. Speech given to IRGC at the Basij on July 30, 2006. *MEMRI* http://memri.org/bin/articles.cgi?Page=archives&Area=sd&ID=SP122506

137. Anthony Cordesman, "Iran in Transition: Uncertain Hostility, Uncertain Threat." *CSIS*. http://www.fas.org/spp/starwars/congress/1998_h/ts050698.htm; "Iran Under Khatami: Weapons of Mass Destruction Terrorism, and the Arab-Israeli Conflict." http://www.iranwatch.org/government/US/Congress/Hearings/sfrc-051498/us-sfrc-eisenstadt-051498.htm

138. Ibid.

139. "Acquaintance with the Head of the Judiciary and his Viewpoints." http://bia-judiciary.ir/En/framework.jsp?SID=41

140. Press Release from Iranian Embassy in Oslo-PDF Format. http://www.iran-embassy-oslo.no/pdf_fil/Biografy%20of%20Iranian%20Ministers.pdf

141. Ibid.

142. Ibid.

143. Ibid.

144. Ibid.

145. "Biography of Iranian Justice Minister Jamal Karimi-Rad.—*BBC Monitoring Middle East—BBC Worldwide Monitoring*,

146. "Biography of Iranian Justice Minister Jamal Karimi-Rad." *BBC Monitoring Middle East*, November 20, 2005 via *Farhang-e Ashti*, October 2005.

147. "Biography of Iranian Justice Minister Jamal Karimi-Rad." *BBC Monitoring Middle East*— Political Supplied by *BBC Worldwide Monitoring*, November 20, 2005 via *Tose'eh*, January 16, 2005.

## Chapter 4

1. Carl Von Clausewitz, *On War*, trans. Colonel J. J. Graham. London and Boston: Routledge & Kegan Paul, 1969, vol. 1, pp. 2 and 23.

2. *Report of the DOD Commission on Beirut International Terrorist Act*, October 23, 1983. December 20, 1983, Part 9, I.C., p. 123.

3. *Army Low Intensity Conflict Study* (unpublished document, 1985) U.S. Department of Defense.

4. Personal Communication with Stefan Possony, October 14, 1984.

5. Brian Jenkins, "Definitions," *Readings on Terrorism*. Fort Leavenworth, Kansas: U.S. Army Command and General Staff College, October 4, 1983, p. 3.

6. An updated document written in Persian by Syed Mehsan Musawi, Temproary Charge d'Affairs, Iranian Embassy in Beirut, addressed to Mr. Louasani, Director General of Asian-African Affairs, Iran.

7. The Revolutionary Organization of Socialist Muslims is allegedly a front for, or ally of, the secular Abu Nidal Organization (Source: "Group Profile: Revolutionary Organization of Socialist Muslims." *Terrorism Knowledge Base*, available at: http://209.235.103.8/Group.jsp?groupID=4242.)

8. The date commemorates the founding of the Islamic Republic of Iran, according to the Iranian calendar.

9. Daniel Pipes, *The Rushdie Affair: The Novel, the Ayatollah, and the West*. Piscataway, NJ: Transaction Publishers, 2003, p. 140.

10. Statement made by Senator Daniel Patrick Moynihan (D-NY) in a statement to the President of the United States, "Resolution Condemning The Threats Against The Author And Publishers Of The 'Satanic Verses' (Senate—February 28, 1989)." available at: http://www.fas.org/irp/congress/1989_cr/s890228-terror.htm

11. "'Satanic Verses' Translator Found Slain; Tokyo Killing Follows Attack on Italian Interpreter of Rushdie Book." *The Washington Post*, July 13, 1991.

12. Ibid.

13. Eugene Robinson, "Norwegian Publisher of 'Satanic Verses' Is Shot." *The Washington Post*, October 12, 1993.

14. "Rushdie Calls For Reprisals on Iran; Shooting of Norwegian Publisher Linked to Satanic Verses." *The Independent* (London), October 12, 1993.

15. "Iranian Reported Killed." *The Washington Post*, August 28, 1989.

16. Patrick E. Tyler, "Iranian Seen as Victim Of Assassination Plan; Cyprus Slaying Was Third Since June." *The Washington Post*, September 9, 1989.

17. Loren Jenkins, "French Ambassador Slain in Midday Beirut; Popular Envoy Shunned Protection." *The Washington Post*, September 5, 1981.

18. "Bomb Rips U.S. Embassy." *St. Louis Post-Dispatch (Missouri)*, April 18, 1983.

19. Thomas L. Friedman, "Counting The Casualties In Beirut And Beyond." *The New York Times*, April 24, 1983.

20. "Pro-Iranian Force Claims Role in Many Attacks In Lebanon." *The Washington Post*, April 20, 1983.

21. "Iranian Guards Bring Revolution To Lebanese Valley." *The Globe and Mail (Canada)*, April 19, 1983.

22. "Don't Kill Frenchman, Shia Clergyman Urges." *The Globe and Mail (Canada)*, March 16, 1987.

23. Stephen Engelberg, "U.S. Links Tehran to Terror Squad." *The New York Times*, November 12, 1989.

24. "Saudi Bomb Blast Kills 5 Americans." *Chicago Sun-Times*, November 14, 1995.

25. "Four Saudis Beheaded in Public for Bombing U.S. Facility." *The Ottawa Citizen*, June 1, 1996.

26. Roula Khalaf and Patti Waldmeir, "Clinton Vows to Catch Bombers: Saudi Blast Kills 19 Americans and Wounds 389 Others." *Financial Times*, June 27, 1996.

27. "Iranian Hit Teams in Turkey." *Middle East Data Project, Inc.*, February 6, 1995.

28. "Gunmen Kill Former Iranian Shah Bodyguard." *United Press International*. October 24, 1986.

29. Ibid.

30. "Iranian Hit Teams in Turkey." *Middle East Data Project, Inc.*, February 6, 1995.

31. "Turkey ousts 2 Iranian diplomats on kidnapping charge." *United Press International*, October 29, 1988.

32. "Iranians assassinated in Turkey." *Middle East Defense News*, April 16, 1990.

33. "Turkish Columnist Who Criticized Islam is Slain." *The Associated Press*, September 4, 1990.

34. "Islamist Terrorists Have Links with Iran: Turkish Police." *Agence France Presse*, March 11, 1996.

35. "Iranian Hit Teams in Turkey." *The Iran Brief*, February 6, 1995.

36. "Iranian Subversion in Turkey." *The Iran Brief*, February 6, 1995.

37. "Iran Blamed for Many Assassinations of Opponents Abroad." *The Associated Press*, March 16, 1993.

38. "Turkey sentences three Islamic radicals to death." *Agence France Presse*, January 7, 2002.

39. "U.N. Urges Tehran to End Political Assassinations Of Opponents Abroad." *Agence France Presse,* November 16, 1993.

40. "Extrajudicial Executions." *Amnesty International report on official secrecy and repression in Iran 1995*, May 30, 1995. http://www.amnestyusa.org/countries/iran/document.do?id=BC7ABDB06436BBB9802569A50071 4EF4

41. "U.N. Urges Tehran to End Political Assassinations of Opponents Abroad." *Agence France Presse*, November 16, 1993.

42. "Iranian Dissident Killed in Ankara." *The Associated Press*, August 28, 1993.

43. Amnesty International, "Amnesty International Report 1995—Iran." *United Nations High Commissioner for Refugees*, 1995. http://www.unhcr.org/home/RSDCOI/3ae6a9f74c.html.

44. "Iran: Amnesty International Concerned About Possible Government Involvement in Deaths of Iranian Nationals." *Amnesty International*, February 28, 1996. http://web.amnesty.org/library/Index/engMDE130071996?OpenDocument&of=COUNTRIES%5CIRAN.

45. "Iranian Kurdish Leader Killed in Baghdad." *Agence France Presse*, August 4, 1994.

46. "Three Iranian Opposition Members Shot Dead in Baghdad." *Agence France Presse*, July 10, 1995.

47. "Iranian Opposition Figure Shot Dead in Baghdad." *Agence France Presse*, March 8, 1996.

48. "Human Rights Questions: Human Rights Situations and Reports of Special Rapporteurs and Representatives: Situation of Human Rights in the Islamic Republic of Iran." *United Nations General Assembly*, October 11, 1996. http://www.unhchr.ch/huridocda/huridoca.nsf/0/61f4b0d4b32382958025670c00538894?OpenDocument.

49. "Human Rights Questions: Human Rights Situations and Reports of Special Rapporteurs and Representatives: Situation of Human Rights in the Islamic Republic of Iran." *United Nations General Assembly*, October 15, 1997.

50. Farouk Choukri, "Car Bomb Kills Six Iranian Opposition Fighters in Iraq, 36 Wounded." *Agence France Press*, June 9, 1999.

51. A Quarterly Publication of the Institute on Religion and Democracy, *Faith and Freedom*, 25(4), Fall 2006. www.ird-renew.org/atf/cf/%7B8548C466-7ECE-4AF1-B844 49C289CE5165%7D/2006%2004%20FF.PDF.

52. "Anglicans Reported Arrested In Iran." *The Associated Press*, August 20, 1980.

53. *The Associated Press*, October 26, 1979.

54. "Son of Anglican Bishop Killed by Gunman." *The Associated Press*, May 7, 1980.

55. "Anglicans Reported Arrested In Iran." *The Associated Press*, August 20, 1980.

56. Julian Nundy, "French Seize Algerian Militants." *The Independent (London)*, November 10, 1993.

57. "Britons Trapped in Arab Hijack Ordeal: Gunmen Threaten to Blow up Kuwaiti Jumbo Stranded in North-East Iran." *The Guardian (London)*, April 6, 1988.

58. Shaul Shay, *Terror in the Name of the Imam*. Hertzliyya: ICT Press. pp. 77–78. [Hebrew].

59. "Insurgents Target Arab-Iraq Ties." *The New York Times*, July 9, 2005.

60. "Al-Ahram Claims Iran Behind Egyptian Ambassador's Murder." *Daily Star Egypt*, January 29, 2007.

61. Patrick E. Tyler, "Killings in Austria, Emirates Laid to Iran; Assassinations Are Said to Bear Marks of Sophisticated Agents." *The Washington Post*, August 2, 1989.

62. Patrick Tyler, "Iranian Killings Are Rare But Done with Precision." *The Guardian (London)*, August 3, 1989.

63. "Iranian Exiles Killed." *Financial Times*, July 9, 1987.

64. "Karachi Gun Attack." *Financial Times*, December 6, 1988.

65. Stephen Engelberg, "U.S. Links Teheran to Terror Squad." *The New York Times*, November 12, 1989.

66. "Iran denies involvement in Karachi assassination of opposition figure." *BBC Summary of World Broadcasts*, June 11, 1993; "Final Report On The Situation Of Human Rights in the Islamic Republic of Iran Prepared By The Special Representative of the Commission on Human Rights." Available online at: http://www.unhchr.ch/Huridocda/Huridoca.nsf/0/3b10d2ce0deea2348025673700654bed?Opendocument.

67. "An Iranian Airline Is Hijacked To Cairo With 280 Aboard." *The New York Times*, August 8, 1984.

68. "Soviets Parade Military Might in Afghan City Diplomats Say." *The Toronto Star*, January 17, 1987. http://web.lexis-nexis.com.ezaccess.libraries.psu.edu/universe/document?_m=88cfa30b47c7fc2be0550d3a9da05f1e&_docnum=4&wchp=dGLzVzz-zSkVA&_md5=d535ce3e85f575e28db6f756f2e38e14.

69. "Iranian Killed." *The Independent (London)*, August 9, 1992.

70. "4 Kurds Slain in Berlin." *The Washington Post*, September 18, 1992.

71. "Two Iranian Diplomats Implicated in anti-Kurdish Attack: Stern." *Agence France Presse*, December 29, 1992.

72. "Slayings Linked to Iran." *The Associated Press*, August 15, 1993.

73. "Brief on Iran-412." Representative Office of The National Council of Resistance of Iran, May 14, 1996.

74. "Murder of Iranian Exile Underlines Risk of Paris." *The Globe and Mail (Canada)*, February 9, 1984.

75. "French Seek Suspect in Slaying of Shah's Nephew." *The Assocciated Press*, December 10, 1979.

76. Shay Shaul, *Terror in the Name of the Imam*. (Hertzliyya: ICT Press, [Hebrew].

77. "Iran: A Hit List Of Opposition In Exile." *IPS-Inter Press Service*, August 9, 1991.

78. Shaul Shay, *Terror in the Name of the Imam*. Hertzliyya: ICT Press, pp. 149–150, [Hebrew].

79. Obituary Page. *Time Magazine*, February 20, 1984. http://www.time.com/time/magazine/article/0,9171,950022,00.html?promoid=googlep.

80. "Emirates' Ambassador To France Assassinated." *The Washington Post*, February 9, 1984.

81. "Mideast Tensions; Iranian Exile Is Slain in Paris." *The New York Times*, October 24, 1990.and "US Court Orders Iran to Pay 311 Million Dollars For Dissident's Killing." *Agence-France Press*, December 21, 2000.

82. "Prosecutor Demands Life Sentence, Links Iran to Slaying." *Associated Press Worldstream*, December 2, 1994.

83. "Patterns of Global Terrorism 1996." Available online at: http://www.fas.org/irp/threat/terror_96/europe.html

84. "German Verdict Indicates Coordinated Policy to Kill Dissidents: Amnesty." *Agence France Presse*, April 10, 1997.

85. G. Boyd, "Iranian Leader Murdered." *Nationwide News Pty Limited, The Austrian* July 20, 1987.

86. "Murder Case Linked to Iran." *The Toronto Star*, July 20, 1987.

87. Hugh Pope, "Tehran Goes Gunning for the Kurds." *The Independent (London)*, June 23, 1993.

88. "Austria Denies Letting Killers Go." *The Independent (London)*, July 14, 1990.

89. "Swiss Orders Arrest of Iranian Ex-Minister." *The Journal of Turkish Weekly*, April 11, 2006. http://www.turkishweekly.net/news.php?id=29587.

90. Michael Wise, "Austria Denies Letting Killers Go." *The Independent*, July 14, 1990.

91. Richard Johns, "Bomb Threatens UK-Iran Relations." *Financial Times (London)*, August 21, 1986.

92. "Iran Terror Campaign Feared After Car Blast." *Nationwide News Pty Limited, The Australian*, July 20, 1987.

93. Karen DeYoung, "Attacks Frighten Iranians in London; Three Opponents of Khomeini Killed." *The Washington Post*, November 1, 1987.

94. "2 Iranians Killed in London." *The Washington Post*, October 4, 1987.

95. Felicity Berringer, "Mail Carrier Is Indicted In Slaying of Iranian Exile." *The Washington Post*, August 29, 1980.

96. Edward A. Gargan, "Victim In Stamford Murder Identified As Missing Dean." *The New York Times*, October 21, 1982.

97. "Bahai death probed," *The Globe and Mail (Canada)*, October 22, 1982.

## Chapter 5

1. Gilles Kepel. *Jihad: The Trail of Political Islam*. Cambridge: Belknap Press, p. 128.

2. "Hezbollah as a strategic arm of Iran." *Intelligence and Terrorism Information Center at the Center for Special Studies (C.S.S.)*, September 8, 2006. Available at: http://www.intelligence.org.il/eng/eng_n/html/iran_hezbollah_e1b.htm

3. Ibid.

4. Dean M. Kaplan. *Hizballah*. The Terrorism Studies Program at George Washington University (unpublished paper).

5. "Hizbullah Secretary-General Hassan Nasrallah: 'The Disarmament of Hizbullah Should Not Be Discussed Now,'" *MEMRI Special Dispatch Series No. 1252*, August 16, 2006. Available at: http://memri.org/bin/articles.cgi?Page=archives&Area=sd&ID=SP125206.

6. "Lebanese military analyst: Hezbollah possess sophisticated weapons," *Associated Press*, August 15, 2007. Available at: http://www.iht.com/articles/ap/2007/08/15/africa/ME-GEN-Lebanon-Hezbollah.php.

7. Intelligence and Terrorism Information Center. http://www.terrorism-info.org.il/site/html/search.asp?isSearch=yes&isT8=yes&searchText=T90&pid=108&sid=13&preview=

8. This last Imam, known as the "Hidden Imam," is presumed to be in occultation rather than deceased, and is expected to return at the End of Days to restore the Shi'ite community to its intended glory.

9. A. Nazir Hamzeh, "Lebanon's Hizbullah: from Islamic revolution to parliamentary accommodation," *Third World Quarterly*, Vol. 14, No. 2, 1993: 5.

10. Hamzeh, 6.

11. John G. Habenstein, "Hezbollah—Party of God" *A Middle Eastern Threat Analysis* by Intellecom Inc. (2002). Accessed via www.intellecom-inc.com on June 10, 2002: 4.

12. Structural information about Hizbllah is from: Magnus Ranstorp "Hizbollah's Command Leadership: Its Structure, Decision-Making and Relationship with Iranian Clergy and Institutions" *Terrorism and Political Violence*, Vol. 6, No. 3 (Autumn 1994), 306–311.

13. Habenstein, op. cit., 4.

14. Habenstein, op. cit., 6.

15. Sami Moubayed. "The Man in Nasrallah's Shadow: A Profile of Sheikh Naim Qasim." *Terrorism Focus*, Jamestown Foundation. Available at: http://www.jamestown.org/terrorism/news/article.php?articleid=2370111

16. Ranstorp, op. cit., 305.

17. Ali Nouri Zadeh. "Imad Mughniyeh: Hizballah's phantom." *Al Sharq al Awsat* online edition, 8.11.06. Available at: http://www.asharqalawsat.com/english/news.asp?section=3&id=5964

18. Jerusalem Center for Public Affairs. "The PLO Weapons Ship from Iran." *Jerusalem Issue Brief*, 1(15), January 7, 2002.

19. Ibid.

20. "Key Leader Profile: Imad Fayez Mugniyah." *Terrorism Knowledge Base*. Available at: http://www.tkb.org/KeyLeader.jsp?memID=5871

21. Bill Roggio. "Imad Mugniyah likely behind the capture of Israeli soldiers." *Counterterrorism Blog*, 7.12.06. Available at: http://counterterrorismblog.org/2006/07/imad_mugniyah_likely_behind_th.php. See Also: Magnus Ranstorp. "Inside Hizballah's Decision-Making." *Counterterrorism Blog*, 7.14.06. Available at: http://counterterrorismblog.org/2006/07/print/inside_hizballahs_decisionmaki_1.php

22. Habenstein, op. cit., pp. 8–9.

23. Rex Hudson. "Terrorist and Organized Crime Groups in the Tri-Border Area (TBA) of South America." *Library of Congress Federal Research Division*, July 2003, p. 14.

24. Jeffrey Fields. "Issue Brief: Islamist Terrorist Threats in the Tri-Border Region." *Issue Brief, Center for Nonproliferation Studies, Monterrey Institute of International Studies*, October 2002. Available at: http://www.nti.org/e_research/e3_16a.html

25. Steve Rodan. "U.S. Mulls Fight of Hezbollah Drug Trade, Funny Money." *Jerusalem Post Service*, September 12, 1997. Accessed via http://www.jewishsf.com/bk970912/imulls.htm on July 15, 2002.

26. Ibid.

27. Jeremy M. Sharp et. al. "Israel-Hamas-Hezbollah: The Current Conflict." *Congressional Research Service CRS Report for Congress*, July 21, 2006.

28. Magnus Ranstorp. "Inside Hizballah's decision-making." *Counterterrorism Blog*, 7.14.06. Available at: http://counterterrorismblog.org/2006/07/print/inside_hizballahs_decisionmaki_1.php

29. "Memorandum Opinion." *Peterson v. Islamic Republic of Iran*, US District Court for the District of Columbia, 2003. Available at: http://perleslaw.com/pdf/peterson.pdf#search=%22Mohtashemi%20october%2023%2C%201983%22

30. Magnus Ranstorp. "Inside Hizballah's decision-making." *Counterterrorism Blog*, 7.14.06. Available at: http://counterterrorismblog.org/2006/07/print/inside_hizballahs_decisionmaki_1.php

31. MEMRI Special Dispatch Series No. 1171. "Iranian Iraqi News Agency Aswathura's Exclusive Interview With Grand Ayatollah Montazeri," 5.24.06. Available at: http://memri.org/bin/articles.cgi?Page=archives&Area=sd&ID=SP117106

32. http://news.bbc.co.uk/2/low/middle_east/2699541.stm

33. Habenstein, op. cit., pp. 6–7.

34. Special Information Paper, Hezbollah Profile of the Lebanese Shiite Terrorist Organization of Global Reach Sponsored by Iran and Supported by Syria, June 2003. www.intelligence.org.il

35. Dan Darling "General Panic" *The Weekly Standard*, October 5, 2005. Available at: http://www.weeklystandard.com/Content/Public/Articles/000/000/006/156kncex.asp

36. Shai Feldman and Yiftah Shapir, eds. *The Middle East Military Balance 2000–2001*. Cambridge: MIT Press, 2001, p. 212.

37. While Hizballah is believed to have fired an Iranian-made C-802 anti-ship missile at an Israeli naval vessel during the July-August 2006 Israel-Hizballah conflict, there is debate as to whether the specific missile used was actually a less-powerful C-701 anti-ship missile, known by its Iranian production name as the *Kowsar*.

38. Habenstein, op. cit., pp. 5–6.

39. Hassan Nasrallah. Speech Broadcast on Al-Manar Television, March 20, 2002.

40. Avi Jorisch. *Beacon of Hatred*. Washington, DC: The Washington Institute for Near East Policy Press, p. 62.

41. Avi Jorisch. "Al-Manar: Hizbullah TV, 24/7". *Middle East Quarterly*, Winter 2004. Available at: http://www.meforum.org/pf.php?id=583

42. Steven Erlanger and Richard A. Oppel, Jr. "A disciplined Hezbollah Surprises Israel with its Training, Tactics and Weapons." *The New York Times*, August 6, 2006. Available at: http://www.nytimes.com/2006/08/07/world/middleeast/07hezbollah.html

43. Ibid.

44. Ibid.

45. Ibid.

46. Ibid.

47. Ibid.

48. Ibid.

49. *Washington Post*. "Suicide Truck Bombing at the US Embassy in Beirut, April 13, 1983." Available at: http://www.washingtonpost.com/ac3/ContentServer?node=world/issues/terrordata&pagename=world/terror&entityId=46&appstat=detail&resulttype=attack&cache12=46_detail_attack

50. *Washington Post*. "Suicide Truck Bombing of US Marine Barracks in Beirut, October 23, 1983." Available at: http://www.washingtonpost.com/ac3/ContentServer?node=world/issues/terrordata&pagename=world/terror&entityId=47&appstat=detail&resulttype=attack&cache12=47_detail_attack

51. *Washington Post*. "Bombing of US Embassy Annex in Kuwait." Available at: http://www.washingtonpost.com/ac3/ContentServer?node=world/issues/terrordata&pagename=world/terror&entityId=48&appstat=detail&resulttype=attack&cache12=48_detail_attack

52. Arlington National Cemetery website. "William Francis Buckley, Lieutenant Colonel, United States Army, Assassinated CIA Station Chief." Available at: http://www.arlingtoncemetery.net/wbuckley.htm

53. *Washington Post*. "Suicide Bomb Attack at US Embassy Compound in Beirut." Available at: http://www.washingtonpost.com/ac3/ContentServer?node=world/issues/

terrordata&pagename=world/terror&entityId=49&appstat=detail&resulttype=attack&cache12=49_detail_attack

54. *Washington Post*. "Restaurant Bombing in Madrid, Spain." Available at: http://www.washingtonpost.com/ac3/ContentServer?node=world/issues/terrordata&pagename=world/terror&appstat=detail&resulttype=attack&entityId=138&cache12=4

55. *Washington Post*. "Hijacking of TWA Flight 847." Available at: http://www.washingtonpost.com/ac3/ContentServer?node=world/issues/terrordata&pagename=world/terror&entityId=50&appstat=detail&resulttype=attack&cache12=50_detail_attack

56. http://www.nti.org/e_research/e3_16a.html

57. http://www.ict.org.il/articles/articledet.cfm?articleid=371

58. http://www.washingtonpost.com/ac3/ContentServer?node=world/issues/terrordata&pagename=world/terror&appstat=detail&resulttype=attack&entityId=147&cache12=19

59. http://www.tkb.org/Incident.jsp?incID=8081

60. http://www.tkb.org/Incident.jsp?incID=7984

61. http://www.tkb.org/Incident.jsp?incID=10256

62. http://www.tkb.org/Incident.jsp?incID=10982

63. http://www.tkb.org/Incident.jsp?incID=15618

64. http://www.tkb.org/Incident.jsp?incID=16944

65. http://www.tkb.org/Incident.jsp?incID=8644

66. http://www.tkb.org/Incident.jsp?incID=16894

67. http://www.tkb.org/Incident.jsp?incID=22852

68. Andrew Mills, "Killing of anti-Syrian leader heightens Lebanon tensions", *USA Today*, November 21rst, 2006, http://www.usatoday.com/news/world/2006-11-21-lebanon_x.htm.

69. Mark Tran and agencies, 'Lebanon mourns assassinated MP, *The Guardian*, June 14th, 2007, http://www.guardian.co.uk/syria/story/0,,2103003,00.html.

70. Independent Media Review Analysis (IMRA), 'Weapons Uncovered on Israel's Northern Border', *IMRA*, January 11th, 2007, http://imra.org.il/story.php3?id=32412.

71. Independent Media Review Analysis (IMRA), 'Hezbollah Bunkers uncovered on Israeli Border', *IMRA*, January 26th, 2007, http://imra.org.il/story.php3?id=32666.

72. Reuters, 'Israel suspects Hezbollah of planting explosives', *Reuters*, February 5, 2007, http://www.reuters.com/article/middleeastCrisis/idUSL05624088.

73. Debka file, 'An Israeli tank force with bulldozers enters enclave between border fence and Lebanese frontier Wednesday night', *Debkafile*, February 7, 2007, http://www.debka.com/section.php?cid=42.

74. For an earlier study, see Yonah Alexander, *Palestinian Religious Terrorism: HAMAS and Islamic Jihad*. Ardsley, NY: Transnational Publishers, Inc., 2002.

75. "In 'revenge' for Sharif Killing. Hamas Calls for Attacks on Jews." *The Jerusalem Post*, April 9, 1998.

76. "Quartet Statement on Palestinian Legislative Council Elections," January 26, 2006.

77. Yaakov Katz, "Israel on Collision Course with Hamas." *Jerusalem Post*, July 19, 2007, available at: http://www.jpost.com/servlet/Satellite?cid=1184766011690&pagename=JPost%2FJPArticle%2FShowFull.

78. For translation, interpretation, and annotation, see Raphael Israeli, "The Charter of Allah: The Platform of the Islamic Resistance Movement (Hamas)" in Yonah Alexander and

Abraham H. Foxman, eds., *The 1988–1989 Annual on Terrorism.* Dordrech, NL: Kluwer Academic Publishers, 1990, pp. 99–134.

79. Muhammad Muslih, "The Foreign Policy of Hamas," *Council on Foreign Relations* (New York City, 1999), p. 17.

80. Kenneth Katzman, "Hamas's Foreign Benefactors." *Middle East Quarterly*, 2(2), June 1995, available at: http://www.meforum.org/article/251.

81. Matthew Levitt, *Hamas: Politics, Charity, and Terrorism in the Service of Jihad.* New Haven, CT: Yale University Press, 2007.

82. The US Treasury Department, Office of Terrorism and Financial Intelligence Website: http://www.ustreas.gov/offices/enforcement/key-issues/protecting/charities_exe-corder_13224-b.shtml#b.

83. "Hamas: The Islamic Resistance Movement." IDF Spokesman, January 1993. Online at: http://www.fas.org/irp/world/para/docs/930100.htm.

84. "Profile: Khaled Meshaal of Hamas," *BBC News Online*, available at: http://news.bbc.co.uk/2/hi/middle_east/3563635.stm.

85. "Profile: Hamas PM Ismail Haniya," *BBC Online*, available at: http://news.bbc.co.uk/2/hi/middle_east/4655146.stm.

86. IDF spokesman.

87. "Abdel Aziz Rantisi," *Jewish Virtual Library*, available at: http://www.jewishvirtuallibrary.org/jsource/biography/Rantissi.html.

88. "Profile: "Hamas's Mahmoud Zahhar." January 27, 2006. *BBC News*. Available at: http://news.bbc.co.uk/2/hi/middle_east/4653706.stm.

89. Jamie Chosak and Julie Sawyer, October 19, 2005. "Hamas' Tactics: Lessons from Recent Attacks." The Washington Institute for Near East Policy, accessed October 10, 2006 at http://www.washingtoninstitute.org/templateC05.php?CID=2382.

90. Roger Gaess, "Interview with Mousa Abu Marzook", *Middle East Policy* 5 (May 1997): pp. 113–129; "Individual Terrorists: Mousa Abu Marzook," 2007, *Investigative Project on Terrorism*, accessed on September 4, 2007 at http://www.investigativeproject.org/profile/106#_ftn5; Steven Greenhouse, "U.S. Detains Arab Tied to Militants," *The New York Times*, July 28, 1995.

91. "Hamas Explosives Expert Dies in Blast." ICT, April 1, 1998, accessed October 3, 2006 online at http://www.ict.org.il/spotlight/det.cfm?id=42.

92. "Palestinian Authority Arrests Killers of Muhi a-Din Sharif." ICT, April 6, 1998, accessed October 3, 2006 online at http://www.ict.org.il/spotlight/det.cfm?id=44.

93. "Middle East Jericho Escapes Recaptured." *BBC News*, August 20, 1998, accessed October 3, 2006 online at http://news.bbc.co.uk/2/hi/middle_east/154781.stm.

94. Institute for Counterterrorism. *Iran and Terrorism.* http://www.ict.org.il/inter_ter/st_terror/iran.htm.

95. Gary C. Gambill. *Sponsoring Terrorism: Syria and Hamas. Middle East Intelligence Bulletin*, 4(10), October 2002. http://www.meib.org/articles/0210_s1.htm

96. Office of Thrift Supervision, U.S. Department of Treasury. "U.S. Designates Five Charities Funding Hamas and Six Senior Hamas Leaders as Terrorist Entities," August 22, 2003. http://www.ots.treas.gov/docs/4/48937.html JS-672

97. U.S. Department of State. "Patterns of Global Terrorism 1997." www.state.gov/www/global/terrorism/1997Report/1997index.html

98. Roger Gaess, "Interview with Mousa Abu Marzook," *Middle East Policy* 5 (May 1997): pp. 113–129; "Individual Terrorists: Mousa Abu Marzook." *2007*

*Investigative Project on Terrorism,* available at http://www.investigativeproject.org/profile/106#_ftn5; Steven Greenhouse, "U.S. Detains Arab Tied to Militants." *The New York Times*, July 28, 1995.

99. The selected chronology is based on material drawn from the database developed by several academic programs directed by Professor Yonah Alexander since the late 1980s. The information has been updated in the post-9/11 period from a variety of other sources as reflected in the citations listed beginning with Footnote 40.

100. William J. Murray, "Trouble in the Holy Land: Christians Also Victims of Islamic Terror," *World Net Daily*, July 16, 2002, http://www.worldnetdaily.com/news/article.asp?ARTICLE_ID=28292.

101. "Seven Israelis Die in Bus Explosion," *The Tribune Online Edition,* July 16, 2002 http://www.tribuneindia.com/2002/20020717/world.htm#8.

102. "Israel Arrests Suspects in University Bombing," *CNN.com*, August 21, 2002, http://archives.cnn.com/2002/WORLD/meast/08/21/mideast/.

103. "Latest Terror Attacks Kill 12," *CNN.com,* August 4, 2002, http://archives.cnn.com/2002/WORLD/meast/08/04/mideast/index.html.

104. "Massacre in Jerusalem," *FactsofIsrael.com*, November 22, 2002, http://factsofisrael.com/blog/archives/000496.html.

105. "Haifa Suicide Bomber Kills 15," *CNN.com*, March 11, 2003, http://www.cnn.com/2003/WORLD/meast/03/05/mideast/.

106. "Palestinian Terrorism—A Wave of Suicide Bombings," *Israel Ministry of Foreign Affairs*, May 19, 2003, http://www.mfa.gov.il/MFA/MFAArchive/2000_2009/2003/5/Palestinian+Terrorism-+A+Wave+of+Suicide+Bombings.htm.

107. "2 Palestinians Arrested in Connection With Terror Attacks," *CNN.com*, August 6, 2003, http://edition.cnn.com/2003/WORLD/meast/08/05/mideast/.

108. Arieh O'Sullivan, "Casualties of War," *The Jerusalem Post*, September 9, 2003, http://info.jpost.com/C002/Supplements/CasualtiesOfWar/2003_09_09_01.html.

109. "15 Killed in Israeli Bus Blasts," *Guardian Unlimited*, August 31, 2004, http://www.guardian.co.uk/israel/Story/0,2763,1294266,00.html.

110. "Terror Attack at Karni Crossing," *Israel Ministry of Foreign Affairs*, Janurary 13, 2005, http://www.mfa.gov.il/MFA/MFAArchive/2000_2009/2005/Terror+attack+at+Karni+Crossing+13-Jan-2005.

111. Scott Wilson, "Suicide Bomber Strikes Israeli Bus Station," *WashingtonPost.com*, August 28, 2005, http://www.washingtonpost.com/wp-dyn/content/article/2005/08/28/AR2005082800252.html.

112. "The Hamas Terror Organization—2006 Update," *Israel Ministry of Foreign Affairs*, March 15, 2007, http://www.mfa.gov.il/MFA/Terrorism+Obstacle+to+Peace/Terror+Groups/The%20HAMAS%20Terror%20Organization%20-%20%202006%20update%2015-Mar-2007 (September 6, 2007).

113. Nissan Ratzlav-Katz, "Gilad Shalit's Second Birthday as a Hostage," *Israel National News*, September 6, 2007, http://www.israelnationalnews.com/News/News.aspx/123513.

114. Kevin Flower, "Rocket Attacks End Calm on Israel-Gaza Border," *CNN.com*, http://edition.cnn.com/2007/WORLD/meast/04/24/hamas.rockets/index.html.

115. Conal Urquhart, "Hamas Declares Victory," *Common Dreams News Center*, June 15, 2007, http://www.commondreams.org/archive/2007/06/15/1892/

## Chapter 6

1. International Atomic Energy Agency (IAEA), *Implementation of the NPT Safeguards Agreement in the Islamic Republic of Iran: Report by the Director General*. GOV/2003/75, November 10, 2003, para. 45.

2. International Atomic Energy Agency (IAEA), *Implementation*. GOV/2003/40, June 6, 2003, p. 7; GOV/2006/53, August 31, 2006, paras. 28–29; GOV/2006/27, April 28, 2006, paras. 33–37.

3. IAEA, *Implementation*. GOV/2003/75, November 10, 2003, para. 46.

4. Leonard Spector and Jaqueline R. Smith, *Nuclear Ambitions*. Colorado: Westview Press, 1990, p. 204.

5. "New Information on Top Secret Projects of The Iranian Regime's Nuclear Program," remarks by Alireza Jafarzadeh, National Council of Resistance of Iran, Washington, DC, August 14, 2002. http://www.iranwatch.org/privateviews/ncri/perspex-ncri-topsecretprojects-081402.htm.

6. IAEA, *Implementation.GOV/2003/6,* September 12, 2003, p. 2.

7. Pierre Goldschmidt and George Perkovich, "Iran Nuclear Showdown," Transcript of briefing. *Carnegie Endowment for International Peace*, January 18, 2006, p.3, http://www.carnegieendowment.org/files/iran2006-01-18.pdf

8. IAEA, *Implementation*. GOV/2006/15, February 27, 2006, p. 6.

9. Goldschmidt and Perkovich, "Iran Nuclear Showdown," transcript of briefing, p. 9.

10. International Atomic Energy Agency, "Communication dated November 26, 2004 received from the Permanent Representatives of France, Germany, the Islamic Republic of Iran, and the United Kingdom concerning the agreement signed in Paris on November 15, 2004." INFCIRC/637, November 26, 2004.

11. IAEA, *Implementation*. GOV/2006/15, February 27, 2006, p. 8.

12. IAEA, *Implementation*. GOV/2006/14, Resolution adopted February 4, 2006, p. 2.

13. IAEA, *Implementation*. GOV/2006/27, April 28, 2006, p. 31.

14. Helene Cooper and John O'Neil, "Iran Reacts Cautiously to Deals on Trade." *New York Times*, June 6, 2006.

15. Nzila Fathi and Helene Cooper, "Iran Given June 29 Deadline to Respond to Anti-Nuke Offer." *New York Times*, June 10, 2006.

16. Helene Cooper, "Russia and China, in Shift, Inch Toward Iran Sanctions." *New York Times*, July 13, 2006.

17. Warren Hoge, "UN Moves Toward Vote on Iran's Atom Program." *New York Times*, July 28, 2006; United Nations Security Council, Resolution 1696 (2006), SC/8792, July 31, 2006. http://www.un.org/News/Press/docs//2006/sc8792.doc.htm

18. William W. Burke-White, "Comment on UN resolution 1696 And Iran's Legal Rights." *Proliferation News*, Carnegie Endowment for International Peace, August 24, 2006.

19. Michael Slackman, "Iran Presents 'New Formula' for Talks." *New York Times*, August 22, 2006.

20. "IAEA Indefinitely Freezes Iran Nuclear Aid Over Plutonium Risk." *Reuters*, November 23, 2006; Nazila Faithi, "Iran Says It Will Build Heavy-Water Reactor Without Agency's Help." *New York Times*, November 24, 2006.

21. Elissa Gootman, "Security Council Approves Sanctions Against Iran over Nuclear Program." *New York Times*, December 23, 2006; United Nations Security Council, Resolution 1737(2006) Adopted on December 23, 2006, S/Res/1737(2006), December 27, 2006.

22. *Reuters*, "Key Points in The UN Security Council Resolution on Iran." *Haaretz*, December 23, 2006.

23. Karl Vick, "Iran Rejects Russia's Proposal on Uranium." *Washington Post*, March 13, 2006.

24. IAEA, *Implementation*. GOV/2004/12, February 20, 2004; Joby Warrick, "Nuclear Program in Iran Tied to Pakistan." *Washington Post*, December 21, 2003.

25. Marvin Miller, "Notes on Centrifuges and Nuclear Proliferation." Revised April 2005, unpublished, private communication.

26. IAEA, *Implementation*. GOV/2004/11, February 24, 2004, paras. 44–46; IAEA, *Implementation*. GOV/2004/34, June 1, 2004, para. 22–26.

27. HEU denotes uranium enriched to 20% or more in the isotope U-235. Natural uranium is mainly the heavier isotope U-238, with 0.72% U-235.

28. IAEA, *Implementation*. GOV/2004/11, March 13, 2004, para. 28.

29. William J. Broad and David E. Sanger, "The Laptop: Decoding Iran's Ambitions; Relying on Computer U.S. Seeks to Prove Iran's Nuclear Aims." *New York Times*, November 13, 2005.

30. IAEA, *Implementation*. GOV/2003/75, November 10, 2003, para. 16.

31. Carla Anne Robbins, "As Evidence Grows of Iran's Program, U.S. Hits Quandary." *Wall Street Journal*, March 18, 2005. http://www.iranfocus.com/modules/news/article.php?storyid=1714

32. Some sources site a relation between MEK and the Israeli intelligence agency, Mossad, starting in about 1996, in which MEK served to disseminate "disinformation" on Iran, e.g., the exposure of Natanz and Arak. "MOSSAD," Iran Didban, 2004. http://www.irandidban.com/master.asp?ID=03864; Scott Ritter, *Target Iran: The Truth About the White House's Plans for Regime Change*. San Francisco: Avalon Publishing Group, Inc., 2006, p. xxv.

33. "New Information on Top Secret Projects of The Iranian Regime's Nuclear Program," remarks by Alireza Jafarzadeh, National Council of Resistance of Iran, Washington, DC, August 14, 2002. http://www.iranwatch.org/privateviews/ncri/perspex-ncri-topsecretprojects-081402.htm.

34. "Mullahs' Top Secret Nuclear Sites and Weapons of Mass Destruction Projects." *Iran Liberation*, NCRI, August 19, 2002. http://www.globalsecurity.org/wmd/library/news/iran/2002/iran-020819-ncri_news.pdf

35. IAEA, *Implementation*. GOV/2003/40, June 6, 2003, paras. 25–26.

36. Ibid., para. 8.

37. Press Conference on Iran's Clandestine Nuclear Projects, the National Council Of Resistance Of Iran, February 20, 2003. http://www.iranwatch.org/privateviews/ncri/perspex-ncri-nuclear-022003.htm

38. Carla Anne Robbins, "As Evidence Grows of Iran's Program, U.S. Hits Quandary." *Wall Street Journal*, March 18, 2005. http://www.iranfocus.com/modules/news/article.php?storyid=1714

39. *Islamic Republic News Agency* (IRNA), February 9, 2003. http://www.iranwatch.org/government/Iran/iran-irna-khatami-yazd-isfahan-hashan-020903.htm

40. IAEA, *Implementation*. GOV/2003/69, September 12, 2003; GOV/2003/75, November 10, 2003, para. 9.

41. William J. Broad and David E. Sanger, "Iran's Boast on Uranium Enrichment Is Put to Test." *New York Times*, February 4, 2007.

42. IAEA, *Implementation*. GOV/2003/69, September 12, 2003; GOV/2003/75, November 10, 2003, para. 9.

43. IAEA, *Implementation*. GOV/2003/69, Resolution adopted by the Board. September 12, 2003.

44. IAEA, *Implementation*. GOV/2003/75, November 10, 2003, para. 13.

45. Ibid., para. 16.

46. Joby Warrick, "Nuclear Program in Iran Tied to Pakistan." *Washington Post*, December 21, 2003; Bill Gertz, "Libyan Sincerity on Arms in Doubt." *Washington Times*, September 9, 2004.

47. *Iran Focus* "'Iran Is Close to A Nuclear Bomb': Iranian scientist," July 13, 2005. http://www.iranfocus.com/modules/news/article.php?storyid=2839

48. Glenn Kessler, "2003 Memo Says Iranian Leaders Backed Talks." *Washington Post*, February 14, 2007; "Rice Denies Seeing Iranian Proposal in '03." *Washington Post*, February 8, 2007; "Washington 'snubbed Iran offer'," *BBC News*, January 18, 2007. http://news.bbc.co.uk/2/hi/middle_east/6274147.stm; Glenn Kessler, "In 2003, U.S. Spurned Iran's Offer of Dialogue." *Washington Post*, June 18, 2006.

49. Barbara Slavin, "Iran, U.S. Holding Talks in Geneva." *USA Today*, May 11, 2003; Barbara Slavin, "Mutual Terror Accusations Halt U.S.-Iran Talks." *USA Today*, May 21, 2003.

50. Glenn Kessler, "U.S. Ready to Resume Talks with Iran, Armitage Says." *Washington Post*, October 29, 2003.

51. Hassan Rohani, "Beyond the Challenges Facing Iran and IAEA Concerning the Nuclear Dossier." Text of speech to the Supreme Cultural Revolution Council, September 30, 2005. http://www.armscontrolwonk.com/file_download/30

52. Chen Kane, "Nuclear Decision Making in Iran: A Rare Glimpse." Brandeis University: Crown Center for Middle East Studies, *Middle East Brief* No. 5, May 2006.

53. IAEA, *Implementation*. GOV/2004/83, November 15, 2004, para. 23.

54. Sharon Squassoni, "Iran's Nuclear Program: Recent Developments." *CRS Report for Congress*, Congressional Research Service, May 18, 2005, p. 2.

55. IAEA, *Implementation*. GOV/2004/11, February 24, 2004, paras 43–44.

56. IAEA, *Implementation*. GOV/2003/63, August 26, 2003, paras. 27, 29.

57. Ibid., para 30.

58. IAEA, *Implementation*. GOV/2003/75, November 10, 2003, p 32; GOV/2003/63, August 26, 2003, para. 18.

59. IAEA, *Implementation*. GOV/2004/83, November 15, 2004, para. 34.

60. IAEA, *Implementation*. GOV/2003/75, November 10, 2003, Annex. 1, pp. 7–8; IAEA, *Implementation*. GOV/2004/79, February 24, 2004, paras. 45–47.

61. IAEA, *Implementation*. GOV/2003/63, August 26, 2003, paras. 7, 32.

62. IAEA, *Implementation*. GOV/2004/83, November 15, 2004, para. 23.

63. IAEA, *Implementation*. GOV/2004/83, November 15, 2004, para. 24.

64. Ibid., para. 25.

65. IAEA, *Implementation*. GOV/2003/75, November 10, 2003, para. 19 and footnote 2.

66. IAEA, *Implementation.* GOV/2003/69, September 12, 2003, para. 3.

67. Robert G. Joseph, Statement Before the House International Relations Committee. Washington DC, March 8, 2006.

68. IAEA, *Implementation.* GOV/2004/11, February 24, 2004, paras 59, 61.

69. Ibid., para 62.

70. IAEA, *Implementation.* GOV/2004/83, November 15, 2004, para 14.

71. IAEA, *Implementation.* GOV/2004/49, June 18, 2004, p. 1.

72. IAEA, *Implementation.* GOV/2004/60, September 1, 2004, paras. 7, 9, 14, 53.

73. IAEA, *Implementation.* GOV/2004/79, Resolution adopted by the Board September 18, 2004.

74. International Atomic Energy Agency, Communication November 26, 2004 from Permanent Representatives France, Germany, the Islamic Republic of Iran, and the United Kingdom. INFCIRC/637, November 26, 2004, p. 3; IAEA, *Implementation.* GOV/2004/90, November 29, 2004; Robert G. Joseph, Statement Before the House International Relations Committee. Washington DC, March 8, 2006.

75. IAEA, *Implementation.* GOV/2005/64, August 11, 2005; IAEA, *Implementation.* GOV/2005/67, September 2, 2005, paras 59–60.

76. Sharon Squassoni, "Iran's Nuclear Program: Recent Developments." *CRS Report for Congress*, Congressional Research Service, May 18, 2005, p. 5.

77. IAEA, *Implementation.*GOV/2005/77, Resolution adopted by the Board. September 24, 2005; British Embassy in Berlin, "E3-EU Statement on Iran," January 13, 2006.

78. Transcript excerpts, *Mosaic*, April 11, 2006. http://209.97.202.24/mosaic/mosaic.php?id=232&con=256&rss=

79. IAEA, *Implementation.* GOV/2006/27, April 28, 2006, para.31.

80. IAEA, *Implementation.* GOV/2006/53, August 31, 2006, paras. 5, 27.

81. Ibid., paras. 2, 6.

82. IAEA, *Implementation.* GOV/2006/64, November 14, 2006, para. 2.

83. Ali Akbar Dareini, "Iran Expands Uranium Enrichment Program." *Associated Press*, December 9, 2006; *RIA Novosti,* "Iranian President Says 3,000 Centrifuges Set at Natanz," December 9, 2006.

84. William J. Broad and David E. Sanger, "Iran's Boast on Uranium Enrichment Is Put to Test." *New York Times*, February 4, 2007.

85. *RIA Novosti*, "Russia Completes Air Defense System Deliveries to Iran—Ivanov." January 16, 2007. http://en.rian.ru/russia/20070116/59156706.html; *Pravda*, "Russia to Sell 29 Air Defense Systems to Iran." December 3, 2005. http://english.pravda.ru/main/18/88/354/16570_Iran.html

86. *Reuters*, "Iran Sets Up 328 Centrifuges at Big Atom Site: Sources." *New York Times*, February 5, 2007.

87. IAEA, *Implementation.* GOV/2004/83, November 15, 2004, para 26.

88. Marvin Miller, *Notes on Centrifuges and Nuclear Proliferation.* Revised April 2005, unpublished, private communication.

89. IAEA, *Implementation.* GOV/2004/11, February 24, 2004, para 44–46.

90. IAEA, *Implementation.* GOV/2006/15, February 27, 2006, para 19.

91. IAEA, *Implementation.* GOV/2004/34, June 1, 2004, paras. 22–26; IAEA, *Implementation.* GOV/2006/27, April 28, 2004, para. 13.

92. IAEA, *Implementation.* GOV/2004/11, February 24, 2004, paras. 46–47.

93. IAEA, *Implementation.* GOV/2004/34, June 1, 2004, Annex. 1 para. 34.

94. William J. Broad and David E. Sanger, "Iran's Boast on Uranium Enrichment Is Put to Test." *New York Times*, February 4, 2007.

95. IAEA, *Implementation*. GOV/2004/83, November 15, 2004, para. 45.

96. IAEA, *Implementation*. GOV/2006/15, February 27, 2006, para. 18.

97. Nasser Karimi, "Iran Advances Could Speed Nuclear Project." *Associated Press*, April 17, 2006.

98. IAEA, *Implementation*. GOV/2006/27, April 28, 2006, para. 14.

99. IAEA, *Implementation*. GOV/2006/38, June 8, 2006, para. 6.

100. Craig Smith, "Foes Say Tehran Builds Fast Uranium Centrifuges." *New York Times*, August 25, 2006; NCRI, "New Revelations on Mullahs' Nuclear Weapon Program." Press Conference, August 24, 2006.

101. IAEA, *Implementation*. GOV/2006/15, February 27, 2006; IAEA, *Implementation*. GOV/2005/87, November 18, 2005, p. 2.

102. IAEA, Statement of the DDG-SG at the Board of Governors Meeting, June 16, 2005.; IAEA, *Implementation*. GOV/2005/87, November 18, 2005, para. 5.

103. NCRI, "Iran Building Nuclear Capable Missiles in Underground Secret Tunnels." November 23, 2005. http://www.ncr-iran.org/content/view/579/76/

104. IAEA, *Implementation*. GOV/2005/87, November 18, 2005, para. 6; IAEA, DDG-SG, Update Brief, January 31, 2006, p. 2; IAEA, *Implementation*. GOV/2006/15, February 27, 2006, para. 22.

105. IAEA, DDG-SG, January 31, 2006, p. 2.

106. IAEA, *Implementation*. GOV/2006/15, February 27, 2006, para. 21.

107. Ibid., para. 22; IAEA, *Implementation*. GOV/2006/27, April 28, 2006.

108. IAEA, DDG-SG, Update Brief, January 31, 2006, p. 2.

109. IAEA, Statement of the DDG-SG at the Board of Governors Meeting. June 16, 2005; IAEA, DD-SG Update Brief, January 31, 2006, p. 2; IAEA, *Implementation*. GOV/2006/27, April 28, 2006, para. 11.

110. IAEA, *Implementation*. GOV/2005/67, September 2, 2005, paras. 13, 16; IAEA, *Implementation*. GOV/2005/87, November 18, 2005, para. 8.

111. IAEA, *Implementation*. GOV/2005/67, September 2, 2005, paras. 17–18.

112. IAEA, *Implementation*. GOV/2005/87, November 18, 2005, para. 12.

113. IAEA, *Implementation*. GOV/2006/27, April 28, 2006, para. 11.

114. USEC, "USEC Inc. Suspends AVLIS Technology Development." News Release, Bethesda, MD, June 9, 1999. http://www.usec.com/v2001_02/Content/News/NewsTemplate.asp?page=/v2001_02/Content/News/NewsFiles/06-09-99b.htm

115. Jack Boureston and Charles D. Ferguson, "Laser Enrichment: Separation Anxiety." *Bulletin of Atomic Scientists*, March/April 2005 pp. 14–18.

116. James Brooke, "South Korean Scientist Calls Uranium Test 'Academic.'" *New York Times*, September 7, 2004.

117. Alireza Jafarzadeh, "Iran Building Nuclear Capable Missiles in Underground Secret Tunnels." November 23, 2005. http://www.ncr-iran.org/content/view/579/76/

118. IAEA, *Implementation*. GOV/2003/63, August 26, 2003, para. 42.

119. Ibid., paras. 42–43; IAEA, *Implementation*. GOV/2003/75, November 10, 2003, para. 36.

120. IAEA, *Implementation*. GOV/2004/83, November 15, 2004, para. 52.

121. IAEA, *Implementation*. GOV/2003/75, November 10, 2003, Annex. 1, paras. 59, 64; IAEA, *Implementation*. GOV/2004/60, September 1, 2004, para. 30.

122. Michael Knapik, "Russia Tells U.S. Officials It Will Not Export Laser., *Nucleanics Week*, 42(10), March 8, 2001.

123. IAEA, *Implementation.* GOV/2004/60, September 1, 2004, paras. 33–35; IAEA, *Implementation.* GOV/2004/83, November 15, 2004, para. 86.

124. IAEA, *Implementation.* GOV/2004/11, February 24, 2004, paras. 49, 53; IAEA, *Implementation.* GOV/2004/34, June 1, 2004, para. 34; IAEA, *Implementation.* GOV/2004/60, September 1, 2004, para. 37; IAEA, *Implementation.* GOV/2004/83, November 15, 2004, para. 51.

125. IAEA, *Implementation.* GOV/2004/60, September 1, 2004, para. 35.

126. IAEA, *Implementation.* GOV/2004/83, November 15, 2004, para. 51; IAEA, *Implementation.* GOV/2004/60, September 1, 2004, paras. 48, Annex. para. 51.

127. IAEA, *Implementation.* GOV/2003/75, November 10, 2003, para. 41.

128. IAEA, *Implementation.* GOV/2005/67, September 2, 2005, para. 10.

129. IAEA, *Implementation.* GOV/2004/83, November 15, 2004, para. 38.

130. IAEA, *Implementation,* GOV/2004/34. June 1, 2004, Annex, para 28.

131. Andrew Koch, "Iran Uranium Source Revealed." *Jane's Defense Weekly*, August 10, 2004.

132. Dafna Linzer, "Findings Could Hurt U.S. Effort Iran." *Washington Post*, August 11, 2004.

133. IAEA, *Implementation.* GOV/2006/27, April 28, 2006, para 8.

134. IAEA, *Implementation.* GOV/2006/15, February 27, 2006, para. 8.

135. Ibid., para. 9; IAEA, *Implementation.* GOV/2005/67, September 2, 2005, para 12.

136. IAEA Board of Governors, *Implementation of the NPT Safeguards Agreement and Relevant Provisions of Security Council Resolution 1737 (2006) in the Islamic Republic of Iran*: Report by the Director General. GOV/2007/8, February 22, 2007, para. 15.

137. IAEA, *Implementation.* GOV/2006/27, April 28, 2006, paras. 24–25; IAEA, *Implementation.* GOV/2006/53, August 31, 2006, para. 12.

138. IAEA Board of Governors, *Implementation of the NPT Safeguards Agreement and Relevant Provisions of Security Council Resolution 1737 (2006) in the Islamic Republic of Iran*: Report by the Director General. GOV/2007/8, February 22, 2007, para. 16.

139. IAEA, *Implementation.* GOV/2006/53, August 31, 2006, para. 17.

140. IAEA, *Implementation.* GOV/2006/64, November 14, 2006, para. 15.

141. IAEA, *Implementation,* GOV/2007/8, February 22, 2007, para. 21.

142. IAEA, *Implementation.* GOV/2003/40, June 6, 2003, paras. 7, 32; IAEA, *Implementation.* GOV/2003/75, November 10, 2003, Annex., Table 1.

143. IAEA, *Implementation.* GOV/2003/75, November 10, 2003, paras. 59, 62; Annex. 1, Table 1.

144. IAEA, Ibid., para. 24.

145. IAEA, *Implementation.* GOV/2003/63, August 26, 2003, para. 21; IAEA, *Implementation.* GOV/2003/75, November 10, 2003, Annex. 1, Table 1.

146. IAEA, *Implementation.* GOV/2003/63, August 26, 2003, para. 21.

147. IAEA, *Implementation.* GOV/2003/40, June 6, 2003, para. 20; IAEA, *Implementation.* GOV/2003/75, November 10, 2003, para. 16; Annex. 1, Table 1;

148. IAEA, *Implementation.* GOV/2003/40, June 6, 2003, para. 23.

149. IAEA, *Implementation.* GOV/2003/75, November 10, 2003, Annex. 1, paras. 27–33.

150. IAEA, *Implementation.* GOV/2003/40, June 6, 2003, paras. 21–24; IAEA, *Implementation.* GOV/2003/63, August 26, 2003, para. 14; IAEA, *Implementation.* GOV/2003/75, November 10, 2003, Annex 1; para. 7; IAEA, *Implementation.* GOV/2004/83, November 15, 2004, para. 71.

151. IAEA, *Implementation.* GOV/2003/75, November 10, 2003, para. 22; Annex. 1, para. 13.

152. IAEA, *Implementation.* GOV/2003/63, August 26, 2003, para. 15; IAEA, *Implementation.* GOV/2003/75, November 10, 2003, paras. 11, 23.

153. IAEA, *Implementation.* GOV/2004/60, September 1, 2004, Annex., paras. 1, 3.

154. IAEA, *Implementation.* GOV/2003/75, November 10, 2003, para. 24; Annex. 1, para. 14; IAEA, *Implementation.* GOV/2004/11, Feburary 24, 2004, para. 16.

155. IAEA, *Implementation.* GOV/2003/40, June 6, 2003, para. 19.

156. IAEA, *Implementation.* GOV/2003/75, November 10, 2003, para. 16.

157. IAEA, Ibid., Annex. 1, paras. 18, 23.

158. Ibid., paras. 16, 26–28; Annex. 1, Table 1, para. 29; IAEA, *Implementation.* GOV/2004/11, February 24, 2004, para. 23; IAEA, *Implementation.* GOV/2004/83, November 15, 2004, para. 71.

159. IAEA, *Implementation.* GOV/2004/11, February 24, 2004, para. 26.

160. IAEA, *Implementation.* GOV/2004/34, June 1, 2004, para. 36.

161. Ibid., para. 16; IAEA, *Implementation.* GOV/2004/60, September 1, 2004, para. 37.

162. IAEA, *Implementation.* GOV/2004/34, June 1, 2004, para. 36, Annex. 1; para. 15; IAEA, *Implementation.* GOV/2004/60, September 1, 2004, para. 37.

163. IAEA, *Implementation.* GOV/2004/60, September 1, 2004, paras. 11–12.

164. IAEA, *Implementation.* GOV/2005/67, September 2, 2005, paras. 22–24; IAEA, *Implementation.* GOV/2006/15, February 27, 2006, paras. 24–25.

165. IAEA, *Implementation.* GOV/2006/27, April 28, 2006, para. 17.

166. IAEA, *Implementation.* GOV/2004/60, September 1, 2004, para. 38.

167. IAEA, *Implementation.* GOV/2006/53, August 31, 2006, para. 17.

168. IAEA, *Implementation.* GOV/2006/64, November 14, 2006, para. 14.

169. Ibid., para 15.

170. IAEA, *Implementation.* GOV/2005/67, September 2, 2005, Annex. 1, p. 14.

171. IAEA, *Implementation.* GOV/2004/11, February 24, 2004, paras. 28–29.

172. *Atomic Power in Space: A History.* U.S. Department of Energy, 1987.

173. "Nuclear Reactors in Space." Briefing Paper #82, Uranium Information Center, May 2006. http://www.uic.com.au/nip82.htm

174. *Nuclear Fuel*, "Po-210 'fingerprint' unlikely, Russian and Western Officials Caution." December 7, 2006. http://www.platts.com/Nuclear/highlights/2006/nucp_nf_120706.xml

175. IAEA, *Implementation.* GOV/2004/11, February 24, 2004, para. 30.

176. IAEA, *Implementation.* GOV/2005/67, September 2, 2005, para. 34.

177. IAEA, *Implementation.* GOV/2003/75, November 10, 2003, para. 20.

178. IAEA, *Implementation.* GOV/2003/75, November 10, 2003, Annex. 1; para. 1; IAEA, *Implementation.* GOV/2004/83, November 15, 2004, para. 9; Mohammed Saeidi, "Nuclear Activities in Iran." Symposium 2005 World Nuclear Association. http://www.world-nuclear.org/sym/2005/saeidi.htm

179. Saeidi, "Nuclear Activities." 2005.

180. IAEA, *Implementation.* GOV/2004/11, February 24, 2004, para. 14; IAEA, *Implementation.* GOV/2004/34, June 1, 2004, para. 31; Annex., paras. 4–5.

181. IAEA, *Implementation.* GOV/2003/75, November 10, 2003, Annex. 1, para. 30.

182. IAEA, *Implementation.* GOV/2004/83, November 15, 2004, paras. 9, 19–21.

183. *Associated Press*, "Iran Should Give Sanctions Serious Response,' China Says." *New York Times*, January 6, 2007.

184. *IRNA*, "Aghazadeh: 270 tons of UF6 produced in Iran." April 9, 2007.

185. IAEA, *Implementation*, GOV/2007/48, August 30, 2007, para. 18.

186. *Iran Watch*, "Information on Two Top Secret Nuclear Sites of the Iranian Regime (Natanz & Arak)." December 2002. http://www.iranwatch.org/privateviews/NCRI/perspex-ncri-natanzarak-1202.htm

187. Ibid.

188. IAEA, *Implementation.* GOV/2003/40, June 6, 2003, paras. 10, 30–31; IAEA, *Implementation.* GOV/2004/83, November 15, 2004, para. 15.

189. IAEA, *Update Brief*, January 31, 2006.

190. *Associated Press*, "Defying U.N., Iran Opens Nuclear Reactor." August 26, 2006; IAEA, *Implementation.* GOV/2006/15, February 27, 2006, para 28.

191. IAEA, *Implementation*, GOV/2007/48, August 30, 2007, para. 21.

192. IAEA, *Implementation.* GOV/2003/75, November 10, 2003, Annex. 1, paras. 76–77.

193. *Associated Press*, "Defying U.N., Iran Opens Nuclear Reactor," August 26, 2006; *Pravda*, "Iran Ignores USA and Doubles Heavy Water Production," August 28, 2006.

194. Michael Jasinski, "Russia's Nuclear and Missile Technology Assistance to Iran." Center for Non-Proliferation Studies.

195. IAEA, *Implementation.* GOV/2003/63, August 26, 2003, paras. 44–46; IAEA, *Implementation.* GOV/2003/75, November 10, 2003, Annex. 1, paras. 64, 68, 71–72.

196. *Reuters*, "IAEA Indefinitely Freezes Iran Nuclear Aid Over Plutonium Risk." November 23, 2006; Nazila Fathi, "Iran Says It Will Build Heavy-Water Reactor Without Agency's Help." *New York Times*, November 24, 2006.

197. IAEA, *Implementation*, GOV/2007/8, February 22, 2007, para. 13.

198. IAEA, *Implementation.* GOV/2004/83, November 15, 2004, para. 63.

199. IAEA, *Implementation.* GOV/2003/63, August 26, 2003, para. 45; IAEA, *Implementation.* GOV/2003/75, November 10, 2003, para. 43; Annex. 1, para. 74; IAEA, *Implementation.* GOV/2004/60, September 1, 2004, para. 38.

200. IAEA, *Implementation.* GOV/2004/34, June 1, 2004, para. 47.

201. IAEA, *Implementation.* GOV/2004/83, November 15, 2004, para. 70.

202. IAEA, *Implementation.* GOV/2003/75, November 10, 2003, para. 44; IAEA, *Implementation.* GOV/2004/34, June 1, 2004, para. 35.

203. See Morteza Aminmansour, "Iran Earthquake safety of Nuclear Power Plants." *Persian* Journal, April 28, 2004.http://www.iranian.ws/cgi-bin/iran_news/exec/view.cgi/2/2182?; "Balakovo Nuclear Power Plant." *Bellona Fact Sheet*, December 28, 1999. http://www.bellona.org/english_import_area/factsheet/international/russia/npps/balakovo/1140457574.6; "Kalinin VVER-1000 Nuclear Power Station." U.S. Nuclear Regulatory Commission, NUREG/IA-0212, Vol. 1, November 2005, p. 8; Kamal Hadad and

Navid Ayobian, "Fuel Burnup and Fuel Pool Shielding Analysis for the Bushehr Nuclear Reactor VVER-1000." *International Journal of Modern Physics E*, 15(4) (2006), p. 925.

204. Aluf Benn, "Focus / Russia's Dangerous Dealings With Iran Go On." *Haaretz* Daily, November 30, 2002.

205. Ali Akbar Dareini, *Associated Press*, "Russia, Iran Sign Nuclear Fuel Deal." *Washington Times*, February 28, 2005.

206. *New York Times*, "Russia Agrees to Send Fuel for Iran Nuclear Plant." September 27, 2006.

207. Ibid.

208. Andrew E. Kramer, "Russia Will Slow Work on Iran's Nuclear Plant." *New York Times*, February 20, 2007.

209. Elaine Sciolino, "Russia Makes Threat to Keep Nuclear Fuel from Iran." *New York Times*, March 19, 2007.

210. "Talks Proseed on International Uranium Enrichment Center." IAEA, March 22, 2007. http://www.iaea.org/NewsCenter/News/2007/russiatalks.html

211. Saeidi, "Nuclear Activities," 2005.

212. Andrew Koch and Jeanette Wolf, "Iran's Nuclear Facilities: A Profile." Center for Non-Proliferation Studies 1998. http://cns.miis.edu/pubs/iranrpt.pdf

213. Ali Akbar, "Iran Discovers New Uranium Deposits." *Associated Press*, May 2, 2002.

214. IAEA, *Implementation*. GOV/2004/83, November 15, 2004, paras. 4, 6.

215. Saeidi, "Nuclear Activities", 2005.

216. IAEA, *Implementation*. GOV/2004/83, November 15, 2004, para. 4.

217. IAEA, Ibid., para. 5.

218. IAEA, DDG-SG, June 16, 2005, p 3.

219. IAEA, *Implementation*. GOV/2005/67, September 2, 2005, para. 26.

220. IAEA, *Implementation*. GOV/2005/67, September 2, 2005, paras. 27–31.

221. *Uranium 2003: Resources, Production and Demand*. Paris: Nuclear Energy Agency of the Organization for Economic Cooperation and Development and the International Atomic Energy Agency (NEA/OECD), 2004.

222. "Iran's Nuclear Fuels Nuclear Fuel Cycle Facilities: A Pattern of Peaceful Intent." U.S. Department of State, 2005, p. 31. www.globalsecurity.org/wmd/library/report/2005/iran-fuel-cycle-brief_dos_2005.pdf.

223. Saeidi, "Nuclear Activities" 2005.

224. Nazila Faithi, "Iran Discovers New Uranium Deposits." *Associated Press*, May 2, 2002.

225. "Iran's Nuclear Fuel Cycle Facilities: A Pattern of Peaceful Intent." U.S. State Department, September 2005. http://abcnews.go.com/images/International/iran_nuclear_report.pdf

226. Amir Taheri "Iran Sleep Walking Into War." *Arab News*, March 11, 2006.

227. Con Coughlin, "Iran Accused of Hiding Secret Nuclear Weapons Site." *Telegraph*, June 13, 2006. www.telegraph.co.uk/news/main.jhtml?xml=/news/2006/06/12/wiran12.xml&sSheet=/news/2006/06/12/ixnews.html

228. Kenneth Timmerman, "Source: Iran Has Secret Uranium Enrichment Sites." *NewsMax.com*, June 13, 2006.

229. United Nations Security Council, Resolution 1747(2007) Adopted on March 24, 2007, S/Res/1747(2006), March 24, 2007.

230. IAEA, *Implementation*, GOV/2004/11, February 24, 2004, para. 37; IAEA, Note by the Secretariat, 2004/Note 17, March 30, 2004, Point 4.

231. United Nations Security Council, Resolution 1737(2006), S/Res/1737(2006), December 27, 2006; United Nations Security Council, Resolution 1747(2007), S/Res/1747(2006), March 24, 2007.

232. Press Conference by Mohammad Mohaddessin, Foreign Affairs Committee Chairman, National Council of Resistance of Iran, November 17, 2004. http://www.iranwatch.org/privateviews/ncri/perspex-ncri-lavizan-111704.htm; IAEA, *Implementation.* GOV/2004/60, September 1, 2004, paras. 6, 42–43, annex. para.46; IAEA, *Implementation.* GOV/2004/83, November 15, 2004, para. 99.

233. IAEA, *Implementation.* GOV/2004/83, November 15, 2004, para. 113.

234. IAEA, *Implementation.* GOV/2004/60, September 1, 2004, paras. 43–44, annex prar 45; Press Conference by Mohammad Mohaddessin, Foreign Affairs Committee Chairman, National Council of Resistance of Iran, November 17, 2004. http://www.iranwatch.org/privateviews/ncri/perspex-ncri-lavizan-111704.htm; IAEA, *Implementation.* GOV/2005/67, September 2, 2005, para. 39.

235. IAEA, *Implementation.* GOV/2005/67, September 2, 2005, paras. 100–101.

236. IAEA, *Implementation.* GOV/2004/83, November 15, 2004, para. 102.

237. IAEA, *Implementation.* GOV/2005/67, September 2, 2005, para. 40; IAEA, DDG-SG. Update Brief, January 31, 2006, p. 2.

238. IAEA, Ibid., para. 38.

239. IAEA, DDG-SG. Update Brief, January 31, 2006, pp. 2–3; IAEA, *Implementation* GOV/2006/27, April 28, 2006, para. 24.

240. IAEA, *Implementation.* GOV/2006/15, February 27, 2006, para. 35.

241. IAEA, Ibid., para. 36; IAEA, *Implementation.* GOV/2006/27, April 28, 2006, para. 25.

242. IAEA, *Implementation.* GOV/2006/53, August 31, 2006, para. 24.

243. IAEA, *Implementation.* GOV/2006/64, November 11, 2006, para. 18.

244. *Reuters*, "Tehran to Allow Iaea Atomic Tests At Iran Center." November 28, 2006. http://today.reuters.com/news/articlenews.aspx?type=worldNews&storyid=2006-11-28T132829Z_01_L28875356_RTRUKOC_0_US-IRAN-NUCLEAR-IAEA.xml&src=rss

245. IAEA, DDG-SG. Update Brief, January 31, 2006; Elaine Sciolino and William Broad, "Atomic Agency Sees Possible Link of Military to Iran Nuclear Work." *New York Times*, February 1, 2006; IAEA, *Implementation.* GOV/2006/15, February 27, 2006, para 39.

246. Carla Anne Robbins, "U.S. Gives Briefing on Iranian Missile to Nuclear Agency." *Wall Street Journal*, July 27, 2005; William Broad and David Sanger, "The Laptop: Decoding Iran's Ambitions: Relying on Computer, U.S. Seeks to Prove Iran's Nuclear Arms." *New York Times*, November 13, 2005; Carla Anne Robbins, "As Evidence Grows of Iran's Program, U.S. Hits Quandary." *Wall Street Journal*, March 18, 2005.

247. Dafna Linzer, "Nuclear Disclosures on Iran Unverified." *Washington Post*, November 19, 2004; Carla Anne Roberts, "Atomic Test: As Evidence Grows Of Iran's Program, U.S. Hits Quandry." *Wall Street Journal*, March 18, 2005.

248. Dafna Linzer, "Strong Leads and Dead Ends in Nuclear Case against Iran." *Washington Post*, February 8, 2006.

249. Broad and Sanger, *New York Times*, 13 Nov 2005.

250. Dafna Linzer, "U.S. Deploy Slide Show to Press Case Against Iran." *Washington Post*, September 14, 2005. A set of briefing slides was obtained by *ABC News*: http://abcnews.go.com/images/International/iran_nuclear_report.pdf

251. Broad and Sanger. *New York Times*, November 13, 2005; *Agence France Presse*, "U.S. Briefs on Alleged Iranian Nuclear Warhead Work: Diplomats (Project 111)," October 8, 2005; IAEA, *Implementation.* GOV/2005/77, September 24, 2005.

252. William J.Broad and David E. Sanger, "The LAPTOP: Recording Iran's Ambitions; Relying on Computer, U.S. Seeks to Prove Iran's Nuclear Aims, " *New York Times*, November 13, 2005.

253. *Agence France Presse*, October 8, 2005.

254. Ibid.

255. Broad and Sanger. *New York Times*, November 13, 2005.

256. Linzer. *Washington Post*, February 8, 2006.

257. Linzer. *Washington Post*, February 8, 2006.

258. Alireza Jafarzadeh, "Iran Hiding a Laser Enrichment Facility Underground in Parchin Military Complex." Strategic Policy Consulting, March 24, 2005. http://www.spcwashington.com/index.php?option=com_content&task=view&id=144&Itemid=26

259. Alireza Jafarzadeh, "Iran Building Capable Missiles in Underground Secret Tunnels." November 23, 2005. http://www.ncr-iran.org/content/view/579/76

260. IAEA, *Implementation.* GOV/2004/83, November 15, 2004, paras. 105, 113; IAEA, *Implementation.* GOV/2005/67, September 2, 2005, para. 41.

261. IAEA, *Implementation.* GOV/2005/87, November 18, 2005, para. 16; IAEA, *Implementation.* GOV/2006/15, February 27, 2006, para. 32.

262. Nazila Fathi and Helene Cooper, "Iran Given June 29 Deadline to Respond to Anti-Nuke Offer." *New York Times*, June 10, 2006

263. Helene Cooper, "Russia and China, in Shift, Inch toward Iran Sanctions." *New York Times*, July 13, 2006.

264. Warren Hoge, "U.N. Gives Iran Deadline to End Nuclear Work." *New York Times*, August 1, 2006.

265. Fred Barbash and Dafna Linzer, "Iran Reportedly Rejects Demands to Halt Nuclear Efforts." *Washington Post*, August 22, 2006.

266. *Reuters*, "Key points in the UN Security Council resolution on Iran." *Haaretz*, December 23, 2006.

267. Resolution 1737—*Entities Involved In The Nuclear Program*: Atomic Energy Organization of Iran (AEOI); Mesbah Energy Company, Provider for IR-40 Reactor; Kalaye Electric; Pars Trash Company; Farayand Technique; Defense Industries Organization (DIO), Controlled by Ministry of Defense and Armed Forces Logistics (MODAFL); 7th of Tir, Subordinate of DIO. *Entities Involved In The Ballistic Missile Program*: Shahid Hemmat Industrial Group (SHIG), Subordinate Entity of Aerospace Industries Group (AIO); Shahid Bagheri Industrial Group (SBIG), Subordinate of AIO; Fajr Industrial Group, Subordinate of AIO; *Persons Involved In The Nuclear Program*: Mohammad Qannadi, AEOI Vice President for Research and Development; Behman Asgarpour, Operational Manager, Arak; Dawood Agha-Jani, Head of the PFEP (Natanz); Ehsan Monajemi, Construction Project Manager, Natanz; Jafar Mohammadi, Technical Adviser to the AEOI; Ali Hajinia Leilabadi, Director General of Mesbah Energy Company; Lt. Gen. Mohammad Mehdi Nejad Nouri, Rector of Malek Ashtar University of Defense Technology (Chemistry Dept.,

Affiliate of MODALF, has conducted Experiments on Beryllium. *Persons Involved In The Ballistic Missile Program:* Gen. Hosein Salimi, Commander of the Air Force, IRGC (Pasdaran); Ahmad Vahid Dastjerdi, Head of the AIO; Reza-Gholi Esmaeli, Head of Trade and International Affairs Dept, AIO; Bahmanyar Morteza Bahmanyar, Head of Finance and Budget Dept., AIO. *Persons Involved In Both The Nuclear And Ballistic Missile Programs*: Maj. Gen. Yahya Rahim Safavi, Commander, IRGC (Pasdaran). UN Security Council, Resolution 1737 (2006) adopted December 23, 2006. http://daccessdds.un.org/doc/UNDOC/GEN/N06/681/42/PDF/N0668142.pdf?OpenElement

268. Mark Heinrich, *Reuters*, "Iran Vows To Pursue Atomic Project Despite Deadline." *Yahoo*, February 21, 2007. http://news.yahoo.com/s/nm/20070221/ts_nm/iran_nuclear1_dc?

269. Ibid., para. 14.

270. IAEA, *Implementation*, GOV/2007/8, February 22, 2007, para. 28.

271. Ibid., paras. 4–10.

272. Ibid., paras. 8–9.

273. United Nations Security Council, Resolution 1747(2007), S/Res/1747(2006), March 24, 2007.

274. Thom Shanker, "Security Council Votes to Tighten Iran Sanctions." *New York Times*, March 25, 2007; United Nations Security Council, Resolution 1747(2007) Adopted on March 24, 2007, S/Res/1747(2006), March 24, 2007.

275. Ibid.

276. Nazila Fathi, "Iran Says It Can Enrich Uranium on an Industrial Scale." *New York Times*, April 10, 2007; Vladimir Isachenkov, "Russia, France Doubt Iran Nuclear Claims." *Associated Press*, April 10, 2007. http://news.yahoo.com/s/ap/20070410/ap_on_re_mi_ea/nuclear_iran_3?; *IranMania*, "UN Nuclear Watchdog; Iran's Program Limited." April 13, 2007. http://www.iranmania.com/News/ArticleView/Default.asp? NewsCode=50894&NewsKind=Current%20Affairs?

277. Dafna Linzer, "Boost in Iran's Capacity to Enrich Uranium Noted." *Washington Post*, March 19, 2007.

278. *Reuters*, "Iran Says Near Unity with EU in Some Nuclear Areas." *New York Times*, April 26, 2007.

279. *Haaretz*, "U.S. Denies Mulling Proposal To Allow Iran To Continue Enrichment." April 25, 2007.

280. *Reuters*, "Iran, EU to Hold Atomic Talks in Turkey." *New York Times*, April 23, 2007.

281. John D. Negroponte, Director of National Intelligence, Unclassified Statement for the Record, Annual Threat Assessment, Senate Select Committee on Intelligence, January 11, 2007, p. 6. http://intelligence.senate.gov/070111/negroponte.pdf

282. Admiral William J. Fallon, Senate Armed Services Committee Hearing on U.S. Central Command Nomination, January 30, 2007. http://www.pacom.mil/speeches/sst2007/070130-fallon-sasc-centcom.shtml

283. Nazila Fathi and Michael Slackman, "Iran's President Criticized over Nuclear Issue." *New York Times*, January 18, 2007; Laura Secor, "Whose Iran?" *New York Times Magazine*, January 28, 2007.

284. Bernard Guetta, "Ali Akbar Velayati, Advisor To The Leader: 'Everything is negotiable,'" *Iran Press Service*. February 14, 2007. http://www.iran-press-service.com/ips/articles-2007/february-2007/ali-akbar-velayati-adviso.shtml

285. Nazila Fathi, "Fuel Rationing in Iran Prompts Lines and Protests." *New York Times*, June 27, 2007.

286. Michael Slackman, "Hard Times Help Leaders In Iran Tighten Their Hold." *New York Times*, September 5, 2007.

287. Joshua Partlow, "Military Ties Iran to Arms in Iraq." *Washington Post*, February 12, 2007; Mark Mazzetti and Michael R. Gordon, "Disputes Emerge on Iran and Roadside Bombs." *New York Times*, February 14, 2007.

288. Michael R. Gordon, "U.S. Says Iran-Supplied Bomb Kills More Troops." *New York Times*, August 8, 2007.

289. Ibid.

290. Anthony Shadid, "With Iran Ascendant, U.S. Is Seen at Fault: Arab Allies in Region Feeling Pressure." *Washington Post*, January 30, 2007.

291. Steven R. Weisman, "U.S. Cautions Foreign Companie on Iran Deals." *New York Times*, March 21, 2007.

292. Steven R. Weisman, "Europe Resists U.S. on Curbing Ties With Iran." *New York Times*, January 29, 2007.

293. Robin Wright, "Iran Unit To Be Labeled 'Terrorist'." *Washington Post*, August 15, 2007.

294. IAEA, *Implementation*. GOV/2007/22, May 23, 2007, paras. 12-13.

295. IAEA, Ibid., paras. 3-5.

296. Joby Warrick, "Tunneling Near Iranian Nuclear Site Stirs Worry." *Washington Post*, July 9, 2007.

297. Michael Adler, *AFP*, "Iran has slowed down its nuclear work: UN nuclear chief ElBaradei." *Yahoo*, July 9, 2007; Mark Heinrich, *Reuters*, "Diplomats say scant recent progress in Iran atom work." *Yahoo*, August 3, 2007.

298. Yossi Melman, Inside intel/ Without fuel, the reactor won't work." Haaretz, July 19, 2007; George Jahn, *Associated Press*. "Russia squeezing Iran on nuclear program." *Philadelphia Inquirer*, August 8, 2007.

299. Guy Faulconbridge, *Reuters*, "Russia delays Iran nuclear plant to 2008." *Yahoo*, July 25, 2007.

300. *Reuters*, "IAEA, Iran Agree Visit At Disputed Reactor Site." *New York Times*, July 13 2007.

301. IAEA, *Implementation*, GOV/2007/48, August 30, 2007, paras. 3-6.

302. *IAEA*, "IAEA Team Concludes Meeting in Tehran." *Press Release*, July 13, 2007; *Associated Press*, "Atomic Agency Says Iran Has Made Concessions." *New York Times*, July 13, 2007.

303. *Reuters*, "Iran Official Rules Out Nuclear "Time Out": Agency." *New York Times*, July 4, 2007.

304. *Reuters*, "Iran to settle IAEA issues in phases." *Khaleei Times Online*, August 24, 2007. www.khaleejtimes.com/. . . /middleeast/2007/August/middleeast_August268.xml§ion=middleeast

305. IAEA, *Communication dated 27 August from the Permanent Mission of the Islamic Republic of Iran to the Agency concerning the text of the "Understandings of the Islamic Republic of Iran and the IAEA on Modalities of Resolution of the Outstanding Issues*, INFCIRC/711, Augusta 27, 2007.

306. IAEA, *Implementation*, GOV/2007/48, August 30, 2007, para. 22.

307. Ibid., para. 11.

308. IAEA, *Implementation*, GOV/2007/48, August 30, 2007, para. 13.

309. Ibid., para. 16.

310. Elaine Sciolino and William J. Broad, "Iran Expanding Its Nuclear Program, Agency Reports." *New York Times*, August 30, 2007.

311. Elaine Sciolino, "Plan Released by Iran and U.N. Atomic Agency Is Faulted." *New York Times*, August 29, 2007.

312. IAEA, *Implementation*, GOV/2007/48, August 30, 2007, paras. 3-6.

313. Ibid.

314. Ibid, para. 9.

315. Ibid., para. 10.

316. Ibid. paras. 23-24.

317. Michael Slackman and Nazilla Faithi, "Iran Reaffirms Its Defiance of West." *New York Times*, September 2, 2007; "On Two Fronts, One Nuclear, Iran Is Defiant." *New York Times*, September 3, 2007.

318. Kenneth Timmerman, Intelcon Preliminary Conference Agenda, 2nd Annual National Intelligence Conference and Exposition, May 7–9, 2006, Bethesda MD http://webzoom.freewebs.com/swnmia/Brochure%20INTELCON%20Conference.pdf

319. Elaine Sciolino, "French Leader Raises Possibility of Use of Force in Iran." *New York Times*, August 28, 2007.

## Chapter 7

1. John D. Negroponte, Director of National Intelligence, Unclassified Statement for the Record, Annual Threat Assessment, Senate Select Committee on Intelligence, 11 January 2007, p. 6. http://intelligence.senate.gov/070111/negroponte.pdf

2. Ballistic missile ranges are as follows: short-range ballistic missile (SRBM)—less than1,000 km; medium-range ballistic missile (MRBM)—1,000–2,500 km; intermediate-range ballistic missile (IRBM)—2,500–3,500 km; intercontinental ballistic missile (ICBM)—greater than 3,500 km.

3. NTI, Missile Chronology 1997. http://www.nti.org/e_research/profiles/Iran/Missile/1788_1812.html

4. Federation of American Scientists, Iran Missile Overview, December 1, 2005. http://www.fas.org/nuke/guide/iran/missile/index.html

5. *GlobalSecurity*, February 19, 2006. http://www.globalsecurity.org/wmd/world/iran/parchin.htm

6. Michael Jasinski, "Russia's Nuclear and Missile Technology Assistance to Iran." Center for Nonproliferation Studies, June 26, 2003. http://cns.miis.edu/research/iran/rusnuc.htm; "The Moscow Summit: Institutions Suspected by the Russian Government of Violating Export Control Legislation." Center for Nonproliferation Studies, August 26, 1998. http://www.cns.miis.edu/research/summit/9firms.htm.

7. United Nations Security Council, Resolution 1737 adopted on December 23, 2006, S/Res/1737(2006). December 27, 2006, http://daccessdds.un.org/doc/UNDOC/GEN/N06/681/42/PDF/N0668142.pdf?OpenElement; *Reuters*, "Key points in the UN Security Council resolution on Iran." *Haaretz*, December 23, 2006.

8. Executive Summary, *Commission To Assess The Ballistic Missile Threat To The United States*, July 15, 1998. http://www.fas.org/irp/threat/missile/rumsfeld/index.html

9. Federation of American Scientists, "SCUD-B/Shahab-1," December 1, 2005. http://www.fas.org/nuke/guide/iran/missile/shahab-1.htm

10. Anthony Cordesman and Khalid R. Al-Rodhan, *Iran's Weapons of Mass Destruction: The Real and Potential Threat*. Washington, DC: CSIS Press, 2006, p. 254.

11. Nuclear Threat Initiative (NTI), Iran Profile, Missile Overview, at http://www.nti.org/e_research/profiles/Iran/Missile/fn3

12. Cordesman and Al-Rodhan, *Iran's Weapons of Mass Destruction*, p. 254.

13. Kenneth Katzman, "Iran's Long Range Missile Capabilities," *Report of the Commission to Assess the Ballistic Missile Threat to the United States*, Appendix 3: Unclassified Working Papers. July 15, 1998, http://www.globalsecurity.org/wmd/library/report/1998/rumsfeld/pt2_katz.htm

14. Cordesman and Al-Rodhan, *Iran's Weapons of Mass Destruction*, p. 255.

15. Ibid.

16. Federation of American Scientists, "SCUD-B/Shahab-1," December 1, 2005. http://www.fas.org/nuke/guide/iran/missile/shahab-1.htm

17. The radius of a circle centered at the intended target into which a missile will land at 50 percent of the time.

18. Federation of American Scientists, "SCUD-B/Shahab-1," December 1, 2005. http://www.fas.org/nuke/guide/iran/missile/shahab-1.htm

19. Federation of American Scientists, "Shahab-2 (Scud C)," December 14, 2006. http://www.fas.org/nuke/guide/iran/missile/shahab-2.htm

20. Cordesman and Al-Rodhan, *Iran's Weapons of Mass Destruction*, p. 256.

21. Federation of American Scientists, "Shahab-2 (Scud C)," December 14, 2006. http://www.fas.org/nuke/guide/iran/missile/shahab-2.htm

22. Cordesman and Al-Rodhan, *Iran's Weapons of Mass Destruction*, p. 257.

23. Ibid., 257.

24. Ibid., 256–257.

25. Ibid., 258.

26. Ibid., 256.

27. Federation of American Scientists, "Shahab-2 (Scud C)," December 14, 2006. http://www.fas.org/nuke/guide/iran/missile/shahab-2.htm

28. Cordesman and Al-Rodhan, *Iran's Weapons of Mass Destruction*, p. 258.

29. Ibid., 259.

30. Federation of American Scientists, "Shahab-3/Zelzal-3," December 14, 2006. http://www.fas.org/nuke/guide/iran/missile/shahab-3.htm

31. "Iran: Shihab-3 Can Hit Anywhere in Israel." *Jerusalem Post*, August 16, 2004.

32. Federation of American Scientists, "Shahab-3/Zelzal-3," December 14, 2006. http://www.fas.org/nuke/guide/iran/missile/shahab-3.htm

33. *Globalsecurity.org*, "Shahab-3/Zelzal-3." http://www.globalsecurity.org/wmd/world/iran/shahab-3.htm

34. Ibid.

35. Ibid., 265.

36. Robert H. Schmucker, "Iran and Its Regional Environment." *Schmucker Technologie*, Peace Research Institute, Frankfurt, March 27, 2006. Available at http://www.hsfk.de/downloads/Panel%201%20-%20Schmucker.pdf

37. Ladane Nasseri and Marc Wolfensberger, "Iran Tests Shahab Missile Capable of Reaching Israel," (Update 5). *Bloomberg*, November 2, 2006.

38. Ibid., 264.

39. Ibid.

40. Federation of American Scientists, Iran Missile Overview, December 1, 2005. http://www.fas.org/nuke/guide/iran/missile/index.html.

41. Cordesman and Al-Rodhan, *Iran's Weapons of Mass Destruction*, p. 260.

42. Ibid., 261.

43. Federation of American Scientists, "Shahab-3/Zelzal-3," December 14, 2006. http://www.fas.org/nuke/guide/iran/missile/shahab-3.htm

44. Cordesman and Al-Rodhan, *Iran's Weapons of Mass Destruction*, p. 261.

45. Ibid., 264.

46. Federation of American Scientists, "Shahab-3/Zelzal-3," December 14, 2006. http://www.fas.org/nuke/guide/iran/missile/shahab-3.htm

47. Cordesman and Al-Rodhan, *Iran's Weapons of Mass Destruction*, p. 266.

48. Ibid.

49. Bill Gertz, "Missiles In Iran of Concern To State." *Washington Times*, September 11, 1997.

50. Michael Eisenstadt, Kenneth Katzman, Kenneth Timmerman, and Seth Carus, "Iran and Iraq," Appendix III: Unclassified Working Papers, Commission to Assess the Ballistic Missile Threat to the United States, March 23, 1998. http://www.fas.org/irp/threat/missile/rumsfeld/pt1_iraq.htm

51. "Shahab-4," *GlobalSecurity*, May 24, 2006. http://www.globalsecurity.org/wmd/world/iran/shahab-4.htm

52. Ibid.

53. MEMRI, *Inquiry and Analysis Series No. 181*, June 17, 2004. http://memri.org/bin/articles.cgi/Page=archivesArea=iaID=IA18104

54. Federation of American Scientists, Iran Missile Overview, December 1, 2005. http://www.fas.org/nuke/guide/iran/missile/index.html

55. Ibid.

56. Charles P. Vick, "Has the No-dong-B/Shahab-4 Finally Been Flight Tested in Iran for North Korea?" *globalsecurity.org*, April 29–May 22, 2006. http://www.globalsecurity.org/wmd/library/report/2006/cpvick-no-dong-b_2006.htm

57. Norimitsu Onishi and David E. Sanger, "6 Missiles Fired By North Korea; Tests Protested." *New York Times*, July 5, 2006.

58. U.S. Department of State, *Adherence and Compliance with Arms Control, Nonproliferation, and Disarmament Agreements*, August 2005, p. 55.

59. Ibid., 55.

60. The Convention on the Prohibition of the Development, Production, Stockpiling and Use of Chemical Weapons and on their Destruction, or Chemical Weapons Convention (CWC), went into force on April 29, 1997.

61. U.S. Department of State, *Adherence and Compliance with Arms Control, Nonproliferation, and Disarmament Agreements*, August 2005, p. 56.

62. Javed Ali, "Chemical weapons and the Iran-Iraq war: A Case Study in Noncompliance." *The Nonproliferation Review*, Spring 2001.

63. Nuclear Threat Initiative, Country Overviews: Iran Biological Capabilities. http://nti.org/e_research/profiles/Iran/Biological/2302.html.

64. Ibid., 51.

65. Ibid., 52.

66. Ibid., 53.

67. Ibid., 55.

68. Ibid., 56.

69. Director of Central Intelligence, *Unclassified Report to Congress on the Acquisition of Technology Relating to Weapons of Mass Destruction and Advanced Conventional Munitions, 1 July through 31 December 2003*. November 2004, p. 13.

70. Nuclear Threat Initiative, Iran Profile: Capabilities (updated February, 2006). 1http://www.nti.org/e_research/profiles/Iran/Chemical/2334.html

71. Unclassified Report to Congress on the Acquisition of Technology Relating to Weapons of Mass Destruction and Advanced Conventional Munitions, 1 January through 30 June 2001. http://web.archive.org/20020601133717/http://www.cia.gov/cia/publications/bian/bian_jan_2002.htm Central Intelligence Agency (USA).

72. *IranWatch*, "Iran's Chemical Program," July 2005. http://iranwatch.org/wmd/wmd-chemicalessay.htm

73. Michael R. Gordon with Stephen Engelberg, "Iran is Said to Try to Obtain Toxins." *New York Times*, August 13, 1989, p. 11; "Says Iran Made Two Attempts to Buy Hazardous Fungi in Netherlands." *Associated Press*, August 15, 1989.

74. Valerie Lincy and Gary Milhollin, "Iran's Forgotten Weapons." *IranWatch*, 1(1), December 2004–January 2005.

75. *IranWatch*, "Iran's Chemical Weapon Page," (updated July 2005). http://www.iranwatch.org/wmd/wmd-chemicalessay.htm

76. The Military Critical Technologies List Part II: Weapons of Mass Destruction Technologies (ADA 3: "Chemical Weapons Technology"—U.S. Department of Defense, Office of the Under Secretary of Defense; Acquisition and Technology, February 1998. As cited in: Federation of American Scientists, *Chemical Weapons Delivery*. http://www.fas.org/cw/delivery.htm

77. Federation of American Scientists, *Chemical Weapons Delivery*. http://www.fas.org/cw/delivery.htm

78. The Military Critical Technologies List Part II: Weapons of Mass Destruction Technologies (ADA 3): "Chemical Weapons Technology"—U.S. Department of Defense, Office of the Under Secretary of Defense: Acquisition and Technology, February 1998. As cited by Federation of American Scientists, *Chemical Weapons Delivery*. http://www.fas.org/cw/delivery.htm

79. Federation of American Scientists, "Chemical Weapons Delivery", http://www.fas.org/cw/delivery.htm

80. The Military Critical Technologies List Part II: Weapons of Mass Destruction Technologies (ADA 3): "Chemical Weapons Technology"—U.S. Department of Defense, Office of the Under Secretary of Defense; Acquisition and Technology, February 1998. As cited in Federation of American Scientists, *Chemical Weapons Delivery*. http://www.fas.org/cw/delivery.htm

81. Eric Croddy, "Weapons of Mass Destruction in the Middle East: CNS brief on WMD in the Middle East." Center for Nonproliferation Studies, Monterey Institute for International Studies, March 1999. http://cns.miis.edu/research/wmdme/syrscud.htm

82. The Arms Control Association, Fact Sheet: Chemical and Biological Weapons at a Glance, September 2002. http://www.armscontrol.org/factsheets/cbwprolif.asp?print

83. Ibid.

84. "Intelligence reports indicate that Iran may be looking to arm its Scud C missile, or its more advanced Shahab-4 missile with more lethal biological weapons. Such missiles are likely to have enough range-payload to give Iran the ability to strike all targets on the southern coast of the Gulf and all of the populated area in Iraq, although not the West. Iran could also reach targets in part of eastern Syria, the eastern third of Turkey, and cover targets in the border area of the former Soviet Union, western Afghanistan, and western Pakistan." As cited in Anthony Cordesman, *Weapons of Mass Destruction in the Middle East: Regional Trends, National Forces, Warfighting Capabilities, Delivery Options and Weapons Effects*. Center for Strategic and International Studies (CSIS), September 2000, Copyright Anthony H. Cordesman. http://csis.org/media/csis/pubs/wmdinmetrends[1].pdf

85. The Arms Control Association, Fact Sheet: *Chemical and Biological Weapons at a Glance*. Published in September 2002. http://www.armscontrol.org/factsheets/cbwprolif.asp?print

86. Nuclear Threat Initiative, Iran: Missile Overview (Updated May 2006). http://www.nti.org/e_research/profiles/Iran/Missile/index.html

87. Ibid.

88. Ibid.

89. Nuclear Threat Initiative, Iran: Missile Overview (Updated May 2006). http://www.nti.org/e_research/profiles/Iran/Missile/index.html

90. John D. Negroponte, Director of National Intelligence, "Annual Threat Assessment of the Director of National Intelligence." Testimony to the Senate Select Committee on Intelligence, February 2, 2006, p. 9.

91. As cited in: Anthony Cordesman, *Weapons of Mass Destruction in the Middle East: Regional Trends, National Forces, Warfighting Capabilities, Delivery Options and Weapons Effects*, Center for Strategic and International Studies. September 2000. Copyright Anthony H. Cordesman. http://csis.org/media/csis/pubs/wmdinmetrends[1].pdf

92. U.S. Department of State, *Adherence and Compliance with Arms Control, Nonproliferation, and Disarmament Agreements*, August 2005, p. 20.

93. Iran ratified the Biological Weapons Convention (BWC) in 1973 and submitted required confidence-building measures (CBM) data in 1998, 1999, and 2002. The Convention on the Prohibition of the Development, Production, and the Stockpiling of Bacteriological (Biological) and Toxic Weapons and their Destruction (usually referred to as just the Biological Weapons Convention (BWC)) was the first multilateral disarmament treaty banning the production of an entire category of weapons (with exceptions for medical and defensive purposes in small quantities). The BWC opened for signature on April 10, 1972 in Moscow, Washington, and London and entered into force on March 26, 1975. As of May 2006 the Convention had 171 parties. The BWC had no stipulation for verification that the signatories were following its provisions. A process of negotiation to add a verification mechanism began in the 1990s, suggesting onsite inspections were needed as well as sanctions for signatories departing from the Convention standards. Early in 2001, the Bush administration withdrew support, claiming that it would interfere with legitimate commercial and biodefense activity.

94. "Unclassified Report to Congress on the Acquisition of Technology Relating to Weapons of Mass Destruction and Advanced Conventional Munitions, 1 July through 31 December 2003," Director of Central Intelligence, November 2004.

95. Ibid.

96. U.S. Department of State, Adherence and Compliance with Arms Control, Nonproliferation, and Disarmament Agreements, August 2005, p. 21.

97. John D. Negroponte, "Annual Threat Assessment of the Director of National Intelligence." Testimony before the Senate Select Committee on Intelligence, February 2, 2006, p. 10.

98 . The Razi Institute for Serums and Vaccines, a facility of the Iranian Research Organization for Science and Technology, produces $100 m worth of vaccines and serums a year. http://www.payvand.com/news/00/oct/1067.html.

99 . U.S. Department of State, Adherence and Compliance with Arms Control, Nonproliferation, and Disarmament Agreements, August 2005, p. 21.

100. U.S. Department of State, Adherence and Compliance with Arms Control, Nonproliferation, and Disarmament Agreements, August 2005, p. 20.

101. Ibid., 21

102. Jonathan B. Tucker, "Bioweapons from Russia: Stemming the flow." *Issues in Science and Technology.* http://www.issues.org/15.3/p_tucker.htm

103. U.S. Department of State, Adherence and Compliance with Arms Control, Nonproliferation, and Disarmament Agreements, August 2005, p. 21.

104. Bill Gertz, "Iran Tests Medium-Range Missile." *Washington Times*, July 23, 1998, p. A1.

## Appendix I

1. "Iran Warns Israel of 'Unimaginable Losses' If Syria Hit." *Agence France Presse*, July 16, 2006.

2. "Iran's Ahmadinejad to Form Group for Investigating Holocaust." *Deutsche Presse-Agentur*, October 20, 2006.

3. "Iran's President Calls Holocaust A 'Myth.'" *United Press International*, December 14, 2005.

4. "Ahmadinejad Calls Israel 'Evil Regime.'" *United Press International*, May 11, 2006.

5. Quote from ISNA—appeared in *Sharq*, taken from: *Special Report 39-Iranian Leaders: Statements and Positions. MEMRI*, December 10, 2005.

6. "Iranian President Tells Holocaust Conference That Israel's Days Are Numbered." *The Daily Telegraph (London)*, December 13, 2006.

7. "The Way Forward in Iraq Stalled." *CNN Situation Room transcript*, December 12, 2006. http://transcripts.cnn.com/TRANSCRIPTS/0612/12/sitroom.03.html

8. Statement from Conference "The World Without Zionism" in Tehran, Iran. *Al-Jazeera News,* October 26, 2005. http://english.aljazeera.net/news/archive/archive?ArchiveId=15816

9. Statement from Conference "The World Without Zionism" in Tehran, Iran. *Al-Jazeera News,* October 26, 2005. http://english.aljazeera.net/news/archive/archive?ArchiveId=15816

10. Statement from Conference "The World Without Zionism" in Tehran, Iran. *The Jerusalem Post*, October 26, 2005. http://www.jpost.com/servlet/Satellite?pagename=JPost%2FJPArticle%2FShowFull&cid=1129540603434

11. Statement from Conference "The World Without Zionism" in Tehran, Iran. *The Jerusalem Post*, October 26, 2005. http://www.jpost.com/servlet/Satellite?pagename=JPost%2FJPArticle%2FShowFull&cid=1129540603434

12. Statement from Conference "The World Without Zionism" in Tehran, Iran. *The Jerusalem Post*, October 26, 2005. http://www.jpost.com/servlet/Satellite?pagename=JPost%2FJPArticle%2FShowFull&cid=1129540603434.

13. Statement from Conference "The World Without Zionism" in Tehran, Iran. *The Jerusalem Post*, October 26, 2005. http://www.jpost.com/servlet/Satellite?pagename=JPost%2FJPArticle%2FShowFull&cid=1129540603434

14. "Israel Should Be Wiped Off Map, Says Iran's President." *The Guardian (London)—Final Edition*, October 27, 2005.

15. "Iranian Leader Turns Back Time In Diatribe on Israel; Quoting Khomeini, He Predicts Destruction." *The International Herald Tribune*, October 28, 2005.

16. "Iran's President Calls Israel A 'Tyrannical Regime,' Dismisses Sanction Threat." *The Associated Press*, May 11, 2006.

17. Ali Akbar Darei, "Iran Leader: Israel Will Be Annihilated." *ABC News International*, April 14, 2006.

18. "Mofaz: Iran gave $ 10m. to Palestinian Terror Groups in '06. Ahmadinejad: Israel Cannot Continue To Exist." *The Jerusalem Post*, April 25, 2006.

19. Nazila Faithi, "Iran's Leader Warns West on Support for Israel." *International Herald Tribune*, October 21, 2006.

20. "Ahmadinejad and Chavez Find New Forums to Display Defiance." *CNN: The Situation Room*, September 21, 2006.

21. "Ahmadinejad: No One Can Stop 'Peaceful' Nuclear Program. Iran Constitutes The Only Existential Threat to Israel Dichter Warns." *The Jerusalem Post*, August 30, 2006.

22. Following are excerpts from an address given by Iranian President Mahmoud Ahmadinejad, which aired on the *MEMRI*, Iranian News Channel on July 18, 2006. http://www.memritv.org/Transcript.asp?P1=1198

23. "European Countries 'Consider Offering Iran Reactor'." *Guardian Unlimited*, May 16, 2006.

24. Patrick Bishop and Sebastien Berger, "Israel fighting 'war against humanity': Iranian President." *National Post*, August 4, 2006.

25. "Ahmadinejad's 'Countdown' For Israel Provokes Outrage." *Deutsche Presse-Agentur*, December 12, 2006.

26. Speech in the town of Islamshahr in southwestern Tehran. *Breitbart News*, October 19, 2005. http://www.breitbart.com/news/2006/10/19/061019140014.r65x4txr.html

27. "Ahmadinejad: Palestinians and "Other Nations" Will Remove Israel." *Deutsche Press-Agentur*, February 11, 2006.

28. "Ahmadinejad Calls Israel 'Evil Regime'." *United Press International*, May 11, 2006.

29. " Iran President Ahmadinejad Warns Israel Against Attacking Syria." *Deutsche Presse-Agenture*, July 14, 2006.

30. Quote from a rally with the President, which aired on the Iranian News Channel, *IRINN*, on August 1, 2006. http://memri.org/bin/articles.cgi?Page=archives&Area=sd&ID=SP122906

31. Iranian President Ahmadinejad on *IRINN* TV: "Lebanon is the Scene of a Historic Test, Which Will Determine the Future of Humanity." MEMRI—Middle East Media Research Institute, July 26, 2006. http://memri.org/bin/latestnews.cgi?ID=SD121206

32. Address to An Audience of His Supporters, Including Members of The Union of Islamic Engineers And Supporters of the Khat-e Emam—*MEMRI*, October 14, 2006. http://memri.org/bin/articles.cgi?Page=archives&Area=sd&ID=SP132806

33. Statement from Conference "The World Without Zionism' in Tehran Iran. *The Jerusalem Post*, October 26, 2005. http://www.jpost.com/servlet/Satellite?pagename=JPost%2FJPArticle%2FShowFull&cid=1129540603434

34. "Ahmadinejad Calls Out To 'Noble Americans' Against Bush Policies." *Al-Bawaba*, November 30, 2006.

35. Address by Iranian President Mahmoud Ahmadinejad on February 11, 2006. MEMRI, February 14, 2006. http://memri.org/bin/articles.cgi?Page=countries&Area=iran&ID=SP109106

36. "Letter To Americans From Ahmadinejad." *Turkish Daily News*, December 1, 2006.

37. Angus McDowall, "Iran's leader hits back at US for 'bloody hands.'" *The Independent (London)*, February 2, 2006.

38. Rally With President Ahmadinejad, aired on *IRINN* on August 1, 2006. *MEMRI*, August 3, 2006. http://memri.org/bin/articles.cgi?Page=archives&Area=sd&ID=SP122906

39. Deutsch, Anthony, "Iranian President Says Tehran Ready to Negotiate over Nuclear Program." *The Associated Press*, May 11, 2006.

40. "Iran President Attacks Us Claims." *BBC News*, February 12, 2007. http://news.bbc.co.uk/2/hi/middle_east/6353923.stm

41. Dareini, Ali Akbar, "Iran Rejects European Incentives to Give Up Uranium Enrichment, Makes Counter Offer." *The Associated Press*, May 18, 2006.

42. "Iran 'Swiftly Seeks Nuclear Goal.'" *BBC News*, February 21, 2007. http://news.bbc.co.uk/2/hi/middle_east/6381477.stm.

43. Hafezi, Parisa, "Iran Condemns UN Nuclear Sanctions." *Reuters*, December 24, 2006. http://today.reuters.com/news/articlenews.aspx?type=topnews&storyid=2006-12-24T093232Z_01_L23866683_RTRIDST_0_NEWS-IRAN-NUCLEAR1-DC.XML

44. Hafezi, Parisa, "Iran Condemns UN Nuclear Sanctions." *Reuters*, December 24, 2006. http://today.reuters.com/news/articlenews.aspx?type=topnews&storyid=2006-12-24T093232Z_01_L23866683_RTRIDST_0_NEWS-IRAN-NUCLEAR1-DC.XML

45. Hughes, Paul, "Iran Rejects Western Bullying In Nuclear Dispute." *DefenseNews.com*, March 9, 2006. http://www.defensenews.com/story.php?F=1588366&C=mideast

46. "Iran Defiant On UN Sanctions; Plans War Games." *Forbes*, January 21, 2007. http://www.forbes.com/afxnewslimited/feeds/afx/2007/01/21/afx3346747.html

47. "Tehran Won't Back Down on nuclear program Ahmadinejad says," *ABC Premium News (Australia)*, January 22, 2007.

48. "Tehran won't back down on Nuclear Program, Ahmadinejad Says." *ABC Premium News (Australia)*, January 22, 2007.

49. Ali Akbar Dareini, "Ahmadinejad Says Iran Ready to Halt Enrichment Program Provided The West Does The Same." *The Associated Press*, February 20, 2007.

50. "Biography of Iranian Defense Minister Brig-Gen Mostafa Mohammad Najjar." *BBC Monitoring Middle East*, November 7, 2005 via *IRNA*, November 2, 2005.

51. "US, Britain, Israel 'Root Cause of All Atrocities.'" *BBC Monitoring International Reports*, November 12, 2006.

52. Speech Given to IRGC at the Basij on July 30, 2006. *MEMRI*: August 2, 2006, http://memri.org/bin/articles.cgi?Page=archives&Area=sd&ID=SP122506

53. Speech Given to IRGC at the Basij on July 30, 2006. *MEMRI*: August 2, 2006, http://memri.org/bin/articles.cgi?Page=archives&Area=sd&ID=SP122506

54. "Lebanon-Security-Council." *IRNA*, August 16, 2006.

55. "US, UK Responsible For Blood of Lebanese Martyrs." *BBC Monitoring Middle East*, August 16, 2006.

56. "Iran's Larijani Says US Cause of Escalation of Insecurity, Terrorism in Mideast." *BBC Monitoring International Reports*, August 4, 2006.

57. "Iran Condemns UN Nuclear Sanctions." *Financial Times*, December 24, 2006. http://www.ft.com/cms/s/7f3d00ee-934d-11db-8a0e-0000779e2340.html

58. "Iran's Presidential Contenders in Their Own Words." *Agence France Presse—English*, June 24, 2005.

59. "Iran Election: Biography of Ali Akbar Hashemi-Rafsanjani." *BBC Monitoring International Reports*, May 17, 2005 via *IRNA*, May 11 2005.

60. Speech Given on December 14, 2001 at Tehran University, Reported on *MEMRI*, January 3, 2002.

61. "Iran's Presidential Contenders in Their Own Words." *Agence France Presse—English*, June 24, 2005.

62. "Iran Election: Biography of Ali Akbar Hashemi-Rafsanjani." *BBC Monitoring International Reports*, May 17, 2005.

63. "Iran Election: Biography of Ali Akbar Hashemi-Rafsanjani." *BBC Monitoring International Reports*, May 17, 2005 via *Hemayat Daily*, January 31, 2005.

64. "Iran Election: Biography of Ali Akbar Hashemi-Rafsanjani." *BBC Monitoring International Reports*, May 17, 2005 via *IRNA*, January 30, 2005.

65. "Profile: Khomeini's Ideal Priest Politician: Rafsanjani, Iran's Pragmatic President." *The Independent*, August 12, 1989.

66. "Rafsanjani-Iran-Nuclear." *Islamic Republic News Agency*, February 3, 2006.

67. Ibid.

68. "Biography of Iranian Justice Minister Jamal Karimi-Rad." *BBC Monitoring Middle East*, November 20, 2005 via *Farhang-e Ashti*, July 2005.

69. "Biography of Iranian Justice Minister Jamal Karimi-Rad." *BBC Monitoring Middle East*, November 20, 2005 via *IRNA*, January 18, 2005.

70. "Iran to Revise IAEA Cooperation." *BBC News*, December 27, 2006. http://news.bbc.co.uk/2/hi/middle_east/6211561.stm

71. Ibid.

72. "In Quotes, Reaction to Iran Sanctions." *BBC News*, December 24, 2006. http://news.bbc.co.uk/2/hi/middle_east/6206777.stm

73. Edith M. Lederer, "Security Council Agrees to Impose Sanctions on Iran for Nuclear Program." *The Associated Press*, December 23, 2006.

74. "Iran Defiant on UN Sanctions; Plans War Games." *Forbes*, January 21, 2007. http://www.forbes.com/afxnewslimited/feeds/afx/2007/01/21/afx3346747.html

75. Ibid.

76. Ibid.

77. "Pakistan's Former Military Leaders Slam Iran Sanctions." *BBC Monitoring International Reports*, December 26, 2006.

78. "Pakistan Never Favors Sanctions on Iran: Official." *Xinhua General News Service*, December 26, 2006.

79. "Palestinian Islamic Jihad Decries 'Unjust Sanctions' on Iran." *BBC Monitoring Middle East*, Political Supplied by *BBC Worldwide Monitoring*, December 24, 2006.

80. "Call for End to 'Nuclear Double Standards.'" *The Gazette (Montreal)*, December 26, 2006.

81. Reese Erlich, Interview with Bashar Al-Assad. *Democracy Now*, June 14, 2006. http://www.democracynow.org/article.pl?sid=06/07/18/1442253

82. Tariq Alhomayed, Interview with King Abdullah II of Jordan, January 24, 2007. http://www.asharq-e.com/news.asp?section=3&id=7773

83. "Azerbaijan Is Against Sanctions on Iran: President Aliyev." *IRNA*, December 26, 2006. http://www.irna.com/en/news/view/line-17/0612260595004004.htm

84. Transcript of an On-the-Record Briefing by Condoleezza Rice, January 12, 2006. http://www.state.gov/secretary/rm/2006/59083.htm

85. Conference Call on UN Sanctions Resolution 1737. Washington DC: *U.S. Department of State*, December 23, 2006. http://www.state.gov/p/us/rm/2006/78246.htm

86. "UN Passes Iran Nuclear Sanctions." *BBC News*, December 23, 2006. http://news.bbc.co.uk/2/hi/middle_east/6205295.stm

87. "Blair says Iran Poses 'Major Strategic Threat' to Mideast." *People's Daily Online*, December 12, 2006. http://english.peopledaily.com.cn/200612/13/eng20061213_331799.html

88. "Senior Iranian Dissident Cleric Criticizes Ahmadinejad on Nuclear Diplomacy, Inflation." *The Associated Press*, January 22, 2007.

89. "Adoption of Iran Security Council Resolution 1737—Explanation of Vote Made by Sir Emyr Jones Parry." *UK Mission To U.S.*, December 23, 2006. http://www.ukun.org/articles_show.asp?SarticleType=17&Article_ID=1383

90. "Monthly News Conference." *People's Daily Online*, December 12, 2006. http://english.peopledaily.com.cn/200612/13/eng20061213_331799.html

91. Statement by Ehud Olmert Made on Official Visit to Germany, December 11, 2006. Quoted in "Holocaust Conference Sparks Outrage." *The Age*, December 13, 2006. http://www.theage.com.au/news/world/holocaust-conference-sparks-outrage/2006/12/13/1165685730562.html

92. "In Quotes: Reaction to Iran Sanctions." *BBC News*, December 24, 2006. http://news.bbc.co.uk/2/hi/middle_east/6206777.stm

93. "Israeli Minister Terms Iran Sanctions As Important Decision." *Xinhua General News Service*, December 23, 2006.

94. "In Quotes: Reaction to Iran Sanctions." *BBC News*, December 24, 2006. http://news.bbc.co.uk/2/hi/middle_east/6206777.stm

95. United Nations Security Council Meeting 5612, New York. *UN.org*, December 23, 2006. http://www.lcnp.org/disarmament/iran/unsc1737statements.pdf

96. "Hu Urges Iran to Respond to UN." *China Daily*, January 5, 2007. http://www.chinadaily.com.cn/china/2007-01/06/content_776076.htm

97. Opening Speech by Angela Merkel, Chancellor of the Federal Republic of Germany, at the 42nd Munich Conference on Security Policy. *German Embassy Site*, February 4, 2006. http://www.germany.info/relaunch/politics/speeches/020506.html

98. "In Quotes: Iran Nuclear Crisis." *BBC News*, March 9, 2006.

99. State of the Nation Address—Moscow. *Radio Free Europe Radio Liberty*, May 10, 2006. http://www.rferl.org/featuresarticle/2006/05/49ccd732-65b4-4581-a9e2-8e919b63e998.html

100. Bilateral Meeting with Russian President Vladimir Putin at G8 Summit in St. Petersburg, Russia. V*oice of America*, July 15, 2006. http://www.voanews.com/english/archive/2006-07/2006-07-15-voa12.cfm?CFID=101161871&CFTOKEN=11781622

101. Colum Lynch, "Dissent Grows at U.N. Over Iran." *The Washington Post*, November 5, 2006. http://www.washingtonpost.com/wp-dyn/content/article/2006/11/04/AR2006110400959.html

102. "Time to Take Iran to UN over Nuclear Issue: French FM." *National Nine News*, March 9, 2006.

103. Ibid.

104. "In Quotes: Iran Nuclear Crisis." *BBC News*, March 9, 2006.

105. "In Quotes: Iran Nuclear Crisis." *BBC News*, March 9, 2006.

106. United Nations Security Council Meeting 5612, New York. *UN.org*, December 23, 2006. http://www.lcnp.org/disarmament/iran/unsc1737statements.pdf

107. Transcript of Director General's Remarks at Conclusion of IAEA Board Meeting, IAEA Headquarters Vienna. *IAEA.org*, Delivered March 8, 2006. http://www.iaea.org/NewsCenter/Transcripts/2006/transcr08032006.html

108. "Bush Warns Iran on Israel." *Agence France-Presse*, March 20, 2006. http://www.breitbart.com/news/2006/03/20/060320195105.4089dcoq.html

109. "Bush Warns Iran to Keep Clear of Iraq." *Sydney Morning Herald*, January 15, 2006. http://www.smh.com.au/news/World/Bush-warns-Iran-to-keep-clear-of-Iraq/2007/01/15/1168709664066.html

110. "Presidential News Conference," *CNN, Show. CNN Newsroom*, 11:00 AM EST, February 14, 2007.

111. "OnlineNewsHour."*PBS*, January 12, 2006. http://www.pbs.org/newshour/bb/middle_east/jan-june06/iran_1-12.html

112. Opening Remarks Before the Senate Appropriations Committee, Washington, DC March 9, 2006. http://www.state.gov/secretary/rm/2006/62900.htm

113. Iranian Nuclear Agency Official Denies Country Installing 3,000 Centrifuges. *The Associated Press*, January 28, 2007.

114. "Reported Damascus Meeting Indicates Hezbollah, Iran and Syria in Crisis Talks." *The Associated Press*, July 27, 2006.

115. Iran Needs Time to Review Plan Calling For A Time-Out to Sanctions, Enrichment. *The Associated Press*, January 28, 2007.

116. "Iran Leader's Comments Attacked." *BBCNews*, October 27, 2005. http://news.bbc.co.uk/2/hi/middle_east/4378948.stm

117. "Report: Russian Diplomat Says Iran Must Always Allow IAEA Nuclear Inspections." *International Herald Tribune*, January 23, 2007. http://www.iht.com/articles/ap/2007/01/23/europe/EU-GEN-Russia-Iran-Nuclear.php

118. "Iran Defiant As Anger Mounts Over Holocaust Forum."*Agence France-Presse*, December 12, 2006. http://www.breitbart.com/news/2006/12/12/061212142536.rhu8rs3p.html.

119. "Blair Tops End of Year EJP Poll." *European Jewish Press*, January 8, 2007, http://www.ejpress.org/article/news/eastern_europe/12736

120. "Blair Says Iran Poses 'Major Strategic Threat' to Mideast." *People's Daily Online*, December 12, 2006. http://english.peopledaily.com.cn/200612/13/eng20061213_331799.html

121. "Statement by the Prime Minister on Statements From the President of Iran—Ottawa, Ontario." *Office of Prime Minister*, December 12, 2006. http://www.pm.gc.ca/eng/media.asp?id=1457

122. "Official Statement on Holocaust Denial Conference Sponsored by Iranian Regime." *WhiteHouse.gov*, December 12, 2006. http://www.whitehouse.gov/news/releases/2006/12/20061212.html

123. "Statement from Vice-President Frattini in Brussels." *Europa-EU*, December 12, 2006. http://europa.eu/rapid/pressReleasesAction.do?reference=IP/06/1772&format=HTML&aged=0&language=EN&guiLanguage=en

## Appendix II

1. "Information on Two Top Secret Nuclear Sites of the Iranian Regime (Natanz and Arak)." *IranWatch*, December 2002. http://www.iranwatch.org/privateviews/NCRI/perspex-ncri-natanzarak-1202.htm

2. Paul Kerr. *Arms Control Today*, March 2003. www.armscontrol.org/act/2003_03/iran_mar03.asp

3. International Atomic Energy Agency (IAEA), *Implementation of the NPT Safeguards Agreements in the Islamic Republic of Iran.*" Report by the Director General, GOV/2003/40, June 19, 2003, p. 2.

4. International Atomic Energy Agency (IAEA), *Implementation.* GOV/2003/40, June 19, 2003, p. 2.

5. IAEA, *Implementation.* GOV/2003/40, June 19, 2003, p. 6.

6. IAEA, *Implementation.* GOV/2003/40, June 19, 2003, p. 2.

7. IAEA, *Implementation.* GOV/2003/40, June 19, 2003, p. 5.

8. IAEA, *Implementation.* GOV/2003/40, June 19, 2003, p. 5; IAEA, *Implementation.* GOV/2003/75, November 10, 2003, p. 5.

9. IAEA, *Implementation.* GOV/2003/40, June 19, 2003; Sharon Squassoni, "Iran's Nuclear Program: Recent Developments." *Congressional Research Service*, November 12, 2003, p. 3.

10. IAEA, *Implementation.* GOV/2003/40, June 19, 2003, p. 4.

11. National Council of Resistance of Iran, Press Conference by Mohammad Mohaddessin, November 17, 2004. http://www.iranwatch.org/privateviews/ncri/perspex-ncri-lavizan-111704.htm; IAEA, *Implementation.* GOV/2004/60, September 1, 2004, paras. 6, 42–43, annex. 46; IAEA, *Implementation.* GOV/2004/83, November 15, 2004, para. 99.

12. IAEA, *Implementation.* GOV/2003/40, June 19, 2003, p. 7.

13. IAEA, *Implementation.* GOV/2003/63, August 26, 2003, p. 8.

14. NCRI, "Information on Newly Detected Nuclear Sites of the Iranian Regime." *National Council of Resistance of Iran*, May 27, 2003. http://www.iranwatch.org/privateviews/NCRI/perspex-ncri-nuclearsites-052703.htm

15. IAEA, *Implementation.* GOV/2003/63, August 26, 2003, p. 8.

16. IAEA, *Implementation.* GOV/2003/63, August 26, 2003, p. 6.

17. IAEA, *Implementation.* GOV/2003/63, August 26, 2003, p. 7.

18. IAEA, *Implementation.* GOV/2003/63, August 26, 2003, p. 7; IAEA, *Implementation.* GOV/2003/75, November 10, 2003, p. 7.

19. National Council of Resistance of Iran (NCRI), "Iran-Nuclear: Iranian Regime's New Nuclear Sites." Remarks of *Alireza Jafarzadeh*, July 8, 2003. http://ncr-iran.org/content/view/568/76/

20. IAEA, *Implementation.* GOV/2003/75, November 10, 2003, p. 3.

21. IAEA, *Implementation.* GOV/2003/63, August 26, 2003, pp. 8, 9.

22. IAEA, *Implementation.* GOV/2004/60, September 1, 2004, pp. 7–8.

23. IAEA, *Implementation.* GOV/2003/63, August 26, 2003, p. 6.

24. IAEA, *Implementation.* GOV/2003/63, August 26, 2003, p. 7.

25. IAEA, *Implementation.* GOV/2003/75, November 10, 2003, p. 8.

26. IAEA, *Implementation.* GOV/2003/63, August 26, 2003, p. 7.

27. IAEA, *Implementation.* GOV/2003/63, August 26, 2003, p. 8.

28. IAEA, *Implementation.* GOV/2003/63, August 26, 2003, p. 4.

29. IAEA, *Implementation.* GOV/2003/69, September 12, 2003, p. 2.

30. IAEA, *Implementation.* GOV/2003/75, November 10, 2003, para. 9.

31. IAEA, *Implementation.* GOV/2004/11, February 24, 2005, p. 5.

32. IAEA, *Implementation.* GOV/2004/11, February 24, 2005, pp. 5–6.

33. IAEA, *Implementation.* GOV/2003/75, November 10, 2003, p. 3; IAEA, *Implementation.* GOV/2004/60, September 1, 2004, p. 6.

34. IAEA, *Implementation.* GOV/2003/75, November 10, 2003, p. 3.

35. IAEA, *Implementation.* GOV/2003/75, November 10, 2003, pp. 4–6; IAEA, *Implementation.* GOV/2004/11, February 24, 2004, p. 5.

36. IAEA, *Implementation.* GOV/2003/75, November 10, 2003, p. 6.

37. IAEA, *Implementation.* GOV/2003/75, November 10, 2003, p. 5; IAEA, *Implementation.* GOV/2004/11, February 24, 2004, p. 4.

38. IAEA, *Implementation.* GOV/2003/75, November 10, 2003, p. 4; Paul Kerr, "With Deadline Looming European Foreign Ministers Strike Deal to Restrict Iran's Nuclear Program." *Arms Control Today,* November 2003. http://www.armscontrol.org/act/2003_11/Iran.asp

39. IAEA, *Implementation.* GOV/2003/75, November 10, 2003, pp. 7–8; IAEA, *Implementation.* GOV/2004/11, February 24, 2004, p. 9.

40. IAEA, *Implementation.* GOV/2003/75, November 10, 2003, p. 7.

41. IAEA, *Implementation.* GOV/2003/75, November 10, 2003, p. 7.

42. IAEA, *Implementation.* GOV/2003/75, November 10, 2003, paras. 42, 44.

43. IAEA, *Implementation.* GOV/2003/75, November 10, 2003, p. 4.

44. IAEA, *Implementation.* GOV/2004/60, September 1, 2004, paras. 43–44, annex. 45; IAEA, *Implementation.* GOV/2004/83, November 15, 2004, para. 102; National Council of Resistance of Iran, Press Conference by Mohammad Mohaddessin, November 17, 2004. http://www.iranwatch.org/privateviews/ncri/perspex-ncri-lavizan-111704.htm

45. IAEA, *Implementation.* GOV/2004/11, February 24, 2004, p. 2.

46. IAEA, *Implementation.* GOV/2004/11, February 24, 2004, p. 10.

47. IAEA, *Implementation.* GOV/2004/11, February 24, 2004, p. 8; IAEA, *Implementation.* GOV/2004/83, November 15, 2004, para. 26.

48. IAEA, *Implementation.* GOV/2004/11, February 24, 2004, p. 8; IAEA, *Implementation.* GOV/2003/75, November 10, 2003, annex. 1, p. 7.

49. IAEA, *Implementation.* GOV/2004/11, February 24, 2004, p. 8.

50. IAEA, *Implementation*. GOV/2004/11, February 24, 2004, p. 4.
51. IAEA, *Implementation*. GOV/2004/11, February 24, 2004, p. 10.
52. IAEA, *Implementation*. GOV/2004/34, June 1, 2004, p. 7.
53. IAEA, *Implementation*. GOV/2004/34, June 1, 2004, pp. 5, 6.
54. IAEA, *Implementation*. GOV/2004/34, June 1, 2004, annex. 1, p. 7.
55. IAEA, *Implementation*. GOV/2004/34, June 1, 2004, pp. 5, 7.
56. IAEA, *Implementation*. GOV/2004/60, September 1, 2004, p. 8.
57. IAEA, *Implementation*. GOV/2004/34, June 1, 2004, pp. 4, 8.
58. IAEA, *Implementation*. GOV/2004/34, June 1, 2004, p. 5.
59. IAEA, *Implementation*. GOV/2004/34, June 1, 2004, p. 5.
60. IAEA, *Implementation*. GOV/2004/34, June 1, 2004, annex. 1, pp. 2–3.
61. IAEA, *Implementation*. GOV/2004/34, June 1, 2004, p. 6, annex pp. 5–6.
62. IAEA, *Implementation*. GOV/2004/60, September 1, 2004, p. 10.
63. IAEA, *Implementation*. GOV/2004/60, September 1, 2004, paras. 6, 42–43, annex. 46; IAEA, *Implementation*. GOV/2004/83, November 15, 2004, para. 99.
64. IAEA, *Implementation*. GOV/2004/83, November 15, 2004, p. 3.
65. IAEA, *Implementation*. GOV/2004/60, September 1, 2004, p. 5.
66. Broad and Sanger. *New York Times*, November 13, 2005.
67. Broad and Sanger. *New York Times*, November 13, 2005.
68. IAEA, *Implementation*. GOV/2004/60, September 1, 2004, pp. 5–6.
69. IAEA, *Implementation*. GOV/2004/60, September 1, 2004, p. 5.
70. IAEA, *Implementation*. GOV/2004/60, September 1, 2004, p. 4.
71. IAEA, *Implementation*. GOV/2004/60, September 1, 2004, p. 7, annex p. 8.
72. IAEA News Center, November 14, 2004. http://www.iaea.org/NewsCenter/Focus/IaeaIran/eu_iran14112004.shtml
73. IAEA, "Communication Dated November 26, 2004 Received From the Permanent Representatives of France, Germany, the Islamic Republic of Iran, and the United Kingdom Concerning the Agreement Signed in Paris on November 15, 2004." INFCIRC/637, November 26, 2004.
74. Dafna Linzer, "Nuclear Disclosures On Iran Unverified." *Washington Post*, November 19, 2004; Carla Anne Robbins, "Atomic Test: As Evidence Grows of Iran's Program, U.S. Hits Quandry." *Wall Street Journal*, March 18, 2005; Carla Anne Robbins, "U.S. Gives Briefing On Iranian Missile To Nuclear Agency." *Wall Street Journal*, July 27, 2005.
75. IAEA, *Implementation*. GOV/2005/67, September 2, 2005, p. 4.
76. IAEA, *Implementation*. GOV/2005/67, September 2, 2005, p. 6.
77. IAEA, *Implementation*. GOV/2005/67, September 2, 2005, p. 5; IAEA, *Implementation*. GOV/2005/87, November 18, 2005, p. 2.
78. Ali Akbar Dareini, "Russia, Iran Sign Nuclear Fuel Deal." *Associated Press*, February 28, 2005.
79. IAEA, *Implementation*. GOV/2005/67, September 2, 2005, p. 6.
80. William Broad and David Sanger, "The Laptop: Decoding Iran's Ambitions: Relying on Computer U.S. Seeks to Prove Iran's Nuclear Aims." *New York Times*, November 13, 2005.
81. INFCIRC/648, "Communication Date August 1, 2005. Received from the Permanent Mission of the Islamic Republic of Iran." August 1, 2005; IAEA, *Implementation*. GOV/2005/67, September 2, 2005, p. 13.

82. IAEA, *Implementation*. GOV/2005/67, September 2, 2005, p. 4.

83. IAEA, *Implementation*. GOV/2005/67, September 2, 2005, p. 10.

84. "E3 Proposal to Iran, August 5, 2005." *Acronym Institute*. http://www.acronym.org.uk/docs/0508/doc03.htm

85. IAEA, *Implementation*. GOV/2005/67, September 2, 2005, p. 12.

86. IAEA, *Implementation*. GOV/2005/67, September 2, 2005, p. 5.

87. IAEA, *Implementation*. GOV/2005/67, September 2, 2005, p. 7.

88. IAEA, *Implementation*. GOV/2005/77, September 24, 2005, p. 2.

89. IAEA, *Implementation*. GOV/2005/77, September 24, 2005; Sharon Squassoni, "Iran's Nuclear Program: Recent Developments." *Congressional Research Service*, Washington DC, November 12, 2003.

90. Chen Kane, "Nuclear Decision Making in Iran: A Rare Glimpse." Brandeis University, *Crown Center for Middle East Studies*, Middle East Brief No. 5, May 2006.

91. Ibid.

92. IAEA, *Implementation*. GOV/2006/15, February 27, 2006, p. 6.

93. IAEA, *Implementation*. GOV/2005/87, November 18, 2005, p. 4; IAEA, *Implementation*. GOV/2006/15, February 27, 2006, p. 7.

94. IAEA, *Implementation*. GOV/2005/87, November 18, 2005, p. 3.

95. Richard Bernstein and David E. Sanger, "New Twist in Iran on Plan for Nuclear Fuel." *New York Times*, December 29, 2005.

96. "Iran Rejects Russian Proposal on Nuclear Program." *Iran Focus*, January 3, 2006. http://www.iranfocus.com/modules/news/article.php?storyid=5115

97. IAEA, *Implementation*. GOV/2006/15, February 27, 2006, para. 35.

98. IAEA, *Implementation*. GOV/2006/15, February 27, 2006, p. 8.

99. IAEA, Update Brief by the Deputy Director General for Safeguards, January 31, 2006, p. 4.

100. IAEA, *Implementation*. GOV/2006/15, February 27, 2006, p. 9.

101. IAEA, *Implementation*. GOV/2006/15, February 27, 2006, p. 7.

102. IAEA, Update Brief by the Deputy Director General for Safeguards, January 31, 2006, p. 3.

103. IAEA, *Implementation*. GOV/2006/15, February 27, 2006, p. 8.

104. IAEA, *Implementation*. GOV/2006/15, February 27, 2006, p. 8.

105. Sharon Squassoni, "Iran's Nuclear Program: Recent Developments." *Congressional Research Service*, Washington DC, April 12, 2006.

106. IAEA, *Implementation*. GOV/2006/14, Resolution adopted—February 4, 2006, p. 2.

107. IAEA, *Implementation*. GOV/2006/15, February 27, 2006, p. 6.

108. IAEA, *Implementation*. GOV/2006/15, February 27, 2006, pp. 6, 9.

109. IAEA, *Implementation*. GOV/2006/15, February 27, 2006, p. 9.

110. IAEA, *Implementation*. GOV/2006/15, February 27, 2006, p. 4.

111. IAEA, *Implementation*. GOV/2006/15, February 27, 2006, p. 9.

112. IAEA, *Implementation*. GOV/2006/15, February 27, 2006, para. 36; IAEA, *Implementation*. GOV/2006/27, February 28, 2006, para. 25.

113. Karl Vick, "Iran Rejects Russia's Proposal on Uranium." *Washington Post*, March 13, 2006.

114. UN Security Council, Presidential Statement SC/8679, March 29, 2006.

115. Mosaic, April 11, 2006. http://www.dahrjamailiraq.com/mosaic/mosaic.php?id=232&con=256

116. Nazila Faithi and Christine Hauser, "Iran Marks Step in Nuclear Development." *New York Times*, April 11, 2006.

117. Transcript of Excerpts from Speech on April 11 and Interview on April 13, 2006. *MEMRI*. http://www.memritv.org/Transcript.asp?P1=1120

118. David Albright, *Prepared testimony before U.S. Senate Committee on Foreign Relations*, May 17, 2006.

119. Nasser Karimi, "Iran Advances Could Speed Nuclear Project." *Associated Press*, April 17, 2006; IAEA, *Implementation*. GOV/2006/38, August 31, 2006, para. 6.

120. IAEA, *Implementation*. GOV/2006/53, August 31, 2006, para 13.

121. IAEA, *Implementation*. GOV/2006/27, April 28, 2006, p. 5.

122. Chen Kane, "Nuclear Decision Making in Iran: A Rare Glimpse." Brandeis University, *Crown Center for Middle East Studies*, No. 5, May 2006.

123. IAEA News Center, 28 April, 2006, p. 1.

124. IAEA, *Implementation*. GOV/2006/27, April 28, 2006, p. 7.

125. IAEA, *Implementation*. GOV/2006/38, June 8, 2006, p. 3; William Broad, "U.N. Finds New Uranium Traces in Iran." *New York Times*, May 13, 2006.

126. Sciolino, Elaine, "Iran Resumes Uranium Enrichment Work." *New York Times*, June 9, 2006.

127. Helene Cooper and John O'Neil, "Iran Reacts Cautiously to Deals on Trade." *New York Times*, June 6, 2006.

128. IAEA, *Implementation*. GOV/2006/38, August 31, 2006, pp. 2–3.

129. IAEA, *Implementation*. GOV/2006/38, August 31, 2006, p. 2.

130. IAEA, *Implementation*. GOV/2006/27, April 28, 2006, p. 5; IAEA, *Implementation*. GOV/2006/38, August 31, 2006, p. 3.

131. Nazila Faithi and Helene Cooper, "Iran Given June 29 Deadline to Respond to Anti-Nuke Offer." *New York Times*, June 10, 2006.

132. Con Coughlin, "Iran Accused of Hiding Secret Nuclear Weapons Site." *Telegraph News*. December 6, 2006. http://www.telegraph.co.uk/news/main.jhtml?xml=/news/2006/06/12/ wiran12.xml&sSheet=/news/2006/06/12/ixnews.html

133. IAEA, *Implementation*. GOV/2006/53, August 31, 2006, para 20.

134. "IAEA Indefinitely Freezes Iran Nuclear Aid over Plutonium Risk." *Reuters*, November 23, 2006; "Iran Offers UN New Nuclear Access." *BBC News*, November 23, 2006.

135. Helene Cooper, "Russia and China, in Shift, Inch toward Iran Sanctions." *New York Times*, July 31, 2006.

136. Hoge, Warren, "UN Moves Toward Vote on Iran's Atom Program." *New York Times*, July 28, 2006; United Nations Security Council, Resolution 1696 (2006), SC/8792, July 31, 2006. http://www.un.org/News/Press/docs//2006/sc8792.doc.htm

137. IAEA, *Implementation*. GOV/2006/53, August 31, 2006, paras. 15, 17.

138. IAEA, *Implementation*. GOV/2006/53, August 31, 2006, para. 4.

139. "Iran's Leader Vows to Continue Nuclear Program." *Associated Press*, August 21, 2006.

140. IAEA, *Implementation*. GOV/2006/53, August 31, 2006, para. 7.

141. Michael Slackman, "Iran Presents 'New Formula' for Talks." *New York Times*, August 22, 2006.

142. Craig T. Smith, "Foes Say Tehran Builds Fast Uranium Centrifuges." *New York Times*, August 25, 2006; NCRI, "New Revelations on the Mullahs' Nuclear Weapon Program." Press Conference, Paris, August 24, 2006.

143. "Defying U.N., Iran Opens Nuclear Reactor." *Associated Press*, August 26, 2006.

144. "Iran Ignores USA and Doubles Heavy Water Production." *Pravda*, August 28, 2006.

145. IAEA, *Implementation*. GOV/2006/53, August 31, 2006, para. 24.

146. IAEA, *Implementation*. GOV/2006/53, August 31, 2006, para. 2.

147. IAEA, *Implementation*. GOV/2006/53, August 31, 2006, para. 6.

148. IAEA, *Implementation*. GOV/2006/53, August 31, 2006, paras. 5, 27.

149. "Russia Agrees to Send Fuel for Iran Nuclear Plant." *New York Times*, September 27, 2006.

150. IAEA, *Implementation*. GOV/2006/64, November 14, 2006, para. 2.

151. IAEA, *Implementation*. GOV/2006/64, November 14, 2006, para. 15.

152. "Is Iran Maintaining a Clandestine Nuclear Fund?" *Spiegel Online*, November 13, 2006. http://www.spiegel.de/international/0,1518,druck-448046,00.html

153. "Iran Strongly Denies German Report on Secret Fund." *IRNA*, November 17, 2006. http://www.payvand.com/news/06/nov/1213.html

154. IAEA, *Implementation*. GOV/2006/64, November 14, 2006, para. 4.

155. "IAEA Indefinitely Freezes Iran Nuclear Aid over Plutonium Risk." *Reuters*, November 23, 2006; Nazila Faithi, "Iran Says It Will Build Heavy-Water Reactor Without Agency's Help." *New York Times*, November 24, 2006.

156. "Iran Offers UN New Nuclear Access. *BBC News*, November 23, 2006; Nazila Faithi, "Iran Says It Will Build Heavy-Water Reactor Without Agency's Help." *New York Times*, November 24, 2006; IAEA, *Implementation*. GOV/2006/64, November 14, 2006, paras. 4, 18.

157. James A. Baker, III, and Lee H. Hamilton, Co-Chairs, *The Iraq Study Group Report*. New York: Vintage Books, December 2006, pp. 52–53. http://graphics8.nytimes.com/packages/pdf/international/20061206_btext.pdf

158. Ali Akbar Dareini, "Iran Expands Uranium Enrichment Program." *Associated Press*, December 9, 2006; "Iranian President Says 3,000 Centrifuges Set at Natanz." *RIA Novosti*, December 9, 2006.

159. Ali Akbar Dareini, *Associated Press*, "Ahmadinejad Opponents Win Elections." *New York Times*, December 21, 2006.

160. Elissa Gootman, "Security Council Approves Sanctions Against Iran over Nuclear Program." *New York Times*, December 23, 2006; United Nations Security Council, Resolution 1737, Adopted on December 23, 2006, S/Res/1737(2006), December 27, 2006.

161. *Reuters*, "Key Points in the UN Security Council Resolution on Iran." *Haaretz*, December 23, 2006.

162. Helene Cooper and Steven R. Weisman, "West Tries a New Tack to Block Iran's Nuclear Agenda." *New York Times*, January 2, 2007.

163. "Second U.S. Carrier Group to Deploy to Gulf: Sources." *Reuters*, January 3, 2007. http://today.reuters.com/news/articlenews.aspx?type=topNews&storyID=2007-01-03T202056Z_01_N03190103_RTRUKOC_0_US-USA-GULF-NAVY.xml

164. President's Address to the Nation, White House, January 10, 2007. http://www.whitehouse.gov/news/releases/2007/01/20070110-7.html

165. Parisa Hafezi, "Iran Wants Atom Talks Without Condition." *Reuters*, *Washington Post*, February 20, 2007.

166. *Associated Press*, "Iran Should Give 'Sanctions Serious Response,' China Says." *New York Times*, January 6, 2007.

167. Ibid.

168. Uzi Mahnaimi and Sarah Baxter, "Revealed: Israel Plans Nuclear Strike on Iran." *Sunday Times*, January 7, 2007. http://www.timesonline.co.uk/article/0,,2089-2535310,00.html

169. Golnaz Esfandian, RFE/RL, "Iran: Former Official, Reformists Criticize Government's Nuclear Policy." *Payvand's Iran News*, January 1, 2007. http://www.payvand.com/news/07/jan/1123.html

170. Yossi Melman, "How to Obtain Nuclear Weapons Without Infuriating the World." *Haaretz*, January 1, 2007.

171. Nazila Faithi and Michael Slackman, "Iran's President Criticized over Nuclear Issue." *The New York Times*, January 18, 2007.

172. Nazila Faithi, "Iran Bars Inspectors; Cleric Criticizes President." *New York Times*, January 25, 2007.

173. *Associated Press*, "Iran Nuclear Program Stalled?" *Washington Times*, January 11, 2007.

174. "Russia Completes Air Defense System Deliveries to Iran—Ivanov." *RIA Novosti*, January 16, 2007. http://en.rian.ru/russia/20070116/59156706.html; "Russia to Sell 29 Air Defense Systems to Iran." *Pravda*, December 3, 2005. http://english.pravda.ru/main/18/88/354/16570_Iran.html

175. *Reuters*, "IAEA Confirms Iran Barred Entry Of 38 Nuclear Inspectors." *Haaretz*, January 22, 2007.

176. *AFP*, "Iran's Nuclear Negotiator Phones UN Watchdog Chief." *Yahoo News*, January 23, 2007. http://news.yahoo.com/s/afp/20070123/wl_mideast_afp/irannuclearpoliticsuniaea_070123141529

177. IAEA Board of Governors, *Implementation of the NPT Safeguards Agreement and Relevant Provisions of Security Council Resolution 1737 (2006) in the Islamic Republic of Iran*. Report by the Director General, GOV/2007/8, February 22, 2007, para. 23.

178. "Dr. ElBaradei Calls for "Timeout" on Iran Nuclear Issue." *IAEA.org*, January 29, 2007. http://www.iaea.org/NewsCenter/News/2007/iran_timeout.html

179. *Reuters*, "Iran Sets Up 328 Centrifuges at Big Atom Site: Sources." *New York Times*, February 5, 2007.

180. *Associated Press*, "Iran's Khamenei Warns U.S. of Retaliation if Attacked." *USA Today*, February 8, 2007.

181. *Associated Press*, "IAEA Suspends Nearly Half of Technical Aid Projects with Tehran." *Haaretz*, February 10, 2007.

182. Molly Moore, "E.U. Nations to Impose Limited Sanctions on Iran." *Washington Post*, February 13, 2007; Valerie Lincy and Gary Milhollin, "Iran's Nuclear Web." *New York Times*, February 13, 2007.

183. Andrew E. Kramer, "Russia Will Slow Work on Iran's Nuclear Plant." *New York Times*, February 22, 2007; "Iran Ready to Settle NPP Debt Issue with Russia." *RNA Novosti*, February 22, 2007.

184. Dafna Linzer, Colum Lynch, and William Branigin, "Iran Continues to Pursue Nuclear Program, Report Finds." *Washington Post*, February 22, 2007; IAEA Board of Governors, *Implementation of the NPT Safeguards Agreement and Relevant Provisions of*

*Security Council Resolution 1737 (2006) in the Islamic Republic of Iran*. Report by the Director General, GOV/2007/8, February 22, 2007.

185. *Associated Press*, "Ahmadinejad: Iran Won't End Nuke Program." *New York Times*, February 25, 2007.

186. *Associated Press*, "India Bans Nuclear Exports to Iran." *Yahoo*, February 21, 2007.

187. *Associated Press*, "Brazil Implements U.N. Sanctions Against Iran." *International Herald Tribune*, February 22, 2007.

188. Con Coughlin, "Ready for war." *Daily Telegraph*, February 24, 2007. http://www.telegraph.co.uk/news/main.jhtml;jsessionid=A5CD1UCUKDEZJQFIQMFCFFOA VCBQYIV0?
xml=/news/2007/02/24/nriran24.xml

189. Elaine Sciolino, "Russia Makes Threat to Keep Nuclear Fuel From Iran." *New York Times*, March 19, 2007.

190. Thom Shanker, "Security Council Votes to Tighten Iran Sanctions." *New York Times*, March 25, 2007; UN Security Council, Resolution 1747 (2007), Adopted March 24, 2007. http://daccessdds.un.org/doc/UNDOC/GEN/N07/281/40/PDF/N0728140.pdf?OpenElement

191. Thom Shanker and William J. Broad, "Iran to Limit Cooperation With Nuclear Inspectors." *New York Times*, March 26, 2007; Nasser Karmi, *Associated Press*, "Iran Partly Suspends Nuclear Pledge." *Washington Post*, March 26, 2007; *Associated Press*, "Iran: Decision to Withhold Information Due to Fear of U.S., Israel Attack." *Haaretz*, March 31, 2007.

192. *Reuters*, "IAEA Pushes Iran to Accept Cameras at Key Atom Site." *New York Times*, March 30, 2007; *AP*, "Iran: Decision to Withhold Information Due to Fear of U.S., Israel Attack." *Haaretz*, March 31, 2007.

193. "Iran's Larijani Holds "Clear Talks" with Solana." *Reuters*, March 26, 2007. http://www.reuters.com/article/idUSL264423320070326

194. Raf Casert, *Associated Press*, " Talks on Iran's Nuclear Program Resume." *Yahoo*. http://news.yahoo.com/s/ap/20070405/ap_on_re_eu/iran_nuclear

195. Nazila Faithi, "Iran Says It Can Enrich Uranium on an Industrial Scale." *New York Times*, April 10, 2007.

196. Vladimir Isachenkov, "Russia, France Doubt Iran Nuclear Claims." *Associated Press*, April 10, 2007. http://news.yahoo.com/s/ap/20070410/ap_on_re_mi_ea/nuclear_iran_3

197. "UN Nuclear Watchdog; Iran's Program Limited." *IranMania*, April 13, 2007. http://www.iranmania.com/News/ArticleView/Default.asp?NewsCode=50894&NewsKind=Current%20Affairs

198. "Aghazadeh: 270 Tons of UF6 Produced in Iran." *IRNA*, April 9, 2007.

199. *Associated Press*, "Iran to Build 2 Nuclear Power Plants." *New York Times*, April 15, 2007.

200. Dafna Linzer, "Boost in Iran's Capacity to Enrich Uranium Noted." *Washington Post*, March 19, 2007.

201. *Reuters*, "Iran, EU to Hold Atomic Talks in Turkey." *New York Times*, April 23, 2007.

202. Sabrina Tavernise, "Iran: Nuclear Negotiators Cautiously Upbeat." *New York Times*, April 27, 2007.

203. *Reuters*, "Iran Says Near Unity with EU in Some Nuclear Areas." *New York Times*, April 26, 2007.

204. "U.S. Denies Mulling Proposal to Allow Iran to Continue Enrichment." *Haaretz*, April 25, 2007.

205. Michael Adler, "EU Chief Solana Meets Iran's Nuclear Negotiator." *Reuters*, April 25, 2007, http://news.yahoo.com/s/afp/20070425/wl_mideast_afp/irannuclearpoliticseu_070425192043

206. Aljazeera.net, "Iran arrests ex-nuclear official," May 2 2007. http://english.aljazeera.net/NR/exeres/276705EB-5E52-4C9A-8D5C-91C34034F03A.htm

207. IAEA, *Implementation*. GOV/2007/22, May 23, 2007, para. 4.

208. Joby Warrick, "Tunneling Near Iranian Nuclear Site Stirs Worry." *Washington Post*, July 9, 2007.

209. Nazila Faithi, "Fuel Rationing in Iran Prompts Lines and Protests." *New York Times*, June 27, 2007.

210. Michael Adler, *AFP*, "Iran has slowed down its nuclear work: UN nuclear chief ElBaradei." *Yahoo*, July 9, 2007; Mark Heinrich, *Reuters*, "Diplomats say scant recent progress in Iran atom work." *Yahoo*, August 3, 2007.

211. IAEA, *Implementation*, GOV/2007/48, August 30, 2007, para. 21.

212. Guy Faulconbridge, *Reuters*, "Russia delays Iran nuclear plant to 2008." *Yahoo*, July 25, 2007.

213. *Reuters*, "IAEA, Iran Agree Visit At Disputed Reactor Site." *New York Times*, July 13 2007; Fredrik Dahl, *Reuters*, "U.N. inspectors revisit Iran's Arak heavy-water site." *Yahoo*, July 30, 2007.

214. Robin Wright, "Iran Unit To Be Labeled 'Terrorist'." *Washington Post*, August 15, 2007.

215. IAEA, *Communication dated 27 August from the Permanent Mission of the Islamic Republic of Iran to the Agency concerning the text of the "Understandings of the* Islamic Republic of Iran and the IAEA on Modalities of Resolution of the Outstanding Issues, INFCIRC/711, August 27, 2007.

216. IAEA, *Implementation*, GOV/2007/48, August 30, 2007, paras. 3-6

217. IAEA, *Communication dated 27 August from the Permanent Mission of the Islamic Republic of Iran to the Agency concerning the text of the "Understandings of the Islamic Republic of Iran and the IAEA on Modalities of Resolution of the Outstanding Issues*, INFCIRC/711, August 27, 2007.

218. Elaine Sciolino, "French Leader Raises Possibility of Use of Force in Iran." *New York Times*, August 28, 2007.

219. IAEA, *Implementation*, GOV/2007/48, August 30, 2007, paras. 3-6.

220. Michael Slackman and Nazila Faithi, "Iran Reaffirms Its Defiance of West." *New York Times*, September 2, 2007; Michael Slackman and Nazila Faithi, "On Two Fronts, One Nuclear, Iran Is Defiant." *New York Times*, September 3, 2007.

# Selected Bibliography

## BOOKS, STUDIES, REPORTS


Afrasiabi, Kaveh L. *Iran's Nuclear Program: Debating Facts Versus Fiction* (Charleston, SC: BookSurge Publishing) 2006.

Alamdari, Kazem. *Why the Middle East Lagged Behind: The Case of Iran* (Lanham, MD: University Press of America) 2005.

Alexander, Yonah, ed. *Combating Terrorism: Strategies of Ten Countries* (Ann Arbor, MI: University of Michigan Press) 2002.

———. *Counterterrorism Strategies: Successes and Failures of Six Nations* (Dulles, VA: Potomac Books Inc.) 2006.

———. *International Terrorism: National, Regional, and Global Perspectives* (Westport, CT: Praeger Publishers) 1976.

———. *Middle East Terrorism: Current Threats and Future Prospects* (Boston, MA: G.K. Hall and Company) 1994.

———. *Middle East Terrorism: Selected Group Profiles* (Washington, DC: JINSA) 1994.

———. *Palestinian Religious Terrorism: A Profile of Hamas and Islamic Jihad* (Ardsley, NY: Transnational Publications) 2002.

———. *Palestinian Secular Terrorism: Profiles of Fatah, Popular Front for the Liberation of Palestine, and Democratic Front for the Liberation of Palestine* (Ardsley, NY: Transnational Publications) 2003.

———. *The Role of Communication in the Middle East Conflict: Ideological and Religious Aspects* (Westport, CT: Praeger Publishers) 1973.

Alexander, Yonah and Brenner, Edgar H., ed. *U.S. Federal Legal Response to Terrorism* (Ardsley, NY: Transnational Publications) 2002.

Alexander, Yonah and Hoenig, Milton, ed. *Super Terrorism: Biological, Chemical, Nuclear* (Ardsley, NY: Transnational Publications) 2001.

Alexander, Yonah and Kittrie, Nicholas N., ed. *Crescent and Star: Arab and Israeli Perspectives on the Middle East* (Brooklyn, NY: AMS Press) 1973.

Alexander, Yonah and Nanes, Allan S., ed. *The United States and Iran: A Documentary History* (Frederick, MD: University Publications of America) 1980.

Alexander, Yonah and Sinai, Joshua. *Terrorism: The PLO Connection* (New York, NY: Crane Russak) 1989.

Alexander, Yonah and Swetnam, Michael S., ed. *Usama bin Laden's al-Qaida: Profile of a Terrorist Network* (Ardsley, NY: Transnational Publications) 2001.

Allison, Graham, et al. *Nuclear Proliferation: Risks and Responsibility.* A Report to the Trilateral Commission (Washington, DC: Trilateral Commission) 2006.

Ansari, Ali M. *Confronting Iran: The Failure of American Foreign Policy and the Next Great Crisis in the Middle East* (Jackson, TN: Basic Books) 2006.

——— *Iran, Islam and Democracy: The Politics of Managing Change* (London: Chatham House) 2006.

Badiozamani, Badi. *Iran and America: Rekindling a Love Lost* (San Diego, CA: East-West Understanding Press) 2005.

Beeman, William O. *The "Great Satan" vs. the "Mad Mullahs": How the United States and Iran Demonize Each Other* (Westport, CT: Praeger Publishers) 2005.

Berman, Ilan. *Tehran Rising: Iran's Challenge to the United States* (Lanham, MD: Rowman & Littlefield Publishers, Inc.) 2005.

Bin Salman al-Saud, Faisal. *Iran, Saudi Arabia and the Gulf: Power Politics in Transition* (London: I.B. Tauris) 2004.

Blake, M. *A Nation Under Siege: Nukes, Mullahs, and the Ultimate Nightmare* (Boston, MA: Blake Press) 2005.

Bowden, Mark. *Guests of the Ayatollah: The Iran Hostage Crisis: The First Battle in America's War with Militant Islam* (New York, NY: Grove Press) 2007.

Buchta, Wilfried. *Who Rules Iran? The Structure of Power in the Islamic Republic* (Washington, DC: Washington Institute for Near East Policy) 2001.

Busch, Nathan E. *No End in Sight: The Continuing Menace of Nuclear Proliferation* (Lexington, KY: University Press of Kentucky) 2003.

Byman, Daniel. *Deadly Connections: States that Sponsor Terrorism* (Cambridge: Cambridge University Press) 2005.

————. *Iran's Security Policy in the Post-Revolutionary Era* (Santa Monica, CA: RAND) 2001.

Chehabi, H.E., Abisaab, Rula Jurdi, Hollinger, Richard, and Harik, Judith. *Distant Relations: Iran and Lebanon in the Last 500 Years* (New York, NY: St. Martin's Press) 2006.

Chubin, Shahram. *Iran's Nuclear Ambitions* (Washington, DC: Carnegie Endowment for International Peace) 2006.

Clawson, Patrick. *Iran's Strategic Intentions and Capabilities* (Honolulu, HI: University Press of the Pacific) 2004.

Clawson, Patrick and Eisenstadt, Michael. *Deterring the Ayatollahs: Complications in Applying Cold War Strategy to Iran* (Washington, DC: Washington Institute for Near East Policy) 2007.

Clawson, Patrick and Rubin, Michael. *Eternal Iran: Continuity and Chaos* (New York, NY: Palgrave Macmillan) 2005.

Clawson, Patrick and Sokolski, Henry. *Checking Iran's Nuclear Ambitions* (Honolulu, HI: University Press of the Pacific) 2004.

Clawson, Patrick and Sokolski, Henry, ed. *Getting Ready for a Nuclear-Ready Iran* (Carlisle, PA: Strategic Studies Institute of the U.S. Army War College) 2005.

Cline, Ray S. and Alexander, Yonah. *Terrorism as State-Sponsored Covert Warfare* (Fairfax, VA: HERO Books) 1986.

Cordesman, Anthony H. *Iran's Developing Military Capabilities* (Washington, DC: Center for Strategic and International Studies) 2005.

———. *Iran's Weapons of Mass Destruction: The Real and Potential Threat* (Washington, DC: Center for Strategic and International Studies) 2006.

Corsi, Jerome R. *Atomic Iran: How the Terrorist Regime Bought the Bomb and American Politicians* (Medford, OR: WND Books) 2005.

Cronin, Stephanie. *Reformers and Revolutionaries in Modern Iran: New Perspectives On The Iranian Left* (Oxford: RoutledgeCurzon) 2004.

Dabashi, Hamid. *Iran: A People Interrupted* (New York, NY: New Press) 2007.

———. *Theology of Discontent: The Ideological Foundation of the Islamic Revolution in Iran* (Piscataway, NJ: Transaction Publishers) 2005.

Davis, Scott C. *The Road from Damascus: A Journey through Syria with Reflections on Radical Islam, Terrorism, Sunnis, Shi'ites, the Hezbollah and the Hamas* (Seattle, WA: Cune Press) 2001.

De Bellaigue, Christopher. *The Struggle for Iran* (New York, NY: New York Review Books) 2007.

Desutter, Paula. *Denial and Jeopardy: Deterring Iranian Use of NBC Weapons* (Honolulu, HI: University Press of the Pacific) 2002.

Diaz, Tom and Newman, Barbara. *Lightning out of Lebanon: Hezbollah Terrorists on American Soil* (New York, NY: Random House) 2005.

Diba, Bahman Aghai. *FAQ About the Nuclear Case of Iran* (Charleston, SC: BookSurge Publishing) 2006.

Drell, Sidney D. *The Gravest Danger: Nuclear Weapons* (Stanford, CA: Hoover Institution Press) 2003.

Emirates Centre for Strategic Studies and Research. *Iran's Nuclear Program: Realities and Repercussions* (Abu Dhabi, UAE: Emirates Center for Strategic Studies) 2007.

Evans, Michael D. and Corsi, Jerome R. *Showdown with Nuclear Iran: Radical Islam's Messianic Mission to Destroy Israel and Cripple the United States* (Nashville, TN: Thomas Nelson) 2006.

Farber, David. *Taken Hostage: The Iran Hostage Crisis and America's First Encounter with Radical Islam* (Princeton, NJ: Princeton University Press) 2004.

Farmanfarmaian, Manucher, and Farmanfarmaian, Roxane. *Blood and Oil: A Prince's Memoir of Iran, from the Shah to the Ayatollah* (New York, NY: Random House) 2005.

Ganji, Babak. *Politics of Confrontation: The Foreign Policy of the USA and Revolutionary Iran* (London: Tauris Academic Studies) 2006.

Gheissari, Ali. *Democracy in Iran: History and the Quest for Liberty* (Oxford: Oxford University Press) 2006.

Goodarzi, Jubin. *Syria and Iran: Diplomatic Alliance and Power Politics in the Middle East* (New York, NY: St. Martin's Press) 2006.

Griffiths, Eldon. *Turbulent Iran: Recollections, Revelations and a Plan for Peace* (Santa Ana, CA: Seven Locks Press) 2006.

Harik, Judith Palmer. *Hezbollah: The Changing Face of Terrorism* (London: I.B. Tauris) 2004.

Harmon, Daniel, Todd, Anne M., and Marty, Martin E. *Ayatollah Ruhollah Khomeini* (New York, NY: Chelsea House Publishers) 2004.

Hassan, George. *Iran: Harsh Arm of Islam* (Santa Ana, CA: Seven Locks Press) 2005.

Heffelfinger, Christopher, ed. *Unmasking Terror: A Global Review of Terrorist Activities* (Washington, DC: Jamestown Foundation) 2004.

Hiro, Dilip. *Iran Under the Ayatollahs* (Oxford: Routledge and Kegan Paul) 1987.

Hitchcock, Mark. *The Coming Crisis: Radical Islam, Oil, and the Nuclear Threat* (Portland, OR: Multnomah) 2006.

Howard, Roger. *Iran Oil: The New Middle East Challenge to America* (London: I.B. Tauris) 2007.

Hroub, Khaled. *Hamas: Political Thought and Practice* (Beirut: Institute of Palestinian Studies) 2000.

Hunter, Shireen. *Iran after Khomeini* (Washington, DC: Center for Strategic International Studies) 1992.

Iklé, Fred Charles. *Annihilation from Within: The Ultimate Threat to Nations* (New York, NY: Colombia University Press) 2006.

Iran Policy Committee. *What Makes Tehran Tick: Islamist Ideology and Hegemonic Interests* (Washington, DC: Iran Policy Committee) 2006.

Jafarzadeh, Alireza. *The Iran Threat: President Ahmadinejad and the Coming Nuclear Crisis* (New York, NY: Palgrave Macmillan) 2007.

James, Bill A. *The Eagle and the Lion: The Tragedy of American-Iranian Relations* (New Haven, CT: Yale University Press) 1988.

Jorish, Avi. *Beacon of Hatred: Inside Hizballah's Al-Manar Television* (Washington, DC: Washington Institute for Near East Policy) 2004.

Kam, Ephraim. *A Nuclear Iran: What Does it Mean, and What Can be Done* (Washington, DC: Institute for National Strategic Studies) 2007.

Katouzian, Homa. *Iranian History and Politics: State and Society in Perpetual Conflict* (Oxford: Routledge Curzon) 2003.

Katz, Samuel M. *The Hunt for the Engineer: The Inside Story of How Israel's Counterterrorist Forces Tracked and Killed the Hamas Master Bomber* (Guilford, CT: The Lyons Press) 2002.

Keddie, Nikki R. *Modern Iran: Roots and Results Of Revolution* (New Haven, CT: Yale University Press) 2006.

Keddie, Nikki R. and Matthee, Rudolph P. *Iran and the Surrounding World: Interactions in Culture and Cultural Politics* (Seattle, WA: University of Washington Press) 2002.

Kile, Shannon L., ed. *Europe and Iran: Perspectives on Non-proliferation* (Oxford: Oxford University Press) 2005.

Kinzer, Stephen. *All The Shah's Men: An American Coup and the Roots of Middle East Terror* (Indianapolis, IN: John Wiley & Sons) 2003.

Laqueur, Walter. *Voices of Terror* (New York, NY: Reed Press) 2004.

Lavoy, Peter R., Sagan, Douglas Scott and Wirtz, James J. *Planning the Unthinkable: How New Powers Will Use Nuclear, Biological, and Chemical Weapons* (Ithaca, NY: Cornell University Press) 2000.

Lennon, Alexander T. J. and Eiss, Camille, ed. *Reshaping Rogue States: Preemption, Regime Change, and U.S. Policy towards Iran, Iraq, and North Korea* (Cambridge, MA: MIT Press) 2004.

Leventhal, Paul and Alexander, Yonah, ed. *Nuclear Terrorism: Defining the Threat* (Washington, DC: Pergamon-Brassey's) 1986.

———. *Preventing Nuclear Terrorism: The Reports and Papers of the International Task Force on Prevention of Nuclear Terrorism* (Lanham, MD: Lexington Books) 1987.

Levitt, Matthew. *Hamas: Politics, Charity, and Terrorism in the Service of Jihad* (Harrisonburg, VA: R.R. Donnelley) 2006.

Litwak, Robert S. *Regime Change: U.S. Strategies through the Prism of 9/11* (Baltimore, MD: John Hopkins University Press) 2007.

Mackey, Sandra. *The Iranians: Persia, Islam and the Soul of a Nation* (New York, NY: Plume) 1998.

Marschall, Christin. *Iran's Persian Gulf Policy: From Khomeini to Khatami* (Oxford: RoutledgeCurzon) 2003.

Melman, Yossi. *The Nuclear Sphinx of Teheran: Mahmoud Ahmadinejad and the State of Iran* (New York, NY: Carrol & Graf) 2007.

Mishal, Shaul and Sela, Avraham. *The Palestinian Hamas: Vision, Violence, and Coexistence* (New York, NY: Colombia University Press) 2006.

Moallem, Minoo. *Between Warrior Brother and Veiled Sister: Islamic Fundamentalism and the Politics of Patriarchy in Iran* (Barkeley, CA: University of California Press) 2005.

Molavi, Afshin. *The Soul of Iran: A Nation's Journey to Freedom* (New York, NY: W.W. Norton and Company Inc.) 2004.

Nabavi, Negin. *Intellectuals And The State In Iran: Politics, Discourse, and the Dilemma of Authenticity* (Gainesville, FL: University Press of Florida) 2003.

Nasr, Seyyed Vali Reza. *The Shia Revival: How Conflicts Within Islam Will Shape The Future* (New York, NY: W.W. Norton and Company Inc.) 2006.

Nincic, Miroslav. *Renegade Regimes: Confronting Deviant Behavior in World Politics*, (New York, NY: Colombia University Press) 2005.

O'Ballance, Edgar. *Islamist Fundamentalist Terrorism, 1979–1995: The Iranian Connection* (New York, NY: New York University Press) 1997.

Pahlavi, Reza. *Winds of Change: The Future of Democracy in Iran* (Washington, DC: Regnery Publishing, Inc.) 2002.

Pelletiere, Stephen. *Hamas and Hizbollah: The Radical Challenge to Israel in the Occupied Territories* (Honolulu, HI: University Press of the Pacific) 2005.

Pollack, Kenneth. *The Persian Puzzle: The Conflict Between Iran and America* (New York, NY: Random House Trade Paperbacks) 2005.

Rahnema, Saeed and Behdad, Sohrab. *Iran after the Revolution: Crisis of an Islamic State* (London: I.B. Tauris) 1996.

Ridgeon, Lloyd. *Religion and Politics in Modern Iran: A Reader* (London: I.B. Tauris) 2005.

Ritter, Scott. *Target Iran: The Truth About the White House's Plan for Regime Change* (New York, NY: Nation Books) 2006.

Roger, Paul. *A War Too Far: Iraq, Iran and the New American Century* (London: Pluto Press) 2006.

Rubin, Uzi. *The Global Reach of Iran's Ballistic Missiles* (Washington, DC: Institute for National Security Studies) 2006.

Rueda, Edwin. *New Terrorism? A Case Study of Al-Qaida and the Lebanese Hezbollah* (Washington, DC: Storming Media) 2001.

Saad-Ghorayeb, Amal. *Hizbu'llah: Politics and Religion* (London: Pluto Press) 2002.

Samore, Gary. *Iran's Strategic Weapons Programmes: A Net Assessment* (Oxford: Routledge) 2005.

Satloff, Robert, ed. *Hamas Triumphant: Implications for Security, Politics, Economy, and Strategy* (Washington, DC: Washington Institute for Near East Policy) 2006.

Schake, Kori N. and Share Yaphe, Judith. *The Strategic Implications of a Nuclear-Armed Iran* (Honolulu, HI: University Press of the Pacific) 2004.

Schirazi, Ashgar. *The Constitution of Iran: Politics and the State in the Islamic Republic* (London: I.B. Tauris) 1998.

Schnorr, Michael. *Iran: Progenitor of the New Cold War* (Bloomington, IN: Authorhouse) 2004.

Schwartz, Milton. *Iran: Political Issues, Nuclear Capabilities, and Missile Range* (London: Nova Science Publishers) 2006.

Sciolino, Elaine. *Persian Mirrors: The Elusive Face of Iran* (New York, NY: Free Press) 2005.

Shai, Shaul. *The Axis of Evil: Iran, Hizballah, and Palestinian Terror* (Piscataway, NJ: Transaction Publishers) 2005.

Shay, Shaul. *The Axis of Evil: Iran, Hizballah, and the Palestinian Terror* (Piscataway, NJ: Transaction Publishers) 2005.

Shirazi, Saeed. *A Concise History of Iran* (Frederick, MD: PublishAmerica) 2005.

Sokolski, Henry D. and Clawson, Patrick. *Checking Iran's Nuclear Ambitions* (Honolulu, HI: University Press of the Pacific) 2004.

Steinberg, Oliver, Steinberg, Anne-Marie, and Steinberg, Paul F. *The Road to Martyr's Square: A Journey into the World of the Suicide Bomber* (Oxford: Oxford University Press) 2005.

Takeyh, Ray. *Hidden Iran: Paradox and Power in the Islamic Republic* (New York, NY: Holt Paperbacks) 2007.

Tapper, Richard. *Islam and Democracy in Iran: Eshkevari and the Quest for Reform* (London: I.B. Tauris) 2006.

Timmerman, Kenneth R. *Countdown to Crisis: The Coming Nuclear Showdown with Iran* (New York, NY: Three Rivers Press) 2006.

Venter, Al. *Iran's Nuclear Option: Tehran's Quest for the Atom Bomb* (Drexel Hill, PA: Casemate) 2005.

Zak, Chen. *Iran's Nuclear Policy and the IAEA: An Evaluation of Program 93+2* (Washington, DC: Washington Institute for Near East Policy) 2002.

Zuhur, Sherifa D. *Iran, Iraq, and the United States: The New Triangle's Impact on Sectarianism and the Nuclear Threat* (Carlisle, PA: Strategic Studies Institute) 2006.

## ARTICLES

Abdo, Geneive. "From Revolution to Revelations: Khatami's Iran Struggles for Reform," *Middle East Report* No. 211, Summer 1999, pp. 7–9.

Aghajanian, Akbar. "Ethnic Inequality in Iran: An Overview," *International Journal of Middle East Studies* 15(2), March 2007, pp. 211–224.

———. "Population Change in Iran, 1966–1986: A Stalled Demographic Transition? *Population and Development Review* 17(4), 1991, pp. 703–715.

Ahmad, Eqbal. "Comprehending Terror," *MERIP Middle East Report* No. 140, 1986, pp. 2–5.

Ahmed, Feroz. "Iran: Subimperialism in Action," *Pakistan Forum* 3(67), 1973, pp. 10–18, 20.

Ajami, Fouad. "Iran: The Impossible Revolution," *Foreign Affairs* 67(2), 1989, pp. 135–155.

Amin, S.H. "The Iran-Iraq Conflict: Legal Implications," *The International and Comparative Law Quarterly* 31(1), 1982, pp. 167–188.

Andriolo, Karin. "Murder by Suicide: Episodes from Muslim History," *American Anthropologist* 104(3), 1982, pp. 736–742.

Arjomand, Said Amir. "History, Structure, and Revolution in the Shi'ite Tradition in Contemporary Iran," *International Political Science Review* 10(2), 1989, pp. 111–119.

Arkin, William M. "Iran and the Virtual Reality of US War Games," *Middle East Report* 197, 1995, pp. 10–13.

Asculai, Ephraim and Landau, Emily, "Developments on the North Korean Nuclear Axis: Parallels with Iran," *Strategic Assessment* 9(4), March 2007 pp. 42–47.

Bakhash, Shaul and Wright, Robin. "The U.S. and Iran: An Offer They Can't Refuse," *Foreign Policy* 108, Autumn 1997, pp. 124–137.

Barr, Cameron. "Stranger than Fiction," *American Lawyer* 12(10), 1990, pp. 70–73.

Beck, Lois. "Revolutionary Iran and Its Tribal Peoples," *Middle East Research and Information Project Reports* 87, 1990, pp. 14–20.

Beeman, William O. "Iran's Religious Regime: What Makes It Tick? Will It Ever Run Down?" *Annals of the American Academy of Political and Social Science* 483, 1986, pp. 73–83.

———. "Iran and the United States: Postmodern Culture Conflict in Action," *Anthropological Quarterly* 76(4), 2003, pp. 671–691.

Berman, Ilan et al. "Iran: Confronting the Threat," *The Journal of International Security Affairs* 11, Fall 2006, pp. 69–74.

Betts, Richard K. "Incentives for Nuclear Weapons: India, Pakistan, Iran," *Asian Survey* 19(11), November 1979, pp. 1053–1072.

Bill, James A. "Iran and the United States: A Clash of Hegemonies," *Middle East Report* 212, Autumn 1999, pp. 44–46.

Chubin, Shahram. "Iran's Security in the 1980s," *International Security* 2(3), 1978, pp. 51–80.

Cirincione, Joseph. "Can Preventive War Cure Proliferation?" *Foreign Policy* 137, July–August 2003, pp. 66–69.

Clawson, Patrick. "Could sanctions work against Tehran? (Employment of UN de facto sanctions against Iran's nuclear ambitions)," *Middle East Quarterly* 14(1), January 2007, pp. 13–20.

———. "Iran's Economy: Between Crisis and Collapse," *Middle East Research and Information Project Reports* 98, 1981, pp. 11–15.

Clawson, Patrick and Rubin, Michael. "Patterns of Discontent: Will History Repeat in Iran?" *Middle East Quarterly* March 2006, no page numbers listed.

Cogan, Charles G. "Not To Offend: Observations on Iran, the Hostages, and the Hostage Rescue Mission—Ten Years Later," *Comparative Strategy* 9(4), 1990, pp. 415–432.

Cottom, Richard. "Goodbye to America's Shah," *Foreign Policy* 34, 1979, p. 314.

Crenshaw, Martha. "The Causes of Terrorism," *Comparative Politics* 13(4), 1981, pp. 379–399.

"Easing of U.S.–Iran Economic Sanctions," *The American Journal of International Law* 94(4), 2000, pp. 699–700.

Ehsani, Kaveh. "High Stakes for Iran," *Middle East Report* 227, Summer 2003, pp. 38–41.

———. "Municipal Matters: The Urbanization of Consciousness and Political Change in Tehran," *Middle East Report* 212, Autumn 1999, pp. 22–27.

El Azhary, M.S. "The Attitudes of the Superpowers towards the Gulf War," *International Affairs* 59(4), 1983 pp. 609–620.

Falk, Richard A. "Khomeini's Promise," *Foreign Policy* 34, 1979, pp. 28–34.

Fatemi, Khosrow. "The Iranian Revolution: Its Impact on Economic Relations with the United States," *International Journal of Middle East Studies* 12(3), 1980, pp. 303–317.

Fuller, Graham E. "The Emergence of Central Asia," *Foreign Policy* 78, 1990, pp. 49–67.

Gharenhbaghian, Morteza. "Oil Revenue and the Militarisation of Iran: 1960–1978," *Social Scientist* 15(4/5), 1987, pp. 87–100.

Green, Jerrold D. "Countermobilization as a Revolutionary Form," *Comparative Politics* 16(2), 1984, pp. 153–169.

Gvosdev, Nikolas K. "A Dose of Realism on Russia," *The Journal of International Security Affairs* 11, Fall 2006, pp. 103–108.

Halliday, Fred. "Iran and the Middle East: Foreign Policy and Domestic Change," *Middle East Report* 220, Autumn 2001, pp. 42–47.

———. "Iran's New Grand Strategy," *Middle East Research and Information Project Middle East Report* 144, 1987 pp. 7–8.

———. "Is Europe Soft on Terrorism?" *Foreign Policy* 115, 1999, pp. 62–76.

———. "The Revolution's First Decade," *Middle East Report* 156, 1989, pp. 19–21.

Himelfarb, Joel. "Slaughter in the Skies," *Near East Report* 34(33), 1990, p. 156.

"Hizballah Prepares Car-Bombs for Europe," *Mednews* 3(11), 1990, pp. 3–4.

Hooglund, Eric. "Iranian Populism and Political Change in the Gulf," *Middle East Report* 174, 1992, pp. 19–21.

———. "Iranian Views of the Arab-Israeli Conflict," *Journal of Palestine Studies* 25(1), 1995, pp. 86–95.

———. "Reagan's Iran: Factions Behind US Policy in the Gulf," *Middle East Report* 151, March 1988, pp. 28–31.

———. "The Islamic Republic at War and Peace," *Middle East Report*, 156, 1989, pp. 4–12.

Hunter, Shireen T. "After the Ayatollah," *Foreign Policy* 1987, pp. 77–97.

"Iran and the Gulf Arabs," *Middle East Report* 156, 1989, pp. 23–24.

"Iran's Nuclear Program," *The American Journal of International Law* 99(1), January 2005, pp. 270–271.

"Iran's Rate of Population Growth—Nearly Four Percent Annually—Is One of the World's Highest," *International Family Planning Perspectives* 15(1), 1989, pp. 41–42.

Johnstone, Diana. "'Little Satan' Stuck in the Arms Export Trap," *Middle East Research and Information Project Middle East Report* 148, 1987, pp. 8–9.

Kamrava, Mehran. "The Civil Society Discourse in Iran," *British Journal of Middle Eastern Studies* 28(2), November 2001, pp. 165–185.

Karsh, Efraim. "Military Power and Foreign Policy Goals: The Iran-Iraq War Revisited," *International Affairs* 64(1), 1987, pp. 83–95.

Katouzian, Homa. "Problems of Political Development in Iran: Democracy, Dictatorship or Arbitrary," *British Journal of Middle East Studies* 22(1/2), 1995, pp. 5–20.

Katz, Mark N. "Iran and America: Is Rapprochement Finally Possible?" *Middle East Policy* 12(4), 2005, pp. 58–65.

Keddie, Nikki R. "Is There a Middle East," *International Journal of Middle East Studies* 4(3), 1973, pp. 255–271.

Kennedy, Edward M. "Statement of Senator Edward M. Kennedy on the Release of Hostage Frank Reed," April 30, 1990, p. 1.

Ladjevardi, Habib. "The Origins of U.S. Support for an Autocratic Iran," *International Journal of Middle East Studies* 15(2), 1983, pp. 225–239.

Lieberman, Samuel S. "Prospects for Development and Population Growth in Iran," *Population and Development Review* 5(2), 1979, pp. 293–317.

Lillich, Richard B. and Bederman, David J. "Jurisprudence of the Foreign Claims Settlement Commission: Iran Claims," *The American Journal of International Law* 91(3), 1997, pp. 436–465.

Lindgren, Henry Clay. "Friends and Enemies' Enemies: Heider's Balance Theory and Middle East Relations," *Political Psychology* (1), No. 2, 1979, pp. 104–105.

McNaugher, Thomas L. "Ballistic Missiles and Chemical Weapons: The Legacy of the Iran-Iraq War," *International Security* 15(2), 1990, pp. 5–34.

Mehran, Golnar. "Social Implications of Literacy in Iran," *Comparative Education Review* 36(2), 1992, pp. 194–211.

Mirsepassi-Ashtiani, Ali. "The Crisis of Secular Politics and the Rise of Political Islam in Iran," *Social Text* 38, 1994, pp. 51–84.

Moens, Alexander. "President Carter's Advisers and the Fall of the Shah," *Political Science Quarterly* 106(2), 1991, pp. 211–237.

Mottahedeh, Roy Parviz. "Iran's Foreign Devils," *Foreign Policy* 38, 1980, pp. 19–34.

Murphy, Richard W. "A Thaw in Iran," *Foreign Policy* 109, Winter 1997, pp. 182–183.

Neff, Donald. "The U.S., Iraq, Israel, and Iran: Backdrop to War," *Journal of Palestine Studies* 20(4), 1991, pp. 23–41.

Niva, Steve. "Between Clash and Co-optation: US Foreign Policy and the Specter of Islam," *Middle East Report* 208, Autumn 1998, pp. 26–29.

Nuckolls, John H. "Post-Cold War Nuclear Dangers: Proliferation and Terrorism", *Science* 267(5201), February 24, 1995, pp. 1112–1114.

"Oil and the Outcome of the Iran-Iraq War," *Middle East Research and Information Project* 125/126, 1984, pp. 40–42.

"Ongoing U.S. Efforts to Curb Iran's Nuclear Program," *The American Journal of International Law* 100(2), April 2006, pp. 480–485.

Orakhelashvili, Alexander. "Oil Platforms: Islamic Republic of Iran v United States of America," *The International and Comparative Law Quarterly* 53(3), July 2004, pp. 753–761.

Perkovich, George. "Can Iran and the United States Bridge the Gulf?" *Foreign Policy* 137, July 2003, p. 65.

———. "Nuclear Proliferation," *Foreign Policy* 112, Autumn 1998, pp. 12–23.

Phares, Walid. "Future Terrorism: Mutant Jihads," *The Journal of International Security Affairs*, 11, Fall 2006, pp. 77–102.

Precht, Henry. "Ayatollah Realpolitik," *Foreign Policy* 70, 1988, pp. 109–128.

Rabil, Robert. "Syria: Buying Time," *The Journal of International Security Affairs* 11, Fall 2006, pp. 75–82.

Ram, Haggay. "Crushing the Opposition: Adversaries of the Islamic Republic of Iran," *The Middle East Journal* 46(3), Summer 1992 pp. 426–439.

Renfrew, Nita M. "Who Started the War?," *Foreign Policy* 66, 1987, pp. 98–108.

"Report: Terrorism Down Overall; Iranian-Backed Attacks Up," *FPI International Report* 10(4), 1990, pp. 5–6.

Rezaei, Ali, "Last Efforts of Iran's Reformists," *Middle East Report* 226, Spring 2003, pp. 40–46.

Roy, Oliver. "Tensions in Iran: The Future of the Islamic Revolution," *Middle East Report* 207, Summer 1998, pp. 38–41.

Salehi-Isfahani, Djavad. "Labor and the Challenge of Economic Restructuring in Iran," *Middle East Report* 210, 1999, pp. 34–37.

Salemeh, Ghassen. "Checkmate in the Gulf War," *Middle East Research and Information Project Reports* 125/126, 1984, pp. 15–21.

Sepehr, Zabih. "Iran's Policy toward the Persian Gulf," *International Journal of Middle East Studies* 7(3), 1976, pp. 345–358.

Shehadi, Philip. "Economic Sanctions and Iranian Trade," *Middle East Research and Information Project* 98, 1981, pp. 15–16.

Shirley, Edward G. "The Iran Policy Trap," *Foreign Policy* 96, 1994, pp. 75–93.

Simon, Jeffrey D. "Misunderstanding Terrorism," *Foreign Policy* 67, 1987, pp. 104–120.

Sirriyeh, Hussein. "Development of the Iraqi-Iranian Dispute, 1847–1975," *Journal of Contemporary History* 20(3), 1985, pp. 483–492.

Stein, Janice Gross. "The Wrong Strategy in the Right Place: The United States in the Gulf," *International Security* 13(3), 1988, pp. 142–167.

Stork, Joe. "Arms Merchants in the Gulf War," *Middle East Research and Information Project Reports* 125/126, 1984, pp. 39–40.

Swearingen, Will D. "Geopolitical Origins of the Iran-Iraq War," *Geographical Review* 78(4), 1988, pp. 405–416.

Tamadonfar, Mehran. "Islam, Law, and Political Control in Contemporary Iran," *Journal for the Scientific Study of Religion* 40(2), June 2001, pp. 205–219.

Thiebaut, Azadeh Kian. "Political and Social Transformations in Post-Islamist Iran," *Middle East Report* 212, Autumn 1999, pp. 36–38.

University of Sussex, Department of International Relations. "U.S. Judgments against Terrorist States," *The American Journal of International Law* Vol. 95, No. 1, 2001, pp. 134–139.

"U.S. Approach to the Non-Proliferation Treaty Review Conference; Concerns about Korean and Iranian Nuclear Programs," *The American Journal of International Law* 99(3), July 2005, pp. 715–718. "U.S. Arms Sales to Iran," *Middle East Research and Information Project* 51, 1977, pp. 15–18. U.S. House of Representatives, Committee on Foreign Affairs, Subcommittee on Europe and the Middle East. "Developments in the Middle East, September 1989," *Washington, DC: U.S. Government Printing Office*, 1990, p. 82.

Wells, Mathew C. "Thermidor in the Islamic Republic of Iran: The Rise of Muhammad Khatami," *British Journal of Middle Eastern Studies* 26(1), May 1999, pp. 27–39.

Wenger, Martha and Anderson, Dick. "The Gulf War," *Middle East Research and Information Project Middle East Report* 148, 1987, pp. 23–26.

Yetiv, Steve A. "The Outcomes of Operations Desert Shield and Desert Storm: Some Antecedent Causes," *Political Science Quarterly* 107(2), 1992, pp. 195–212.

Zabih, Sepehr. "Aspects of Terrorism in Iran," *Annals of the American Academy of Political and Social Science* 463, 1982, pp. 84–94.

# Index

## About the Authors

YONAH ALEXANDER is director of the Inter-University Center of Terrorism Studies, a consortium of academic institutions in over forty countries. He is also a senior fellow and director of the International Center for Terrorism Studies at the Potomac Institute for Policy Studies in Arlington, Virginia, a senior fellow at the Homeland Security Policy Institute at The George Washington University and co-director of the Inter-University Center of Legal Studies at the International Law Institute in Washington, DC.

Formerly a professor and director of terrorism studies at the State University of New York and The George Washington University, Dr. Alexander has also held academic appointments at many other institutions in the United States and abroad. Educated at Columbia University (PhD), University of Chicago (MA), and Roosevelt University of Chicago (BA), he founded and edited three international journals on terrorism, political communication, and minority and group rights. He has now published ninety-five books, the latest on *Counterterrorism Strategies: Successes and Failures of Six Nations* (2006), and *Evolution of U.S. Counterterrorism Policy*, Three Volumes (2007).

MILTON HOENIG is a nuclear physicist and a Washington, DC-based consultant. He holds a PhD from Cornell University, was a professor of physics at the University of Massachusetts in North Dartmouth, and served in the U.S. Arms Control and Disarmament Agency at the end of the Carter Administration. At the Natural Resources Defense Council, he coauthored the first three volumes of the

*Nuclear Weapons Databook.* He was scientific director of the Nuclear Control Institute in Washington and served as an advisor to its Task Force on Prevention of Nuclear Terrorism. Dr. Hoenig is the author of numerous articles and has spoken at many conferences and seminars. With Yonah Alexander, he edited the book, *Super Terrorism: Biological, Chemical, and Nuclear* (2001).

**DATE DUE**